This guide to the coast path from Plymouth to Poole (217¼ miles) covers the third part, the South Devon and Dorset section, of the 630-mile South-West

Coast Path (SWCP) and is the final book in this series. The first edition was walked, researched and written by **HENRY STEDMAN** (far left) and **JOEL NEWTON** (left) accompanied by Henry's dog, **DAISY**. They also researched and wrote the two other books in this SWCP series, plus numerous other Trailblazer guides.

This **second edition** of *Dorset & South Devon Coast Path* was rewalked and updated by **DANIEL MCCROHAN**. Daniel is a hardened hiker and widely-published travel writer who has now worked on eight Trailblazer guides, and authored more than 30 Lonely Planet books to destinations as far flung as Tibet and Mongolia. He specialises in China, where he lived for more than a decade, but he is from the UK and relishes any opportunity he gets to explore the

British countryside. Daniel hiked and camped his way along the whole coast path for this latest trip, accompanied for much of the Jurassic Coast section by his fossil-loving seven-year-old daughter Yoyo, who has now walked all, or part of, no fewer than five national trails.

Catch up with their adventures at 🖳 danielmccrohan.com, or track down Daniel on Twitter (@daniel mccrohan).

Authors

Dorset & South Devon Coast Path (SWCP Part 3)

First edition: 2013; this second edition 2018

Publisher Trailblazer Publications
The Old Manse, Tower Rd, Hindhead, Surrey, GU26 6SU, UK
info@trailblazer-guides.com, www.trailblazer-guides.com

British Library Cataloguing in Publication Data
A catalogue record for this book is available from the British Library

ISBN 978-1-905864-94-2

© Trailblazer 2013, 2018: Text and maps

Series Editor: Anna Jacomb-Hood
Editor & layout: Anna Jacomb-Hood **Cartography**: Nick Hill **Proof-reading**: Jane Thomas
Index: Anna Jacomb-Hood **Photographs (flora)**: © Bryn Thomas
All other photographs: © Daniel McCrohan unless otherwise indicated

The maps in this guide were prepared from out-of-Crown-copyright Ordnance Survey maps amended and updated by Trailblazer.

Acknowledgements

From Daniel Hugs and kisses to my darling daughter Yoyo for joining me on yet another fabulous Trailblazer adventure, and for introducing me to the fascinating world of ammonites, belemnites and crinoids – I hope your dreams of becoming the next Mary Anning come true. Thanks, too, to my mum, to Sam and Heidi, and to Cat and Steve Allan for helping with everything back in Guildford, and to Taotao and Dudu in China for their love and patience at such a trying time. Thanks to fellow authors Henry Stedman and Joel Newton for their magnificent work on the previous edition and huge gratitude to the team at Trailblazer HQ, particularly Anna Jacomb-Hood, Nick Hill, Jane Thomas and, of course, Bryn Thomas. And thank you, too, to all the Trailblazer readers who wrote in with comments and suggestions, in particular, David Mallinson, Helen Older, David Schaehe, Roland Thorpe and Janine Watson – keep 'em coming!

A request

The author and publisher have tried to ensure that this guide is as accurate and up to date as possible. Nevertheless, things change. If you notice any changes or omissions that should be included in the next edition of this book, please write to Trailblazer (address above) or email us at 🖳 info@trailblazer-guides.com. A free copy of the next edition will be sent to persons making a significant contribution.

Warning: coastal walking and long-distance walking can be dangerous

Please read the notes on when to go (pp13-16) and on outdoor safety (pp78-81). Every effort has been made by the authors and publisher to ensure that the information contained herein is as accurate and up to date as possible. However, they are unable to accept responsibility for any inconvenience, loss or injury sustained by anyone as a result of the advice and information given in this guide.

Updated information will be available on: 🖳 www.trailblazer-guides.com

Photos – Front cover On the path between West Bay and Burton Freshwater.
This page: Durdle Door. **Previous page**: The white cliffs at Old Harry Rocks.
Overleaf: Resting up at Burton Freshwater. (Photos © Daniel McCrohan).

Printed in China; print production by D'Print (☎ +65-6581 3832), Singapore

Dorset & South Devon
COAST PATH

SW COAST PATH PART 3 – PLYMOUTH TO POOLE

97 large-scale maps & guides to 48 towns and villages

PLANNING – PLACES TO STAY – PLACES TO EAT

HENRY STEDMAN, JOEL NEWTON
& DANIEL McCROHAN

TRAILBLAZER PUBLICATIONS

INTRODUCTION

Contents

PART 4: ROUTE GUIDE AND MAPS

Contents

ABOUT THIS BOOK

This guidebook contains all the information you need. The hard work has been done for you so you can plan your trip from home without spending hours on the internet or perusing the usual pile of books, maps and guides.

When you're all packed and ready to go, there's comprehensive public transport information to get you to and from the trail and 97 detailed route maps and 30 town plans to help you find your way along it. The guide includes:

● All standards of accommodation with reviews of campsites, hostels, B&Bs, guesthouses and hotels
● Walking companies if you want an organised tour and baggage-transfer services if you just want your luggage carried
● Itineraries for all levels of walkers
● Answers to all your questions: when to go, degree of difficulty, what to pack, and how much the whole walking holiday will cost
● Walking times in both directions and GPS waypoints
● Cafés, pubs, tearooms, takeaways, restaurants and shops for buying supplies
● Rail, bus and taxi information for all places along the path
● Street plans of the main towns both on and off the path
● Historical, cultural and geographical background information

---

❏ MINIMUM IMPACT FOR MAXIMUM INSIGHT

Man has suffered in his separation from the soil and from other living creatures ... and as yet he must still, for security, look long at some portion of the earth as it was before he tampered with it.
Gavin Maxwell, *Ring of Bright Water*, 1960

Why is walking in wild and solitary places so satisfying? Partly it is the sheer physical pleasure: sometimes pitting one's strength against the elements and the lie of the land. The beauty and wonder of the natural world and the fresh air restore our sense of proportion and the stresses and strains of everyday life slip away. Whatever the character of the countryside, walking in it benefits us mentally and physically, inducing a sense of well-being, an enrichment of life and an enhanced awareness of what lies around us.

All this the countryside gives us and the least we can do is to safeguard it by supporting rural economies, local businesses, and low-impact methods of farming and land-management, and by using environmentally sensitive forms of transport – walking being pre-eminent.

In this book there is a detailed and illustrated chapter on the wildlife and conservation of the region and a chapter on minimum-impact walking, with ideas on how to tread lightly in this fragile environment; by following its principles we can help to preserve our natural heritage for future generations.

INTRODUCTION

This book covers the last 217¼ miles (350km) of the South-West Coast Path (SWCP), Britain's longest national trail. The walk described begins on the Devon–Cornwall border, at Plymouth and, having navigated Devon's entire southern coastline, enters the county of Dorset at Lyme Regis, before finishing at South Haven Point, overlooking Poole Harbour. Together with the two other books in this series, the entire 630 miles of the SWCP is covered.

This book covers the last 217¼ miles of the 630-mile South-West Coast Path

There are few, if any, stretches of the British coastline that can offer the walker such variety, such interest – and such beauty – as this third and final leg of the coast path. From sun-drenched promenades to wild, remote cliff-tops, through ancient 'apple-pie' villages, tiny thatched hamlets and smart, friendly Georgian resorts, this path has it all. Indeed it is difficult to think of another section of any national trail that so comprehensively lives up to that well-worn cliché of the travel industry: that there is something for everyone. For historians the trail begins – most appropriately, given the many famous journeys that have departed from the same spot – at the Mayflower Steps,

The South Devon stretch of the Coast Path is sprinkled with tempting little beaches, like this one by the Cary Arms at Babbacombe (Map 35).

in Plymouth's timeless Barbican district, and passes through such fascinating towns as medieval Dartmouth, home to the UK's only Royal Naval college, and Teignmouth, the last place in mainland England to be successfully invaded by a foreign power. Castles, caves, barrows, burial mounds, ships, stone circles, historic harbours and old hostelries – all lie on the path and all offer something to intrigue and captivate the history buff.

Similarly, geologists also have plenty that they'll find engrossing – and indeed you don't need to be an expert in stone or strata to enjoy them. Not only is the English Riviera (see box p146) the home of a Global Geopark but across the River Exe there's the Jurassic Coast World Heritage Site, where the very rocks you step on can take you on a 185-million-year geological journey. Steep and precipitous cliffs of orange, grey and white change their hue with each passing geological era; and if these don't 'rock' your world, within these very cliffs are fossils of strange and unfamiliar beasts that once dominated the Earth: a long-vanished land of soaring pterodactyls rather than swooping peregrines, where plesiosaurs, not porpoises, cruised the seas, and the endemic scelidosaurus once roamed where sheep now ruminate.

❏ **The South-West Coast Path**

As the crow flies, the distance between Minehead (the official start point of the South West Coast Path) and South Haven Point (the official end point) is only around 90 miles long. So why would anyone wish to spend weeks on end walking the 630-mile coastal route between the same two points? The answer is simple: the SWCP is one of the most beautiful trails in the UK

Around 70% of those 630 miles are spent either in national parks or regions that have been designated an Area of Outstanding Natural Beauty. The variety of places crossed by the SWCP is extraordinary too: from sunkissed beaches to sandy burrows, holiday parks to fishing villages, esplanade to estuary, on top of windswept cliffs and under woodland canopy, the scenery that one travels through has to be the most diverse of any of the national trails.

Maintaining such a monumental route is no easy task, with thousands of signposts and waymarks, hundreds of bridges, gates and stiles, and more than 25,000 steps! The task of looking after the trail falls to a dedicated team from the official body, Natural England (see p55). Another important organisation, and one that looks after the rights of walkers, is the South West Coast Path Association (see p46), a charity that fights for improvements to the path and offers advice, information and support to walkers. They also campaign against many of the proposed changes to the path and help to ensure that England's right-of-way laws (which ensure that the footpath is open to the public – even though it does, on occasion, pass through private property) are fully observed.

History of the path

In 1948 a government report recommended the creation of a footpath around the entire South-West peninsula to improve public access to the coast which, at that time, was pretty dire. It took until 1973 for the Cornwall Coast Path to be declared officially open and another five years for the rest of the South-West Coast Path to be completed. The section covered in this book, Dorset & South Devon, is the third part that most coastal walkers complete, though it was one of the earliest sections opened to the public, back in 1974.

The wildlife of today is not without its merits either, from the lovely deer of Lulworth to otters in Axmouth. And while man has done more than his fair share of shaping and utilising the land you pass through, he has also been careful to protect it too, with numerous Sites of Special Scientific Interest, several nature reserves and no fewer than three Areas of Outstanding Natural Beauty – with each encompassing mile after mile of epic panoramas,

Set in stone – an ammonite in Lyme Regis.

jagged sea stacks, and bountiful, beckoning beaches. There are also such spectacular delights as the curious Undercliffs, moulded by landslides and decorated by the free hand of nature into a truly English jungle; the south coast's high-

---

The origins of the path, however, are much older than its official designation. Originally, the paths were established – or at least adopted, as the paths themselves had been connecting coastal villages for centuries – by the local coastguards in the 19th century; they needed a path that hugged the shoreline closely to aid them in their attempts to spot and prevent smugglers from bringing contraband into the country. The coastguards were unpopular in the area as they prevented the locals from exploiting a lucrative if illegal activity, to the extent that it was considered too dangerous for them to stay in the villages; as a result, the authorities were obliged to build special cottages for the coastguards that stood (and, often, still stand) in splendid isolation near the path – but well away from the villages.

The lifeboat patrols also used the path to look out for craft in distress (and on one famous occasion used the path to drag their boat to a safe launch to rescue a ship in distress). When the coastguards' work ended in 1856, the Admiralty took over the task of protecting England's shoreline and thus the paths continued to be used.

The route – Minehead (Somerset) to Poole Harbour (Dorset)

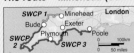

The SWCP officially begins at Minehead in Somerset (its exact starting point marked by a sculpture that celebrates the trail), heads west right round the bottom south-west corner of Britain then shuffles back along the south coast to South Haven Point, on the tip of Shell Bay, overlooking Poole Harbour in Dorset.

On its lengthy journey around Britain's south-western corner the SWCP crosses national parks such as Exmoor as well as regions that have been designated Areas of Outstanding Natural Beauty (including North, South and East Devon AONB and the Cornwall and Dorset AONBs) or Sites of Special Scientific Interest (Braunton Burrows being just one example – an area that also enjoys a privileged status as a UNESCO Biosphere Reserve), and even two UNESCO World Heritage sites: the Jurassic Coast of East Devon and Dorset, and the old mining landscape of Cornwall and West Devon. *(cont'd overleaf)*

❏ **The South-West Coast Path** (cont'd from p9)

Other features passed on the way include the highest cliffs on mainland Britain (at Great Hangman – also the highest point on the coast path at 318m/1043ft, with a cliff-face of 244m), the largest sand-dune system in England (at Braunton Burrows), England's most westerly point (at Land's End) and Britain's most southerly (at the Lizard), the 18-mile barrier beach of Chesil Bank, one of the world's largest natural harbours at Poole, and even the National Trust's only official naturist beach at Studland!

The path ends at South Haven Point, its exact finish marked by a second SWCP sculpture. The path also takes in four counties – Somerset, Devon, Cornwall and Dorset – and connects with over 15 other long-distance trails, including the newly formed England Coast Path. The southern section from Plymouth to Poole also forms part of the 3125-mile long European E9 Coastal Path that runs on a convoluted route from Portugal to Estonia.

Walking the South-West Coast Path

In terms of difficulty, there are those people who, having never undertaken such a trail before, are under the illusion that coastal walking is a cinch; that all it involves is a simple stroll along mile after mile of golden beach, the walker needing to pause only to kick the sand out from his or her flipflops or buy another ice-cream. The truth, of course, is somewhat different, for coastal paths tend to stick to the cliffs above the beaches rather than the beaches themselves (which is actually something of a relief, given how hard it is to walk across sand or shingle). These cliffs make for some spectacular walking but – given the undulating nature of Britain's coastline, and the fact that the course of the SWCP inevitably crosses innumerable river valleys, each of which forces the walker to descend rapidly before climbing back up again almost immediately afterwards – some exhausting walking too. Indeed, it has been estimated that anybody who completes the entire SWCP will have climbed more than four times the height of Everest (35,031m to be precise, or 114,931ft) by the time they finish!

Given these figures, it is perhaps hardly surprising that most people take around eight weeks to complete the whole route and few do so in one go; indeed, it is not unusual for people to take years or even decades to complete the whole path, taking a week or two here and there to tackle various sections until the whole trail is complete.

est point, Golden Cap; and the iconic natural architecture of Durdle Door, Stair Hole and Lulworth Cove.

But if all the above sound a bit too worthy, for those after less cerebral pleasures the path also cuts through such quintessential seaside resorts as Exmouth, Sidmouth and the English Riviera (Torquay, Paignton and Brixham) – a land of doughnuts and dodgems, arcades and amusements, candy floss and crazy golf.

Another joy of the coast path is the food, with fish in Brixham so fresh you can taste the salt of the ocean. Crab sandwiches, pints of real ale and cream teas galore can be savoured all along the path, especially in the thatched villages of Beer, Abbotsbury and West Lulworth, all of which prove that nature doesn't have the monopoly on beauty and defy you not to change your plans and spend a night in their cosy embrace.

Of course such rewards aren't gained without a fight and there are a couple of tough stretches of walking that must be completed before you can say

INTRODUCTION

you've conquered the path. But those of you who started in Minehead, the beginning of the SWCP, will know that, whatever the hardships faced, the treasures of this endlessly fascinating path, are always worth any effort expended.

How difficult is the path?

The South-West Coast Path is just a (very, very) long walk, so there's no need for crampons, ropes, ice axes, oxygen bottles or any other climbing paraphernalia, because there's no climbing involved. All you need to complete the walk is some suitable clothing, a bit of money, a rucksack full of determination and a half-decent pair of calf muscles.

The part of the SWCP that is covered by this book is perhaps the one with the most variety. Topographically speaking, there are plenty of steep ups-and-downs as well as large flat areas of walking on seaside promenades. While the Riviera (see box p146) provides walkers with an unbroken swathe of civilisation, this book is bookended by two remote sections where settlements are scarce and amenities are few and far between. These two sections, from Mount Batten Point to Salcombe and from Lulworth Cove to Swanage, require a little

Signposting is good: look for the acorn symbol. This signpost points the way to Golden Cap (see p239) which, at 191m (627ft), is the highest point on the south coast of England.
(Photo ©Yoyo McCrohan)

advanced planning to ensure you have something to eat and somewhere to rest your head for the night. Still, with the path well signposted (look for the acorn symbol) all the way along and the sea keeping you company for the entire stretch, it's difficult to get lost (though it's always a good idea to take a compass or GPS unit, just in case).

As with any walk, you can minimise the risks by preparing properly. Your greatest danger on the walk is likely to be from the weather, which can be so unpredictable in this corner of the world, so it is vital that you dress for inclement conditions and always carry a set of dry clothes with you. Not pushing yourself too hard is important too, as over-exertion leads to exhaustion and all its inherent dangers (see pp78-81), so plan an itinerary that matches your abilities rather than your (over-) ambitions. In terms of orientation, the South-West Coast Path is very well signposted, so you shouldn't lose your way. However, we think that the distances the signposts have written on them can be of questionable accuracy so are not always to be trusted; indeed sometimes even the spelling on the signposts is wrong. But in terms of helping you find your way, the signposts on the SWCP do a terrific job and the trail authorities are to be congratulated both on this and on the maintenance of the trail in general.

How long do you need?

People take an average of around 18 days to complete the walk; count on three weeks in total to give you time to travel there and back. Of course, if you're fit

People take an average of around 18 days to complete the walk

there's no reason why you can't go a little faster, if that's what you want to do, and finish the walk in 15 days or even less, though you will end up having a different sort of trek from most of the other people on the trail. For whilst theirs might be a fairly relaxing holiday, yours will be more of a sport. What's more, you won't have much time to laze in the sun on the beaches, scoff scones in tearooms, visit an attraction or two, or sup local beers under the shade of a pub parasol.

There's nothing wrong with the fast approach, of course, but do make sure you **don't push yourself too fast, or too far.** That road leads only to exhaustion, injury or, at the absolute least, an unpleasant time.

When deciding how long to allow for the trek, those intending to camp and carry their own luggage shouldn't underestimate just how much a heavy pack can slow them down. On p34 and p35 there are some suggested itineraries cov-

See pp34-5 for some suggested itineraries covering different walking speeds

ering different walking speeds. If you have only a few days, don't try to walk it all; concentrate instead on one area such as the coast path through Dorset, the Riviera (see box p146), or the less-demanding section from Plymouth to Salcombe or Dartmouth.

When to go

SEASONS

'My shoes are clean from walking in the rain.' **Jack Kerouac**

Britain is a notoriously wet country and South-West England does nothing to crush that reputation. Few walkers manage to complete the walk without suffering at least one downpour; two or three per walk are more likely, even in summer. That said, it's equally unlikely that you'll spend a week in the area and not see any sun at all; even the most cynical of walkers will have to admit that, during the **walking season** at least, there are more sunny days than showery ones.

The season starts at Easter and builds to a crescendo in August, before steadily tailing off in October. Few people attempt the entire path after the end of October though there are still plenty of people on day walks. Many places close in November for the winter.

There is one further point to consider when planning your trip. Firstly, remember that most people set off on the trail at a weekend. This means that **you'll find the trail quieter during the week** and as a consequence you may find it easier to book accommodation.

Spring

Find a dry fortnight in springtime (around the end of March to mid June) and you're in for a treat. The wild flowers are coming into bloom, lambs are skipping in the meadows and the grass is green and lush.

Of course, finding a dry week in spring is not easy but occasionally there's a mini-heatwave at this time. Another advantage with walking at this time is that there will be fewer walkers and finding accommodation is relatively easy, though do check that the hostels, campsites and B&Bs are open. Easter is the exception; the first major holiday in the year when people flock to the coast.

Summer

Summer, on the other hand, can be a bit *too* busy, at least in the towns and tourist centres, and over a weekend in August can be both suffocating and insufferable. Still, the chances of a prolonged period of sunshine are of course higher at this time of year than any other, the days are longer, and all the facilities and public transport are

From huge family-friendly caravan parks to remote farmers' fields like this one at East Prawle, campers are spoilt for choice.

❏ FESTIVALS AND ANNUAL EVENTS

April
● **Budleigh Salterton Jazz Festival** (🖥 budleighjazzfestival.org)

May
● **Dart Music Festival, Dartmouth** (🖥 dartmusicfestival.co.uk)
● **Brixham Pirate Festival** (🖥 brixham pirates.com) Live music, historic re-enactments and very large gathering of pirates.
● **Lyme Regis Fossil Festival** (🖥 fossilfestival.com; mostly free) A weekend of fossil-hunting walks, talks, displays and a fossil fair.
● **Lyme Regis Jazz & Blues Festival** (🖥 lymeregisjazzfestival.co.uk)

June
● **Exmouth Festival** (🖥 exmouthfestival.org.uk) Annual 9-day festival of music, theatre, film and dance, showcasing local talent. In May or June
● **Teignmouth Folk Festival** (🖥 efestivals.co.uk/festivals/teignmouthfolk)
● **Dawlish Arts Festival** (🖥 dawlish artsfestival.org.uk) Festival of arts, crafts, theatre, classical music, gospel and jazz; held late May to early June
● **Shaldon Festival** (🖥 shaldonfestival .co.uk) Weekend of classical music featuring established professionals as well as choral workshops for amateurs.
● **Wessex Folk Festival, Weymouth** (🖥 wessexfolk.co.uk)

July
● **Budleigh Music Festival, Budleigh Salterton** (🖥 budleighmusicfestival.co.uk) Week-long classical music festival.
● **Dorset Seafood Festival, Weymouth** (🖥 dorsetseafood.co.uk)
● **Camp Bestival, Lulworth Castle** (🖥 campbestival.net) Music, comedy and many other events held over a long weekend in late July.
● **Paignton Festival** (🖥 paigntonfestival.com) Week-long festival of music, dance, games and shows.
● **Square and Compass Stone Carving Festival, Worth Matravers** (🖥 squareand compasspub.co.uk) Two weeks late July to early August (see p300)

August
● **British Firework Championships, Plymouth** (🖥 britishfireworks.co.uk)
● **Sidmouth Folk Week** (🖥 sidmouthfolkweek.co.uk)
● **Burton Bradstock Festival of Music & Art** (🖥 burtonbradstockfestival.com)
● **Shaldon Water Carnival** (🖥 www.shaldonwatercarnival.co.uk) First Saturday in August.

September
● **Budleigh Salterton Literary Festival** (🖥 budlitfest.org.uk)
● **Swanage Folk Festival** (🖥 swanagefolkfestival.com) Annual shindig with numerous musicians, dance & music workshops.
● **International Agatha Christie Festival** (🖥 iacf-uk.org) Week-long celebration of the author's works in and around Torquay.

October
● **Dartmouth Food Festival** (🖥 dartmouthfoodfestival.com)
● **Torbay Festival of Poetry** (🖥 torbaypoetryfestival.co.uk) Torquay & Brixham.
● **Beer Rhythm & Blues Festival** (🖥 beerblues.co.uk)

November
● **Teignmouth Jazz & Blues Festival** (🖥 teignmouthjazz.org)

operating. Our advice is this: if you're flexible and want to avoid seeing too many people on the trail, avoid the school holidays, which basically means ruling out the tail end of July, all of August and the first few days of September. Alternatively, if you crave the company of other walkers, summer will provide you with the opportunity of meeting plenty, though do remember that you **must book your accommodation in advance**, especially if staying in B&B-style accommodation. Despite the higher-than-average chance of sunshine, take clothes for any eventuality – it will probably still rain at some point.

Autumn

September is a wonderful time to walk; many tourists have returned home and the path is clear. The weather is often sunny too, at least at the beginning of September. The first signs of winter will be felt in October but there's nothing really to deter the walker. In fact there's still much to entice you, such as the colours of the heathland, which come into their own in autumn; a magnificent blaze of brilliant purples and pinks, splashed with the occasional yellow flowers of gorse (it is more usual in spring but can thrive in autumn). By the end of October, however, the weather will begin to get a little wilder and the nights will start to draw in. Most campsites and some B&Bs and hostels may close.

Winter

November can bring crisp clear days which are ideal for walking, although you'll definitely feel the chill when you stop on the cliff tops for a break. Winter temperatures rarely fall below freezing but the incidence of gales and storms definitely increases. You need to be fairly hardy to walk in December and January and you may have to alter your plans because of the weather. By February the daffodils and primroses are already appearing but even into March it can still be decidedly chilly if the sun is not out.

While winter is definitely the low season with many places closed, this can be an advantage; very few people walk at this time of year, giving you long stretches of the trail to yourself. When you do stumble across other walkers they are as happy as you to stop and chat. Finding B&B accommodation is easier as you will rarely have to book more than a night ahead (though it is still worth checking in advance as some B&Bs close out of season), but if you are planning to camp, or are on a small budget, you will find places to stay much more limited.

WEATHER

Before departing on your walk, tell yourself this: at some point on my walk it is going to **rain**. That's not to say it will, but at least if it does you won't be too disappointed and will hopefully have come

Whatever the weather there are numerous welcoming pubs to detain you along the way.

INTRODUCTION

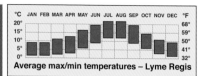

Average max/min temperatures – Lyme Regis

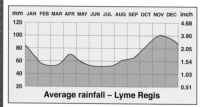

Average rainfall – Lyme Regis

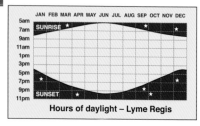

Hours of daylight – Lyme Regis

prepared for this, clothes-wise. Besides, walking in the rain can be fun, at least for a while: the gentle drumming of rain on hood can be quite relaxing, the path is usually quiet, and if it really does chuck it down at least it provides an excuse to linger in tearooms and have that extra scone. And as long as you dress accordingly and take note of the safety advice given on pp78-81, walking in moderate rain is no more dangerous than walking at any other time – though do be careful, particularly on exposed sections, if the path becomes slippery or the wind picks up.

DAYLIGHT HOURS

If walking in winter, autumn or even early spring, you must take account of how far you can walk in the available light. It won't be possible to cover as many miles as you would in summer. Conversely, in the summer months there is enough available light until at least 9pm. Remember, too, that you will get a further 30-45 minutes of usable light before sunrise and after sunset depending on the weather.

(**Below**): You may wish to avert your eyes as you hurry along the beach at Studland. (Photo © Henry Stedman)

Practical information for the walker

ROUTE FINDING

For most of its length the coast path is well signposted. At confusing junctions the route is usually indicated by a finger-post sign with

'coast path' written on it. At other points, where there could be some confusion, there are wooden waymark posts with an acorn symbol and a yellow arrow to indicate in which direction you should head. The waymarking is the responsibility of the local authorities along the trail who have a duty to maintain the path. Generally they do a good job but occasionally you will come across sections of the trail where waymarking is ambiguous, or even non-existent, but with the detailed trail maps and directions in this book and the fact that you always have the sea to one side it would be hard to get really lost.

Using GPS with this book

Given the above, modern Wainwrights may scoff at those who use GPS technology, but more open-minded walkers will accept that it can be an inexpensive, well-established if non-essential, navigational aid. In no time at all a GPS receiver with a clear view of the sky will establish your position and altitude in a variety of formats, including the British OS grid system, to within a few metres.

The maps in the route guide include numbered waypoints; these correlate to the list on pp318-20, which gives the latitude/longitude position in a decimal minute format as well as a description. Where the path is vague, or there are several options, you will find more waypoints. You can download the complete list of these waypoints for free as a GPS-readable file (that doesn't include the text descriptions) from the Trailblazer website: 🖳 trailblazer-guides.com (click on GPS waypoints).

It's also possible to buy state-of-the-art digital mapping to import into your GPS unit, assuming that you have sufficient memory capacity, but it's not the most reliable way of navigating and the small screen on your pocket-sized unit will invariably fail to put places into context or give you the 'big picture'.

Bear in mind that the vast majority of people who tackle this path do so perfectly well without a GPS unit. Instead of rushing out to invest in one, consider putting the money towards good-quality footwear or waterproofs instead.

ACCOMMODATION

The trail guide (Part 4) lists a fairly comprehensive selection of places to stay along the length of the trail. You have three main options: camping, using B&Bs/guesthouses/hotels, or staying in hostels/bunkhouses. Few people stick to just one of these options the whole way, preferring, for example, to camp most of the time but spend the odd night in a guesthouse, or perhaps use hostels where possible (as there are only a few on this stretch of the path) but splash out on a B&B where necessary.

When booking accommodation that is far from the path, remember to ask if a pick-up and drop-off service is available (usually only B&Bs provide this service); at the end of a tiring day it's nice to know a lift is available to take you to your accommodation rather than having to traipse another two or three miles off the path to get to your bed for the night.

The facilities' table on pp32-3 provides a quick snapshot of what type of accommodation is available in each of the towns and villages along the way,

---

❑ **Should you book your accommodation in advance?**

With the exception of campsites, which rarely need booking, it's essential that you have your night's accommodation booked by the time you set off in the morning. Nothing is more deflating than to arrive at your destination at the day's end only to find that you've then got to walk a further five miles or so, or even take a detour, because everywhere is booked. For this reason, it would pay to cast an eye over the list of festivals and events (see box p14) in towns and villages on the path as accommodation will be particularly hard to find at those times. Note that, as well as the annual events mentioned, a number of the towns, especially those near estuaries such as Dartmouth, host regattas, during which time they can also become very busy.

Outside the high season (ie the summer period coinciding with the long school holidays in the UK), and particularly in April/May or September, as long as you're flexible and willing to take what's offered, with maybe even a night or two in a hostel if that's all there is, you should get away with booking **B&B-style accommodation** just a few nights in advance, or indeed just the night before. If planning to walk in the high season (and also over a weekend) you should book as soon as you can, especially if you want to stay in a particular place. However, many places don't accept advance bookings for one night in the peak season/at weekends so actually for this route it may be hard to book in advance for a single-night stay. Online booking is also often for a minimum of two nights so for anything less than this you may have to contact the place direct.

If planning to stay in **hostels**, it's worth checking in advance that they will be open, though most on this route are open all year. It's also well worth phoning at least one night before, and well before that if it's a weekend or the peak season, to make sure the hostel isn't fully booked.

Campers have more flexibility and can usually just turn up and find a space there and then, though ringing in advance adds some peace of mind.

while the tables on p34 and p35 provide some suggested itineraries. The following is a brief introduction to what to expect from each type of accommodation.

Camping

There are campsites all the way along this section of the South West Coast Path, meaning it's entirely feasible to camp the whole way, although not many people camp every single night for the whole walk. You're almost bound to get at least one night where the rain falls relentlessly, soaking equipment and sapping morale, and it is then that some campers opt to spend the next night drying out in a hostel or B&B. There are, however, many advantages with camping. It's more economical, for a start, with most campsites charging £10 or less for hikers (though some large holiday parks can charge double that in high season). There's rarely any need to book either, except possibly in the very high season, and even then you'd be very unlucky not to find somewhere.

Campsites vary; some are just a quiet corner of a farmer's field, while others are full-blown holiday parks with a few spaces put aside for tents. Showers are nearly always available, occasionally for a fee though more often than not included in the rate. Note that **wild camping** (ie not in a regular campsite) is not allowed. However, some hikers do still do this, being careful to set up camp late in the evening and leave without trace early in the morning.

Camping is fabulous fun, but it's not an easy option; the route is wearying enough without carrying your accommodation around with you. You could look into employing a baggage-transfer company (see p28), though this rather negates two of the main advantages of camping – affordability and flexibility – as it will cost you more and means you have to tell the company, at least a day before, of your next destination – and stick to it – so that you and your bag can be reunited every evening. The best thing to do is to just pack as lightly as possible – bring nothing but the absolute essentials.

Hostels and bunkhouses

It isn't really feasible to plan to stay in a hostel (or bunkhouse) every night on this walk, at least at the beginning, as there is only one bunkhouse (at East Soar Farm, near Salcombe), though there are six places with hostels: Plymouth, Beer, Portland, Weymouth, West Lulworth and Swanage. However, they are great places to stay in when you get the chance; especially good for meeting fellow walkers to swap stories and compare blisters.

As well as five independent hostels, there are four YHA (Youth Hostel Association) hostels en route. If you associate YHAs with cold, crowded dorms, uncomfortable beds and lousy food, be prepared to think again. Many of them provide good meals (breakfast is usually served 7.30-9am and evening meals 6-8pm) and a number are also licensed, but if you prefer to self-cater most have a fully equipped kitchen and some have a shop selling emergency groceries, snacks and souvenirs. In addition they now have a whole range of extra facilities from drying rooms to televisions and internet access.

Dorms usually have bunk beds sleeping 4-6 people but increasingly, hostels also have some private rooms. Toilet and shower facilities are still generally shared (but are usually very clean, especially at YHAs) but all YHA hostels on this route have at least one room with en suite facilities.

The curfew (usually 11pm) can be annoying but many YHA hostels now utilise access codes on their doors to offer residents more freedom.

Most of the hostels on this path are open all year but at certain times the YHA hostels are only open to prebooked sole-use groups. In fact at any time of the year they may be fully booked with schools or other groups, so contact the YHA or the relevant hostel to check the situation.

If you're walking alone hostels work out far cheaper than B&Bs, even taking into account the added cost of breakfast, but if there are two or more of you it can be just as expensive as staying in a B&B; see also opposite.

Hostel membership & bookings You don't have to be a YHA member to stay at YHAs, but it does give you a discount (typically £3 per night). Despite the name, anybody of any age can join the YHA. This can be done at any hostel or by contacting the **Youth Hostels Association of England and Wales** (☎ 01629-592700, ☎ 0800-019 1700, 🖥 yha.org.uk). Annual membership costs £20/10 per adult/under-26 (£15/5 if paying by direct debit).

YHA hostels are easy to book online, but booking by phone through the central switchboard often involves spending a frustrating amount of time on hold. If you're able to call the hostel direct, do so.

Bed and breakfast accommodation

Bed and Breakfasts (**B&Bs**) are a great British institution and many of those along the South-West Coast Path are absolutely charming. Nearly all the B&Bs on this route have either en suite rooms or rooms with private facilities. (In this book we have stated where a B&B has rooms with shared facilities, so rare are they on the trail.)

The rooms usually contain either a double bed (known as a double room), or two single beds (known as a twin room, though these can sometimes be pushed together to create a double bed). Triple rooms are for three people and quad rooms are for four or more. Triple/quad rooms usually contain a double bed and either a single bed or a bunk bed; occasionally there are three or four single beds.

Note that in winter some B&Bs close; for those that stay open, make sure beforehand that they will have their heating in your room turned on!

Increasingly B&B proprietors are able to cater for specific dietary requirements – eg if you're vegetarian, or have to have a gluten-free diet – but you need to tell the B&B owner beforehand. The rate virtually always includes breakfast; an evening meal (usually around £15-20) is sometimes provided at the more remote or bigger places, but generally only if you book in advance. Alternatively, if you want to eat out, there's nearly always a pub or restaurant nearby or, if it's far, the B&B owner may give you a lift to and from the nearest place with food.

The difference between a B&B and a **guesthouse** is minimal, though some of the better guesthouses are more like hotels, offering evening meals and a lounge for guests. **Pubs** and **inns** also offer bed and breakfast accommodation and prices are generally no more than in a regular B&B.

Hotels usually *do* cost more than B&Bs, however, and some can be a little perturbed with a bunch of smelly trekkers turning up and treading mud into their carpet. Most on the South-West Coast Path, however, are used to seeing trekkers and welcome them warmly.

Rates Rates in this guide are quoted on a **per person** (pp) basis, assuming two people are sharing a room. Solo walkers should note: single rooms are not easy to find and you will often end up in a double/twin room and are likely therefore to have to pay a **single occupancy rate**; this is often the room rate less about £10, or may even be the full room rate in peak season. B&B accommodation in this guide starts at around £30pp for the most basic B&Bs (from £20pp room only), rising to around £60pp for the most luxurious places; most charge around £35-45pp. Rates in guesthouses, pubs and inns are similar to B&Bs but hotel tariffs start at around £45pp and can go up to £200pp for a room with a sea view in the summer. Note that at some hotels the rate is room only.

Most places have their own website and offer online/email **booking** but for many you will need to phone to book a room especially for a single-night stay. Most places ask for a deposit (about 50%) which is generally non-refundable if you cancel at short notice. Some places may charge 100% if the booking is for one night only and many require a stay of at least two nights for an advance booking. Always let the owner know as soon as possible if you have to cancel your booking so they can offer the bed to someone else.

Hotels and guesthouses generally take credit or debit cards but most smaller B&Bs only accept cheques by post, or payment by bank transfer, for the deposit; the balance can be settled with cash or a cheque.

Airbnb

The rise and rise of Airbnb (🖳 airbnb.co.uk) has seen private homes and apartments opened up to overnight travellers on an informal basis. While accommodation is primarily based in cities, the concept is spreading to tourist hotspots in more rural areas, but do check thoroughly what you are getting and the precise location. While the first couple of options listed may be in the area you're after, others may be far too far afield for walkers. At its best, this is a great way to meet local people in a relatively unstructured environment, but do be aware that these places are not registered B&Bs, so standards may vary, yet prices may not necessarily be any lower than the norm.

FOOD AND DRINK

Stay in a B&B and you'll be filled to the gills with a cooked **'full-English' breakfast**. This tends to follow a choice of cereals that will have been laid out for you to graze on while you wait for the main event, which usually consists of a plateful of eggs, bacon, sausages, mushrooms, tomatoes and possibly baked beans or black pudding, with toast and butter, and all washed down with coffee, tea and/or juice. Enormously satisfying the first time you try it, but by the fourth or fifth morning you and your arteries may start to prefer a lighter continental breakfast. *(cont'd on p24)*

PLANNING YOUR WALK

❏ FOOD AND DRINK IN DEVON AND DORSET

Traditional food

As a major centre of farming and fishing, it's not surprising that the South-West is an important supplier of food to the rest of Britain and can boast some pretty fine local specialities.

Say 'Devon' to most Brits and in addition to images of sparkling coastlines and rolling hills, the county's name will also conjure up the delights of **clotted cream** – best enjoyed as part of a traditional **cream tea** with a scone or two and some whortleberry jam. This is certainly a speciality, **whortleberry** being the local name for the wild bilberry (though they go by several other names including blueberry, heidelberry, huckleberry, hurtleberry and wimberry) and locally they're called 'worts' or 'urts'.

Dairy products as a whole are plentiful in this corner of the country including delicious yoghurts and ice-cream. **Blue Vinney** is Dorset's most renowned cheese, best eaten with some **Dorset knob biscuits** (today made by only one producer, Moores Biscuits, based near Bridport), or for something sweeter you could try **Dorset apple cake** – and, just to make sure that no artery is left unclogged, enjoy it with a dollop of Dorset clotted cream.

From the sea, **South Devon crab** is reputed to be the tastiest in the world and **smoked eels** are a speciality in these parts too. The county's mature farmhouse cheeses, ice-creams and cottage loaves ensure that, no matter how hard you push yourself on the walk, you won't lose too much weight. Even if you're on a tight budget the ubiquitous fish & chips can be satisfying if cooked with fresh fish. At the other end of the scale there are plenty of fine-dining restaurants around the coast offering mouth-watering dishes concocted from locally caught fish.

Beer

The process of brewing beer is believed to have been in Britain since the Neolithic period and is an art local brewers have been perfecting ever since.

Real ale (also known as cask ale) is beer that has been brewed using traditional methods. Real ales are not filtered or pasteurised, a process which removes and kills all the yeast cells, but instead undergo a secondary fermentation in their casks at the pub, which enhances the natural flavours and brings out the individual characteristics of the beer. It's served at cellar temperature with no artificial fizz added, unlike keg beer which is pasteurised and has the fizz added by injecting nitrogen dioxide.

● **Devon** Devon is thought to have approximately 30 breweries and micro-breweries operating within its borders. Amongst the more celebrated is **Dartmoor Brewery** (🖥 dartmoorbrewery.co.uk), family owned, situated in the centre of the national park and the highest brewery in England (at 1400ft/427m above sea level). From this vantage point they brew their famous Jail Ale (4.8%), as well as Dartmoor IPA (4%).

Closer to the coast at Honiton, **Otter Brewery** (🖥 otterbrewery.co.uk) produces five regular brews including their easy-drinking 'session' ale, Otter Bitter (3.6%), and the ever-popular Otter Ale (4.5%). Meanwhile, based near Kingsbridge, **South Hams Brewery** (🖥 southhamsbrewery.co.uk) brews, amongst others, Devon Pride (3.8%) and Wild Blonde (4.4%).

Located in Newton Abbot, **Teignworthy Brewery** (🖥 teignworthybrewery.com) produces six regular cask ales including Beachcomber (4.5%) and Reel Ale (4%) as well as more than 20 seasonal ales. For the brave, their dark Russian Imperial Porter is a staggering 13%!

Based in Paignton, **Bays Brewery** (🖥 baysbrewery.co.uk) produces three permanent beers – Gold (4.3%), Devon Dumpling (5.1%) and Bays Topsail (4%). The

Dolphin Inn (pp144-5), in Dartmouth, serves beers from its brewery – **Bridgetown Brewery** (🖥 venture-inns.com/the-brewery.html), in nearby Totnes.

● **Dorset** Real ale aficionados are just as well catered for over the border in Dorset. Scattered along the coast path you will come across **Hall & Woodhouse** (🖥 hallwoodhouse.co.uk) pubs, which stock several of their own-brewed Badger Ales, including Tanglefoot (4.9%) and Fursty Ferret (4.4%).

Just by the Devon–Dorset border, **Lyme Regis Brewery** (🖥 lymeregisbrewery .com) operates from premises near the old Town Mill in Lyme Regis. Beers include Cobb (3.9%) and Town Mill (4.5%).

Heading east, **Palmers Brewery** (🖥 palmersbrewery.com), based in Bridport, has been perfecting ale for over 200 years. Calling on such experience they produce five fine ales including Dorset Gold (4.5%), Copper Pale Ale (3.7%) and Tally Ho! (5.5%), a strong dark ale which was first brewed in 1949.

Weymouth's **Dorset Brewing Company**'s (🖥 dbcales.com) award-winning ales include Durdle Door (5%), Jurassic (4.2%), and even a lager titled Chesil (4.1%).

Inland from here, in the Dorset village of Piddlehinton, **Piddle Brewery** (🖥 piddlebrewery.co.uk) produces four year-round cask ales including Piddle (4.1%) and the more hoppy Cocky (4.3%), while right at the end of your walk, why not celebrate with a pint from **Isle of Purbeck Brewery** (🖥 isleofpurbeckbrewery.com), which produces beers from its brewery beside Bankes Arms (p309) in Studland. Ales to look for include Fossil Fuel (4.1%) and Purbeck IPA (4.8%).

Cider

A pint of cider on this section of the walk is almost as obligatory as blisters. **Scrumpy**, or rough cider, is a particular form of cider, easy to differentiate from the weaker, more mass-market keg ciders, being cloudy, fizz-free and with bits floating in it too! The only thing to remember before drinking scrumpy is that it should be done so in moderation – it's powerful stuff. After you've drunk it, you'll be lucky to remember anything at all.

● **Devon** Look out for products from **Sandford Orchards** (🖥 sandfordorchards .co.uk), such as the cloudy Devon Scrumpy (6%), and their biggest seller, the sparkling and clear Devon Red (4.5%).

● **Dorset** Meanwhile, in Dorset, look for ciders fermented at **Marshwood Vale Cider** (🖥 marshwoodvalecider.com), such as the bottled and sweet Dorset Kingfisher (7%) and the medium Dorset Tit (7.2%).

A must for cider aficionados is **Castle Inn** (see p289) at Lulworth; however, the inn was being taken over by new owners at the time of research. Fingers crossed they will have the same commitment to supporting traditional local cider-makers and continue to stock a wide range of traditional draught ciders and perries (produced from perry pears as opposed to apples) from Dorset, Somerset, Hampshire and Herefordshire. Pressed and ripened in Dorset they stock the popular Cider by Rosie (6.5%), whilst favourites from the surrounding counties include beverages produced by Westons Cider (🖥 westons-cider.co.uk) such as Westons Old Rosie Scrumpy (7.3%) and Westons Country Perry (4.5%) from Herefordshire, and the Maverick (ginger and chilli) Cider (4%) produced by Orchard Pig (🖥 orchardpig.co.uk) in Somerset.

The Square and Compass, in Worth Matravers (p300), is also very proud of the cider they stock and with good reason as they press their own ciders in the back garden; they also host an annual cider festival in November.

(Cont'd from p21) If you have had enough of these cooked breakfasts and/or plan an early start, ask if you can have a **packed lunch** instead of breakfast. Your landlady or hostel can usually provide one at an additional cost (unless it's in lieu of breakfast), though of course there's nothing to stop you preparing your own lunch (a penknife is very handy for this), or going to a pub (see below) or café.

Whatever you do for lunch, don't forget to leave some room for a **cream tea** (see box p22) or two, a morale, energy and cholesterol booster all rolled into one delicious package. To describe it as simply a pot of tea accompanied by scones served with cream and jam is to totally ignore the history, ceremony and joy of this Titan of teatime. The jury is out on whether you should put the jam on first or the cream – but either way, do not miss the chance of at least one cream tea.

Pubs are as much a feature of the walk as seagulls and sheep, and in some cases they are as much a tourist attraction as any castle or cove. Most pubs have become highly attuned to the desires of trekkers and offer lunch and evening meals (often with a couple of local dishes and usually some vegetarian options), some locally brewed real ales (and/or ciders), a garden to relax in on hot days and a roaring fire to huddle around on cold ones. The standard of the food varies widely, though is usually served in big portions, which is often just about all trekkers care about at the end of a long day. In many of the villages the pub is the only place to eat out. Note that pubs may close in the afternoon, especially in the winter months, so check in advance if you are hoping to visit a particular one, and also if you are planning lunch there as food serving hours can change.

That other great British culinary institution, the **fish 'n' chip shop**, can be found in virtually every town on the trail. As well as these, there are **restaurants** and **takeaways** in the larger towns en route and also in some of the villages.

> ❏ **Opening hours**
> The opening days and hours for pubs, restaurants and cafés mentioned in Part 4 are as accurate as possible but often if the weather is bad, or there is no demand, places will close early or not open at all so it is worth checking in advance, especially if there are few eating places in the area. See also box p26.

Self-catering

There is a shop of some description in most of the places along the route, though most are small (and often combined with the post office) and whether you'll be able to find precisely what you went in for is uncertain. If self-catering, therefore, your menu for the evening will depend upon what you found in the store that day. Part 4 details what shops are on the path.

Drinking water

Be careful: on a hot day in some of the remoter parts after a steep climb or two you'll quickly dehydrate, which is at best highly unpleasant and at worst mightily dangerous. Always carry some water with you and in hot weather drink 3-4 litres a day. Don't be tempted by the water in the streams; if the cow or sheep faeces in the water don't make you ill, the chemicals from the pesticides and fertilisers used on the farms almost certainly will.

Using iodine or another purifying treatment will help to combat the former, though there's little you can do about the latter. It's a lot safer to fill up from taps instead, all of which are safe to drink from in England, including those in public toilets (although the annoying rise in automated warm-water hand-washing machines makes re-filling water bottles an impossible task).

Look out for handy **water taps** located on some tourist beaches along the coast path, and note that, in Dorset particularly, rows of beach huts often have a water tap behind them. We've marked some water taps on our maps.

MONEY

There are several **banks** on the trail and most are equipped with an **ATM** (cash machine). You'll also find ATMs in many shops and stores though these tend to charge (typically £1.85) to withdraw money. You can also withdraw money over the counter at **post offices** (providing your bank is affiliated – most UK banks are). Another way of getting money in your hand is to use the **cashback** system: find a store or a pub that will accept a debit card and ask them to advance cash against the card. Some will, especially if you buy something; some won't.

Most local shops, cafés and pubs accept cards these days, but few B&Bs do so it's important to carry plenty of **cash** with you, though do keep it safe and out of sight (preferably in a moneybelt).

A **chequebook** could prove very useful as back-up, so that you don't have to keep on dipping into your cash reserves, especially as most B&Bs don't accept credit/debit cards.

Getting cash at post offices

Several banks have agreements with the Post Office allowing customers to make cash withdrawals free of charge using a debit card at branches throughout the country. Given that many towns and villages have post offices but may not have banks, this is a very useful facility.

You can find a full list of participating banks and a list of post office branches with an ATM on the Post Office website (🖥 postoffice.co.uk, click on Products & Services, then Branch and Banking services); alternatively check with the Post Office Helpline (☎ 0345-611 2970).

OTHER SERVICES

Thanks to the rise of smartphones, internet cafés seem to be a thing of the past, but you'll still find **public internet access** in the libraries along the trail. Most pubs, cafés and B&Bs also have **free wi-fi** for customers who have their own devices. Towns have at least one **supermarket** and most villages have a **grocery store**. You'll sometimes find a **phone box** near these shops, though you will almost definitely need a card (credit, debit, BT or prepaid) as many phone boxes no longer accept coins. Calls from a phone box cost a minimum of 60p (including a 40p connection charge; thereafter 10p a minute).

There are **outdoor equipment shops** in most large towns en route.

PLANNING YOUR WALK

WALKING COMPANIES

It is, of course, possible to turn up with your boots and backpack at Plymouth and just start walking, with little planned save for your accommodation (see box on p18). The following companies, however, are in the business of making your holiday as stress-free and enjoyable as possible. Several companies offer what are known as **self-guided holidays** (see pp28-9), where your accommodation, transport at the start/end of the walk and baggage transfer along the trail are

---

❑ Information for foreign visitors

● **Currency** The British pound (£) comes in notes of £100, £50, £20, £10 and £5, and coins of £2 and £1. The pound is divided into 100 pence (usually referred to as 'p', pronounced 'pee') which comes in silver coins of 50p, 20p, 10p and 5p, and copper coins of 2p and 1p.

● **Money** Up-to-date **rates of exchange** can be found on 🖥 www.xe.com/currency converter, at some post offices, or at any bank or travel agent.

● **Business hours** Most **village shops** are open Monday to Friday 9am-5pm and Saturday 9am-12.30pm, though some open as early as 7.30/8am; many also open on Sundays but not usually for the whole day. Occasionally you'll come across a local shop that closes at lunchtime on one day during the week, usually a Wednesday or Thursday; this is a throwback to the days when all towns and villages had an 'early closing day'. **Supermarkets** are open Monday to Saturday 8am-8pm (often longer) and on Sunday from about 9am to 5 or 6pm, though main branches of supermarkets generally open 10am-4pm or 11am-5pm.

Main **post offices** generally open Monday to Friday 9am-5pm and Saturday 9am-12.30pm though where the branch is in a shop PO services are sometimes available whenever the shop is open; **banks** typically open at 9.30/10am Monday to Friday and close at 3.30/4pm, though in some places both post offices and banks may open only two or three days a week and/or in the morning, or limited hours, only. **ATMs (cash machines)** located outside a bank, shop, post office or petrol station are open all the time, but any that are inside will be accessible only when that place is open. However, ones that charge, such as Link machines, may not accept foreign-issued cards.

Pub hours are less predictable as each pub may have different opening hours. However, most pubs on the Path open daily 11am-11pm (some close at 10.30pm on Sunday) but **some close in the afternoon** especially in the winter months.

The last entry time to most **museums and galleries** is usually half an hour, or an hour, before the official closing time.

● **National holidays** Most businesses in the South-West are shut on 1st January, Good Friday and Easter Monday (March/April), first and last Monday in May, last Monday in August, 25th December and 26th December.

● **School holidays** State-school holidays in England are generally as follows: a one-week break late October, two weeks over Christmas and the New Year, a week mid February, two weeks around Easter, one week at the end of May/early June (to coincide with the bank holiday at the end of May) and five to six weeks from late July to early September. Private-school holidays fall at the same time, but tend to be slightly longer.

● **Documents** If you are a member of a National Trust organisation in your country bring your membership card as you should be entitled to free entry to National Trust properties and sites in the UK (see p57).

---

arranged for you. Detailed information and maps are also provided as a matter of course, thereby allowing you to just turn up and start marching! These are useful for those who simply don't have the time to organise their trip,

No matter how much information is provided by the self-guided companies – or indeed this book – the chances are you will learn and appreciate much more in the company of an experienced and knowledgeable guide. **Guided walking tours** (see p29) are ideal for those who want the extra safety, security and companionship that comes with walking in a group.

● **EHICs and travel insurance** Although Britain's National Health Service (NHS) is free at the point of use, that is only the case for residents. All visitors to Britain should be properly insured, including comprehensive health coverage. The European Health Insurance Card (EHIC) entitles EU nationals (on production of the EHIC card so ensure you bring it with you) to necessary medical treatment under the NHS while on a temporary visit here – probably until Brexit is complete, that is. For details, contact your national social security institution. However, this is not a substitute for proper medical cover on your travel insurance for unforeseen bills and for getting you home should that be necessary. Also consider cover for loss and theft of personal belongings, especially if you are camping or staying in hostels, as there may be times when you'll have to leave your luggage unattended.

● **Weights and measures** In Britain milk is sold in pints (1 pint = 568ml), as is beer in pubs, though most other **liquids** including petrol (gasoline) and diesel are sold in litres. **Distances** on road and path signs are given in miles (1 mile = 1.6km) rather than kilometres, and yards (1yd = 0.9m) rather than metres. The population remains divided between those who still use inches (1 inch = 2.5cm), feet (1ft = 0.3m) and yards and those who are happy with millimetres, centimetres and metres; you'll often be told that 'it's only a hundred yards or so' to somewhere, rather than a hundred metres or so. Most **food** is sold in metric weights (g and kg) but the imperial weights of pounds (lb: 1lb = 453g) and ounces (oz: 1oz = 28g) are frequently displayed too. The **weather** – a frequent topic of conversation – is also an issue: while most forecasts predict temperatures in Celsius (C), many people continue to think in terms of Fahrenheit (F; see the temperature chart on p16 for conversions).

● **Smoking** The ban on smoking in public places relates not only to pubs and restaurants, but also to B&Bs, hostels and hotels. These latter have the right to designate one or more bedrooms where the occupants can smoke, but the ban is in force in all enclosed areas open to the public – even if they are in a private home such as a B&B. Should you be foolhardy enough to light up in a no-smoking area, which includes pretty well any indoor public place, you could be fined £50, but it's the owners of the premises who carry the can if they fail to stop you, with a potential fine of £2500.

● **Time** During the winter, the whole of Britain is on Greenwich Mean Time (GMT). The clocks move one hour forward on the last Sunday in March, remaining on British Summer Time (BST) until the last Sunday in October.

● **Telephone** The international country access code for Britain is ☎ 44 followed by the area code minus the first 0, and then the number you require. Within Britain, to call a landline number with the same code as the landline phone you are calling from, the code can be omitted: dial the number only. If you're using a mobile phone that is registered overseas, consider buying a local SIM card to keep costs down. See box p42.

● **Emergency services** For police, ambulance, fire or coastguard dial ☎ 999 or ☎ 112.

PLANNING YOUR WALK

Accommodation, meals, transport to and from the trail and baggage transfer are usually included in the price. Be warned, however, that the standards of accommodation, the distances walked each day and the age of the clients that companies attract often vary widely, so do check each company carefully to make sure you choose that one that is right for you.

Baggage transfer

For those who don't fancy being burdened while on the path, it is possible to arrange to have your luggage transferred to the end of each day's destination.

The main baggage company on the SWCP is the aptly named **Luggage Transfers** (☎ 01326-567247, 🖳 luggagetransfers.co.uk), who cover the whole of the path. Transfer costs start at £17 for a short 2-bag transfer; a small discount is made for only one bag. Next-day bookings are taken up until 6.30pm. They also have an LT Taxi booking service (🖳 lttaxis.co.uk) which means you can book for your luggage transfers and yourselves all in one place.

Alternatively, some of the taxi companies listed in this guide can provide a similar service within a local area if you want a break from carrying your bags for a day or so. Also, don't rule out the possibility of your B&B/guesthouse owner taking your bags ahead for you. Some are happy to do so and, depending on the distance, they may make no charge at all, or charge £10-15; this may be less than a taxi so is worth enquiring about.

Self-guided holidays

(See p26) The companies below offer **tailor-made holidays** in addition to the packages mentioned.

● **Absolute Escapes** (☎ 0131-240 1210, 🖳 absoluteescapes.com; Edinburgh) Offer walks along the path from Exmouth to Lyme Regis and Lyme Regis to Poole.

● **Celtic Trails** (☎ 01291-689774, 🖳 celtictrailswalkingholidays.co.uk; Chepstow) Long-established company that offers the whole path and in sections.

● **Contours Walking Holidays** (☎ 01629-821900, 🖳 contours.co.uk; Derbyshire) Offer the path in sections and the entire length; also dog-friendly walks.

● **Encounter Walking** (☎ 01208-871066, 🖳 encounterwalkingholidays.com; Cornwall) Offer walks along the entire path and in sections.

● **Explore Britain** (☎ 01740-650900, 🖳 explorebritain.com; Co Durham) Organises several treks around the South-West peninsula including Sidmouth to Portesham, a 6-night inn-to-inn walking tour with two nights at Lyme Regis.

● **Footpath Holidays** (☎ 01985-840049, 🖳 footpath-holidays.com; Wiltshire) Operate a range of walking holidays including inn-to-inn itineraries for the whole path and single-centre holidays from the Purbeck peninsula, Dartmouth and Sidmouth. They also offer short breaks.

● **Footscape** (☎ 01935 817618, 🖳 footscape.co.uk; Sherborne) Offer bespoke, independent, walking holidays along the Jurassic coast and also dog-walking holidays.

● **High Point Holidays** (☎ 07483-241945, 🖳 highpointholidays.co.uk; Somerset) Offer a range of walks (4-7 days) along the Jurassic Coast Path.

● **Let's Go Walking!** (☎ 01837-880075, 🖳 letsgowalking.com; North Tawton, Devon) Offer walks along the entire path and in parts.

● **Macs Adventure** (☎ 0141-530 8886, 🖳 macsadventure.com; Glasgow) Have walks covering the whole SWCP including Plymouth to Brixham, Exmouth to Lyme Regis, Lyme Regis to Poole, with varying itineraries to suit.

● **Nearwater Holidays** (☎ 01326-279278, 🖳 nearwaterwalkingholidays.co.uk; Truro) Walks covering the whole path as well as sections.

● **Responsible Travel** (☎ 01273-823700, 🖳 responsibletravel.com; Brighton) Offer walks along the whole path and in sections.

● **Sherpa Expeditions** (☎ 020-8875 5070, 🖳 sherpaexpeditions.com; London) Offer 8-day holidays from Lyme Regis to Lulworth Cove.

● **The Discerning Traveller** (☎ 01865-515618, 🖳 discerningtraveller.co.uk; Oxford) Walks from Exmouth to Lyme Regis and Exmouth to Lulworth Cove for five or eight nights. They also offer a separate 'Purbeck' tour between Lulworth Cove and Studland.

● **Walk the Trail (formerly BW Holidays)** (☎ 01326-567252, 🖳 www.walk thetrail.co.uk; Helston) Holidays of any itinerary length from short breaks to the entire SWCP and all routes in between.

● **Westcountry Walking Holidays** (☎ 0330-350 1348, 🖳 westcountry-walk ing-holidays.com; Norfolk) Specialise in the South West Coast Path and Pembrokeshire Coast Path. Arrange tours along the whole path as well as in sections according to requirements.

Group/guided walking tours

● **Footpath Holidays** (see opposite) Fully guided tours in South Devon and in Dorset on the Purbeck peninsula.

● **HF Holidays** (☎ 0845-470 8558, 🖳 hfholidays.co.uk; Herts) Offer a seven-night 'Dorset Coast Path' walk along the Jurassic Coast and a centre-based holiday from their country house at Lulworth Cove, as well as walks in South Devon from Plymouth to Brixham.

● **Jurassic Coast Walking** (☎ 01425-655779, 🖳 jurassiccoastwalking.co.uk; Purbeck) Arranges and guides short walking holidays for small groups, with the focus on Purbeck.

● **South Devon Walking Holidays** (☎ 01752-897034, 🖳 blackadonbarns.co .uk/out-and-about/activities/south-devon-walking-holidays; Devon) Specialise in groups walking between Plymouth and Dartmouth/Brixham. Holidays include Plymouth to Dartmouth for six nights.

● **Trexx Walking Holidays** (☎ 01305-783129, 🖳 rob@trexx.co.uk; Weymouth) Provide walks (Oct-Mar) led by the owner of The Esplanade (see p278), a local man who has been visiting the area's beauty spots all his life. Two- or three-day tours cover the coast between Charmouth and Lulworth Cove although other sites can also be visited and itineraries can be tailor-made.

Budgeting

England is not a cheap place to go travelling and the accommodation providers on the South-West Coast Path are more than used to seeing tourists and charge accordingly. You may think before you set out that you are going to try to keep your budget to a minimum by camping every night and cooking your own food but it's a rare trekker who sticks to this rule. Besides, the B&Bs and pubs on the route are amongst the path's major attractions and it would be a pity not to sample the hospitality in at least some of them. If you really want to keep costs to a minimum, consider walking out of season when accommodation rates are often cheaper.

   If the only expenses of this walk were accommodation and food, budgeting for the trip would be a piece of cake. Unfortunately, in addition there are all the little extras that push up the cost: beer, cream teas, stamps and postcards, internet use, phone costs, buses here and there, ferry rides, baggage transfer, laundry, souvenirs, entrance fees... it's surprising how much all of these things add up.

CAMPING

You can survive on less than £15 per person (pp) if you use the cheapest campsites (or wild camp), don't visit a pub, avoid all museums and tourist attractions, and cook all your own food from staple ingredients. Even then, unforeseen expenses will probably nudge your daily budget above this figure. Include the occasional pint, and perhaps a pub meal every now and then, and the figure will be nearer £20-25pp a day.

HOSTELS AND BUNKHOUSES

Rates at the hostels (both independent and YHA) en route start from £12pp but can be much higher in peak season; YHA rates are now very fluid depending on demand. Breakfast at hostels is about £7.50 and a two-course evening meal (where available) may cost £8-15. The only bunkhouse charges £45pp including breakfast and supper. This means that, overall, it can cost around £30-35pp per day, or £40-50pp to live in a little more comfort and enjoy the odd beer or two. However, since it isn't possible to stay in a hostel or bunkhouse every night on this section of the coast path, anticipate a higher daily budget if you choose to stay in a B&B.

B&Bs, PUBS, GUESTHOUSES AND HOTELS

B&B rates start at around £30pp (based on two sharing) per night but can be twice or even three times this, particularly if you are walking by yourself and are thus liable to pay a single occupancy supplement (see p21). Add on the cost of lunch and dinner and you should reckon on about £45-50pp minimum per day. Staying in a guesthouse or hotel would probably push the minimum up to £55-60pp.

Itineraries

Part 4 of this book has been written from west to east, though there is of course nothing to stop you from tackling it in the opposite direction, and there are advantages in doing so – see below.

To help plan your walk see the **colour maps and gradient profiles** (at the end of the book) and the **table of town and village facilities** (pp32-3), which gives a run-down on the availability of services including accommodation.

You could follow one of the suggested itineraries (see p34 & p35) which are based on preferred type of accommodation and walking speeds or, if tackling the entire walk seems a bit ambitious, you can tackle it a day or two at a time. To help you, we discuss the highlights of the Dorset & South Devon Coast Path on pp36-7 and you can use public transport to get to the start and end of the walk. The public transport map and service details are on pp51-4.

Once you have an idea of your approach turn to Part 4 for detailed information on accommodation, places to eat and other services in each village and town on the route. Also in Part 4 you will find summaries of the route to accompany the detailed trail maps.

WHICH DIRECTION?

It's more common for walkers attempting the entire SWCP to start from Minehead and finish at South Haven Point and this is the way the route is described in Part 4. Furthermore, the prevailing wind usually comes from the west so, by walking in this direction, you'll find you have the weather behind you for the section described in this book, pushing you on rather than driving in your face. That said, if this is your first taste of the coast path – and you think you're going to continue one day and complete the rest of the 630-mile trek – you may prefer to start at South Haven Point and finish at Plymouth.

Those who prefer to swim against the tide of popular opinion and walk east to west should find it easy to use this book too.

SUGGESTED ITINERARIES

The itineraries in the boxes on p34 and on p35 are based on different accommodation types (camping and B&B-style accommodation), with each divided into three alternatives depending on your walking speed. They are only suggestions so feel free to adapt them. **Don't forget** to add your travelling time before and after the walk.

VILLAGE AND

Place name (Places in brackets are a short walk off the Coast Path)	Distance from previous place (if in brackets nearest point on the trail used) approx miles	km	Cash Machine (ATM)/Bank (£ = charge)	Post Office	Tourist Information Centre (TIC)/ Point (TIP)/
Plymouth			✔	✔	TIC
Wembury	10¾	17.25		✔	
(Noss Mayo/N Ferrers)	(2)	(3.25)	✔		
Ch'borough/Bigbury	15¼	24.5	✔£		
Outer Hope	5	8	✔£	✔	
Salcombe	8	13	✔	✔	TIC
(East Prawle)	(6)	(9.75)			
Beesands	12¼	19.75			
Torcross	½	.075		✔	
(Slapton)	(2½)	(4)			
Strete	3½	5.75		✔	
Stoke Fleming	2½	4		✔	
Dartmouth	4¼	6.75	✔	✔	TIC
Kingswear	FERRY		✔		
Brixham	11	17.75	✔	✔	TIP
Paignton	5¾	9.25	✔	✔	TIP
Torquay	2¾	4.5	✔	✔	TIC
(St Marychurch)	(6)	(9.75)	✔	✔	
Maidencombe	8	13			
Shaldon	3¼	5.25	✔	✔	TIC
Teignmouth	–	–	✔	✔	TIP
Dawlish	3¾	6	✔	✔	TIC
Dawlish Warren	1¾	2.75	✔£		
Cockwood/Starcross	2½	4			
Exmouth	FERRY		✔	✔	TIC
Budleigh Salterton	5½	9	✔	✔	TIC
Sidmouth	7	11.25	✔	✔	TIC
Branscombe Mouth	6½	10.5			
Beer	2¼	3.5	✔£	✔	
Seaton	1½	2.5	✔	✔	TIC
Lyme Regis	7	11.25	✔	✔	TIC
Charmouth	3	4.75	✔£	✔	
Seatown/(Chideock)	4¼ (½)	6.75 (1)		✔	
Eype Mouth	2	3.25			TIP
West Bay	1¼	2	✔£		
(Burton Bradstock)	(1¼)	(2)	✔£	✔	
West Bexington	5½	8.75			
Abbotsbury	3¾	6		✔	TIP
Fortuneswell/Portland	13	21	✔	✔	
Weymouth	14¾	23.75	✔	✔	
Osmington/Os Mills	4¾	7.75			
Lulworth	6¼	10	✔£		
(Kimmeridge)	(7¼)	(11.75)			
(Worth Matravers)	(5½)	(8.75)			
Swanage	13½	21.75	✔	✔	TIC
South Haven Point	7½	12			
TOTAL DISTANCE	217¼ miles	350km			

TOWN FACILITIES

Eating Place	Food Store	Campsite	Hostels	B&B-style accommodation	Place name
✔ = one		✔	YHA/	✔ = one;	(Places in
✔✔ = two			H (Ind Hostel)/	✔✔ = two	brackets are a
✔✔✔ = three +			B (Bunkhouse)	✔✔✔ = three+	short walk off the Coast Path)
✔✔✔	✔		H	✔✔✔	Plymouth
✔	✔	✔		✔✔✔	Wembury
✔✔✔	✔			✔✔✔	(Noss Mayo/N Ferrers)
✔✔✔	✔	✔		✔✔	Ch'borough/Bigbury
✔✔✔	✔			✔✔✔	Outer Hope
✔✔✔	✔	✔		✔✔✔	Salcombe
✔✔	✔	✔		✔	(East Prawle)
✔	✔			✔✔	Beesands
✔✔✔	✔			✔✔	Torcross
✔	✔	✔		✔	(Slapton)
✔	✔	✔		✔✔✔	Strete
✔✔✔	✔	✔		✔✔✔	Stoke Fleming
✔✔✔	✔			✔✔✔	Dartmouth
✔✔✔	✔				Kingswear
✔✔✔	✔	✔		✔✔✔	Brixham
✔✔✔	✔	✔		✔✔✔	Paignton
✔✔✔	✔			✔✔✔	Torquay
✔✔✔	✔			✔	(St Marychurch)
✔				✔	Maidencombe
✔✔✔	✔	✔		✔✔✔	Shaldon
✔✔✔	✔			✔✔✔	Teignmouth
✔✔✔	✔			✔✔✔	Dawlish
✔✔✔	✔			✔	Dawlish Warren
✔✔✔	✔			✔✔	Cockwood/Starcross
✔✔✔	✔	✔	B	✔✔✔	Exmouth
✔✔✔	✔	✔		✔✔	Budleigh Salterton
✔✔✔	✔			✔✔✔	Sidmouth
✔	✔			✔	Branscombe Mouth
✔✔✔	✔	✔	YHA	✔✔✔	Beer
✔✔✔	✔	✔		✔✔✔	Seaton
✔✔✔	✔	✔		✔✔✔	Lyme Regis
✔✔✔	✔	✔		✔✔✔	Charmouth
✔✔✔	✔	✔		✔✔✔	Seatown/(Chideock)
✔	✔	✔		✔	Eype Mouth
✔✔✔	✔	✔		✔✔✔	West Bay
✔	✔	✔		✔✔✔	(Burton Bradstock)
✔✔				✔	West Bexington
✔✔✔	✔			✔✔✔	Abbotsbury
✔✔✔	✔	✔	YHA/H	✔✔✔	Fortuneswell/Portland
✔✔✔	✔		H	✔✔✔	Weymouth
✔		✔		✔	Osmington/Os Mills
✔✔✔	✔	✔	YHA	✔✔✔	Lulworth
✔✔		✔		✔	(Kimmeridge)
✔✔		✔		✔	(Worth Matravers)
✔✔✔	✔		YHA/H	✔✔✔	Swanage
					South Haven Point

PLANNING YOUR WALK

CAMPING

	Relaxed			Medium			Fast		
Night	**Place**	**Approx Distance** miles	km	**Place**	**Approx Distance** miles	km	**Place**	**Approx Distance** miles	km
0	Plymouth			Plymouth			Plymouth		
1	Wembury*	10¾	17.25	Wembury*	10¾	17.25	Wembury*	10¾	17.25
2	Bigbury	15¼	24.5	Bigbury	15¼	24.5	Bigbury	15¼	24.5
3	Salcombe*	12½	20	Salcombe*	12½	20	East Prawle*	18½	29.75
4	East Prawle*	7	11.25	East Prawle*	7	11.25	Stoke Flm'g	13¼	21.25
5	Slapton*	8¾	14	Stoke Fleming	13¼	21.25	Brixham	15¼	24.5
6	Stoke Fleming	4½	7.25	Brixham	15¼	24.5	Shaldon	16½	26.5
7	Brixham	15¼	24.5	Goodrington*	4½	7.5	Budleigh Sn	13½	21.75
8	Goodrington*	4½	7.5	Shaldon*	12½	20	Seaton*	17¼	27.75
9	Shaldon*	12½	20	Exmouth*	8	13	Seatown	14¼	23
10	Exmouth*	8	13	Budleigh Sn*	5½	9	East Fleet	19¼	31
11	Budleigh Sn*	5½	9	Beer	16	25.5	Fortuneswell*§	16	25.75
12	Ladram Bay▲	7	11.25	Charmouth	11½	18.5	Durdle Door	16	25.75
13	Beer	9	14.5	West Bay	7	11.25	Kimmeridge§§	7¼	11.75
14	Charmouth	11½	18.5	East Fleet	16½	26	Worth Matrvs**	7½	12
15	West Bay	7	11.25	Fortuneswell*	6¼	10	S Haven Pt†	13½	21.5
16	West Fleet*	14	22.5	Osmington M§	19½	31.5			
17	Fortuneswell*	8½	13.5	Durdle Door	6¼	10			
18	Fortuneswell*§	9¾	15.75	Kimmeridge§§	7¼	11.75			
19	Osmington M	9¾	15.75	Worth Matrvs**	7½	12			
20	Durdle Door	6¼	10	S Haven Point†	13½	21.5			
21	Kimmeridge§§	7¼	11.75						
22	Worth Matrvs**	7½	12						
23	S Haven Point†	13½	21.5						

▲ Ladram Bay Holiday Park (see p204)

§ After Isle of Portland circuit

* On this chart we have **not** included in the mile counts the distance from the path to the campsite, which can be a mile or more. The campsites that are a significant distance off the path are marked with an asterisk. Consult the route guide for distances. Remember to factor these into your walk when calculating the distance you will walk for any one stage.

** Open mid summer only (see p300)   §§ Distance via Lulworth Ranges

† From S Haven Point cross to Sandbanks for buses to Poole or Bournemouth (p313)

THE BEST DAY AND WEEKEND WALKS

We think that this leg of the South-West Coast Path is the most varied of the three and thus deserves to be walked in its entirety. But, if you don't have the time for that, the following will allow you to savour at least some of the joys of this walk.

The routes on pp36-7 are designed to link up with public transport (see pp50-4) at both their start and finish; the only places where there are no services are Bigbury-on-Sea, West Bexington and Kimmeridge. The lack of services to Kimmeridge is particularly annoying as it sits at the end of possibly the most spectacular stage, over the Lulworth Ranges. But if you have a weekend free you can take one path through the ranges on one day – then walk back to Lulworth Cove on the alternative (inland) trail the next.

STAYING IN B&B-STYLE ACCOMMODATION

	Relaxed			Medium			Fast		
Night	Place	Approx Distance miles km		Place	Approx Distance miles km		Place	Approx Distance miles km	
0	Plymouth			Plymouth			Plymouth		
1	Wembury	10¾	17.25	Wembury	10¾	17.25	Wembury	10¾	17.25
2	Bigbury	15¼	24.5	Bigbury	15¼	24.5	Bigbury	15¼	24.5
3	Hope Cove	5	8	Salcombe	13	21	Salcombe	13	21
4	Salcombe	8	13	Torcross	12¾	20.5	Stoke Flem'g	18¾	30
5	Torcross	12¾	20.5	Dartmouth	10¼	16.5	Brixham	15¼	24.5
6	Dartmouth	10¼	16.5	Brixham	11	17.5	Maidencombe	16½	26.5
7	Brixham	11	17.75	Torquay	8½	13.75	Exmouth	11¼	18.25
8	Torquay	8½	13.75	Teignmouth	11¼	18.25	Sidmouth	12½	20
9	Teignmouth	11¼	18.25	Exmouth	8	13	Seaton	10¼	16.5
10	Exmouth	8	13	Sidmouth	12½	20	Seatown	14¼	23
11	Budleigh Sn	5½	9	Seaton	10¼	16.5	Abbotsbury	12½	20
12	Sidmouth	7	11.25	Lyme Regis	7¼	11.75	Fortuneswell	13	21
13	Beer	8¾	14	West Bay	10	16	Weymouth§	14¾	23.75
14	Lyme Regis	8½	13.75	Abbotsbury	9½	15.25	Lulworth	11	17.75
15	Seatown	7¼	11.5	Fortuneswell	13	21	Kimmeridge	7¼	11.75
16	Abbotsbury	12½	20	Weymouth§	14¾	23.75	Swanage	13½	21.75
17	Fortuneswell	13	21	Lulworth Cove	11	17.75	S Haven Pt†	7½	12
18	Portland Bill	4	6.5	Kimmeridge	7¼	11.75			
19	Weymouth	8	13	Swanage	13½	21.75			
20	Lulworth	11	17.75	S Haven Pt†	7½	12			
21	Kimmeridge*	7¼	11.75						
22	Swanage	13½	21.75						
23	S Haven Point†	7½	12						

§ After Isle of Portland circuit   * Distance via Lulworth Ranges
† From S Haven Point cross to Sandbanks for buses to Poole or Bournemouth (p313)

❏ Crossing rivers

As you may expect from a coastal walk, the path from Plymouth to South Haven Point (Poole Harbour), particularly Plymouth to Exmouth, is interrupted fairly frequently by rivers that bisect the path on their way down to the sea. The coast path uses ferries to cross these waterways which actually provide a welcome relief (and a sit-down!) from all your exertions.

In summer, getting a ferry is generally not a problem (though some don't operate daily and some only operate limited hours); but walk outside the high season and it's a different story: in places, particularly at the beginning of the walk, the ferries do not run all year. In these instances, trekkers must either resort to the (often infrequent) public transport, or take a lengthy diversion inland to a point where the river can be crossed, then return to the coastline to pick up the path again.

In this book we describe these alternative walking routes at the appropriate places in the guide – as well as looking at the public transport options. Remember to add extra days to your trek should you need to take any of these alternative routes.

Note that services are often seasonal and not always daily so check in advance before you plan any of these walks.

Day walks

● **Bigbury-on-Sea to Salcombe**   13 miles/21km (see pp114-24)
One of the remotest sections on the path, but just divine, beginning at pretty Bigbury and culminating in a saunter round Bolt Tail and Bolt Head, with Hope Cove a lovely place for lunch.

● **Brixham to Torquay**   8½ miles/13.6km (see pp155-69)
For those who fancy an easy, largely horizontal day strolling from one seaside resort to the next, with a camera in one hand and an ice-cream in the other, this is the heart of the English Riviera.

● **Exmouth to Sidmouth**   12½ miles/20km (see pp197-211)
Not the easiest of walks, but one that takes in some spectacular scenery, refreshments at Budleigh Salterton – and the gateway to a World Heritage Coast.

● **Sidmouth to Seaton**   10¼ miles/16.5km (see pp211-21)
A tough trek but the rewards are ample, with the settlements of Branscombe Mouth and Beer lovely places to recover after some stiff strolling on undulating, natural terrain.

● **Seaton to Lyme Regis**   7 miles/11.5km (see pp221-33)
One of the best – if not the best – walk on the path, taking in the sublime natural beauty of the phenomenon known as the Undercliffs.

● **Lyme Regis to Seatown (& Chideock)**   7¼ miles/11.75km (see pp233-40)
A short (3hr) and relatively easy walk through some lovely coastal scenery culminating in a conquest of the south coast's highest point, Golden Cap.

● **Portland Circuit**   9¾ miles/15.75km (see pp268-72)
One of the oddest walks on the path, beginning and ending at Fortuneswell and taking in prisons, housing estates and boulder fields as well as some lovely walking on this idiosyncratic isle.

● **Weymouth to Lulworth Cove**   11 miles/17.75km (see pp279-89)
A contender for the most photogenic walk in the book with a straightforward stroll to Osmington Mills followed by the tough chalk rollercoaster leading to delightful Durdle Door and lovely Lulworth.

● **Lulworth Cove to Kimmeridge Bay**   7¼ miles/11.75km (see pp289-98)
Cliff-top strolling doesn't get more awe-inspiring than this stiff hike through the ranges; just make sure you go when they're open (usually weekends only). Transport from Kimmeridge Bay is limited but the walk can be combined with the first of the alternative routes around the ranges (13½ miles/21.75km) for one very long but immensely satisfying circular walk.

● **South Dorset Ridgeway (West Bexington to Osmington) 17 miles/27.4km (see pp251-4)**
For those who are fed up with coastal walking but love burial barrows, hillforts, stone circles and other prehistoric constructions. A lovely, lovely walk.

Weekend walks

● **Salcombe to Dartmouth**   **23 miles/37km (see pp124-45)**
One of the best couple of days on the South Devon coastline, very diverse with
some fairly strenuous climbing in places, lots of easy flat walking too – and
plenty of places for refreshments on the way.

● **Sidmouth to Lyme Regis**   **17½ miles/28.2km (see pp211-33)**
Dreamy landscapes, pretty beaches, remote combes, lovely villages and the
delightful Undercliffs to finish. This reasonably taxing but short walk is packed
with interest.

● **Lyme Regis to Abbotsbury 19½ miles/31.4km (see pp233-50 & pp254-9)**
Once past Charmouth this difficult-in-places stroll takes in some delicious
Dorset countryside, with Golden Cap and Chesil Beach just two of the many
highlights on the way. Abbotsbury is the perfect end to any walk, too.

● **Lulworth Cove to Swanage**   **20¾ miles/33.4km (see pp289-308)**
Arguably the best weekend walk on the path, though only if the ranges are open
(which they usually are at weekends). Spectacular, wild, remote, delightful hiking through the Isle of Purbeck, bookended by two lovely settlements. Your calf
muscles may curse that you undertook such a testing trek – but your eyes, and
your soul, will be forever grateful.

SIDE TRIPS

The SWCP isn't the only walking trail to meander through Devon and Dorset.
Indeed, at times the coast path is bisected by other trails or even shares its route
with other paths.

A glance at an OS map will give you an idea of the many paths in the region
but below is a brief description of the main ones you may encounter.

● **Erme-Plym Trail/The Two Moors Way** The Erme-Plym Trail begins in
Wembury on the South Devon coast and travels as far north as Ivybridge (15
miles in all) where The Two Moors Way begins. Climbing onto Dartmoor can
be strenuous but the effort is worth it.

The trail then heads north, traversing the length of Dartmoor to
Drewsteignton before passing through Morchard Bishop and Witheridge, even-
tually entering Exmoor from the south before culminating in Lynmouth.
Splendid scenery and real solitude are just two of the joys of this trip.

● **Avon Estuary Walk** A pretty 7½-mile hike (Bigbury-on-Sea to Bantham)
which circumvents the need to catch a ferry across the River Avon (see
pp114-16).

● **John Musgrave Heritage Trail** A 35-mile inland trail that bypasses Torbay
by linking Brixham with Maidencombe, crossing the River Dart twice and taking in Totnes and plenty of splendid Devonshire countryside as it does so.
Established in 2005 in memory of John Musgrave, a local walking enthusiast
and former chair of the South Devon Group of Ramblers.

● **Templer Way** An 18-mile path that links Haytor on Dartmoor with the coast
at Teignmouth, following the journey taken by the granite quarried there during

the 19th century on its way to being exported; Templer, by the way, was the family name of those responsible for the canals and tramways that formed the granite's route.

● **Exe Estuary Trail** (🖥 exetrail.co.uk) This cycle path and walkway around the River Exe (Exmouth to Dawlish; see pp192-4) is useful when the ferry between Starcross and Exmouth is not operational – though it's a decent-enough stroll in its own right too.

● **Monarch's Way** (🖥 monarchsway.50megs.com) A whopping 615-mile route which follows in the footsteps of King Charles II who, having been defeated at the Battle of Worcester in 1651, was being pursued by Cromwell's Parliamentarians. The Way passes through the Cotswolds and the Mendips before arriving on the south coast at Charmouth. It then follows the coast path around Bridport before going inland and finally traversing the South Downs to Shoreham – from where the monarch escaped to France.

● **Macmillan Way** (🖥 macmillanway.org) This 290-mile path links England's east coast and Boston in Lincolnshire with Chesil Beach and Abbotsbury in Dorset; the path also has tributaries leading off the main route to Banbury, Bath and Barnstaple. Set up in aid of Macmillan Cancer Support, so far over £350,000 has been raised from walkers' sponsorship!

● **The Jubilee Trail** Launched in 1995, this 90-mile path connects the Somerset and Hampshire borders and in doing so slices through Dorset, purposefully following, wherever possible, what were previously little-known pathways. The jubilee of the title is the 60th anniversary of the founding of the Ramblers' Association (see box p46), now called Ramblers.

● **The Hardy Way** This 212-mile trail (🖥 thehardyway.co.uk) passes through the Dorset countryside that inspired Thomas Hardy's semi-fictional Wessex, the backdrop to his novels.

● **The Purbeck Way** (🖥 dorsetforyou.com/purbeckway) A Y-shaped pathway, this time passing through the stunning and varied scenery of the Isle of Purbeck, starting at Wareham Quay and ending either at Ballard Down (east of Swanage), or Chapman's Pool (near St Aldhelm's Head).

TAKING DOGS ALONG THE PATH

The South-West Coast Path is a dog-friendly path but taking a dog does require some planning: it is a long walk and some places have restrictions on whether dogs can go on a beach or not, and regulations that a dog must be on a lead and owners must clean up after their dog.

See pp315-17 for detailed information on long-distance walking with a dog and p28 for self-guided holidays with a dog. Also worth looking at are 🖥 www.doggydevon.co.uk and 🖥 dorsetdogs.org.uk.

What to take

'When you have worn out your shoes, the strength of the shoe leather has passed into the fiber of your body. I measure your health by the number of shoes and hats and clothes you have worn out.' **Ralph Waldo Emerson**

Deciding how much to take can be difficult. Experienced walkers know that you should take only the bare essentials but at the same time you should ensure you have all the equipment necessary to make the trip safe and comfortable.

KEEP YOUR LUGGAGE LIGHT

Veteran backpackers know that there is some sort of complicated formula governing the success of a trek, in which the enjoyment of the walk is inversely proportional to the amount carried.

Carrying a heavy rucksack slows you down, tires you out and gives you aches and pains in parts of the body that you didn't even know existed. It is imperative, therefore, that you take a good deal of time packing and that you are ruthless when you do; if it's not essential, don't take it.

HOW TO CARRY IT

If you are using the baggage-transfer service, you must check what their regulations are regarding the weight and size of the luggage you wish them to carry.

Even if you are using this service, you will still need to carry a small **daypack**, filled with those items that you will need during the day: water bottle or pouch, this book, sun-screen, sun hat, wet-weather gear, some food, camera, money and so on.

If you have decided to forego the baggage-transfer service you will have to consider your **rucksack** even more carefully. Ultimately its size will depend on where you are planning to stay and how you are planning to eat. If you are camping and cooking for yourself you will probably need a 65- to 75-litre rucksack, which should be large enough to carry a small tent, sleeping bag, cooking equipment and food. Those not carrying their home on their back should find a 40- to 60-litre rucksack sufficient.

When choosing a rucksack, make sure it has a stiffened back and can be adjusted to fit your back comfortably. Don't just try the rucksack out in the shop: take it home, fill it with things and then try it out around the house and take it out for a short walk. Only then can you be certain that it fits. Make sure the hip belt and chest strap (if there is one) are fastened tightly as this helps distribute the weight more comfortably with most of it being carried on your hips. Carry a small daypack inside the rucksack as this will be useful to carry things in when leaving the main pack at the hostel or B&B.

Most rucksacks these days have a **waterproof rucksack cover** 'built in' to the sack, but they tend to be thin and unable to cope with sustained rain or big downpours so consider buying an extra separate one too. Lining your bag with a **bin liner** is another sensible, cut-price idea. It's also a good idea to keep everything wrapped in plastic bags and put these in a bin-bag inside the rucksack. That way, even if it does pour with rain, everything should remain dry.

FOOTWEAR

Boots

Many hikers swear that only a decent pair of strong, durable trekking boots are good enough to survive the rigours of trails such as the South-West Coast Path. In fact, it's perfectly feasible (and often a lot more comfortable, particularly in summer) to complete the walk in a pair of trainers, as long as they have a good grip. They won't, of course, be waterproof, but they tend to dry quickly (far quicker than other, heavier footwear), so you should always be able to start your walk each morning with dry shoes. If you do go down the hiking boot route, make sure your boots are waterproof: these days most people opt for a synthetic waterproof lining (Gore-Tex or similar), though a good-quality leather boot with dubbin should prove just as reliable in keeping your feet dry.

Whatever footwear you choose, the most important thing to remember is to make sure that your shoes/boots are properly worn in before you start your trip. Never start a multi-day hike like this in brand-new shoes!

Hiking-boot wearers will probably want an extra pair of shoes or trainers to wear off the trail. This is not essential but if you are using the baggage-transfer service and you've got room in your luggage, why not?

Flipflops are handy to bring along for wearing around campsites or for using in shared shower blocks.

Socks

If you haven't got a pair of the modern hi-tech walking socks the old system of wearing a thin liner sock under a thicker wool sock is just as good. Bring a few pairs of each.

CLOTHES

In a country notorious for its unpredictable climate it is imperative that you pack enough clothes to cover every extreme of weather, from burning hot to bloomin' freezing. Modern hi-tech outdoor clothes come with a range of fancy names and brands but they all still follow the basic two- or three-layer principle, with an inner base layer to transport sweat away from your skin, a mid-layer for warmth and an outer layer to protect you from the wind and rain.

A thin lightweight **thermal top** of a synthetic material is ideal as the base layer as it draws moisture (ie sweat) away from your body. Cool in hot weather and warm when worn under other clothes in the cold, pack at least one thermal top. Over the top in cold weather a mid-weight **polyester fleece** should suffice.

Fleeces are light, more water-resistant than the alternatives (such as a woolly jumper), remain warm even when wet and pack down small in rucksacks; they are thus ideal trekking gear.

Over the top of all this a **waterproof jacket** is essential. 'Breathable' jackets cost a small fortune (though prices are falling all the time) but they do prevent the build-up of condensation.

Leg wear

Many trekkers find trekking **trousers** an unnecessary investment; any light, quick-drying trouser should suffice. Jeans are heavy and dry slowly and are thus not recommended. A pair of waterproof trousers *is* more than useful, however, while on really hot sunny days you'll be glad you brought your **shorts**. Thermal **long johns** take up little room in the rucksack and could be vital if the weather starts to close in.

Gaiters are not essential but, again, those who bring them are always glad they did, for they provide extra protection when walking through muddy ground and when the vegetation around the trail is dripping wet after bad weather or morning dew.

Underwear

Three or four changes of underwear is likely to be sufficient. Because backpacks can cause bra straps to dig painfully into the skin, women may find a **sports bra** more comfortable.

Other clothes

You might want to consider a woolly **hat** and **gloves** – you'd be surprised how cold it can get up on the cliffs even in summer – and don't forget a sun hat! **Swimwear** is also worth bringing if you fancy taking advantage of some of the wonderful beaches, and quirky outdoor lidos, en route.

TOILETRIES

Once again, take the minimum. **Soap**, **towel**, **toothbrush** and **toothpaste** are pretty much essential (although those staying in B&Bs will find that most provide soap and towels anyway). Some **toilet paper** could also prove vital on the trail, particularly if using public toilets (which occasionally run out).

Other items: **razor**; **deodorant**; **tampons/sanitary towels** and a high factor **sun-screen** (see p81) should cover just about everything.

FIRST-AID KIT

A small first-aid kit could prove useful for those emergencies that occur along the trail. This kit should include **aspirin** or **paracetamol**; **plasters** for minor cuts; Compeed, Second Skin or some other **treatment for blisters**; a **bandage** or elasticated joint support for supporting a sprained ankle or a weak knee; **antiseptic wipes**; **antiseptic cream**; **safety pins**; **tweezers** and **scissors**.

PLANNING YOUR WALK

GENERAL ITEMS

Essential

Everybody should have a **water bottle or pouch**, some **emergency food**, a **map** (though this book has that covered), a **torch** (particularly if walking during shorter winter days, or if camping), a **whistle** for emergencies (see p80 for details of the international distress signal), a **mobile phone** (for emergencies if nothing else; see box below), **spare batteries and/or chargers** for all your devices, a **penknife** and an ordinary **wristwatch** with an alarm (if that phone battery might not always be charged). A **walking pole** or **sticks** will take the strain off your knees.

It is a good idea to carry a **tide table** with you; they can be purchased for about £1.30 from newsagents or TICs in coastal areas. Tide times are also available online at 🖳 www.tidetimes.org.uk. If you know how to use it properly, you'll find a **compass** handy.

Useful items and luxuries

Suggestions here include a **book** for days off or on train and bus journeys, a **camera**, a pair of **sunglasses**, **binoculars** and a **radio** or **iPod/MP3 player**.

CAMPING GEAR

Both campers and those intending to stay in the bunkhouse en route will find a **sleeping bag** essential. A two- to three-season bag should suffice for summer.

In addition, campers will also need a decent bivvy bag or **tent**, a **sleeping mat**, a **towel** (microfleece travel towels are the best), fuel and **stove**, and a camping **cookware** set.

MONEY

Both banks and ATMs (cash machines) are fairly common along the Dorset & South Devon Coast Path. Not everybody accepts **debit** or **credit cards** as payment – though most hotels, restaurants, cafés and pubs now do and also some B&Bs/guesthouses. As a result, you should carry a fair amount of **cash** with you, just to be on the safe side. A **cheque book** from a British bank is useful in those places where debit/credit cards are not accepted.

Crime on the trail is thankfully rare but it's always a good idea to carry your money safely in a **moneybelt**.

❏ **Mobile phone reception and internet connections**
Mobile phone reception and 3G/4G coverage is much better than on the Cornwall section of the SWCP, but there are some areas here where you won't get any signal at all, so make sure that you don't need to rely solely on your phone or mobile device.

Most B&Bs, cafés and pubs have free wi-fi access for customers, as do some larger campsites (though often with a daily charge). You can also get online at all public libraries; their wi-fi is free, but they sometimes charge for internet use on their computer terminals.

DOCUMENTS

National Trust and English Heritage memberships, as well as student cards and YHA hostel cards could all save you money on the trail. Some sort of ID, such as a driving licence, could also prove useful. You need to show photographic ID when you check into all YHA hostels and most independent hostels.

MAPS

It would be perfectly possible to walk long stretches of the coastal path unaided by map or compass. Just keep the sea to your right (or left, depending on which way you're heading) and you can't go too far off track. The hand-drawn maps in this book, though, which cover the trail at a scale of 1:20,000, will hopefully provide sufficient aid in areas where navigation is slightly more problematic.

Having extra maps with you will paint a more fulfilling picture of your surroundings and will allow you to plan more effectively for any accommodation or other facilities that lie off the trail. **Ordnance Survey** (🖳 ordnance surveyleisure.co.uk) produce their maps to two scales: the 1:25,000 Explorer series in orange and the 1:50,000 Landranger in pink (which is less useful for trekking purposes). Alongside the paper versions they also produce an 'Active' edition of both, which is 'weatherproof' (covered in a lightweight protective plastic coating). Those needed for the stretch of the SWCP covered by this book are Explorer: Outdoor Leisure OL20 South Devon; 110 Torquay & Dawlish; OL115 Exmouth & Sidmouth; OL116 Lyme Regis & Bridport; and OL15 Purbeck & South Dorset.

❏ Digital mapping

There are several software packages on the market today that provide Ordnance Survey maps for a PC or smartphone. The two best known are Memory Map and Anquet. Maps are supplied electronically, on DVD, USB media, or by direct download over the internet. The maps are then loaded into an application, also available by download, from where you can view them, print them and create routes on them.

The real value of digital maps, though, is the ability to draw a route directly onto the map from your computer or smartphone. The map, or the appropriate sections of it, can then be printed with the route marked on it, so you no longer need the full versions of the OS maps (though the SWCP AZ Adventure Series map, see p44, provides the same thing). Additionally, the route can be viewed directly on the smartphone or uploaded to a GPS device. Most modern smartphones have a GPS chip so you will be able to see your position overlaid onto the digital map on your phone. Almost every device with built-in GPS functionality now has some mapping software available for it. One of the most popular manufacturers of dedicated handheld GPS devices is Garmin, who have an extensive range. Prices vary from around £100 to £600.

Smartphones and GPS devices should complement, not replace, the traditional method of navigation (a map and compass) as any electronic device can break or, if nothing else, run out of battery. Remember that the battery life of your phone will be significantly reduced, compared to normal usage, when you are using the built-in GPS and running the screen for long periods. **Stuart Greig**

If you don't feel that such precise cartography is needed the Landranger may be a more suitable choice; of the fourteen to cover the SWCP you will need the following six: OL21 Plymouth & Launceston; OL202 Torbay & South Dartmoor; OL192 Exeter & Sidmouth; OL193 Taunton & Lyme Regis; OL194 Dorchester & Weymouth; and OL195 Bournemouth & Purbeck.

The **AZ Adventure Series** (🖥 www.az.co.uk) has five booklets with OS maps, each to a scale of 1:25,000, for the whole of the SWCP; the main difference from standard OS maps is that the booklets have an index. The South Devon map covers Plymouth to Lyme Regis and the Dorset one covers Lyme Regis to South Haven Point.

Harvey Maps (🖥 harveymaps.co.uk) produce a series of maps that cover all the designated National Trails to a scale of 1:40,000. For full coverage of the SWCP you will need three maps, but if you are intending to walk the section covered by this book only the Plymouth to Poole Harbour map will suffice; there is also a digital map for this section of the path. This, of course, will save on weight and cost compared to buying the four OS maps, though the OS has more detail and will show you what is further inland.

While it may be extravagant to buy all the OS maps, Ramblers (see box p46) allows members to borrow up to ten maps for up to six weeks at just 50p per map, or £1 for waterproof maps. However, public libraries in Britain have some OS maps and members can borrow these for free.

RECOMMENDED READING

Below is a by no means exhaustive but hopefully helpful introduction to some of the literature relating to the SWCP and, in particular, the Dorset & South Devon Coast Path.

Guidebooks
It doesn't include any maps, but if you're willing to carry a separate map then the most detailed guide to the accommodation, tide tables and other useful information on the entire SWCP is the South West Coast Path Association's companion to the path, called *The Complete Guide To The South West Coast Path*, which at the time of research cost £15. Alongside this annual guide they also produce and sell pamphlets for each section which can be found in tourist information centres en route or ordered online (🖥 southwestcoastpath.org.uk).

Flora, fauna and geology
For identifying obscure plants and peculiar-looking beasties as you walk, Collins and New Holland publish a pocket-sized range to Britain's natural riches. Both series contain a wealth of information.

The **Collins Gem** series are tough little books; current titles include guides to *Trees*, *Birds*, *Mushrooms*, *Wild Flowers*, *Wild Animals*, *Insects* and *Butterflies*. In addition, for any budding crustacean connoisseur there is a *Seashore* book; there is also a handbook to the *Stars*, which could be of particular interest for those who are considering sleeping under them. Also in the Collins series, there's an adapted version of Richard Mabey's classic bestseller

Food for Free – great for anyone intent on getting back to nature, saving the pennies, or just with an interest in what's edible outside of a supermarket. You could also consult *Wild Food: Foraging for Food in the Wild*, written by Jane Eastoe and published by the National Trust.

New Holland's Concise range covers many of the same topics as the Gem series, comes in a waterproof plastic jacket and also includes useful quick reference foldout charts.

For books that are more **specific to the walk**, *Wildlife of the Jurassic Coast* by Bryan Edwards is available in local tourist information offices, while *Where to Watch Wildlife in Devon* by Robert Hesketh is one of the several books dealing with the nature in that county.

If you need help grappling with the complex **geology** (see pp57-62) you'll encounter, *The Official Guide to the Jurassic Coast: Dorset and East Devon's World Heritage Coast (Walk Through Time Guide)* by Denys Brunsden is available both locally and online, while *Dorset and East Devon: Landscape and Geology* by Malcolm Hart is a more recent addition to the subject. You'll probably also be interested in *Discover Dorset Fossils* by Richard Edmonds, or the tiny but useful paperback *Finding Fossils in Lyme Bay* by Robert Coram.

A Guide to Fossil Collecting in England and Wales, by Craig Chapman and Steve Snowball, is an excellent beginner's guide and can be bought from the UK Fossils website (⌨ ukfossils.co.uk).

Autobiography
With the Falklands War imminent Mark Wallington set off to walk the SWCP in an attempt to impress a girl that he had met at a party. Accompanied by the more-loathed-than-loved Boogie the dog, man and beast survive all that the path can throw at them on a diet of tinned soup and Kennomeat. *Travels with Boogie: 500 Mile Walkies* is Wallington's humorous account of his own time spent on the trail. If you have walked and camped or have ever walked a long distance with a dog many of the author's anecdotes will ring true – a light-hearted and thoroughly enjoyable read. Another dog goes walking in *Two feet, four paws*, Spud Talbot-Ponsonby's tale of her time circumnavigating Britain.

The Tarka Trail is a local path named after Henry Williamson's much-loved *Tarka the Otter*, just one of many books in which Williamson's extraordinary ability to evoke the Devonshire countryside gilds every page.

History
One thousand years of farming, quarrying and the Home Guard are crammed into Felicity Goodall's *Lost Devon*, which is good for those with an interest in the lost heritage of the county.

Derrick Warren's *Curious Devon* examines the quirkier side of the county, as does his *Curious Dorset*, while for something a little darker there's John Van Der Kiste's *Grim Almanac of Devon* that recounts 366 of the county's more macabre episodes. A more general tome on Dorset is Cecil North Cullingford's *A History of Dorset*.

❏ SOURCES OF FURTHER INFORMATION

Online information
● 🖳 www.nationaltrail.co.uk/south-west-coast-path The official and most useful website to Britain's longest national trail. Good for background information and has the latest news on the path, details about river crossings and army ranges, as well as lots of information on accommodation, itineraries and distance and timing calculators.
● 🖳 www.southwestcoastpath.org.uk The site for the **South-West Coast Path Association (SWCPA)**, a registered charity that exists to support users of the path. Many of the features on the official site are replicated here – distance calculators, river-crossing details etc – though there is much more detail here too. The Association is also very active politically, pressurising government bodies to ensure that the path is highly maintained along its length. Membership is available at £22/29 for single/joint memberships and includes a copy of their guidebook and twice-yearly newsletters.
● 🖳 jurassiccoast.org Website dedicated to Britain's first natural World Heritage Site with good explanations on the geology of the region and just why it is of such global importance.
● See also p56 for details of the websites for the various Areas of Outstanding Natural Beauty on this section of the path. These are good for background information on the geology, flora and fauna of the region.

Tourist information centres (TICs) and points (TIPs)
As one of the busiest tourist areas of the country, the South-West is reasonably well served by tourist information centres: **Plymouth** (see p89); **Salcombe** (see p120); **Dartmouth** (see p142); **Torquay** (see p165); **Shaldon** (see p176); **Dawlish** (see p185); **Exmouth** (see p195); **Budleigh Salterton** (see p202); **Sidmouth** (see p208); **Seaton** (see p219); **Lyme Regis** (see p228); **Swanage** (see p304).

There are also some **tourist information points** where it is possible to pick up leaflets about local attractions. TIPs are often at caravan parks and may also be in libraries, where there isn't a tourist information centre. Some attractions have a **visitor centre** with information about that particular place.

For general information visit: 🖳 www.visitdevon.co.uk and/or 🖳 www.visit-dorset.com.

Organisations for walkers
● **Backpackers' Club** (🖳 backpackersclub.co.uk) A club aimed at people who are involved, or interested, in lightweight camping through walking, cycling, skiing and canoeing. They produce a quarterly magazine, provide members with a comprehensive advisory and information service on all aspects of backpacking, organise weekend trips, offer discounts for maps and at outdoor stores, and also publish a farm-pitch directory. Membership costs £15 a year (£20 for a family; £8.50 for under 18s).
● **The Long Distance Walkers' Association** (🖳 ldwa.org.uk) Membership (£13 a year; family and international membership £19.50) includes a copy of their journal *Strider* three times per year giving details of challenge events and local group walks as well as articles on the subject. Members also receive a discount on maps and also on the *UK Trailwalker's Handbook* which details 730 trails across the UK.
● **Ramblers** (formerly Ramblers' Association; 🖳 ramblers.org.uk) Looks after the interests of walkers throughout Britain. They publish a large amount of useful information including their quarterly *Walk* magazine. The website also has a discussion forum and members can borrow OS maps. Membership costs £34.50/45.50 individual/joint; concessionary rates are £20.50/27.50 individual/joint.

The South West Coast Path – An Illustrated History recounts, in probably rather too much detail for the layman, the struggle to establish Britain's longest national trail.

One of the most entertaining reads on one aspect of the history of this coastline is *The Dinosaur Hunters: A True Story of Scientific Rivalry and the Discovery of the Prehistoric World* by Deborah Cadbury, detailing the work of Mary Anning, Gideon Mantell et al and their rivalry in the 19th century.

Fiction

The two counties have been fairly blessed with bestselling authors. Thomas Hardy began the trend, his novels and short stories nearly always set in his fictional Wessex – which is essentially Dorset and the surrounding counties but with the names changed. Hardy's hometown of Dorchester, for example, became 'Casterbridge' in his novels, while Weymouth is 'Budmouth' in his novel *Far from the Madding Crowd*, and is also Eustacia Vye's hometown in *The Return of the Native*. Portland, by the way, is the 'Isle of Slingers'.

Hardy's book sales, however, are outstripped by those of another homegrown talent, Agatha Christie. Once again her homeland features prominently in her books; indeed, the Imperial Hotel at her home town of Torquay appears in three of her novels, *Peril at End House*, *The Body in the Library* and *Sleeping Murder*, while Burgh Island is the setting for two of her thrillers, *And Then There Were None* and *Evil Under the Sun*.

Thomas Hardy's practice of changing local place-names (while otherwise remaining true to the local geography) was emulated by his fellow Victorian, J Meade Falkner, in his most famous work, *Moonfleet*. Written at the end of the 19th century, this children's story is set in a small Dorset village (based on East Fleet behind Chesil Beach) and involves smuggling, kidnapping – and an awful lot of intrigue. Falkner stayed in Abbotsbury while he wrote the novel.

Set in the same location, though this time in 1962, before the sexual revolution really took off, *On Chesil Beach* is by one of Britain's most celebrated contemporary novelists, Ian McEwan, and concerns the wedding night of two twenty-somethings, their fears and dreams.

Further west, Lyme Regis is the home of Sarah Woodruff, better known as *The French Lieutenant's Woman* in the novel by John Fowles. She spends her days on The Cobb, staring out to sea, in disgrace because of her affair with the Frenchman Varguennes, who, unbeknown to her until later, was already married; it is while standing there that she is spied by Charles Smithson and his fiancée, Ernestina Freeman, and a close relationship between Charles and Sarah ensues. The novel is perhaps most remarkable in that the author offers three different endings. It was made into a film in 1981 starring Jeremy Irons and Meryl Streep.

For something much lighter, PG Wodehouse's *Thank you, Jeeves* is the first to feature the eponymous butler-cum-hero; indeed, the story begins with Jeeves leaving Bertie Wooster's service because of the latter's incessant playing of the banjolele, finding employment instead with Bertie's old chum Lord 'Chuffy' Chuffnell. Bertie retreats to one of Chuffy's cottages in Dorset – and the usual wonderfully entertaining chaos ensues.

PLANNING YOUR WALK

Getting to and from the Coast Path

All the major towns along the coast path are reasonably well served by rail and/ or coach services from the rest of Britain. Travelling by train or coach is the most convenient way to get to the trail as you do not need to worry about where to leave your car, how safe it will be while you're walking, or how to get back to it at the end of your holiday. Choosing to travel by public transport is also choosing to help the environment; a creative step in minimising your impact on the countryside. It can also be an enjoyable experience in itself. How many of us have fond memories of relaxing to the regular rattle of the train wheels while sleepily watching the scenery pass by?

NATIONAL TRANSPORT

By train

The main Devon line (operated by Great Western Railways, ☎ 0345-700 0125, 🖵 gwr.com) runs from London Paddington through Exeter to **Plymouth**, with

PLANNING YOUR WALK

❏ **GETTING TO BRITAIN**

● **By air** The best international gateway to Britain for the Dorset & South Devon Coast Path is London; its most convenient airports are Heathrow (🖵 heathrowairport.com) and Gatwick (🖵 gatwickairport.com).

Exeter Airport (🖵 exeter-airport.co.uk), Southampton (🖵 southamptonairport.com) and Bournemouth (🖵 bournemouthairport.com) are closer to the walk and have international flights though mostly from Europe only.

● **From Europe by train** Eurostar (🖵 eurostar.com) operates a high-speed passenger service via the Channel Tunnel between Paris, Brussels and Lille and London. The Eurostar terminal in London is at St Pancras International with connections to the London Underground and to all other main railway stations in London. Trains to Dorset and Devon leave from Paddington station (Great Western Railway) and also from Waterloo (South Western Railway); see below for details.

There are also various rail services from mainland Europe to Britain; for more information contact your national rail provider or Railteam (🖵 railteam.eu).

● **From Europe by coach** Eurolines (🖵 eurolines.com) have a wide network of long-distance bus services connecting over 500 destinations in 25 European countries to London (Victoria Coach Station).

● **From Europe with a car** There are **ferry services** that operate between: Santander/Roscoff and Plymouth; Cherbourg/St Malo/Caen and Poole/Portsmouth; Le Havre and Portsmouth; Calais and Dover; Dunkirk and Dover; Rotterdam/Zeebrugge and Hull; Dublin and Liverpool. Look at 🖵 ferrysavers.com or 🖵 www .directferries.com for a full list of companies and services.

Eurotunnel (🖵 eurotunnel.com) operates 'le shuttle', a **shuttle train service** for vehicles via the Channel Tunnel between Calais and Folkestone (4/hr; 35 mins).

branch lines connecting major towns on the coast path. There are several services every day as well as a night train (the Night Riviera, Sun-Fri). Cross Country (☎ 0844-811 0124, 🖥 crosscountrytrains.co.uk) operates services from Scotland, the North-East, Manchester and the Midlands to Bournemouth, Exeter and Plymouth. To access Dorset, and **Poole** or **Weymouth** from London, South Western Railway (☎ 0345-600 0650, 🖥 southwesternrailway.com) run regularly and direct from London Waterloo.

National rail enquiries (☎ 0345-748 4950, 🖥 nationalrail.co.uk) is the only number or website you really need to find out all timetable and fare information. The 'Buy now' button on the website transfers you to the relevant train operator's website where you can buy tickets online.

Rail **tickets** are generally cheaper if you book them well in advance and also if you buy online. Most discounted tickets carry some restrictions (such as travelling on a particular train) so check what they are before you purchase them. It is best to buy tickets through the relevant companies or at any rail station. However, they can also be bought online at 🖥 thetrainline.com.

It is possible to buy a train ticket that includes bus travel at your destination: for further information visit the **Plusbus** website (🖥 www.plusbus.info).

If you think you'll want a **taxi** when you arrive consult the town guides included in this book, many of which have taxi numbers in their transport sections. Alternatively, visit 🖥 www.traintaxi.co.uk.

By coach
National Express (☎ 0871-781 8178, 🖥 nationalexpress.com) is the principal coach (ie long-distance bus) operator in Britain. Travel by coach is usually cheaper than by rail but does take longer. See box below for details of services to Devon and Dorset.

❏ **Useful National Express services**
Note: not all stops are listed

035 London to Poole via Bournemouth (10/day); some continue to **Swanage** (1-2/day), and **Weymouth** (1/day)
205 Heathrow Airport to Poole via Bournemouth, 12/day
206 Gatwick Airport to Poole via Portsmouth, Southampton & Bournemouth, 5/day
304 Liverpool to **Weymouth** via Birmingham & Bournemouth, 1/day
315 Eastbourne to Helston via Portsmouth, Southampton, Bournemouth, Poole, **Weymouth**, Dorchester, Bridport, Exeter, **Plymouth** & Falmouth, 1/day
328 Blackpool to **Plymouth** via Manchester, Bristol & Taunton, 1/day
330 Nottingham to Penzance via Bristol, **Plymouth** & Newquay, 1/day
333 Blackpool to **Bournemouth** via Manchester, Poole, 1/day
336 Edinburgh to **Plymouth** via Glasgow, Carlisle, Taunton & Exeter, 1/day
404 London Victoria to **Plymouth** via Heathrow Airport, Bath, Bristol Airport, Exeter, Newton Abbot, **Torquay, Paignton** & Totnes, 1/day
501 London Victoria to Totnes (4/day) via Heathrow, Exeter, **Starcross** (1/day), **Dawlish** (1/day) and Teignmouth (1/day), **Torquay** (5/day) & **Paignton** (5/day) plus 1/day to **Brixham**
531 Newcastle to **Plymouth** via Leeds, Birmingham, Gloucester & Bristol, 1/day

To get the cheapest fares you need to book in advance. You can purchase tickets from coach and bus station ticket offices, National Express agents (including post offices and some tourist information centres), directly from the driver (though not always, so do check with locals in advance), by telephone, or online. An easier option is to print your ticket yourself at home. Known as an e-ticket, you should be able to do this direct from the National Express website.

Megabus (🖳 uk.megabus.com) provides low-cost coach services to Paignton, Torquay and Plymouth.

By car

The route options for driving to Dorset and Devon depend largely on your starting point; the main problem is that the roads can get very crowded in the summer months. A good road atlas will be required to navigate Devon and Dorset's country lanes. You can get detailed driving directions from the AA website (🖳 theaa.com/route-planner/index.jsp) by clicking on the route planner. Parking your car can be a problem; there are long-stay car parks in Plymouth, Bournemouth and Poole but this means you will have to go back to the car park at the end of your walk. Overall it's probably easier and cheaper and certainly better for the environment to use public transport.

LOCAL TRANSPORT

Bus services

Both Devon and Dorset have reasonable public transport networks linking most of the coastal villages. There are usually several buses per day in the summer, though fewer in winter. This is great news for the walker as it opens up the possibility of walking along the coast path from a fixed base. Note, however, that the stretch between Wembury and Salcombe has very limited public transport options, as does the stretch between Lulworth Cove and Swanage.

Timetables   Three timetables cover southern Devon. If walking the whole path you will need all of them. Starting from Plymouth you will need: **South Hams** (pink), which covers Plymouth to Torquay; **Teignbridge** (blue), which covers Brixham to the Exe Estuary and Exeter; and **East Devon** (green), that covers Exeter and Exmouth to Lyme Regis. Once in Dorset you will need the Southern Dorset Area timetable only.

In both counties you can pick the timetables up for free from bus stations, railway stations and tourist information centres. The timetables can also be either ordered online or downloaded from Devon County Council (🖳 traveldevon.info/bus/timetables) and Dorset County Council (🖳 dorsetforyou.gov.uk/travel-dorset/bus/bus-timetables-and-operators). The service numbers of the most useful buses are given in the table on pp51-2, and on p54 so you can flip straight to the page you need in the actual timetable.

Bus companies and customer helplines   If the contact details in the box on pp51-2, or p54, prove unsatisfactory, you can contact **traveline** (☎ 0871-200 2233, open daily 8am-8pm but calls cost 12p per minute; 🖳 traveline.info), which has public transport information for the whole of the UK or, just for the south-west (🖳 travelinesw.com).

Public transport at a glance

The public transport map (p53) and the services table (below and on p52 and p54) are designed to make it easy for you to plan your day using public transport. Use the map to see which towns are covered by each service and then turn to the table to check that service's frequency. Take time to read the table carefully: some services run only one day a week, while others don't run at weekends. The definition of a summer service depends on the company and the route; in some cases it is from Easter to October but in others it's May/July to September – again, always check before you plan to use a summer service.

Note that bus services do change from year to year. Use this information as a rough guide and confirm details with the bus operators before travelling.

For information about tide timetables, see p42.

❏ PUBLIC TRANSPORT SERVICES

Note: not all stops are listed. Also that details about the various ferry services on this section of the SWCP are provided, where relevant, in Part 4.

Bus services

Axe Valley Mini Travel (☎ 01297-625959)

885 Axminster to Beer via Seaton & Beer Cross, Mon-Sat 8/day

899 Sidmouth to Seaton via Sidford, Branscombe, Beer & Beer Quarry Caves, Mon-Fri 4/day plus 2/day during term-time, Sat 3/day

Damory Coaches (☎ 01258-452545, 🖳 www.damory.co.uk)

30 (Breezer; see p54) Weymouth to Swanage via Osmington, Durdle Door (Holiday Park), Lulworth Cove, West Lulworth, Wool, Wareham & Corfe Castle, late July to mid Sep, daily 4/day
(See Wilts & Dorset Bus Company for details of the other Breezer services)

First in Wessex Dorset & South Somerset (🖳 www.firstgroup.com/wessex-dorset-south-somerset)

1 Weymouth to Portland via Wyke Regis, Easton & Southwell, Mon-Sat 5-6/hr, Sun 3-4/hr

5 Weymouth to Dorchester via Osmington, Mon-Sat 5/day

8 Weymouth to Chickerell, Mon-Fri 4/hr, Sat 3/hr, Sun 1/hr

10 Dorchester to Weymouth, Mon-Sat 4/hr, Sun 1/hr

X51 (**Jurassic Coaster**) Dorchester to Axminster via Bridport, Chideock, Charmouth & Lyme Regis, Apr-Sep Mon-Fri 6/day, Sat & Sun 5/day, Oct-Mar Mon-Sat 7/day

X52 (**Jurassic Coaster**) Exeter to Lyme Regis via Sidmouth, Beer Cross & Seaton, Mon-Sat 2/day

X53 (**Jurassic Coaster**) Axminster to Weymouth via Lyme Regis, Charmouth, Chideock, Bridport, West Bay, Burton Bradstock, Swyre, Abbotsbury, Portesham & Chickerell, Apr-Sep Mon-Sat 5/day plus 2/day Lyme Regis to Weymouth, Sun 5/day plus 2/day Bridport to Weymouth, Oct-Mar daily 6/day

X54 (**Jurassic Coaster**) Weymouth to Poole via Osmington, Wool railway station & Wareham, Mon-Sat 4/day *(services continued overleaf)*

PLANNING YOUR WALK

PLANNING YOUR WALK

❏ PUBLIC TRANSPORT SERVICES

Bus services *(cont'd from p51)*
First in Wessex Dorset & South Somerset *(cont'd)*

X55 (**Jurassic Coaster**) Weymouth to Wool railway station via Osmington, Durdle Door & Lulworth Cove, late May to early Sep daily 3/day

500 (**Jurassic Coaster**) Bowleaze Cove to Weymouth Pavilion (connects with the 501), May-Sep daily 1/hr

501 (**Jurassic Coaster**) Weymouth (Pavilion) to Portland Bill via Wyke Regis, Portland, Easton & Southwell, late May to early Sep daily 4-8/day, Apr & May weekends only

510 (**SLOWcoaster**) Bridport to Weymouth via West Bay, Freshwater, Burton Bradstock, Hive Beach, Abbotsbury, Ferrybridge & Portland, late May to early Sep, daily 3/day

Stagecoach South West (🖥 www.stagecoachbus.com)

2 Newton Abbot to Exeter Bus Station via Teignmouth, Dawlish, Dawlish Warren & Starcross, Mon-Sat 3/hr, Sun 1/hr

3 Plymouth to Dartmouth via Brixton, Yealmpton, Aveton Gifford, Kingsbridge, Torcross, Slapton, Slapton Turn, Strete, Blackpool & Stoke Fleming, Mon-Sat 11/day, summer Sun 2/day Kingsbridge to Dartmouth.

9 Exeter to Honiton via Sidmouth, Mon-Sat 1/hr

9A Exeter to Lyme Regis via Sidmouth, Sidford, Seaton & Axmouth, Mon-Sat 1/hr, Sun 4/day plus 1/day to Seaton and 2/day from Sidmouth

hop12 Newton Abbot to Brixham via Torquay, & Paignton, Mon-Sat 6/hr, Sun 4/hr

18/18A Kingswear to Brixham, Mon-Sat 2/hr, Sun 1/hr

20 Taunton to Seaton via Honiton, Mon-Sat 3/day

hop22 Dawlish Warren to Paignton via Teignmouth, Shaldon, St Marychurch, Maidencombe & Torquay, Mon-Sat 1/hr plus 2/hr St Marychurch to Paignton, Sun 1/hr

46 Exeter Bus Station to Torquay, Mon-Sat 4/day

48 Plymouth to Wembury via Plymstock, Mon-Sat 6/day

56 Exeter St David's Station to Exmouth via Exeter Bus Station, Exeter Airport, & Lympstone, Mon-Sat 1/hr, Sun 1/hr to Exeter Airport, Sun 1/hr

56B Exeter St David's Station to Sidmouth via Exeter Bus Station, Exeter Airport & Honiton, late May-mid Sep Sun 3/day

57 Exeter Bus Station to Brixington via Topsham, Lympstone & Exmouth, Mon-Sat 4/hr, Sun 2/hr (Stagecoach Gold)

58 Exeter to Budleigh Salterton via Exmouth, Mon-Fri 5/day

X64 Exeter to Dartmouth via Newton Abbot & Totnes, Mon-Sat 6/day. Sun 2/day

Stagecoach Gold (SG) Plymouth to Torquay via Totnes, Ivybridge & Paignton, Mon-Sat 2/hr, Sun 1/hr

120 Paignton Bus Station to Kingswear (for ferry to Dartmouth), Mon-Sat 1/hr

157 Exmouth to Sidmouth via Budleigh Salterton, Mon-Sat 1/hr, Sun summer 4/day

357 Exmouth to Budleigh Salterton, daily 1/hr

164 Totnes to Kingsbridge, Sun 2/day, 1/day continues to Salcombe; see also Tally Ho

Rail River Link Bus (🖥 www.dartmouthrailriver.co.uk/tours/no100-bus-service)

100 Totnes to Paignton, Apr to end Oct daily 9/day, late Oct to Apr Mon-Fri 5/day

South West Coaches (🖥 www.southwestcoaches.co.uk)

206A/B Weymouth circular route to Wyke Regis, Mon-Sat 2/hr *(cont'd on p54)*

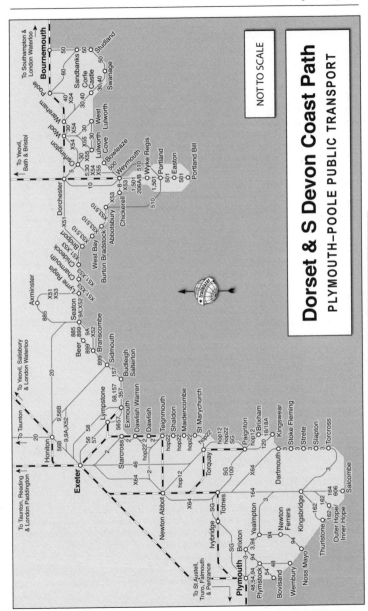

Dorset & S Devon Coast Path
PLYMOUTH–POOLE PUBLIC TRANSPORT

NOT TO SCALE

PLANNING YOUR WALK

❑ PUBLIC TRANSPORT SERVICES

Bus services *(cont'd from p52)*

Tally Ho Coaches (☎ 01548-853081, 💻 www.tallyhocoaches.co.uk/busservice)

162 Kingsbridge Bus Station circular route via Thurlestone, Outer Hope & Inner Hope, Mon-Sat 3/day

164 Totnes to Kingsbridge Bus Station, Mon-Sat 7-8/day; see also Stagecoach

606 Kingsbridge Bus Station to Salcombe, Mon-Sat 10/day

Target Travel (☎ 01752-242000, 💻 www.targettravel.co.uk)

54 Plymouth to Bovisand via Plymstock & Jennycliff, late July to early Sep daily 8/day, mid June to late July and Sep weekends only 8/day

94 Plymouth Bus Station to Noss Mayo via Plymstock, Brixton, Yealmpton & Newton Ferrers, Mon-Sat 3/day

Wilts & Dorset Bus Company (Mon-Fri 8am-6.30pm ☎ 01202-338420, 💻 www .morebus.co.uk, 💻 www.purbeckbreezer.co.uk)
Note: the 30 Breezer service is operated in conjunction with Damory (see p51)

40 (Breezer) Swanage to Poole via Corfe Castle & Wareham, Apr-Oct daily 1/hr, Nov-Mar Mon-Sat 1/hr, Sun 5/day

50 (Breezer) Swanage bus station to Bournemouth Station via Studland, Shell Bay (ferry) & Sandbanks (ferry), Apr-late Oct daily 1-2/hr, late Oct-late Mar Mon-Sat 1/hr, Sun 6/day

60 (Breezer) Sandbanks (ferry) to Poole via Canford Cliffs, Apr-Oct daily 1/hr, Oct-Mar Mon-Sat 1/hr

Rail services

Note: not all stops are listed and not all trains stop at all stops listed

Great Western Railway (☎ 0345-700 0125, 💻 gwr.com)

- London Paddington to Plymouth via Reading, Castle Cary, Taunton, Tiverton Parkway, Exeter St David's, Newton Abbot & Totnes, daily approx 1/hr
- Newton Abbot to Paignton via Torquay, daily 1-3/hr
- Exeter St David's to Penzance via Newton Abbot & Plymouth, daily 1-3/hr
- Exmouth (The Riviera Line) to Paignton via Exeter, Starcross, Dawlish Warren, Dawlish, Teignmouth, Newton Abbot, Torre & Torquay, Mon-Fri 19/day, Sat 13/day, Sun 6/day to all stops plus additional services to some stops
- Exeter St David's to Exmouth (The Avocet Line) via Exeter Central, Topsham, Exton, Lympstone Commando & Lympstone Village, Mon-Sat 1-2/hr, Sun 1/hr; note some stops are request only
- Barnstaple to Exmouth (The Tarka Line) via Exeter, Mon-Sat 10/day
- Penzance to Plymouth via Redruth, Truro, Par & Bodmin Parkway, 14-15/day
- Bristol Temple Meads to Weymouth via Bath Spa, Bradford-on-Avon, Frome & Castle Cary, Mon-Sat 7/day, Sun 4/day

South Western Railway (☎ 0345-600 0650, 💻 southwesternrailway.com)

- London Waterloo to Weymouth via Bournemouth, Poole, Wareham, Wool & Dorchester South, Mon-Sat 2/hr, Sun 1/hr (not all services stop at every station)
- London Waterloo to Exeter via Salisbury, Crewkerne, Axminster & Honiton (not all services stop at every station), daily 1/hr

Cross Country Trains (💻 crosscountrytrains.co.uk

- Birmingham to Plymouth via Bristol, Exeter, Newton Abbot, & Totnes, daily 1/hr
- Birmingham to Bournemouth via Reading & Southampton, daily 1/hr

THE ENVIRONMENT AND NATURE

2

Conserving the Dorset & South Devon Coast Path

Britain is an overcrowded island and England is the most densely populated part of it. As such, the English countryside has suffered a great deal of pressure from both over-population and the activities of an ever more industrialised world. Thankfully, there is some enlightened legislation to protect the surviving pockets of forest and heathland.

Beyond these fragments, it is interesting to note just how much man has altered the land he lives on. Whilst the aesthetic costs of such intrusions are open to debate, what is certain is the loss of biodiversity that has resulted. The last wild boar was shot a few centuries ago; add to its demise the extinction of bear and wolf as well as, far more recently, a number of other species lost or severely depleted and you get an idea of just how much an influence man has over the land and how that influence is all too often used negatively.

There is good news, however. In these enlightened times when environmental issues are quite rightly given more precedence, many endangered species, such as the otter, have increased in number thanks to the active work of voluntary conservation bodies. There are other reasons to be optimistic; the environment is no longer the least important issue in party politics and this reflects the opinions of everyday people who are concerned about issues such as conservation on both a local and global scale.

CONSERVATION SCHEMES – WHAT'S AN AONB?

It is perhaps the chief joy of this walk that much of it is spent in an Area of Outstanding Natural Beauty. But what exactly is this designation and what protection do designations such as this actually confer?

Natural England (🖥 gov.uk/government/organisations/natural-england) is the single body responsible for identifying, establishing and managing National Parks, AONBs, NNRs, SSSIs and Special Areas of Conservation (SACs), see p56.

National parks

The highest level of landscape protection is the designation of land as a national park (🖥 nationalparks.gov.uk). There are 15 in Britain of which nine are in England. This designation recognises the national importance of an area in terms of landscape, biodiversity and as a recreational resource. It does not signify national ownership and these are not uninhabited wildernesses, making conservation a knife-edged balance between protecting the environment and the rights and livelihoods of those living in the park. There are, alas, no national parks on this stretch of the coast path.

Areas of Outstanding Natural Beauty

The second level of protection is Area of Outstanding Natural Beauty (AONB; 🖥 landscapesforlife.org.uk), of which there are 38 in England and Wales and three (South Devon 🖥 southdevonaonb.org.uk; East Devon 🖥 eastdevonaonb .org.uk; and Dorset 🖥 dorsetaonb.org.uk) on this section of the SWCP.

The primary objective of AONBs is conservation of the natural beauty of a landscape. As there is no statutory administrative framework for their management, this is the responsibility of the local authority within whose boundaries they fall.

As well as many AONBs this section of coast is also blessed with its very own **Geopark** (see box p150), of which there are only eight in the UK.

(Around 33% of the English coastline has been defined a **Heritage Coast**; this is a non-statutory designation but it shows that the designated area is of interest because of its scenic beauty, wildlife or general heritage; South Devon, East Devon, West Dorset and Purbeck are all Heritage Coasts.)

National Nature Reserves and Sites of Special Scientific Interest

The next level of protection includes National Nature Reserves (NNRs) and Sites of Special Scientific Interest (SSSIs).

There are 224 **NNRs** in England, of which Axmouth to Lyme Regis Undercliffs, Berry Head to Sharkham Point, Dawlish Warren and Slapton Ley, Durlston and Studland are all covered by this book.

There are over 4100 **SSSIs** in England. SSSIs are a particularly important designation as they have some legal standing. They are managed in partnership with the owners and occupiers of the land who must give written notice before initiating any operations likely to damage the site and who cannot proceed without consent from Natural England. There are plenty of SSSIs along this stretch of the SWCP, including 14 on the Jurassic Coast (such as Sidmouth to Beer SSSI and the South Dorset Coast SSSI that encompasses Kimmeridge Bay) and numerous SSSIs on the South Devon shore including Plymouth Sound, the Taw–Torridge, Yealm, Exe, Erme and Otter estuaries, the points at Wembury, Prawle and Start, the stretches of coastline from Bolt Head to Bolt Tail, Hallsands to Beesands, Roundham Head – and around Dawlish Warren.

Special Area of Conservation (SAC; 🖥 jncc.defra.gov.uk/page-23) is an international designation which came into being as a result of the 1992 Earth Summit in Rio de Janeiro, Brazil. This European-wide network of sites is designed to promote the conservation of habitats, wild animals and plants, both on land and at sea. More than 200 land sites in England have been designated as SACs including South Hams, Blackstone Point near Dartmouth, Beer Quarry Caves (see p216), Chesil and the Fleet, and St Alban's Head to Durlston Head and Sidmouth to West Bay.

THE ENVIRONMENT & NATURE

Campaigning and conservation organisations

A number of voluntary organisations started the conservation movement in the mid 19th century and they are still at the forefront of developments. Independent of government but reliant on public support, they can concentrate their resources either on acquiring land which can then be managed purely for conservation purposes, or on influencing political decision-makers by lobbying and campaigning.

Managers and owners of land include well-known bodies such as the **National Trust** (NT; 🖳 nationaltrust.org.uk) that owns over 600 miles of coastline including Wembury, Noss Mayo, Salcombe to Hope Point, South Milton Sands in South Hams, Hallsands to Beesands, Bolberry Down, Branscombe, Overbecks in Salcombe, Orcombe Point, Studland Beach, Purbeck Countryside and, inland, the Hardy Monument (see p253); the **Royal Society for the Protection of Birds** (RSPB; 🖳 rspb.org.uk), the **Campaign to Protect Rural England** (CPRE; 🖳 cpre.org.uk) and the **Woodland Trust** (🖳 woodland-trust .org.uk).

The Wildlife Trusts (🖳 wildlifetrusts.org) are the umbrella organisation for the 47 wildlife trusts in the UK that manage nature reserves and run marine conservation projects. The sole purpose of the **Marine Conservation Society** (🖳 mcsuk.org) is to protect the seas and shores as well as the wildlife in and around them so they also run marine conservation projects.

Geology

EONS, ERAS AND PERIODS

The Earth is four and a half billion years old, give or take the odd thousand years. To make such a huge timespan more manageable, geologists have divided these four and a half billion years into four different **eons**, with each at least half a billion years or more in length; the **Phanerozoic eon** (from 570 million years to the present day) is the most relevant for this walk.

These eons are then further subdivided into **eras**, each spanning several hundred million years – and the cliffs, rocks and fossils found along this 217¼-mile stretch of coast date from three of these eras: the **Palaeozoic** (570-250 million years ago), the **Mesozoic** (250-65 million years ago), and the **Cenozoic** (65 million years ago to the present day).

Without wishing to complicate matters any further, these geological eras are further divided into **periods**. The length of each period varies because the divisions aren't arbitrary, but are defined by distinctive changes in the types of rocks and fossils that can be found in the layers. As you probably know, when you look at a cliff-face you'll notice that it has lines running horizontally through it. These lines are layers of sediment that have been laid down over time, with the oldest at the bottom and the newest at the top.

Geologists are able to identify how long ago each of those layers was formed, and from the type of rock and fossils found in each layer they can determine what the terrain and the climate were like – and what creatures roamed the Earth at that time.

Palaeozoic era

The Palaeozoic era is divided into six main periods. Starting from the oldest they are: the Cambrian, Ordovician, Silurian, Devonian, Carboniferous and Permian.

The Cambrian period stretched for 70 million years (570-500 million years ago) and was characterised by the first shellfish and, for the first time, fossils which can be found in great numbers. On the other hand the Permian period spans only 30 million years (280-250 million years ago) and is characterised by the widespread existence of reptiles and amphibians.

On this walk you'll come across significant geological evidence of two of these Palaeozoic periods: the **Devonian** (415-360 million years ago) is represented by the limestone sites between Plymouth and the River Exe (Berry Head, Daddyhole Cove, Hope's Nose); while the red cliffs near Dawlish Warren, which are actually fossilised sand dunes, date from the **Permian period** (290-250 million years ago).

The Mesozoic Era and the Jurassic Coast

The Mesozoic era is the one that will be of most interest to the walker on this route. It is divided into three periods, **Triassic**, **Jurassic** and **Cretaceous** and it's fair to say that these periods could be described – by the layman at least – as the most interesting of all geological periods, when the great dinosaurs roamed the Earth (the Mesozoic is commonly called the 'Age of the Reptiles'), the supercontinent of Pangaea began the split into the separate continents we know today, and birds and mammals also made their first appearance.

So what is it that makes the coastline of Devon and Dorset so special to geologists today? Well, there is, of course, the wealth of fossils and rocks from each of these periods that can be found along this stretch of southern British shoreline. Perhaps, more importantly, this evidence is both exposed and readily accessible.

The erosion so prevalent along most coastlines is partly responsible for this, the millennia of wind, weather and waves exposing the various strata of the three periods. But in part this is also due to a geological phenomenon called an **unconformity**.

At some point during the Cretaceous period, rocks were first tilted then eroded, leading to the complete disappearance on certain stretches of the coast of Jurassic rock. As such, in certain places (such as at Sidmouth) on the coast there are Cretaceous rocks (ie the youngest rocks of the Mesozoic era) lying directly atop Triassic rocks (ie the oldest rocks).

Thus, while geology is impossible to escape and there are several sites between Plymouth and Exmouth that are of interest to rock-hounds, the subject becomes truly spectacular once you arrive at Orcombe Point (see Map 41,

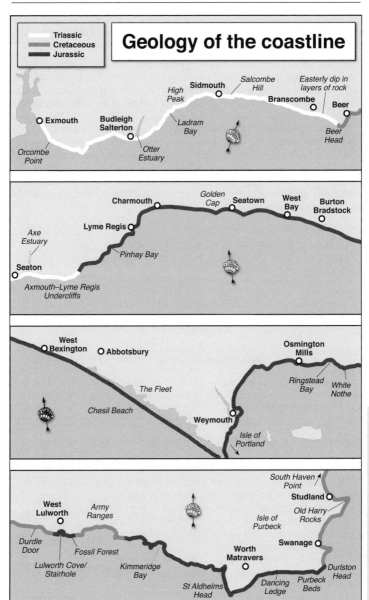

Geology of the coastline

Triassic
Cretaceous
Jurassic

Exmouth · Orcombe Point · Budleigh Salterton · Otter Estuary · Ladram Bay · High Peak · Sidmouth · Salcombe Hill · Branscombe · Easterly dip in layers of rock · Beer · Beer Head

Seaton · Axe Estuary · Axmouth–Lyme Regis Undercliffs · Lyme Regis · Charmouth · Pinhay Bay · Golden Cap · Seatown · West Bay · Burton Bradstock

West Bexington · Abbotsbury · The Fleet · Chesil Beach · Weymouth · Isle of Portland · Osmington Mills · Ringstead Bay · White Nothe

West Lulworth · Durdle Door · Lulworth Cove/Stairhole · Fossil Forest · Army Ranges · Kimmeridge Bay · St Aldhelms Head · Worth Matravers · Isle of Purbeck · Dancing Ledge · Purbeck Beds · Durlston Head · Swanage · Old Harry Rocks · Studland · South Haven Point

THE ENVIRONMENT & NATURE

p199), just east of Exmouth, and the official start of the Jurassic Coast that's marked, as you will discover, by a geoneedle unveiled by Prince Charles. The following is a site-by-site guide to the coast, organised by geological period.

Triassic Period (250-200 million years ago) During this period Devon was located near to the centre of a super-continent: Pangaea. The county was part of a huge, hot and arid desert through which seasonal flash floods would sweep, depositing large amounts of sediment – mud and stone – as they carved their way through the landscape.

The red and orange rock that you see at the western end of the Jurassic Coast is indicative of the harsh, barren conditions in which they were formed. The few creatures that survived the mass extinction at the end of the Permian period began to dominate during the Triassic period; dinosaurs also began to evolve at this time. The period ended as it had begun, however, with a mass extinction – volcanic activity, an asteroid strike and climate change are all held up as possible culprits.

❏ **Where to see evidence of the Triassic Period**
● **Orcombe Point** The red mudstone and sandstone at Orcombe provide evidence of the harsh desert environment of the Triassic.
● **Budleigh Salterton** Here one finds Triassic pebble-beds overlain with red sandstone.
● **Otter Estuary** Formed of Triassic sandstone; a fossilised 'Devon rhynchosaur', a stocky dinosaur up to 2m in length with a powerful beak, was also found buried here.
● **Ladram Bay** The impressive red sea stacks here are made of Triassic sandstone, the result of erosion by the sea.
● **Sidmouth to Beer** This stretch provides a great example of the unconformity (see p58), with the cliff's colours changing from orange Triassic rock to the white chalk of the Cretaceous period.
● **The Undercliffs** Beginning at the Axe estuary in the late Triassic period, 7 miles and 25 million years later you arrive near Pinhay Bay in the early Jurassic! Just to complete the Mesozoic set, landslips also expose Cretaceous chalk.

Jurassic Period (200-140 million years ago) As sea levels rose and tropical oceans flooded the deserts, Pangaea began to split, with the landmass that would become the modern-day Americas separated from that which would become Europe, while in between these continents the Atlantic Ocean formed. With an increase in the length and number of coastlines, the continental climate changed from desert to tropical, lush forests, allowing life to thrive. Birds first took to the wing at this time, dinosaurs stalked the land and mammals also first entered the fray.

This is also the period of the **ammonite**, one of the most common fossils found on beaches today. Luckily for all these creatures, there was no mass extinction at the end of the Jurassic period.

Ammonite

❏ **Where to see evidence of the Jurassic Period**
● **Beaches** At Lyme Regis, Charmouth and Seatown you can hunt the ancient fossilised remains of marine reptiles below the Jurassic Blue Lias cliffs.
● **Portland** One huge slab of Jurassic rock.
● **Weymouth to Ringstead Bay** The geological folds and faults en route consist of Jurassic clays, limestones and sandstones.
● **Osmington Mills** The fossilised burrows and markings of marine animals can be seen on the beach here.
● **Durdle Door/Stair Hole/Lulworth Cove** Jurassic limestone and Cretaceous chalk prove more resistant than the clays and sands that the sea have eroded away, leaving these impressive natural wonders.
● **Fossil Forest** Near Lulworth Cove, this is one of the most complete records of a fossil forest in the world.
● **Kimmeridge Bay** The clay found in these cliffs now gives its name to this type of rock the world over: Kimmeridgian. Meanwhile, the rocks found here were once the base of a tropical ocean.

Cretaceous Period (140-65 million years ago) The most important event in this period occurred midway through it: the South-West of England tilted eastwards, the Atlantic expanded and the whole area became covered by one vast ocean. Billions of algae living in the sea prospered before their skeletons sank to the sea floor to form chalk – the youngest rock of this period (the Latin for chalk is *creta*).

Hospitable conditions on land enabled the largest and most ferocious of dinosaurs to flourish; flowering plants also began to develop. Another mass extinction at the end of the period, however, led to the end of the reptiles' reign; the dawn of the Cenozoic era – and the reign of the mammals – was upon us.

Cenozoic era
The Cenozoic era is divided into two periods, the **Tertiary** (65-1.8 million years ago) and the **Quaternary** (1.8 million years ago to the present day). During the Tertiary period mammals began to dominate the Earth and great shifts in the terrain led to the formation of some of the great mountain ranges,

❏ **Where to see evidence of the Cretaceous Period**
● **High Peak, Salcombe Hill and Branscombe** Due to the unconformity, upper Greensand (ie Cretaceous sandstone) and chalk lie directly on top of distinctively red Triassic mudstone.
● **Beer Head** Here's an anomaly: chalk cliffs in the midst of red Triassic rocks.
● **Golden Cap** Upper Greensand lies directly on top of darker Jurassic clay on this, the SWCP's highest peak; the greensand supposedly glowing at night.
● **White Nothe** Cretaceous chalk and sandstone on top of Jurassic clay.
● **The Purbeck Beds** Here you'll find a fossilised record of mammal evolution at the dawn of the Cretaceous Period with the fossils of fish, amphibians, reptiles and even dinosaur footprints; mixture of Cretaceous and Jurassic rock.
● **Old Harry Rocks** Impressive chalk stacks.

THE ENVIRONMENT & NATURE

such as the Alps. The great folds in the terrain that run through the Isle of Purbeck at the end of the walk were also formed at this time.

The above is obviously a remarkably simplified description of the geology of the area. For those who wish to delve deeper there are several very good books (see Recommended reading, p45).

Flora and fauna

With a varied topography that encompasses a full range of landscapes from windblasted moor to wetland marsh, hogback cliffs to wooded valleys, muddy estuaries to mobile sand dunes, you can begin to appreciate why the South-West can boast such a rich and varied countryside, with several unique species of flora and thriving populations of mammals and birds that, elsewhere in the UK, struggle to survive.

The following is not in any way a comprehensive guide – if it were, you would not have room for anything else in your rucksack – but merely a brief run-down of the more commonly seen flora and fauna on the trail, together with some of the rarer and more spectacular species.

TREES

Like most of Britain, Dorset and Devon would once have been covered in woodland and forest. Much of this woodland has of course long since vanished, having been cleared by our ancestors. Less than 10% of Dorset, for example, is covered in woodland today; and the figure is even lower – around 6% – in East Devon.

However, some of that cleared woodland grew back again several hundred years ago and is now known as ancient woodland. The presence of bluebells, wood anemones and other particular flowering plants are indicators that there has been tree cover for a very long time (the estimate we hear most frequently is 'over 400 years').

Despite man's interference, there are some surprisingly fine patches of woodland on the coast path. The most interesting species is the **oak** (family name *Quercus*), which was originally planted as coppice or scrub. Oak woodland is a diverse habitat and not

❏ **Oak leaves showing galls**
Oak trees support more kinds of insects than any other tree in Britain and some affect the oak in unusual ways. The eggs of gall-flies cause growths known as galls on the leaves. Each of these contains a single insect. Other kinds of gall-flies lay eggs in stalks or flowers, leading to flower galls, growths the size of currants.

exclusively made up of oak. In Dorset the most prolific species of oak is **sessile oak** (*Quercus petraea*). Unfortunately, the two counties have been hit in recent years by a disease know colloquially as 'sudden oak death', and many of the trees have had to be felled to prevent further spread.

BIRCH (WITH FLOWERS)

Another tree affected by disease in recent years is the **ash** (*Fraxinus excelsior*). Ash dieback disease first appeared on these shores in 2012 and has now spread right across Britain including Devon and Dorset. In Denmark, where the disease appears to have originated, up to 90% of trees have been infected.

Other trees that flourish here include **downy birch** (*Betula pubescens*), its relative the **silver birch** (*Betula pendula*), **holly** (*Ilex aquifolium*) and **hazel** (*Corylus avellana*) which has traditionally been used for coppicing (the periodic cutting of small trees for harvesting).

HAZEL (WITH FLOWERS)

FLOWERS

The extraordinary geology of the area ensures that a wide diversity of plants is able to thrive too. Whatever ground a plant prefers, be it chalk, clay, shingle, woodland mulch or the acid soils below Golden Cap and the dunes of Studland Beach, there is something for them on this stretch of southern British coastline. Spring is the time to come and see the spectacular displays of colour on the South-West Coast Path, when most of the flowers are in bloom.

Alternatively, arrive in August and you'll see the heathers carpeting patches of the moors in a blaze of purple flowers, picked out with the brilliant yellow of the gorse bush; the latter will have been a feature of the landscape since spring.

Woodland and hedgerows

From March to May **bluebells** (*Hyacinthoides non-scripta*) proliferate in some of the woods along the trail, providing a wonderful spectacle.

The white **wood anemone** (*Anemone nemorosa*) – wide open flowers when sunny but closed and drooping when the weather's dull – and the yellow **primrose** (*Primula vulgaris*) also flower early in spring. **Red campion** (*Silene dioica*), which flowers from late April, can be found in hedgebanks along with

THE ENVIRONMENT & NATURE

rosebay willowherb (*Epilobium angustifolium*) which also has the name fire-weed due to its habit of colonising burnt areas.

In scrubland and on woodland edges you will find **bramble** (*Rubus fruticosus*), a common vigorous shrub responsible for many a ripped jacket thanks to its sharp thorns and prickles. **Blackberry** fruits ripen from late summer to autumn. Fairly common in scrubland and on woodland edges is the **dog rose** (*Rosa canina*) which has a large pink flower, the fruits of which are used to make rose-hip syrup.

Look out, too, on the water in streams or rivers for the white-flowered **water crow-foot** (*Ranunculus penicillatus pseudofluitans*) which, because it needs unpolluted, flowing water, is a good indicator of the cleanliness of the stream.

Other flowering plants to look for in wooded areas and in hedgerows include the tall **foxglove** (*Digitalis purpurea*) with its trumpet-like flowers, **forget-me-not** (*Myosotis arvensis*) with tiny, delicate blue flowers, and **cow parsley** (*Anthriscus sylvestris*), a tall member of the carrot family with a large globe of white flowers which often covers roadside verges and hedge banks.

Heathland and scrubland

There are three species of heather. The most dominant is **ling** (*Calluna vulgaris*) with tiny flowers on delicate upright stems. The other two species are **bell heather** (*Erica cinera*) with deep purple bell-shaped flowers and **cross-leaved heath** (*Erica tetralix*) with similarly shaped flowers of a lighter pink, almost white colour. Cross-leaved heath prefers wet and boggy ground. As a result, it usually grows away from bell heather which prefers well-drained soils.

Heather is an incredibly versatile plant which is put to many uses. It provides fodder for livestock, fuel for fires, an orange dye and material for bedding, thatching, basketwork and brooms. It is still sometimes used in place of hops to flavour beer and the flower heads can be brewed to make good tea. It is also incredibly hardy and thrives on the denuded hills, preventing other species from flourishing. Indeed, at times, highland cattle are brought to certain areas of the moors to graze on the heather, allowing other species a chance to grow.

On Portland there is also the **Portland sea lavender** (*Limonium recurvum*), a purple-flowered species first discovered in 1832, that flowers in abundance on the cliff edges on the eastern side of the island just north of the Bill between July and August – and which doesn't exist anywhere else in the world.

Grassland

There is much overlap between the hedge/woodland-edge habitat and that of pastures and meadows. You will come across **common birdsfoot-trefoil** (*Lotus corniculatus*), **Germander speedwell** (*Veronica chamaedrys*), **tufted** and **bush vetch** (*Vicia cracca* and *Vicia sepium*) and **meadow vetchling** (*Lathyrus pratensis*) in both. Often the only species you will see in heavily grazed pastures are the most resilient.

Of the thistles, in late summer you should come across the **melancholy thistle** (*Cirsium helenoides*) drooping sadly on roadside verges and hay meadows. Unusually, it has no prickles on its stem. The **yellow rattle** is aptly named,

Bell Heather
Erica cinerea

Heather (Ling)
Calluna vulgaris

Thrift (Sea Pink)
Armeria maritima

Rosebay Willowherb
Epilobium angustifolium

Common Vetch
Vicia sativa

Forget-me-not
Myosotis arvensis

Rowan (tree)
Sorbus aucuparia

Spear Thistle
Cirsium vulgare

Red Campion
Silene dioica

Early Purple Orchid
Orchis mascula

Foxglove
Digitalis purpurea

Sea Holly
Eryngium maritimum

Common Dog Violet
Viola riviniana

Common Centaury
Centaurium erythraea

Honeysuckle
Lonicera periclymemum

Ramsons (Wild Garlic)
Allium ursinum

Germander Speedwell
Veronica chamaedrys

Herb-Robert
Geranium robertianum

Lousewort
Pedicularis sylvatica

Self-heal
Prunella vulgaris

Scarlet Pimpernel
Anagallis arvensis

Sea Campion
Silene maritima

Bluebell
Hyacinthoides non-scripta

Hogweed
Heracleum sphondylium

Dog Rose
Rosa canina

Meadow Buttercup
Ranunculis acris

Gorse
Ulex europaeus

Tormentil
Potentilla erecta

Birdsfoot-trefoil
Lotus corniculatus

Ox-eye Daisy
Leucanthemum vulgare

Common Ragwort
Senecio jacobaea

Primrose
Primula vulgaris

Cowslip
Primula veris

Colour photos (following pages)

● **C4 Left, top**: On the rugged coast between Hope and Salcombe. **Bottom**: Colourful pubs, Turnchapel (p97). **Right, top**: Playground of the rich – luxury yachts fill the harbour at Salcombe. **Bottom**: Hiking from Bigbury-on-Sea to catch the Cockleridge Ham ferry (p114).

● **C5 (clockwise from top left)**: **1**. Burgh Island is joined to Bigbury-on-Sea at low tide by a lovely sand spit. **2**. Swimmers soak up the sun at the Shoalstone sea water pool (p152). **3**. Steam railway, Paignton. **4**. Fossils placed by Mary Anning's grave in Lyme Regis (p227). **5**. Huge ammonites at Dinosaurland (p227). **6**. The century-old Babbacombe Cliff Railway.

● **C6 (clockwise from top left)**: **1**. Portland Bill Lighthouse (p271). **2**. Looking east from the top of Golden Cap (p239). **3**. Dancing Ledge (p303). **4**. Grandiose Creech Grange Farm (Map 76b). **5**. The coast-hugging railway, Dawlish. **6**. The quiet village of Shaldon (p176).

● **C7 Left, top**: Hikers sweep their way around Anvil Point Lighthouse (p305). **Bottom**: The boulder-strewn Isle of Portland. **Right, top**: Day-trippers scale East Cliff up the precarious path from West Bay. **Bottom**: Relaxing by the chalk pinnacles of Old Harry Rocks.

C6

LULWORTH
COVE 3
DURDLE DOOR 1½

THE WARREN
SCRATCHY
BOTTOM 1¼

COAST
PATH

for the dry seedpods rattle in the wind, a good indication for farmers that it is time to harvest the hay.

Other widespread grassland species include **harebell** (*Campanula rotundifolia*), delicate yellow **tormentil** (*Potentilla erecta*) and **devil's-bit scabious** (*Succisa pratensis*). Also keep an eye out for orchids such as the **fragrant orchid** (*Gymnaadenia conopsea*) and **early purple orchid** (*Orchis mascula*).

Dunes

Dunes are formed by wind action creating a fragile, unstable environment. Among the first colonisers is **marram grass** (*Ammophila arenaria*) which is able to withstand drought, exposure to wind and salt spray and has an ability to grow up through new layers of sand that cover it.

Other specialist plants are **sea holly** (*Eryngium maritimum*), **sea spurge** (*Euphorbia paralias*) and **sea bindweed** (*Calystegia soldanella*). The one thing that these seemingly indomitable plants can't tolerate is trampling by human feet; stay on the path which is nearly always well marked through dunes.

MAMMALS

The south-west is blessed with wildlife. The Lulworth Ranges play host to two of our largest mammal species, one native, one imported. The former is the **roe deer** (*Capreolus capreolus*), the most common of deer species in England. It is quite easy to distinguish from the other species, mainly due to its diminutive size (standing around 65cm to the shoulder), red-brown coat in summer and small antlers (around 25cm), white rump and short tail. Its nocturnal habits, however, mean that you will still be lucky to see one.

Britain's only other native deer, the **red deer** (*Cervus elaphus*), is also present in Devon and Dorset, mainly in Exmoor but also in patches throughout the two counties.

The exotic **sika deer** (*Cervus nippon*) also thrives in the Lulworth Ranges. They are believed to have come from herds that arrived in 1895 at Hyde House and the following year at Brownsea Island in Poole Harbour. Few people realised that the deer could swim to the mainland; together with further escapees from Hyde House they were able to establish themselves on the ranges and nearby areas. Considered sacred in Japan – where they originally hail from – they find the conditions so benign on the ranges that they are now having to be culled before their numbers become unmanageable.

The South-West, in particular Exmoor, is also renowned as the spiritual home of the **otter** (*Lutra lutra*). The county was the home of the author Henry Williamson – creator of *Tarka the Otter* – and Devon today is proud to be associated with this most graceful of British carnivores. It wasn't always like this, however, and for much of the 20th century (and before) the otter was persecuted because it was (wrongly) believed to have an enormously detrimental effect on fish stocks.

THE ENVIRONMENT & NATURE

(Opposite) Top: The beach east of the headland at famous Durdle Door (see p282). **Bottom left**: Almost within reach: Scratchy Bottom. **Right**: The coast path sculpture marking the end of the South-West Coast Path at Sandbanks (p312, photo © Henry Stedman).

Today the otter is enjoying something of a renaissance thanks to concerted conservation efforts. At home both in salt water and fresh water, they are a good indicator of an unpolluted environment. It is unlikely that you'll spot one on your walk, although there are records of sightings all along the path. The Erme River, which you wade across on the path, is a particularly good spot to see one, according to records, and Devon is renowned as one of the otter's main strongholds.

Seeing any of the above requires patience and no little amount of luck. One creature that you will definitely see along the walk, however, is the **rabbit** (*Oryctolagus cuniculus*). Most of the time you'll get nothing more than a brief and distant glimpse of their white tails as they race for the nearest warren at the sound of your footfall since they're timid by nature. Because they are so numerous, however, the laws of probability dictate that you will at some stage during your walk get close enough to observe them without being spotted; trying to take a decent photo of one of them, however, is a different matter.

If you're lucky you may also come across **hares** (*Lepus europaeus*), often mistaken for rabbits but much larger, more elongated and with longer ears and back legs. There are populations of hares all over the arable parts of the South-West – look out for them around the Lulworth Ranges and the Kimmeridge area – though nowhere are they common.

Like the otter, the **water vole** (*Arvicola terrestris*) has both been a major character in a well-known work of fiction (in this case 'Ratty' from Kenneth Grahame's classic children's story *Wind in the Willows*) and has suffered a devastating drop in its population. Their numbers had originally declined due to the arrival in the UK countryside of the mink from North America, which successfully adapted to living in the wild after escaping from local fur farms. Unfortunately, the mink not only hunts water voles but is small enough to slip inside their burrows. Thus, with the voles afforded no protection, the mink was able to wipe out an entire riverbank's population in a matter of months. (Incidentally, this is another reason why protecting the otter is important: they kill mink.) A programme is now in place in which the water vole and its habitat is not only protected but the mink are being trapped and killed.

Another native British species that has suffered at the hands of a foreign invader is the **red squirrel** (*Sciurus vulgaris*), a small, tufty-eared native that has been usurped by its larger cousin from North America, the **grey squirrel** (*Sciurus carolinensis*). The only place where it might be possible to see the red squirrel is on Brownsea Island in Poole Harbour – at the very end of the coast path.

The ubiquitous **fox** (*Vulpes vulpes*) is now just as at home in the city as it is in the country. While usually considered nocturnal, it's not unusual to encounter one during the day. Another creature of the night that you may occasionally see is the **badger** (*Meles meles*). Relatively common throughout the British Isles, these sociable mammals with their distinctive black-and-white striped muzzles live in large underground burrows called setts, appearing around sunset to root for worms and slugs.

The nocturnal **bat**, of which there are 17 species in Britain, is protected by law. Your best chance of spotting one is at dusk while there's still enough light in the sky to make out their flitting forms as they fly along hedgerows, over rivers and streams and around street lamps in their quest for moths and insects. The commonest species in Britain is the **pipistrelle** (*Pipistrellus pipistrellus*).

Keep a look out for other fairly common but little seen species such as the carnivorous **stoat** (*Mustela erminea*), its diminutive cousin the **weasel** (*Mustela nivalis*), the **hedgehog** (*Erinaceus europaeus*) – these days, alas, most commonly seen as roadkill – and any number of species of **voles**, **mice** and **shrews**.

Out at sea

The high cliffs are also a great place from which to look out over the sea. Searching for seals is an enjoyable and essential part of cliff walking. You'll spot lots of grey lobster-pot buoys before your first seal, but it's worth the effort. **Atlantic grey seals** (*Halichoerus grypus*) relax in the water, looking over their big Roman noses with doggy eyes, as interested in you as you are in them. Twice the weight of a red deer, a big bull can be over 200kg. On calm, sunny days it's possible to follow them down through the clear water as they dive, as elegant in their element as they are clumsy on land. Seals generally come ashore only to rest, moult their fur, or to breed. Devon is your best chance of seeing one, though there are small pockets of them as far east as Poole and beyond.

A cliff-top sighting of Britain's largest fish is also a real possibility, but is more chilling than endearing! **Basking sharks** (*Cetorhinus maximus*) can grow to a massive 36ft (11 metres) and weigh seven tonnes, and their two fins, a large shark-like dorsal fin followed by a notched tail fin, are so far apart it takes a second look to be convinced it's one fish. But these are gentle giants cruising slowly with open jaws, filtering microscopic plankton from the sea. You are most likely to see one during late spring and summer when they feed at the surface during calm, warm weather. No fewer than 15 sightings were recorded off Devon and Cornwall in the summer of 2016, and though you are most likely to spy them in the waters off Cornwall, a beautiful specimen was spotted off West Bexington in Dorset. Look out for coloured or numbered tags, put on for research into this sadly declining species, and report them to the website given in the box below.

Taking a longer view and with some good luck, watch the sea for dolphins, porpoises or even a whale. **Harbour porpoises** (*Phocoena phocoena*)

❏ **Reporting wildlife sightings**

Report basking shark or marine turtle sightings to the website of the Marine Conservation Society (⌨ mcsuk.org). Remember to note any tags you've spotted. Reports are greatly appreciated. If you see any of the other large marine creatures – such as dolphins, whales or seals – you can report them online through Seaquest Southwest, part of the Devon Biodiversity Records Centre (⌨ dbrc.org.uk). With any report give the location, number and the direction they were heading in.

If you come across a stranded marine animal such as a dolphin or porpoise, don't approach it but contact either British Divers Marine Life Rescue (office hours ☎ 01825-765546, out of office hours ☎ 07787 433412, ⌨ bdmlr.org.uk) or the RSPCA hotline (☎ 0300-123 4999, ⌨ rspca.org.uk).

THE ENVIRONMENT & NATURE

and **bottlenose dolphins** (*Tursiops truncatus*) both visit the offshore waters. One such dolphin, nicknamed George, has been turning up along the Dorset coast for years and even became something of a tabloid celebrity when he settled in the waters off Beer one summer.

Other cetaceans you may catch a glimpse of are **Risso's dolphins** (*Grampus griseus*), **common dolphins** (*Delphinus delphis*), **striped dolphins** (*Stenella coeruleoalba*), **orcas** or **killer whales** (*Orcinus orca*) and **pilot whales** (*Globicephala melaena*) but, be warned, they are fiendishly difficult to tell apart: a brief glimpse of a fin is nothing like the 'whole animal' pictures shown in field guides.

REPTILES

Dorset and Devon both have populations of all six British reptile species: smooth snake, grass snake, adder, sand lizard, common lizard and slow worm. Of the above, by far the rarest is the **sand lizard**, though wonderfully Dorset is its stronghold. Unremarkable most of the time, during the mating season the male's sides become a vivid green. Confined largely to the heathlands of Dorset, there is a small population on Studland on the last day of the walk.

The **adder** (*Vipera berus*) is the only poisonous snake of the three mentioned above. They pose very little risk to walkers – indeed, you should consider yourself extremely fortunate to see one, providing you're a safe distance away. They bite only when provoked, preferring to hide instead. The venom is designed to kill small mammals such as mice, voles and shrews, so deaths in humans are very rare but a bite can be extremely unpleasant and occasionally dangerous to children or the elderly. You are most likely to encounter them in spring when they come out of hibernation and during the summer when pregnant females warm themselves in the sun. They are easily identified by the striking zigzag pattern on their back. Should you be lucky enough to encounter one (they enjoy basking on clifftops and on the moors), enjoy it but leave it undisturbed.

The **grass snake** (*Natrix natrix*) is the largest British species, growing up to over a metre in length. Olive-grey in colour with short black bars down each side and orange or yellow patches just below the head, they are harmless, relying not on venom or biting for defence but instead give off a foul odour if disturbed.

The **slow-worm** (*Anguis fragilis*) must be one of the more unusual creatures in the British Isles – a reptile that is called a worm, looks like a snake but is actually a legless lizard! Silver-grey with a dark line down the centre of the back and along each side, it is common in Devon and Dorset, where it feeds on slugs, worms and insects.

BIRDS

In and around the fishing villages

The wild laugh of the **herring gull** (*Larus argentatus*) is the wake-up call of the coast path. Perched on the rooftops of the stone villages, they are a reminder of the link between people and wildlife, the rocky coast and our stone and concrete towns and cities. Shoreline scavengers, they've adapted to the increasing waste thrown out by human society. Despite their bad reputation it's worth taking a closer look at these fascinating, ubiquitous birds. How do they keep their pale grey and white plumage so beautiful feeding on rubbish? Nobel-prize-winning animal behaviourist Nikko Tinbergen showed how the young pecking at the red dot on their bright yellow bills triggers the adults to regurgitate food. In August the newly fledged brown young follow their parents begging for food. Over the next three years they'll go through a motley range of plumages, more grey and less brown each year till they reach adulthood. But please don't feed them and do watch your sandwiches and fish & chips – they are quite capable of grabbing food from your hand.

Village harbours are a good place for lunch or an evening drink after a hard day on the cliffs. Look out for the birds who are equally at home on a rocky shore or in villages, such as the beautiful little black-and-white **pied wagtail** (*Motacilla alba*) with its long, bobbing tail. Also looking black from a distance as they strut the beach are **jackdaws** (*Corvus monedula*). Close up, however, they are beautiful with a grey nape giving them a hooded look and shining blue eyes. They are very sociable: you will often see them high up in the air in pairs or flocks playing tag or performing acrobatic tricks.

Small, dark brown and easy to miss, the **rock pipit** (*Anthus petrosus*) is one of our toughest birds, as it feeds whilst walking on the rocks between the land and the sea. They nest in crevices and caves along the rocky coastline.

Seen on or from the sea cliffs

Walking on the coastal path leads you into a world of rock and sea, high cliffs with bracken-clad slopes, exposed green pasture, dramatic drops and headlands, sweeping sandy beaches and softer country around the estuaries. Stunning **stonechats** (*Saxicola torquata*) with black, white and orange colouring are common on heath and grassy plains where you may hear their distinctive song, which is not dissimilar to two stones being clacked together.

STONECHAT
L: 135MM/5.25"

Twittering **linnets** (*Carduelis cannabina*) with their bright red breasts and grey heads fly ahead and perch on gorse and fences. The vertiginous swoops of the path mean it's often possible to be at eye level, or even look down on, birds and mammals. Watch for **kestrels** (*Falco tinnunculus*), hovering on sharp brown wings, before plummeting onto their prey.

At eye level the black 'moustache' of the powerful slate-grey-backed **peregrine** (*Falco peregrinus*) is sometimes visible. At a glance it can be mistaken for a pigeon, its main prey. But the power and speed of this, the world's fastest bird, soon sets it apart. In the late summer whole families fly over the cliffs. In mid winter look for them over estuaries where they hunt ducks and waders. Despite the remote fastness of the cliffs, peregrines have suffered terribly. Accidental poisoning by the pesticide DDT succeeded where WWII persecution for fear they would kill carrier pigeons failed, and they were almost extinct by

THE ENVIRONMENT & NATURE

GUILLEMOT
L: 450MM/18"

the end of the 1960s. Their triumphant return means not only a thriving population on their traditional sea cliffs, but more and more nesting in our cities on man-made cliffs, such as tower blocks and cathedrals. Coast-path walkers have seen them swooping around the Undercliffs near Lyme Regis.

Cliff ledges, a kind of multi-storey block of flats for birds, provide nesting places safe from marauding land predators such as foxes and rats. It's surprising just how close it's possible to get to **fulmars** (*Fulmarus glacialis*), which return to their nesting ledges in February for the start of the long breeding season that goes on into the autumn. Only in the depth of winter are the cliffs quiet. Fulmars are related to albatrosses and like them are masters of the air. You can distinguish them from gulls by their ridged, flat wings as they sail the wind close to the waves with the occasional burst of fast flapping. Fulmars are incredibly tenacious at holding their nesting sites and vomit a stinking oily secretion over any intruders, including rock-climbers! The elegant **kittiwake** (*Rissa tridactyla*), the one true seagull that never feeds on land, is another cliff nester, identified by its 'dipped in ink' black wingtips.

Black above, white below, **manx shearwaters** (*Puffinus puffinus*) make globe-encircling journeys as they sail effortlessly just above even the wildest sea.

Small and fast on hard-beating wings, black and white **guillemots** (*Uria troile*) and **razorbills** (*Alca torda*) shoot out from their nesting ledges hidden in the cliffs. Guillemots have a long thin bill and razorbills a heavy half circle bill. Large colonies of guillemots, kittiwakes, razorbills, and a few puffins inhabit the cliff ledges near Durlston Head, just before Swanage. Purbeck also has several small colonies of puffins.

Less lovely in most people's eyes, though undeniably magnificent, the big, rapacious **great black-backed gulls** (*Larus marinus*) cruise the nesting colonies for prey. Star of the sea show, however, has to be the big, sharp-winged, Persil-white **gannets** (*Morus bassanus*) cruising slowly for fish, then suddenly plunging with folded wings into the sea. Their strengthened skulls protect them from the huge force of the impact with the water. Gannets, together with storm petrels, shearwaters and skuas are often seen from Portland Bill.

Two birds more familiar from the artificial cliffs of our cities can be seen here in their natural habitat – **house martins** (*Delichon urbica*), steely-blue backed like a **swallow** (*Hirundo rustica*), but with more V-shaped wings and a distinctive white rump. And **rock doves** (*Columba livia*). These are so mixed with **town pigeons** (*Columba livia domestica*) it's hard to say if any 'pure' wild birds remain, but many individuals with the characteristic grey back, small white rump and two black wing bars can be seen.

Where the path drops steeply to a rocky bay, **oystercatchers** (*Haematopus ostralegus*), with their black and white plumage and spectacular carrot-coloured bill, pipe in panic when they fly off. This is also a good spot to get close to **shags** (*Phalacrocorax aristotelis*) and **cormorants** (*Phalacrocorax carbo*), common all round the coast, swimming low and black in the water. Shags are smaller and are always seen on the sea – cormorants are also on rivers and estuaries – and in the summer have a crest whilst cormorants have a white patch near their tail and a white face. Close up, these oily birds shine iridescently; shags are green, cormorants are purple. They are a primitive species and since their feathers are not completely waterproof both have to dry their bodies after time in the sea; their heraldic pose, standing upright with half-spread wings on drying rocks is one of the special sights of the coast path.

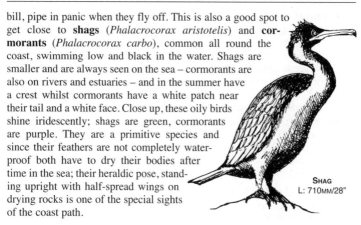

SHAG
L: 710MM/28"

In pastures, combes and woods

The one species that enjoys more publicity than any other on the coast path is the **cirl bunting** (*Emberiza cirlus*). Its rarity and declining numbers – by 1989 there were only 118 breeding pairs – led to the establishment of some large conservation efforts and you'll come across several cliff-top fields on the trail that have been entirely given over to their protection. Labrador Bay (four miles south of Teignmouth), Prawle Point, Maidencombe, Berry Head, Wembury, Jenny Cliff, and Stoke Point near Noss Mayo, are all good places to spot this smallish bird with a yellow-streaked head and green breast band – like a small yellowhammer. The programme is ongoing but there are now thought to be more than one thousand pairs. They are also found at Slapton Ley National Nature Reserve (see p133) where you

CORMORANT
L: 900MM/36"

may also spot **Cetti's warblers** (*Cettia cetti*) and **Greater crested grebes** (*Podiceps cristatus*).

On your walk you'll find that the path frequently rises up onto rich green pasture. **Skylarks** (*Alauda arvensis*) soar tunefully – almost disappearing into the spring sky, while in winter small green-brown **meadow pipits** (*Anthus pratensis*) flit weakly, giving a small high-pitched call.

Spring also brings migrant **wheatears** (*Oenanthe oenanthe*): they are beautiful with their grey and black feathers above, buff and white below, and unmistakable when they fly and show their distinctive white rump. **Buzzard** (*Buteo buteo*) soar up with their tilted, broad round wings, giving their high, wild 'ke-oow' cry.

THE ENVIRONMENT & NATURE

Ravens (*Corvus corax*) cronk-cronk over the cliffs and are distinguished from more common **carrion crows** (*Corvus corone*) by their huge size and wedge-shaped tail.

In the woods you'll find all three native species of **woodpecker** – **green**, **great** and **lesser spotted** (*Picus viridis* and *Dendrocopos major* and *minor* respectively); the two latter are very much wedded to the woods, while the former, with its laughing call, can often be seen on the moors looking for insects.

In spring familiar birds such as **robins** (*Erithacus rubecula*), **blackbirds** (*Turdus merula*), **blue** and **great tits** (*Parus major* & *caeruleus*), **chaffinches** (*Fringila coelebs*) and **dunnocks** (*Prunella modularis*) are joined by the small green **chiffchaff** (*Phylloscopus collybita*); it's not much to look at but is one of the earliest returning migrants and unmistakably calls its own name in two repeated notes.

In and around estuaries

Descending to the long walk round the estuaries you move into a different, softer world of shelter and rich farmland. Best for birds in winter, they are a welcome refuge from the ferocity of the worst weather for wildlife and people.

There are large flocks of ducks – whistling **wigeon** (*Anas penelope*), a combination of grey and pinky brown, with big white wing patches in flight – and waders like the brown **curlew** (*Numenius arquata*) with its impossibly long, down-curved beak and beautiful sad fluting call, evocative of summer moors.

The **redshank** (*Tringa totanus*), **greenshank** (*Tringa nebularia*), golden and grey **plover** (*Pluvialis sp.*), and black-tailed and bar-tailed **godwit** (*Limosa sp.*) can also be seen in winter. Look out for the big black, white and chestnut **shelduck** (*Tadorna tadorna*), and for the tall grey **heron** (*Ardea cinerea*), hunched at rest or extended to its full 175cm as it slowly, patiently stalks fish in the shallows.

A real rarity ten years ago, another species of heron, the stunning white **little egret** (*Egretta garzetta*) is now unmissable on estuaries. Here the more common gull is the nimble **black-headed gull** (*Larus ridibundus*), with its elegant cap, dark in summer but pale in winter. In summer, terns come: the big **sandwich tern** (*Sterna sandvicensis*) with its shaggy black cap and loud rasping call, and the smaller sleeker **aerobatic common tern** (*Sterna hirundo*).

BUTTERFLIES AND MOTHS

Butterflies are an unexpected treat on the SWCP. Not only are they numerous, but there are several different varieties too. Portland alone plays host to two butterfly reserves, Broadcroft Quarry and the Perryfields Reserve (both, alas, off the path), home of the rare and fussy silver-studded blue and the island's very own **moth**, the Portland ribbon wave. Small blues, chalkhill blues and common blues are also present, and migrants such as clouded yellow and painted lady may also put in an appearance.

The most famous butterfly in the region is the orange and brown heath fritillary, which has declined rapidly over the last 30 years in the UK, but which is thriving in the combes of north Devon and around Thurlestone.

MINIMUM IMPACT & OUTDOOR SAFETY

3

Minimum impact walking

By visiting this rural corner of England you are having a positive impact, not just on your own well-being but on local communities as well. Your presence brings money and jobs into the local economy and also pride in and awareness of the region's environment and culture.

However, the environment should not just be considered in terms of its value as a tourist asset. Its long-term survival and enjoyment by future generations will only be possible if both visitors and local communities protect it now. The following points are made to help you reduce your impact on the environment, encourage conservation and promote sustainable tourism in the area.

ECONOMIC IMPACT

Rural businesses and communities in Britain have been hit hard in recent years by a seemingly endless series of crises. Most people are aware of the countryside code – not dropping litter and closing the gate behind you are still as pertinent as ever – but in light of the economic pressures that local countryside businesses are under, there is something else you can do: **buy local**.

Look and ask for local produce (see box pp22-3) to buy and eat. Not only does this cut down on the amount of pollution and congestion that the transportation of food creates – so-called 'food miles' – but also ensures that you are supporting local farmers and producers, the very people who have moulded the countryside you have come to see and who are in the best position to protect it. If you can find local food which is also organic so much the better.

Money spent at local level – perhaps in a market, or at the greengrocer, or in an independent pub – has a far greater impact for good in that community than the equivalent spent in a branch of a national chain store or restaurant. It would be going too far advocate that walkers boycott the larger supermarkets, which after all do provide local employment, but it's worth remembering that smaller businesses in rural communities rely heavily on visitors for their very existence. If we want to keep these local shops and post offices, we need to use them.

ENVIRONMENTAL IMPACT

A walking holiday in itself is an environmentally friendly approach to tourism. The following are some ideas on how you can go a few steps further in helping to minimise your impact on the environment while walking the Coast Path.

Use public transport whenever possible

While we recognise that public transport along this section of the South-West Coast Path is not great, using it is preferable to taking a car as it benefits everyone: visitors, locals and the environment.

Never leave litter

Leaving litter shows a total disrespect for the natural world and others coming after you. As well as being unsightly, litter kills wildlife, pollutes the environment and can be dangerous to farm animals. Please carry a plastic bag so you can dispose of your rubbish in a bin in the next village. It would be very helpful if you could pick up litter left by other people too.

● **Is it OK if it's biodegradable?** Not really. Apple cores, banana skins, orange peel and the like are unsightly, encourage flies, ants and wasps and ruin a picnic spot for others.

● **The lasting impact of litter** A piece of orange peel left on the ground takes six months to decompose; silver foil 18 months; a plastic bag 10 years; clothes 15 years; and an aluminium can 85 years.

Respect all wildlife

Care for all wildlife you come across along the path; it has as much right to be there as you. As tempting as it may be to pick wild flowers, leave them in place so the next people who pass can enjoy them too. Don't break branches off or damage trees in any way. If you come across wildlife, keep your distance and don't watch for too long. Your presence can cause considerable stress, particularly if the adults are with young, or in winter when the weather is harsh and food is scarce. Young animals are rarely abandoned. If you come across young birds, keep away so that their mother can return.

Outdoor toiletry

As more and more people discover the joys of walking in the natural environment issues such as how to go to the loo outdoors rapidly gain importance. How many of us have shaken our heads at the sight of toilet paper strewn beside the path, or even worse, someone's dump left in full view? Human excrement is not only offensive to our senses but, more importantly, can infect water sources.

Where to go The coast path is a high-use area and many habitats will not benefit from your fertilisation. As far as 'number twos' are concerned try whenever possible to use public toilets. There is no shortage of public toilets along the coast path and they are all marked on the trail maps. However, there are those times when the only time is now.

If you have to go outdoors help the environment to deal with your deposit in the best possible way by following a few simple guidelines.

● **Choose your site carefully** It should be at least 30 metres away from running water and out of reach of the high tide and not on any site of historical or archaeological interest. Carry a small trowel or use a sturdy stick to dig a small hole about 15cm (6") deep to bury your faeces in. Faeces decompose quicker when in contact with the top layer of soil or leaf mould; by using a stick to stir loose soil into your deposit you will speed decomposition up even more. Do not squash it under rocks as this slows down the decomposition process. If you have to use rocks as a cover make sure they are not in contact with your faeces.

● **Pack out toilet paper and tampons** Toilet paper takes a long time to decompose whether buried or not. It is easily dug up by animals and may then blow into water sources or onto the trail. The best method for dealing with used toilet paper is to pack it out. Put it in a paper bag placed inside a plastic bag and then dispose of it at the next toilet. Tampons and sanitary towels also need to be packed out in a similar way. They take years to decompose and may also be dug up and scattered about by animals.

ACCESS

Britain is a crowded cluster of islands with few places where you can wander as you please. Most of the land is a patchwork of fields and agriculture and the environment through which the Dorset & South Devon Coast Path marches is no different. However, there are countless public rights of way, in addition to the main trail, that criss-cross the land.

This is fine, but what happens if you feel a little more adventurous and want to explore the moorland, woodland and hills that can also be found near the walk. Access to the countryside has always been a hot topic in Britain. In the 1940s soldiers coming back from the Second World War were horrified and disgruntled to find that landowners were denying them the right to walk across the moors; ironically the very country that they had been fighting to protect. Since then it has been an ongoing battle and it is a battle that was finally won (for the most part) as new legislation came into force in 2005 granting public access to thousands of acres of Britain's wildest land.

All those who enjoy access to the countryside must respect the land, its wildlife, the interests of those who live and work there and other users; we all share a common interest in the countryside. Knowing your rights and responsibilities gives you the information you need to act with minimal impact.

Old milestone in miles, furlongs and poles. In case you've forgotten, 40 poles make one furlong and eight furlongs equal one mile.

© DANIEL MCCROHAN

❏ THE COUNTRYSIDE CODE

The Countryside Code, originally described in the 1950s as the Country Code, was revised and relaunched in 2004, in part because of the changes brought about by the CRoW Act (see p78); it was updated again in 2012, 2014 and also 2016. The Code seems like common sense but sadly some people still appear to have no understanding of how to treat the countryside they walk in. An adapted version of the 2016 Code, launched under the logo 'Respect. Protect. Enjoy.', is given below:

Respect other people
● **Consider the local community and other people enjoying the outdoors** Be sensitive to the needs and wishes of those who live and work there. If, for example, farm animals are being moved or gathered keep out of the way and follow the farmer's directions. Being courteous and friendly to those you meet will ensure a healthy future for all based on partnership and co-operation.
● **Leave gates and property as you find them and follow paths unless wider access is available** A farmer normally closes gates to keep farm animals in, but may sometimes leave them open so the animals can reach food and water. Leave gates as you find them or follow instructions on signs. When in a group, make sure the last person knows how to leave the gate. Follow paths unless wider access is available, such as on open country or registered common land (known as 'open access land'). Leave machinery and farm animals alone – if you think an animal is in distress try to alert the farmer instead. Use gates, stiles or gaps in field boundaries if you can – climbing over walls, hedges and fences can damage them and increase the risk of farm animals escaping. If you have to climb over a gate because you can't open it always do so at the hinged end. Also be careful not to disturb ruins and historic sites.

Stick to the official path across arable/pasture land. Minimise erosion by not cutting corners or widening the path.

Protect the natural environment
● **Leave no trace of your visit and take your litter home** Take special care not to damage, destroy or remove features such as rocks, plants and trees. Take your litter with you (see p74); litter and leftover food don't just spoil the beauty of the countryside, they can be dangerous to wildlife and farm animals.

Fires can be as devastating to wildlife and habitats as they are to people and property – so be careful with naked flames and cigarettes at any time of the year. Never make a camp fire; the deep burn damages turf and destroys flora and fauna.
● **Keep dogs under effective control** This means that you should keep your dog on a lead or keep it in sight at all times, be aware of what it's doing and be confident it will return to you promptly on command.

Across farmland dogs should always be kept on a short lead. During lambing time they should not be taken with you at all. Always clean up after your dog and get rid of the mess responsibly – 'bag it and bin it'. (See also pp315-17).

Enjoy the outdoors
● **Plan ahead and be prepared** You're responsible for your own safety: be prepared for natural hazards, changes in weather and other events. Wild animals, farm animals and horses can behave unpredictably if you get too close, especially if they're with their young – so give them plenty of space.
● **Follow advice and local signs** In some areas there may be temporary diversions in place. Take notice of these and other local trail advice. Walking on the SWCP is pretty much hazard-free but you're responsible for your own safety so follow the simple guidelines outlined on pp79-80.

Rights of way

As a designated National Trail the coast path is a public right of way. A public right of way is either a footpath, a bridleway or a byway. The Dorset & South Devon section of the South West Coast Path is a footpath for almost all its length which means that anyone has the legal right to use it on foot only.

Rights of way are theoretically established because the owner has dedicated them to public use. However, very few paths are formally dedicated in this way. If members of the public have been using a path without interference for 20 years or more the law assumes the owner has intended to dedicate it as a right of way. If a path has been unused for 20 years it does not cease to exist; the guiding principle is 'once a highway, always a highway'.

On a public right of way you have the right to 'pass and repass along the way' which includes stopping to rest or admire the view, or to consume refreshments. You can also take with you a 'natural accompaniment', which includes a dog, but it must be kept under close control (see opposite).

Farmers and land managers must ensure that paths are not blocked by crops or other vegetation, or otherwise obstructed, that the route is identifiable and the surface is restored soon after cultivation. If crops are growing over the path you have every right to walk through them, following the line of the right of way as closely as possible.

If you find a path blocked or impassable you should report it to the appropriate highway authority. Highway authorities are responsible for maintaining footpaths. In Devon and Dorset the highway authorities are the respective county councils. The council is also the surveying authority with responsibility for maintaining the official definitive map of public rights of way.

Wider access

The access situation to land around the coast path is a little more complicated. Trying to unravel and understand the seemingly thousands of laws and acts is never easy in any legal system. Parliamentary Acts give a right to walk over certain areas of land such as some, but by no means all, common land and some specific places such as Dartmoor and the New Forest. However, in other places, such as Bodmin Moor and many British beaches, right of access is not written in law. It is merely tolerated by the landowner and could be terminated at any time.

Some landowners, such as the Forestry Commission, water companies and the National Trust, are obliged by law to allow some degree of access to their land. Land covered by schemes such as the Environmental Stewardship Scheme, formerly the Countryside Stewardship Scheme, gives landowners a financial incentive to manage their land for conservation and to provide limited public access. There are also a few truly altruistic landowners who have allowed access over their land and these include organisations such as the RSPB, the Woodland Trust, and some local authorities. Overall, however, access to most of Britain's countryside is forbidden to Britain's people, in marked contrast to the general rights of access that prevail in other European countries.

Right to roam

For many years groups such as Ramblers (see box p46) and the British Mountaineering Council (🖥 thebmc.co.uk) campaigned for new and wider access legislation. This finally bore fruit in the form of the Countryside and Rights of Way Act of November 2000, colloquially known as the CRoW Act, which granted access for 'recreation on foot' to mountain, moor, heath, down and registered common land in England and Wales. In essence it allows walkers the freedom to roam responsibly away from footpaths, without being accused of trespass, on about four million acres of open, uncultivated land.

There may be a good reason why you shouldn't take a short cut.

On 28th August 2005 the South-West became the sixth region in England and Wales to be opened up under this act; however, restrictions may still be in place from time to time – check the situation on 🖥 www.gov.uk/right-of-way-open-access-land/use-your-right-to-roam.

Outdoor safety

AVOIDANCE OF HAZARDS

Swimming

If you are not an experienced swimmer or familiar with the sea, plan ahead and swim at **beaches** where there is a lifeguard service, such as Exmouth, Teignmouth and Dawlish Warren. On such beaches you should swim between the red and yellow flags as this is the patrolled area. Don't swim between black and white chequered flags as these areas are only for surfboards. A red flag flying indicates that it is dangerous to enter the water. If you are not sure about anything ask one of the lifeguards; after all they are there to help you.

If you are going to swim at unsupervised beaches never do so alone and always take care; some beaches are prone to strong rips. Never swim off headlands or near river mouths as there may be strong currents. Always be aware of changing weather conditions and tidal movement (see box opposite). The South-West has a huge tidal range and it can be very easy to get cut off by the tide.

If you see someone in difficulty do not attempt a rescue until you have contacted the coastguard (see box p80). Once you know help is on the way try to assist the person by throwing something to help them stay afloat. Many beaches have rescue equipment located in red boxes; these are marked on the trail maps.

For a safer place to swim, look out for outdoor swimming pools, known as **lidos**. Plymouth's Art-Deco, salt-water Tinside Lido (p86) is a striking example, but there's also a small lido in Teignmouth (p178). There are also free-to-use

❏ Tides

Tides are the regular rise and fall of the ocean caused by the gravitational pull of the moon. They are actually very long waves which follow the path of the moon across the ocean. Twice a day there is a high tide and a low tide and there are approximately 6¼ hours between high and low water.

Spring tides (derived from the German word *springen* meaning 'to jump') are tides with a very large range that occur just after the full- and new-moon phases when the gravitational forces of the sun and the moon line up. Spring tides occur twice every month; high tides then are higher and low tides lower than normal. Neap tides occur halfway between each spring tide and are tides with the smallest range, so you get comparatively high low tides and low high tides. They occur at the first and third quarters of the moon when the sun, moon and earth are all at right angles to each other, hence the gravitational forces of the sun and moon are weakened.

sea-water lidos by Plymouth's Royal William Yard (p86) and just outside Brixham (p152).

Walking alone

If you are walking alone you must appreciate and be prepared for the increased risk. It is always a good idea to leave word with somebody about where you are going; you can always ring ahead to book accommodation and let them know you are walking alone and what time you expect to arrive. Don't forget to contact whoever you have left word with to let them know you've arrived safely. Carrying a mobile phone can be useful though you cannot rely on getting good reception (see box p42).

Safety on the coast path

Sadly every year people are injured walking along the trail, though usually it's nothing more than a badly twisted ankle. Landslides are rare but not unknown (see p222). Parts of the path can be pretty remote, however, and it certainly pays to take precautions when walking. Abiding by the following rules should minimise the risks.

● Avoid walking on your own if possible.
● Make sure that somebody knows your plans for every day you are on the trail. This could be a friend or relative whom you have promised to call every night or the B&B or hostel you plan to stay in at the end of each day's walk. That way, if you fail to turn up or call, they can raise the alarm.
● If the weather closes in suddenly and fog or mist descends while you are on the trail and you become uncertain of the correct trail, do not be tempted to continue. Just wait where you are and you'll find that mist often clears, at least for long enough to allow you to get your bearings.

If you are still uncertain and the weather does not look like improving, return the way you came to the nearest point of civilisation and try again another time when conditions have improved.
● Always fill your water bottle or pouch at every available opportunity and ensure you have some food such as high-energy snacks.

- Always carry a map, torch, whistle and wet-weather gear with you.
- Wear footwear with good grip.
- Be extra vigilant with children.
- Always keep dogs on leads on clifftops.
- Avoid walking and sitting directly below steep unstable-looking cliffs where possible.

Dealing with an accident

- Use basic first aid to treat the injury to the best of your ability.
- Try to attract the attention of anybody else who may be in the area. The **international distress (emergency) signal** is six blasts on a whistle, or six flashes with a torch.
- If possible leave someone with the casualty while others go to get help. If there are only two people, you have a dilemma. If you decide to get help, leave all spare clothing and food with the casualty.
- In an emergency dial ☎ 999 and ask for the coastguard. They are responsible for dealing with any emergency that occurs on the coast or at sea. Make sure you know exactly where you are before you call.
- Report the exact position of the casualty and their condition.

WEATHER AND WEATHER FORECASTS

The trail suffers from extremes of weather so it's vital that you always try to find out what the weather is going to be like before you set off for the day. It is a good idea to pay attention to **wind and gale warnings**. The wind on any coastline can get very strong and if it is strong it is advisable not to walk, particularly if you are carrying a pack which can act as a sail. If you are on a steep incline or above high cliffs it is also dangerous. Even if the wind direction is inland it can literally blow you right over (unpleasant if there are gorse bushes around!); or if it suddenly stops or eddies (a common phenomenon when strong winds hit cliffs) it can cause you to lose your balance and stagger in the direction in which you have been leaning, ie towards the cliffs!

Another hazard on the coast is **sea mist or fog** which can dramatically decrease visibility. If a coastal fog blows over take extreme care where the path runs close to cliff edges.

Most hotels, some B&Bs and TICs will have pinned up somewhere a summary of the **weather forecast**. Alternatively you can get a forecast through 🖥 bbc.co.uk/weather, or 🖥 metoffice.gov.uk/weather.

Pay close attention to the weather forecast and alter your plans for the day accordingly. That said, even if the forecast is for a fine sunny day, always assume the worst and pack some wet-weather gear.

BLISTERS

It is important to break in new boots/shoes before embarking on a long trek. Make sure they are comfortable and try to avoid getting them wet on the inside. Air your feet at every opportunity, keep them clean and change your socks regularly; using talcum powder can help to keep them dry. If you feel any hot spots, stop immediately and apply a few strips of zinc oxide tape and leave it on until the 'hot spot' is pain free or the tape starts to come off. If you have left it too late and a blister has developed you should surround it with Compeed or any other blister kit to protect it from abrasion. Popping it can lead to infection. If the skin is broken keep the area clean with antiseptic and cover with a non-adhesive dressing material held in place with tape.

HYPOTHERMIA, HYPERTHERMIA & SUNBURN

Also known as exposure, **hypothermia** occurs when the body can't generate enough heat to maintain its normal temperature, usually as a result of being wet, cold, unprotected from the wind, tired and hungry. It is usually more of a problem in upland areas such as on the moors. Hypothermia is easily avoided by wearing suitable clothing, carrying and eating enough food and drink, being aware of the weather conditions and checking the morale of your companions.

Early signs to watch for are feeling cold and tired with involuntary shivering. Find some shelter as soon as possible and warm the victim up with a hot drink and some chocolate or other high-energy food. If possible give them another warm layer of clothing and allow them to rest until feeling better.

If allowed to worsen, strange behaviour, slurring of speech and poor coordination will become apparent and the victim can easily progress into unconsciousness, followed by coma and death. Quickly get the victim out of any wind and rain, improvising a shelter if necessary. Rapid restoration of bodily warmth is essential and best achieved by bare-skin contact: someone should get into the same sleeping bag as the patient, both having stripped to their underwear, putting any spare clothing under or over them to build up heat. Send urgently for help.

Hyperthermia occurs when the body generates too much heat, eg heat exhaustion and heatstroke. Not ailments that you would normally associate with England, these are serious problems nonetheless.

Symptoms of **heat exhaustion** include thirst, fatigue, giddiness, a rapid pulse, raised body temperature, low urine output and, if not treated, delirium and finally a coma. The best cure is to drink plenty of water. The darker your urine the more you should drink.

Heatstroke is more serious. A high body temperature and an absence of sweating are early indications, followed by symptoms similar to hypothermia (see above) such as a lack of coordination, convulsions and coma. Death will follow if treatment is not given instantly. Sponge the victim down, wrap them in wet towels, fan them and get help immediately.

The sun in the South-West can be very strong. The best way to avoid **sunburn** – and the extra risk of developing skin cancers that sunburn brings – is to keep your skin covered at all times in light, loose-fitting clothing, and to cover any exposed areas of skin in sunscreen (with a minimum factor of 30). Sunscreen should be applied regularly throughout the day. Don't forget your lips, nose, ears, the back of your neck, and even under your chin to protect you against rays reflected from the ground. Most importantly of all, always wear a hat!

ROUTE GUIDE & MAPS

Using this guide

While this guide has been divided into stages, each of which approximates a day's walk, they are meant as a guide only. To plan an itinerary that better suits your pace, fitness and the time you have available, please see the 'Suggested itineraries' section on p31.

The **route summaries** below describe the trail between significant places and are written as if walking the coast path from Plymouth to South Haven Point (Poole Harbour). To enable you to plan your own itinerary, **practical information** is presented clearly on the trail maps. This includes walking times, all places to stay, camp and eat, as well as shops where you can buy supplies. Further service **details** are given in the text under the entry for each place.

For a condensed overview of this information see the town and village facilities table on pp32-3.

TRAIL MAPS

Scale and walking times

The trail maps are to a scale of 1:20,000 (1cm = 200m; $3^{1}/_{8}$ inches = one mile). Walking times are given along the side of each map and the arrow shows the direction to which the time refers. Black triangles indicate the points between which the times have been taken. **See the note on walking times in the box opposite**.

The time-bars are a tool and are not there to judge your walking ability. There are so many variables that affect walking speed, from the weather conditions to how many beers you drank the previous evening. After the first hour or two of walking you will be able to see how your speed relates to the timings on the maps.

Up or down?

Other than when on a track or bridleway the trail is shown as a dotted line. An arrow across the trail indicates the slope; two arrows show that it is steep. Note that the arrow points towards the higher part of the trail. If, for example, you are walking from A (at 80m) to B (at 200m) and the trail between the two is short and steep it would be shown thus: A— — — >> — — – B. Reversed arrow heads indicate a downward gradient.

GPS waypoints

The numbered GPS waypoints refer to the list on pp318-20.

> ❏ **Important note – walking times**
> Unless otherwise specified, **all times in this book refer only to the time spent walk-ing**. You will need to add 20-30% to allow for rests, photography, checking the map, drinking water etc. When planning the day's hike count on 5-7 hours of actual walking.

Accommodation

Apart from in large towns where some selection of places has been necessary, almost every place to stay that is within easy reach of the trail is marked. Details of each place are given in the accompanying text.

The number of **rooms of each type** is indicated as follows: **S** = single bed, **T** = twin beds, **D** = double bed, **Tr** = triple room (for three people) and **Qd** = quad (for four). Note that most of the Tr/Qd rooms have a double bed and one/two single beds or bunk beds; thus for a group of three or four, two people may have to share the double bed but the room can also be used as a double or twin.

Rates quoted are **per person** (pp) based on two people sharing a room for a one-night stay; rates are almost always discounted for longer stays. Where a single room (sgl) is available the rate for that is quoted if different from the per person rate. The rate for single occupancy (sgl occ) of a double/twin is general-ly higher, and the rate for three or more sharing a room may be lower. Unless specified, rates are for B&B. At some places the only option is a room rate; this will be the same whether one or two people share.

Many places do not accept **advance bookings** for a single-night stay at peak times; the minimum is often two, or even, three nights. However, if you turn up on the day, or even call a few nights before, they may accept a booking.

Most B&Bs don't accept **credit/debit cards** but hotels usually do.

The text also mentions whether the premises have **wi-fi** (WI-FI); if a **bath** is available (🛁) in, or for, at least one room; and whether **dogs** (🐾) are welcome. Most places will not take more than one dog in a room and also accept them subject to prior arrangement. Some make an additional charge (usually per night but occasionally per stay) while others may require a deposit which is refund-able if the dog doesn't make a mess. See also pp315-17.

Prices for **camping** vary from site to site. Some charge per pitch (and some-times with an additional charge for a second person), some per person. Note that

> ❏ **Food and drink planning**
> Remember, to plan ahead: certain stretches of the walk are virtually devoid of eating places (Kingswear to Brixham, Seaton to Lyme Regis, Abbotsbury to Wyke Regis, Lulworth Cove to Kimmeridge Bay and from there to Swanage, as well as the South Dorset Ridgeway) so read ahead about the next day's walk to make sure you never go hungry. See also box p22.
> The **opening days and hours** for pubs, restaurants and cafés mentioned are as accurate as possible but often if the weather is bad, or there is no demand, places will close early or not open at all so it is worth checking in advance, especially if there are few eating places in the area.

the larger holiday parks, whose priorities lie with longer-stay families and groups, do still often have special rates for hikers that are cheaper than the rates advertised on their websites, so if calling up to reserve a tent pitch, always make it clear that you are walking the coast path. However, you rarely need to book campsites in advance, especially if you're walking alone, though calling ahead the morning before you arrive is good for peace of mind.

Other features

Features are marked on the map when pertinent to navigation. In order to avoid cluttering the maps and making them unusable not all features have been marked each time they occur.

The route guide

PLYMOUTH   [map p91]

*'Plymouth is indeed a town of considera-
tion, and of great importance to the public.
The situation of it between two very large
inlets of the sea, and in the bottom of a
large bay [...] is very remarkable for the
advantage of navigation.'*

Daniel Defoe, *A Tour through the
Whole Island of Great Britain*

Lying between the mouths of the rivers Plym and Tamar, Plymouth is a modern city with a rich and eventful past. The city's growth and prosperity are forever indebted to its proximity to – and relationship with – the sea. Not just as the famous departure point of the Pilgrim Fathers (see box p88) but also as a hub for trade (the commercial dockyards are amongst the largest in Europe) and, foremost, as a vital naval base: with a tradition that dates back to the very inception of the Royal Navy, there is much to see and do in this historic city.

The first record of habitation in the area, Sudtone (Saxon for 'South Farm'), situated on the site of the present-day Barbican, can be found in the Domesday Book (1086). Initially just a small fishing village, its strategically important location soon brought prosperity and – despite bouts of plague, cholera and smallpox trimming the ever-burgeoning population as well as a concerted attempt at destruction by the Luftwaffe during the Plymouth Blitz – the town has continued to swell in size.

Much of this success is down to its situation at the mouths of two rivers, a crucial location that the nascent Royal Navy in the 17th century was quick to recognise. Her Majesty's Naval Base (HMNB) Devonport opened in 1690, with further docks being built in 1727, 1762 and 1795. Isambard Kingdom Brunel then designed the Great Western Docks (1844-50) and in 1854 the Keynham Steam Yard, built for the construction of steam ships, was also completed. It's hardly surprising, then, that most of the town's defining moments are sea based, from the defeat of the Spanish Armada (1588; see box opposite) to the sailing of the Mayflower (1620; see box p88) as well as the heroic resistance the city showed in WWII when, despite 59 German bombing sorties, it still played a full part in the Battle of the Atlantic and was a major embarkation point on D-Day.

Unfortunately, where the Luftwaffe flattened Plymouth some ugly buildings have sprouted and a large chunk of the town is actually fairly nondescript and pretty much devoid of charm. Thankfully, the **seafront** remains one of the more interesting and beautiful parts; and the area around the **Mayflower Steps**, known as **The Barbican**, is one of Plymouth's oldest, prettiest and most vibrant, with plenty of bars and restaurants in which to conduct any last-minute planning for your walk.

What to see and do

The Hoe The green expanse that separates the modern-day city centre from the sea, The Hoe is best known for playing host to Francis Drake's game of bowls in 1588 (see box below). It is also the place where, during the Plymouth Blitz of WWII, Nancy Astor, MP for the city and great friend of TE Lawrence (of Arabia) danced with servicemen, defiantly proclaiming that the city would go on despite the bombing.

Lighthouse lovers will be impressed by the red-and-white-striped **Smeaton's Tower** (daily 10am-5pm; £4). Originally the third lighthouse to be put on Eddystone Rocks, which lie 14km south-west of Rame Head, it was dismantled in 1882 and the upper portions of the tower were rebuilt on The Hoe. John Smeaton, incidentally, after whom the tower is named, was the original builder of the tower way back in 1759.

Other notable sites on The Hoe include a three-tier **belvedere** (a structure that was deliberately designed to command a view), built in 1891, and the **Drake Statue** (1884), sculpted by one of the Victorian era's most

---

❏ Francis Drake, the Spanish Armada and that famous game of bowls

The Elizabethan era was a time of turmoil. The major European powers were often at war, with religion frequently the cause. The two main protagonists at this time were Protestant England and Catholic Spain. The latter controlled the Netherlands where Protestant ideals were popular. England, as was their wont, aided the Dutch Protestants who were being hunted by the Spanish Inquisition, and it was this decision – as well as the beheading of the Catholic Mary Queen of Scots, ordered by the Protestant Queen Elizabeth I in 1587 – that led to King Philip II of Spain's decision to 'defend Catholicism' by invading England.

One of Queen Elizabeth I's most feared seamen was Sir Francis Drake. A buccaneering adventurer and hero to the English, the Spanish considered him a menace and he was a constant thorn in their side. Conducting his own personal Protestant crusade, by 1588 he had already harassed and harried many Spanish boats in the West Indies, occupied the ports of Cadiz and Corunna, destroying 37 Spanish ships as he did so, and plundered the treasures of Spain wherever he found them, describing his wish to 'singe the king of Spain's beard'.

King Philip II's Spanish Armada set sail from Lisbon in May 1588; their ships were attacked by English and Dutch boats throughout their journey. Struggling through, the Spanish were eventually spotted off The Lizard and the news of their arrival swiftly reached Plymouth, where the English navy was waiting. Famously, Drake purportedly scoffed on being told of the arrival of the Armada, and chose to finish his game of bowls, claiming he could do so and defeat the Spanish. A much debated incident, if it did actually happen it is possible that Drake would have known that the tide of the Tamar was against him – so preventing his boats from accessing the Channel until it turned – and thus recognised that he had ample time to complete his game.

History doesn't record whether Drake won his game of bowls. The outcome of the battle, however, is certain. Fighting between the Spanish and English navies went on for eight days before the Spaniards finally had to admit defeat, their navy beaten, burnt and scattered. To make matters worse, because of westerly winds many of the defeated boats couldn't return straight home, but instead had to sail around the tip of Scotland and down the coast of Ireland where they were further battered by storms – as well as being attacked by the English in Ireland. Drake meanwhile sailed home a hero, his legend forever cemented in English naval history for establishing England's dominance of the Atlantic – and refusing to end a game of bowls.

pre-eminent producers of commemorative statues, Joseph Boehm. Many **war memorials** also adorn the area, fittingly so when one considers the number of servicemen and women to have departed from (and hopefully returned to) the city on various campaigns and missions over the years.

Overlooked by the Smeaton Tower is **Tinside Lido** (☎ 01752-261915, 🖥 every oneactive.com/centre/tinside-lido; end May to mid Sep Mon-Fri noon-6pm, Sat-Sun & school hols 10am-6pm, plus Wed 6-7.30pm), a striking Art Deco outdoor swimming pool that opened in 1935. Following years of neglect the pool became a Grade II-listed building before being renovated and reopened in 2005. If that's not quirky enough for you, consider taking a bracing dip in the small, sea-fed **tidal pool** by Royal William Yard.

The Hoe is also the site of the **British Firework Championships** (see p14) in August. It is a competition between the country's professional firework companies that, for two nights, light up the skies above Devon.

The Royal Citadel At The Hoe's eastern end is the Royal Citadel. A large and impressive limestone fort, it was built in the late 1660s on the orders of Charles II in response to the second Dutch War (1664-7). Encompassing a previous fort that Drake had requested to be built in the 16th century, its guns bear down on the town as well as out to sea, most likely as a reaction to Plymouth's Parliamentarian leanings during the English Civil War. Still militarily operational today, you can only visit the fort on **guided tours** (🖥 citadel.yapsody .com; Apr-Sep Mon, Tue, Thur & Sun 2.30pm; £6), which are available just four times a week and last for around two hours. You have to book online, but then pay in

---

❏ The coast path through Plymouth

While the route for this book starts at the Mayflower Steps, the South-West Coast Path begins way back at Minehead, in Somerset, and thus on its way travels through the centre of Plymouth. Initially this 2¾-mile trail is a little confusing, the lack of coast path signs not helping. That said, the city has worked hard to add some quirky features to what is already a walk stuffed with points of interest.

The path begins at **Cremyll Ferry** by Admiral's Hard. Having wiped your feet on the welcome mat positioned there, you come to a fried breakfast expertly rendered in wool on the wall of *Elvira's Café* (Mon-Thur & Sat 8am-2.30pm, Fri 7.30am-2.30pm, Sun 8.30am-2.30pm) – look just below the main sign for the café. Said to be the home of the fry-up, the café has also been immortalised in a Beryl Cook painting. Unsurprisingly, the breakfasts here are particularly good. Close by you come to the **Codeword Pavement**, where messages between sailors and their loved ones at home have been carved, in shorthand, into the pavement.

Taking a right before The Vine pub, onto Strand St and then a left onto Cremyll St leads to **Royal William Yard**, passing **Ede Vinegar Works** (owned by the same family for six generations) on the way. Named after King William IV (who stands overlooking the entrance), the yard was built, mostly from reclaimed land, to supply the navy with beef, biscuits and beer – with a brewery, bakery and slaughterhouse on site. The path, now well signposted, goes on a circuit of the yard, allowing walkers to explore its historic buildings (some of which now house cafés and restaurants), before emerging from it again at the **Artillery Tower**, built to protect the harbour and yard but now a *restaurant* (see p94).

There's a small **tidal pool** (see above) that you can swim in, just beside the tower, while nearby is *The Hutong Café* (Mon & Wed-Fri 7.30am-5pm, Sat & Sun 8am-5pm), which has a modern European-café menu, but takes its inspiration from the cafés found in the traditional alleyways of old Beijing, where the owners used to live (*hutong* means 'narrow lane' in Chinese).

cash on the day. Note that as The Citadel is still a working fort, tours may be cancelled without notice and that photography is also prohibited.

The Barbican The Barbican is the old harbour area of the city and the heart of the old town. Fortuitously escaping much of the bombing inflicted on Plymouth during WWII, the mazes of narrow **cobbled streets** (reputed to be the most extensive collection of cobbled thoroughfares in the UK) still exist in the originally medieval layout of what was then the town of Sutton. The former location of Plymouth's fish market, the area is now more of a draw to those seeking art, antiques and alcohol.

Speaking of the latter, if Plymouth marks the end of your walk, and you feel that a celebratory tipple is in order the venerable **Plymouth Gin Distillery** (☎ 01752-665292, 🖳 plymouthgin.com; Mon-Sat

10am-5pm, Sun 11am-5pm), on Southside St, has been knocking out grade-A booze to discerning punters since 1793 and runs 40-minute distillery **tours** (booking recommended; daily 11.30am, 12.30pm, 2.30pm & 3.30pm plus Mon-Sat 10.30am & 4.30pm; £7) round its building, which partly dates back to the mid 15th century. The building, incidentally, and more than a little ironically, was also where the Puritan Pilgrim Fathers supposedly spent their last night before embarking for America.

Only a couple of minutes away, **Elizabethan House**, 32 New St, retains much of its original structure and is kitted out in suitable period furniture. However, it was closed for extensive renovations at the time of research and is unlikely to reopen before the end of 2018; contact Plymouth Arts & Heritage Service (☎ 01752-304774, 🖳 plymhearts.org/elizabethan-house) for further details.

From the Artillery Tower, the route takes a left and leads past the smart Georgian terraces of Durnford St, where Sir Arthur Conan-Doyle worked as a doctor – which explains the **Sherlock Holmes' quotes** in the pavement. A hard right after **Stonehouse Barracks** leads you onto Millbay Rd, with Millbay Docks on the right; at the next roundabout is the **Wall of Stars** celebrating the famous figures – Bing Crosby and Judy Garland to name but two – who have arrived in the dock on the cruise ships that still call in here. Just past it is the **Ingot Sculpture**, a squat block of dozens of bars of gold bullion, celebrating the flow of British bullion that used to pass through the docks almost daily. The sculpture, alas, is made of iron.

Moving to the next roundabout, to return to the waterfront you need to turn right onto West Hoe Rd. The road leads you past the **Wall of Industrial Memories**, celebrating the heritage of the Millbay area.

You now join Hoe Rd, which you follow all the way to The Barbican, passing the lovely **Tinside Lido** (see opposite) on your right and **The Hoe** (see p85) and **The Royal Citadel** (see opposite) on your left.

There are still some quirky little sights on the way, including a **cross** in the pavement to celebrate 1999's total eclipse of the sun and a marble **scallop shell** in the wall near the start of The Barbican, which celebrates the fact that Plymouth was one of only two English ports licensed by the king from which pilgrims were allowed to embark when heading to Santiago de Compostela on the Way of St James. The shell is the symbol of St James, the patron saint of pilgrims. Another patron saint is celebrated in the same wall a little further down: **Stella Maris, the Virgin, Star of the Sea**, patron saint of seafarers, was rescued from a lost cargo of marble and now sits illuminated by the pole star shining above.

Pilgrims would pray to these saints for protection during their journeys; although your journey is mostly land based, it can't hurt to ask for their help on your forthcoming expedition, just in case.

ROUTE GUIDE AND MAPS

Next to the pedestrian walkway which crosses Sutton Harbour, the **Mayflower Steps** commemorate the Pilgrim Fathers' departure for the New World in 1620. The steps consist of a portico that was built in 1934 and a platform hanging out over the water's edge.

Nearby, above the tourist information centre (see opposite) and open the same hours, you will find the **Mayflower Museum** (£3), covering three floors telling the story of the Pilgrim Fathers. It also has a balcony from which you can gaze out over the bustle below.

Not technically part of The Barbican but just across the walkway from the Mayflower Steps is the **National Marine Aquarium** (Map 1; ☎ 0844-893 7938, ☐ national-aquarium.co.uk; daily summer 9.30am-6pm, rest of year 10am-5pm; £15.95, 10% off tickets bought online in advance). The UK's largest, it houses a tank that contains 2.5 million litres of water! The Atlantic Ocean display, as it is known, is home not only to tiger and nurse sharks, stingrays and barracuda but also a full-sized replica of a WWII plane. There are regular talks and feedings as well as a 4D cinema.

Services
As you'd expect, Plymouth has just about every amenity you need, though you may have to head into the less attractive, pedestrianised, new part of the city for some.

❑ The Mayflower and the Pilgrim Fathers
Most visitors to Plymouth – and certainly every American tourist in the city – are aware that amongst the first, and most famous Europeans to settle in America (a group now celebrated as the Pilgrim Fathers) set sail from Plymouth in 1620. What is less well-known, perhaps, is the background to their emigration... and why they felt compelled to head for the New World in the first place.

The pilgrimage has its roots in Henry VIII's rejection of the Catholic Church back in 1534, an act that led to England becoming a Protestant country for the first time. Puritanism, the ideology followed by the Pilgrim fathers, emerged soon afterwards during the reign of Henry VIII's daughter, Elizabeth I. As the name suggests, the Puritans felt that Henry VIII's Church of England was neither strict nor pious enough for their rather fanatical tastes. This stance angered both Elizabeth and her successor, James I, and it wasn't long before the Puritans were being persecuted for their beliefs.

In 1609 a number of Puritans headed for Leiden in the Netherlands to seek a land where they could practise their faith in peace. Unfortunately, whilst the persecutions were less common, they were still unhappy with the tolerance and levity of their Dutch hosts; and more worrying still for the Puritans was the way their offspring were being assimilated into Dutch culture. There seemed to be only one solution: to build their own community, away from the persecution and profanity (as they saw it) of Europe, in the New World.

Plymouth's role in their story is actually both fortuitous and fairly minor. Setting sail from Southampton in *The Mayflower* and *The Speedwell* in August 1620, they only docked in Plymouth due to a storm that damaged the already old and leaking boats as they navigated The Channel. Fully stocked, and with the decision made to leave *The Speedwell* behind, a total of 102 passengers and crew (not all of whom were Puritans) finally left the city on 6th September 1620, reaching Cape Cod 66 days later to found the community they had dreamed of, in Massachusetts.

Alas, the Pilgrim Fathers' travails didn't end there. Weakened by their journey and unprepared for winter, half of them died within the first four months of landing. However, those who did survive owed their survival to the natives, a relationship cemented in the Pilgrims' first harvest of 1621 – a ceremony which would go on to become the basis for the American festival of Thanksgiving.

The **tourist information centre** (☎ 01752-306330, 🖳 visitplymouth.co.uk; Apr-Oct Mon-Sat 9am-5pm, Sun 10am-4pm, Nov-Mar Mon-Fri 9am-5pm, Sat 10am-4pm) offers accommodation booking and is handily placed right by the Mayflower Steps on The Barbican and is one of the friendliest and most helpful on the entire walk.

There are plenty of **banks** with **ATMs** in the city.

Also in The Barbican area, there's a small McColl's **supermarket** (daily 7am-10pm), at 49-50 Southside St, which contains a **sub post office** (Mon-Fri 9am-5.30pm, Sat 9am-12.30pm). The **main post office** (Mon-Sat 9am-5.30pm, Sun 10.30am-2.30pm) is inside WH Smith, at 73-75 New George St.

Other **supermarkets** include a Tesco Express (daily 6am-11pm) on Notte St, and a large Aldi (Mon-Sat 8am-10pm, Sun 10am-4pm) on Union St.

The main **Central Library** (☎ 01752-305901, 🖳 plymouth.gov.uk/libraries; Mon-Fri 8.30am-6pm, Sat 9am-5pm), on the corner of Armada Way and Mayflower St, has **internet access** (£1.10 for 15 mins plus two print-outs) and free **wi-fi**.

The city's signature **shopping centre**, Drake Circus (Mon-Wed & Fri-Sat 9am-6pm, Thur 9am-8pm, Sun 10.30am-4.30pm), is at one end of New George St, and contains supermarkets, pharmacies, bookshops, clothes shops and cafés.

For **camping/trekking** supplies head to New George St, where you'll find Millets at No 40 and Trespass at No 34.

Back nearer the waterfront, the most convenient of Plymouth's **launderettes** is Hoegate Laundromat (☎ 01752-223031; Mon-Fri 8.30am-6pm, Sat 9am-1pm) at 55 Notte St.

For a **bookshop** with a dash of history, seek out The Book Cupboard (☎ 01752-226311, 🖳 secondhandbooksplymouth.co.uk; Mon-Sat 10.30am-4.30pm, Sun 10.30am-4pm), a treasure trove of second-hand reading material housed inside the 16th-century, stone-walled Old Custom House by the harbour.

Transport

[See also pp50-4] Stagecoach's 48 **bus** service runs to Wembury whilst their No 3 journeys along the coast as far as Dartmouth. Note that getting public transport to most coastal destinations between Plymouth and Salcombe and then from there to Torcross is not easy. If you want to avoid an area so devoid in public transport Stagecoach's Stagecoach Gold service will take you to Torquay and the English Riviera. Target Travel's No 94 operates to Noss Mayo.

Plymouth railway station is an easy 10-minute walk north of Royal Parade; walk straight up Armada Way and follow the signs. Trains depart frequently for Exeter and London, as well as west to Penzance and the rest of Cornwall. For stations on the south Devon coast, change at Newton Abbot.

Newly opened in 2016, **Plymouth Coach Station** is at 165 Armada Way, just north of Cornwall St, and has direct services to many towns and cities in the country with carriers such as National Express (see box p49) and Megabus.

The **ferry to Mount Batten Point** (see box p94) leaves from just south of the Mayflower Steps. Close by is the departure point for the **Cawsand Ferry** (daily 9am, 10.30am, noon, 1.30pm, 3pm & 4.30pm; 30 mins; £4 one-way), which shuttles passengers to the village of Cawsand in Cornwall.

For a **taxi**, try Plymouth Taxis (☎ 01752-606060, 🖳 plymouthtaxis.com) or Need a Cab (☎ 01752-666222, 🖳 needacab 247.com).

Where to stay

Hostels   There are two hostels in Plymouth, almost side-by-side on Union St. The better of the two is the smaller, more modern *Staykation* (☎ 01752-269333, 🖳 staykation.co.uk; 2D/1 x 2-, 1 x 3-, 1 x 4-, 1 x 5-, 1 x 6-bed dorms; shared facilities; WI-FI), at No 94, which has double rooms (£35-40 for two sharing) as well as dorm beds (£20pp), and is clean and well-run. There's a decent self-catering kitchen, a small living area and laundry facilities, but breakfast is not provided. Nearby

Plymouth Backpackers (☎ 01752-213033, 🖳 plymouthbackpackershotel.co.uk; 6T, 2 x 4-, 2 x 6-, 1 x 10-, 1 x 12-bed dorms, most rooms en suite; WI-FI; dorm beds/private rooms from £15pp/18pp), at No 102, also has a self-catering kitchen plus a large TV room, laundry service and a complimentary toast-and-cereal breakfast. It's cheaper than Staykation, but a bit run down and rather gloomy.

B&Bs There are B&Bs aplenty and many are well situated for both the path and the city centre. A useful resource is 🖳 plymouthbedandbreakfast.co.uk.

Two near West Hoe Park are *The Firs* (☎ 01752-262870, 🖳 thefirsinplymouth .co.uk; 3S/3D or T/1Tr/1Qd, some share facilities; WI-FI; 🐾; £35-45pp, sgl occ £60-90), at 13 Pier St; and *The Caraneal*

(☎ 01752-663589, 🖳 caranealplymouth.co .uk; 8D/2T; WI-FI; £30-35pp, sgl occ from £40), at 12-14 Pier St.

Those more central are generally based along Citadel Rd. Facing Hoe Park are *George Guesthouse* (☎ 01752-661517, 🖳 georgeguesthouse.com; 1S/1T/3Tr/1Qd; most en suite but two share a bathroom; ✎; WI-FI; 🐾; £25-30pp, sgl from £30, sgl occ room rate), at No 161, and *Pub On The Hoe* (☎ 01752-202405, 🖳 thepubonthehoe .co.uk; 2D/1Tr; WI-FI; 🐾; room only £30-43pp, sgl occ room rate), at No 159; breakfast (£1.95-7.95) is not included in the rate but is available from 8am.

Towards the western end of Citadel Rd, there are more options such as *Kynance House* (☎ 01752-266821, 🖳 kynancehouse.co.uk; 6S/18D or T/2Qd; ✎; WI-FI; 🐾; £31-50pp, sgl/sgl occ from

PLYMOUTH MAP KEY

Where to stay
4 Plymouth Backpackers
5 Staykation
6 The Firs
7 The Caraneal
10 Duke of Cornwall Hotel
11 Caledonia Guesthouse
12 Kynance House
13 Invicta Hotel
14 The Bowling Green
15 Pub on the Hoe
16 George Guesthouse
29 Casa Mia Guesthouse
30 Four Seasons
31 Mayflower
32 Seymour

Where to eat & drink
1 Elvira's Café
2 The Hutong Café
3 Artillery Tower
8 By the Park

Where to eat & drink *(cont'd)*
9 The Wet Wok
15 Pub on the Hoe
18 La Roux
21 Yukisan
22 Favourite Food
24 Eastern Eye
25 Arribas
26 Barbican Steakhouse
27 Thai House
28 Barbican Kitchen (in Plymouth Gin Distillery)
33 Hakka
35 Barbican Pasty Co
36 The Ship
37 Rakuda Kitchen
38 The Village
39 The Navy Inn
41 The Flower Café
43 Jacka Bakery
44 Barbican Fish & Chicken
45 Harbourside
46 The Harbour
47 Cap'n Jaspers
48 Monty's Café

Where to eat & drink *(cont'd)*
50 B-Bar (in Barbican Theatre)
51 Boathouse Café
52 Dutton's

Other
17 Tesco Express
19 Millets
20 Trespass
23 Hoegate Laundromat
28 Plymouth Gin Distillery
34 The Book Cupboard
40 McColls & Post Office
42 Elizabethan House
49 Tourist Information Centre; Mayflower Museum
50 Barbican Theatre

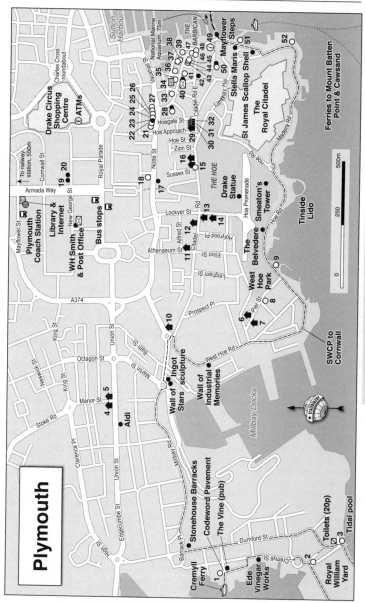

Plymouth

Drake Circus Shopping Centre

Charles Cross roundabout

£ ATMs

Sutton Harbour

National Marine Aquarium, 75m

THE BARBICAN

Mayflower Steps

Stella Maris Scallop Shell

St James Scallop Shell

Vauxhall St

Cornwall St

To railway station, 550m

Armada Way

Mayflower St

Library & Internet

Plymouth Coach Station

WH Smith & Post Office

Bus stops

New George St

Royal Parade

Hoegate St

Hoe Approach

Hoe St

Notte St

Zion St

Sussex St

Lockyer St

Athenaeum St

Alfred St

Holyrood Pl

Elliot St

Citadel Rd

Leigham St

Prospect Pl

West Hoe Rd

A374

Octagon St

Bath St

Martin St

King St

King St

Neswick St

Manor St

Aldi

Stoke Rd

Clarence Pl

Union St

Union St

Edgecumbe St

Millbay Rd

Wall of Ingot Stars sculpture

Wall of Industrial Memories

Millbay Docks

SWCP to Cornwall

THE HOE

Drake Statue

The Hoe Promenade

Smeaton's Tower

The Belvedere

West Hoe Park

Pier St

Lambhay Hill

Citadel Rd E

The Royal Citadel

Hoe Rd

Madeira Rd

Tinside Lido

Ferries to Mount Batten Point & Cawsand

Stonehouse Barracks

Codeword Pavement

The Vine (pub)

Cremyll Ferry

Ede Vinegar Works

Barrack Pl

Durnford St

Cremyll St

Royal William Yard

Toilets (20p)

Tidal pool

500m

250

0

ROUTE GUIDE AND MAPS

★ trailblazer

£50/75), at 107-11, and on Athenaeum St, *Caledonia Guesthouse* (☎ 01752-229052, 🖳 info@thecaledonia.co.uk; 1S/5D/3T; WI-FI; £30-50pp, sgl/sgl occ £45-70), at No 27.

Closer to The Barbican, but still on Citadel Rd, there is another selection of guesthouses including *Seymour* (☎ 01752-667002, 🖳 seymourguesthouse.co.uk; 2S/2D/3T, most en suite; WI-FI; from £32pp, sgl occ from £42), at No 211, *Mayflower* (☎ 01752-667496, 🖳 mayflowerguesthouse .co.uk; 2S/7D or T; WI-FI; from £32.50pp, sgl £37-45, sgl occ from £45), at No 209, *Four Seasons* (☎ 01752-223591, 🖳 four seasonsguesthouse.co.uk; 2S/3D/2D or T; WI-FI; 🐾; £32.50-34pp, sgl £35-48, sgl occ £45-48), at No 207, and *Casa Mia* (☎ 01752-265742, 🖳 casamiaguesthouse.co .uk; 2S/2D or T/3D; WI-FI; £30-38pp, sgl from £35, sgl occ £40-45), at No 201.

Hotels The grand, 150-year-old *Duke of Cornwall Hotel* (☎ 01752-275850, 🖳 www.thedukeofcornwall.co.uk; 12S/42D/14T/4Qd; ☛; WI-FI; 🐾; £42.50-60pp, sgl/sgl occ from £82/87) is owned by the Best Western chain and is on Millbay Rd, at the western end of Citadel Rd.

Closer to The Hoe, but much smaller, are *The Bowling Green* (☎ 01752-209090, 🖳 www.thebowlinggreenplymouth.com; 1S/1T/4D; ☛; WI-FI; Mar/Apr to end Sep; room only from £35pp, sgl/sgl occ from £50), an elegant Georgian building at 9-10 Osborne Place, but they don't offer breakfast, and *Invicta Hotel* (☎ 01752-664997, 🖳 invictahotel.co.uk; 4S/8D/6D or T/1Tr; ☛; WI-FI; 🐾; £50-55pp, sgl from £65, sgl occ £75-100), next door at 11-12 Osborne Place.

Where to eat and drink

The Barbican is the place to go for food or a drink, though other fine eateries are dotted around town.

Snacks & takeaways For **pasties** head to *Barbican Pasty Co* (☎ 01752 225339, 🖳 barbicanpastyco.co.uk; Feb-Dec daily from 10am), on Southside; they do more than a dozen varieties, including traditional Cornish. Get your **fish & chips** fix at *Harbourside* (Sun-Mon 11am-10pm, Tue-Thur 11am-10.30pm, Fri-Sat 11am-11pm), 35 Southside St, or next door at *Barbican Fish & Chicken*. Both have restaurant seating too. There's also a takeaway fish & chips kiosk (daily 11am-10pm) attached to *The Harbour Restaurant* (see p93).

You can get takeaway **Thai** noodles at *B-Bar* (☎ 01752-242021, 🖳 b-bar.co.uk; food daily noon-9pm) in the Barbican Theatre on Castle St. Their noodle boxes start at £7.50, but they have restaurant seating too.

For late-night takeaway **kebabs**, head to *Favourite Food* (Mon-Thur 5pm-2am, Fri-Sat 5pm-4am, Sun 5pm-midnight), on Notte St.

Cafés The most famous of the lot is the open almost all hours *Cap'n Jaspers* (☎ 01752-262444, 🖳 capn-jaspers.co.uk; Mon-Sat 7.30am to midnight, Sun 8am to midnight), a no-frills harbourside café that's been serving up great-value burgers (£1.80-4.95), hot rolls (£1.80-3.85), tea (70p) and coffee (£1) since 1978. There's no indoor seating, but there are plenty of sheltered tables beside it.

Also overlooking the harbour, is *Boathouse Café* (☎ 01752-600560, 🖳 the boathousecafe.co.uk; daily 8am-8pm, Oct-Mar 9am-3pm; note all hours are weather dependent), a bright, modern, all-glass affair which specialises in freshly caught fish and shellfish.

Slightly further back along the coast path, on a perch high above the harbour and at the foot of the Royal Citadel, *Dutton's*

ROUTE GUIDE AND MAPS

❏ **Where to stay: the details**

Unless specified, B&B-style accommodation is either en suite or has private facilities; ☛ means at least one room has a bath; 🐾 signifies that dogs are welcome in at least one room but always by prior arrangement, an additional charge may also be payable (see also pp315-17); WI-FI means wi-fi is available in the property, though not always reliably in every room.

(☎ 01752-255245, 🖳 duttonsplymouth.co.uk; summer daily 9.30am-7pm, winter 10am-5pm but again depending on the weather; 🐕) is housed in a Grade II-listed former artillery store that was built in 1847. There are fabulous views across the sea to Mount Batten Point from the café's garden, which comes complete with two neighbouring cannons.

In amongst the narrow lanes of The Barbican you'll find numerous other cafés, including ***Jacka Bakery*** (☎ 01752-262187; Wed-Mon 9am-4pm), at 38 Southside St, thought to be Britain's oldest bakery (dating from the 1600s) but which now serves good coffee alongside its famously fresh breads. There's also ***Monty's Café*** (☎ 01752-252877, 🖳 montyscafeplymouth.co.uk; Mon-Sat 9am-5.30pm, Sun 9am-4pm), at 13 The Barbican, with some standout all-day breakfasts as well as sandwiches and ciabattas (£5-6), and ***The Flower Café*** (☎ 01752-253788; summer daily 9.30am-5pm, winter hours variable; 🐕), at 46 Southside St, a cute friendly little place with a small back garden.

Further afield, ***La Roux*** (☎ 01752-220411, 🖳 larouxplymouth.co.uk; Mon-Wed 8am-4pm, Thur 8am-8pm, Fri 8am-midnight, Sat 8am-5pm, Sun 11am-4pm; winter hours variable) is a tiny but charming corner café and wine bar at 33 Notte St, while ***By The Park*** (☎ 01752-251185, 🖳 bytheparkcafe.com; summer daily 9.30am-4.30/5pm, winter Tue-Fri to 4pm, Sat & Sun to 5pm), at 26 Pier St, does wonderful cakes and cream teas as well as lunches and hot and cold drinks.

If you're walking the coast path from the Cremyll Ferry, ***Elvira's Café*** and ***The Hutong Café*** are both right en route (see box p86).

Pubs & bars On Southside St, ***The Navy Inn*** (☎ 01752-301812; food Mon-Sat noon-7.30pm, Sun till 6pm) has won awards for its food. It's nothing flash – just a traditional pub with real ales and a seemingly ordinary pub-grub menu – but the results are excellent and the atmosphere is always lively. An added bonus is the terrace on the first floor with views along the waterfront.

Opening out onto the waterfront, ***The Ship*** (☎ 01752-667604, 🖳 www.theshipplymouth.co.uk; food summer daily noon-9pm, rest of year Mon-Sat noon-3pm & 6-8pm, Sun noon-8pm) has a great location, although the atmosphere inside is rather stale. No matter; most punters grab a table outside instead, overlooking the harbour. The fish & chips here were voted the best of any pub in the UK in 2013; they're still pretty good. Practically next door, ***Rakuda Kitchen*** (☎ 01752-221155, 🖳 rakudabar.com; food daily summer 9.30am-10pm, winter hours variable) is more of a bar-restaurant than a pub, but with the same great outdoor seating spot as The Ship. Food-wise, it's burgers, grilled meats, fish and pasta. For drinks, it's all about the cocktails.

Away from the tourists, ***Pub On The Hoe*** (see Where to Stay; food Mon-Thur noon-3pm & 5-9pm, Fri-Sun noon-9pm) has a selection of real ales and good honest pub grub.

Restaurants Next door to The Navy Inn, ***The Village*** (☎ 01752-667688, 🖳 thevillagerestaurantplymouth.co.uk; daily summer 11.30am-10.15pm, reduced hours in winter), at 32 Southside St, is an excellent **seafood** restaurant which also does a terrific roast beef on Sundays. Good seafood can also be had at ***The Harbour*** (☎ 01752-228556, 🖳 harbourbarbican.co.uk; daily 11am-10pm; 🐕), a modern, high-ceilinged, family-friendly restaurant right at the water's edge. Mains are affordable (£10-18), and if you're in a hurry there's a fish & chips takeaway kiosk attached.

Back on Southside St, ***Barbican Kitchen*** (☎ 01752-604448, 🖳 barbicankitchen.com; Mon-Sat noon-2.30pm & Mon-Thur 6-9.30pm, Fri & Sat 5-10pm) is located inside **Plymouth Gin Distillery** (p87). It's a quality place with a menu focusing on hearty British countryside fare such as slow-cooked lamb shoulder (£17.95), west-country chicken breast with asparagus (£17.50) and beer-battered fish & chips (£13.95).

A short walk away, on Notte St, ***Barbican Steakhouse*** (☎ 01752-222214,

🖳 barbicansteakhouse.com; Mon-Thur 4.30-10.30pm, Fri-Sat 4.30-11pm) does a mouthwatering 12oz rib-eye for £15.25.

For **Indian** cuisine, try *Eastern Eye* (☎ 01752-262948, 🖳 easterneyeplymouth.com; Mon-Thur noon-2pm & 6pm-midnight, Fri & Sat 6pm-2am, Sun 6pm-midnight) on Notte St. For **Thai** food, head to nearby *Thai House* (☎ 01752-661600, 🖳 thethaihouse.co.uk; Mon-Thur 6-10pm, Fri & Sat 6-10.30pm), and for **Mexican**, try *Arribas* (☎ 01752-603303, 🖳 arribasmexican.co.uk; daily noon-10pm), also on the same strip.

There are plenty of **Chinese** options, including *Hakka* (☎ 01752-224777; daily noon-3pm & 6-9pm), at 13 Southside St, an upmarket Cantonese joint with delicious home-made dim sum. If that doesn't take your fancy, there are two other Chinese restaurants in the same building.

For Chinese cuisine with a sea view, *The Wet Wok* (☎ 01752-664456, 🖳 wetwokchineserestaurant.co.uk; open daily noon-2pm & 6-11pm) is perched directly below the coast path on Hoe Rd.

On Notte St, meanwhile, *Yukisan* (☎ 01752-250240, 🖳 yukisan.co.uk; Mon-Thur 11.30am-2.30pm & 5-10pm, Fri-Sat 11.30am-10.30pm, Sun noon-9.30pm), established in 2004, was the first **Japanese** restaurant in town and is still going strong. As well as two generic Oriental-style dining rooms, they have a traditional Japanese dining room, with low tables and floor cushions for seats.

Further afield, but worth the walk, *Artillery Tower* (☎ 01752-257610, 🖳 artillerytower.co.uk; Wed-Sat 7.15-9.30pm), is one of the more discreet places in the city, and is set in a 15th-century defensive tower (see box p86) on the sea wall, overlooking Plymouth Sound. Evening meals are set at £38.50 for two courses, or £42.50 for three, and include dishes such as loin of lamb, roasted field mushrooms, and dived scallops.

PLYMOUTH TO WEMBURY [MAPS 1-6]

For such a lovely trek, this initial **10¾-mile (17.25km; 4¼hrs)** leg is a bit of an inauspicious start. True, there may be the occasional stroller who will swoon at this saunter through the city's unsung suburbs and praise the opportunity it provides to plod through Plymouth's less picturesque parts. But for most people the start of their 217¼-mile odyssey is little more than a fairly mundane trudge through an unappealing industrial estate followed by an only-slightly-more-interesting hike through the suburban sprawl that precedes Mount Batten Point.

You can, of course, opt to take the ferry (see box below) from The Barbican to Mount Batten Point, and if time is short this would be a good decision. It does, after all, completely cut out the dullest stretch of this stage (possibly, some may argue, of the entire SWCP), and leaves you with just its more appetising latter half along the eastern edge of Plymouth Sound and on past Heybrook Bay to Wembury.

❏ The ferry to Mount Batten Point

The ferry to Mount Batten Point (boat ☎ 07930-838614, 🖳 mountbattenferry.co.uk; £1.50, 🐾 free) is not actually part of the coast path – though many trekkers treat it as such to cut out the rather dull walking through Plymouth. Crossings depart every 30 minutes (summer Mon-Fri 7.30am-11pm, Sat 9am-11pm, Sun 9am-10.30pm; winter Mon-Thur 7.30am-6.15pm, Fri 7.30am-11pm, Sat 9am-11pm, Sun 9am-6.15pm), and take around 10 minutes.

But if you do have the time – and you're serious about completing the walk described in this book – you should probably attempt the whole stage, from Mayflower Steps to Wembury: taking a short-cut before you've even begun walking is no way to begin a challenge such as this. And besides, the path is not entirely without interest. There's the signage, for one thing, which for some unknown reason is by far the best on the entire coast path. Why anyone designed such a variegated array of signposts and waymarks is anyone's guess – but the fact is the path is marked with signposts made from huge recycled navigation beacons, some Communist-style iron star plaques and even giant metal sycamore keys. It's all rather bizarre – but they do serve to provide much-needed distractions for this stage. The city authorities have also gone to some length to provide interest to this section and are to be applauded for their efforts. On the first half of this stage, for example, you'll come across a holy shrine, a wall of poetry and a rhino sculpture. There's also a 19th-century 'castle', situated between the neighbouring lakes of Hooe and Radford; with swans drifting lazily nearby this is, in most people's opinions, the prettiest part of this stage (though you'll have to compose your photos carefully if you want to exclude all the rude graffiti with which it's been embellished down the years).

After Mount Batten Point matters improve and the countryside for the first time starts to dominate. While the bucolic beauty of this stage's second half is still interrupted on occasion – most noticeably by the holiday park at Bovisand – it is, on the whole, a largely rustic, gentle ramble, and much more characteristic of the trek to come. So strap on those boots, tighten the shoulder straps and get going: you've got 217¼ miles to go, and these paths don't walk themselves.

Before you set off, though, make sure you check the ferry times (see box opposite and pp101-2) for this section of the path.

The route

Beginning at the **Mayflower Steps**, the path leaves the busy delights of The Barbican behind by crossing the lock gates that secure Sutton Harbour, passing

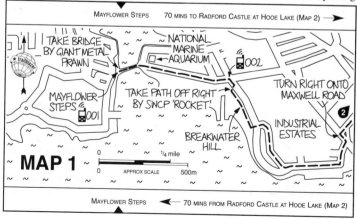

the huge **National Marine Aquarium** on the left on its way to the **Wallsend** and Cattedown **industrial estates**. (You may be surprised to find that the former is actually an SSSI, see p56, a disused quarry clearly showing the development of Devonian Plymouth limestone.) It's not the only surprise on this section of the trail: the **giant 'rocket' SWCP waypoint** leading you on to **Breakwater Hill** was once a navigational beacon for sailors

Oreston Rhino sculpture

and now serves much the same purpose for landlubbing trekkers. A section of speeding through an industrial estate, past a quirky **SWCP bench**, then sepa-

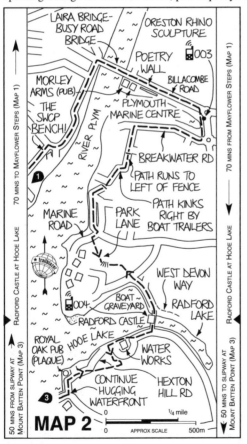

MAP 2

rates you from **Laira Bridge** and a crossing of the Plym. A **poetry wall** lines busy Billacombe Rd, which brightens an otherwise unpleasant stretch.

You leave this thoroughfare at **Oreston Rhino**, a sculpture which celebrates the prehistoric fossils of lion, ox, elephant, hippo, camel and, yes, rhino, that have been found in the caves near the city. Heading down Breakwater Rd, it's not long before the banks of **Hooe Lake** are reached, which you then hug most of the way to the neat suburb of Turnchapel (see opposite). On the way you pass **Radford Castle**, originally built for the 'keeper', a member of staff of nearby Radford House, who was responsible for looking after the estate's moorings and quays. Shortly after, by Hooe Green, a pub, *The Royal Oak* (☎ 01752-491577; **food** Mon-Fri noon-2.30pm & 5.30-6.30pm, Sat noon-6.30pm, Sun to 6pm; WI-FI; 🐾) has a **plaque** on its wall facing the path – one of several such plaques that decorate the walls around here. It is a large-scale re-creation of a medallion issued by John Smeaton (see p85), builder of Eddystone Lighthouse, which he gave to his highly skilled workers to prevent them being taken by press-gangs – hired thugs employed to force men into the military service. The pub dates from 1799 and welcomes coast-path walkers. It does food and real ales and overlooks Hooe Green and the corner of the harbour, otherwise known as Hooe Lake.

You'll soon pass through the delightfully colourful, narrow streets of **Turnchapel**, where two fine pubs – the cool-blue *Boringdon Arms* (☎ 01752-402053, 🖥 boringdon-arms.net; **food** Mon-Sat noon-3pm & 6-9pm, Sun noon-3pm; WI-FI; 🐾), which does **B&B** (3D/2Tr/1Qd; two en suite, rest share facilities; from £30pp inc for sgl occ) and the bright-yellow *Clovelly Bay Inn* (☎ 01752-402765; 🐾 ; bar Mon-Thur 6-11pm, Fri-Sat noon-3pm & 6-11pm, Sun noon-4pm & 7-10.30pm; **food** Mon-Thur 6-9pm, Fri & Sat noon-3pm & 6-9pm, Sun noon-2.30pm & 7-9pm) – vie for your attention.

It's not long before you arrive at **Mount Batten Point** (see box below). You'll find several more places to eat round here though we advise holding off until you're strolling on the **Jennycliffs** and reach the no-frills, but very popular *Jennycliff Café* (Map 3; ☎ 01752-402358; daily 9am-6pm, winter till 4pm), with the best views over the Sound and a great-value menu including omelettes (£4.40-4.80), full breakfasts (£3.80-4.90) and baked potatoes. Cash only.

After Mount Batten Point the path changes character and finally becomes the rustic ramble you were hoping for. True, Plymouth is still a huge looming presence over your right shoulder. The large naval contingent in the Sound and the helicopters swooping overhead further ensure that you aren't free of the city shackles just yet. But climbing away from Mount Batten Point the path is soon dodging amongst woods and meadows rather than warehouses and marinas.

❑ **Mount Batten Point**

Though today it seems little more than an unprepossessing pimple of grassy rock, Mount Batten Point actually has a lengthy history, as a few of its old buildings may suggest. Indeed, excavations indicate that this spot was the location for the very earliest trade the British had with Europe. From the late Bronze Age right through to the Roman era, archaeologists at Mount Batten Point have found evidence of a market that lead some to suggest that this spot could be the 'Tamaris' mentioned by Ptolemy in his *Geographica* (often cited as the world's earliest guidebook). The most obvious building here today, however, the austere **Mount Batten Tower**, is significantly younger, having been constructed in 1652 to protect the burgeoning new settlement around Plymouth Harbour.

Skip forward a few hundred years and the waters off Mount Batten Point were used to test the first sea-plane models, and an air station was subsequently established here. A **monument in the shape of a propellor** from a Sunderland flying boat, situated at the very end of the point, celebrates the RAF's tenure.

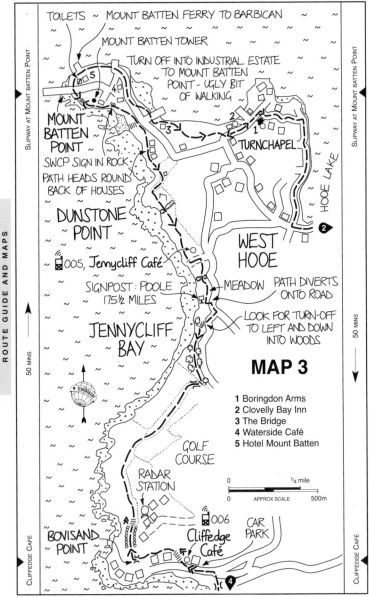

TOILETS ~ MOUNT BATTEN FERRY TO BARBICAN

MOUNT BATTEN TOWER

TURN OFF INTO INDUSTRIAL ESTATE
TO MOUNT BATTEN
POINT - UGLY BIT
OF WALKING

SLIPWAY AT MOUNT BATTEN POINT

MOUNT
BATTEN
POINT

TURNCHAPEL

SWCP SIGN IN ROCK
PATH HEADS ROUND
BACK OF HOUSES

DUNSTONE
~ POINT ~

HOOE LAKE

005, Jennycliff Café

WEST
HOOE

SIGNPOST: POOLE
175½ MILES

MEADOW   PATH DIVERTS
ONTO ROAD

LOOK FOR TURN-OFF
TO LEFT AND DOWN
INTO WOODS

JENNYCLIFF
~ BAY ~

MAP 3

★ trailblazer

1 Boringdon Arms
2 Clovelly Bay Inn
3 The Bridge
4 Waterside Café
5 Hotel Mount Batten

GOLF
COURSE

RADAR
STATION

0   ¼ mile
0   APPROX SCALE   500m

BOVISAND
~ POINT ~

006
Cliffedge Café

CAR
PARK

SLIPWAY AT MOUNT BATTEN POINT

50 MINS

50 MINS

CLIFFEDGE CAFÉ

CLIFFEDGE CAFÉ

This rural idyll is interrupted by naval defences near **Bovisand Point**, which is home to the seasonal *Cliffedge Café* (Wed-Sun & bank hols 10am-3pm) and its neighbouring holiday park – which in turn plays host to *Café Bovisands* (☎ 01752-862679; Mon-Thur 10am-4pm, Fri 10am-8pm, Sat & Sun 9.30am-5pm) and a **shop** (generally Apr-Sep daily 9am-5pm); note that the opening

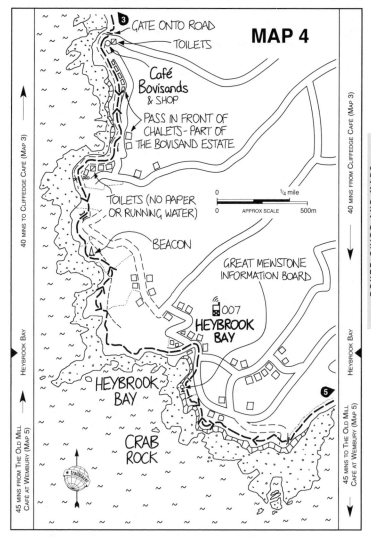

MAP 4

GATE ONTO ROAD
TOILETS
Café Bovisands & SHOP
PASS IN FRONT OF CHALETS - PART OF THE BOVISAND ESTATE
TOILETS (NO PAPER OR RUNNING WATER)
BEACON
GREAT MEWSTONE INFORMATION BOARD
007
HEYBROOK BAY
HEYBROOK BAY
CRAB ROCK

0 ¼ mile
APPROX SCALE
0 500m

trailblazer

40 MINS TO CLIFFEDGE CAFÉ (MAP 3)

40 MINS FROM CLIFFEDGE CAFÉ (MAP 3)

HEYBROOK BAY

HEYBROOK BAY

45 MINS FROM THE OLD MILL CAFE AT WEMBURY (MAP 5)

45 MINS TO THE OLD MILL CAFE AT WEMBURY (MAP 5)

days/hours for both vary, particularly in the winter, so check in advance. But it's not long before you are once again away from civilisation on a reasonably flat path heading via **Heybrook Bay** to round **Wembury Point**.

The island out to sea, by the way, is **Great Mewstone**, now uninhabited but once occupied by one Sam Wakeman, who was exiled there for seven years as punishment for some misdemeanour and paid his rent by supplying rabbits for the table of the local manor. There is a painting of the island by JMW Turner, dated 1816, which is now in the National Gallery of Ireland, Dublin.

With **Wembury Marine Conservation Area** to the right, rising ground to the left and an easy flat path ahead, it's a pleasant final stretch to *The Old Mill Café* (☎ 01752-863280, 🖳 oldmillwembury.co.uk; Apr-end Oct daily 10.30am-4.30pm, Nov-Mar weekends & hols 11am-4pm), a 150-year-old watermill turned eatery. The small **Wembury Marine Centre** (☎ 01752-862538, 🖳 wem burymarinecentre.org; Apr-Oct daily 10am-5pm; free) next door gives a kid-friendly introduction to the coastline conservation.

The road to Wembury runs steeply up the hill from here – or you can continue along the coast path to the mouth of the Yealm, from where a much flatter path heads inland to the village. Alternatively, you can carry on down to the ferry launch and the continuation of the trail.

WEMBURY   [map opposite, top]

An unassuming little place nestling in the shadow of Plymouth and its suburbs, Wembury has been around for a long time – some flint tools have been found hereabouts which proves that man has been stomping around since at least the Mesolithic era (10,000-4000BC).

Little happens here in Wembury but it's a pleasant-enough place, if a little too uphill from the coast for most tired trekkers. **Knighton Stores** (daily 7am-8pm) is well stocked, and doubles up as the **post office** (same hours).

Stagecoach's No 48 **bus** service (see pp50-4) travels between the village and Plymouth.

Campers can head to *Pilgrims Rest Camping & Caravan Site* (☎ 01752-863429, 🖳 www.pilgrimsrest.co.uk; limited WI-FI; 🐾 OK if on lead; Jan-Nov) with pitches for £10 per tent and up to two people; a shower costs 20p.

For **B&B**, try *Wembury Bay B&B* (☎ 01752-863392, 🖳 wemburybaybedand breakfast.yolasite.com; 1D/1T share facilities, 1T en suite; 🛏; WI-FI; from £35pp, sgl occ from £49), at 2 Warren Close. Other options include *Seahorses* (☎ 01752-863038, 🖳 seahorsesbb.yolasite.com; 1D/1Qd; 🛏; WI-FI; from £35pp, sgl occ from £40pp), at 10 Hawthorn Park Rd, and *107 Southland Park Road* (☎ 01752-862036; 1D or T; WI-FI; from £30pp, sgl occ from £40). Wembury Cars (see p109) also do B&B from *1 Barton Close* (☎ 01752-863710, 🖳 lorraine.pitcher123@btinternet .com; 1T; 🛏; WI-FI; 🐾; from £30pp, sgl occ from £35).

For **food**, the village pub, *The Odd Wheel* (☎ 01752-863052, 🖳 theoddwheel .co.uk; food Mon-Fri noon-2.30pm & 5-9pm, Sat noon-9pm, Sun to 8.30pm; WI-FI; 🐾 lounge bar only) does some great dishes including a mean Sunday roast. Also stocks a selection of real ales.

TACKLING THE YEALM

Ferry details

For the coast path you need the Warren Point to Noss Mayo service (the service from Warren Point to Newton Ferrers will still get you across the river, but

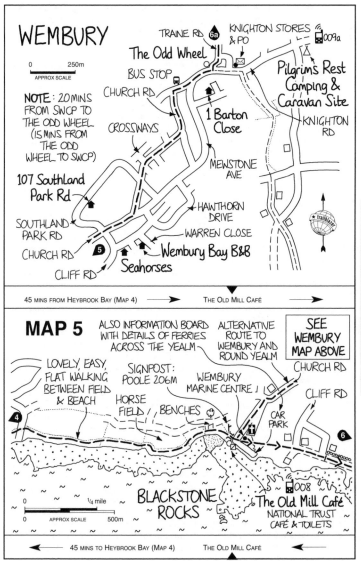

WEMBURY

TRAINE RD 6a

KNIGHTON STORES & PO

009a

The Odd Wheel

0   250m
APPROX SCALE

BUS STOP

NOTE: 20 MINS FROM SWCP TO THE ODD WHEEL (15 MINS FROM THE ODD WHEEL TO SWCP)

CHURCH RD

CROSSWAYS

Pilgrim's Rest Camping & Caravan Site

KNIGHTON RD

1 Barton Close

107 Southland Park Rd

MEWSTONE AVE

SOUTHLAND PARK RD

HAWTHORN DRIVE

CHURCH RD 5

WARREN CLOSE

Wembury Bay B&B

CLIFF RD   Seahorses

trailblazer

45 MINS FROM HEYBROOK BAY (MAP 4) →   THE OLD MILL CAFÉ →

MAP 5

ALSO INFORMATION BOARD WITH DETAILS OF FERRIES ACROSS THE YEALM

ALTERNATIVE ROUTE TO WEMBURY AND ROUND YEALM

SEE WEMBURY MAP ABOVE

LOVELY, EASY, FLAT WALKING BETWEEN FIELD & BEACH

SIGNPOST: POOLE 206M

HORSE FIELD / BENCHES

WEMBURY MARINE CENTRE

CHURCH RD

CLIFF RD

4

CAR PARK

6

BLACKSTONE ~ ROCKS ~

008

The Old Mill Café
NATIONAL TRUST CAFÉ & TOILETS

0   ¼ mile
0   APPROX SCALE   500m

← 45 MINS TO HEYBROOK BAY (MAP 4)   THE OLD MILL CAFÉ ←

ROUTE GUIDE AND MAPS

further away from the coast path than the Noss Mayo one). The ferry (☎ 07817-132757; £3.50; 🐾 free) operates daily from Easter/Apr to the end of September 10am-4pm but at times this may be restricted to 10am-noon & 3-4pm.

Bus details

If you miss the ferry, and don't want to walk around the estuary, you can take Stagecoach's No 48 from Wembury to Plymstock then change for Target Travel's No 94 to Noss Mayo; see pp50-4.

Walking around the Yealm   [Map 5 p101, Map 6a, pp104-5]

The **9-mile (14.5km; 4hrs)** diversion is not without its attractions including some pleasant walking on the **Erme-Plym Trail** (see p37). However, overall there are times, particularly when you reach the Devonshire village of Brixton, that the coast path seems an awfully long way away and it won't be long before you'll be yearning for the sound of the sea again.

The trail begins by The Odd Wheel pub, at the eastern end of Wembury, where a small country lane, Traine Rd, runs north away from the village to Wembury Rd. Opposite the junction here, the Erme-Plym Trail continues along a pathway down the side of Treetop Cottage, through a forest, across an open field with a pond, and on to a wooded track towards tiny **Spriddlestone**.

Turn right then left and continue across **Cofflete Creek** to the busy A379, where you turn right to reach the historic village of **Brixton**. There's **camping** available at *Brixton Caravan & Camping* (☎ 01752-402732; 🐾 ; £6 per pitch, £4pp) and, beside the 15th-century St Mary's Church, is the friendly **Brixton Village Stores** (Mon-Sat 7am-7.30pm, Sun 8am-noon), which incorporates the local **post office** (Mon-Wed & Fri 9am-noon, Thur 1-3pm) and even has a small *café*-like area by the window where you can sit and eat whatever you purchased in the shop while staff make you a cup of coffee or pot of tea.

Brixton also has a standout pub: *The Foxhound Inn* (☎ 01752-880271, 🖥 foxhoundinn.co.uk; WI-FI; 🐾 bar area; food served Mon-Sat noon-2pm, Sun to 2.30pm & Sun-Thur 6-9pm, Fri & Sat 6-9.30pm), an award-winning 200-year-old real-ale pub with a continually revolving line of guest ales, as well as one – Redcoat – that's brewed by the landlord and always on tap.

From Brixton the path continues along the Erme-Plym Trail which you rejoin beside Brixton Stores (don't be tempted to walk along the A379 as it has no pavement), heading through fields of crops and pheasants on your way to a small country lane that you join at **Gorlofen**. This you leave via a steep climb up a field, rejoining the A379 at **Yealmpton**. Stagecoach's No 3 and Target Travel's No 94 call here (see pp50-4).

A lovely stretch now follows as you say goodbye to the Erme-Plym for the last time, briefly heading west back along the A379 then down **Stray Park** to the end to reach a lovely wooded track on the right that heads, via some charmingly overgrown quarry works, to **Puslinch Bridge**, where you actually cross the Yealm. Much of the next section is, alas, on roads (albeit quiet country roads) as you climb steeply out of the valley, diverting off the road briefly to cross a couple of fields before returning to the tarmac for the long but hilly straight stretch to the **Water Tower** at Butts Park and the B3186 leading down (right) to **Newton Ferrers** (see pp104-5).

Sticking to the road, you skirt the end of Newton Creek to reach the even tinier settlement of **Noss Mayo** (see pp104-5) – at the end of which, of course, lies the **ferry launch** and a reunion with the coast path.

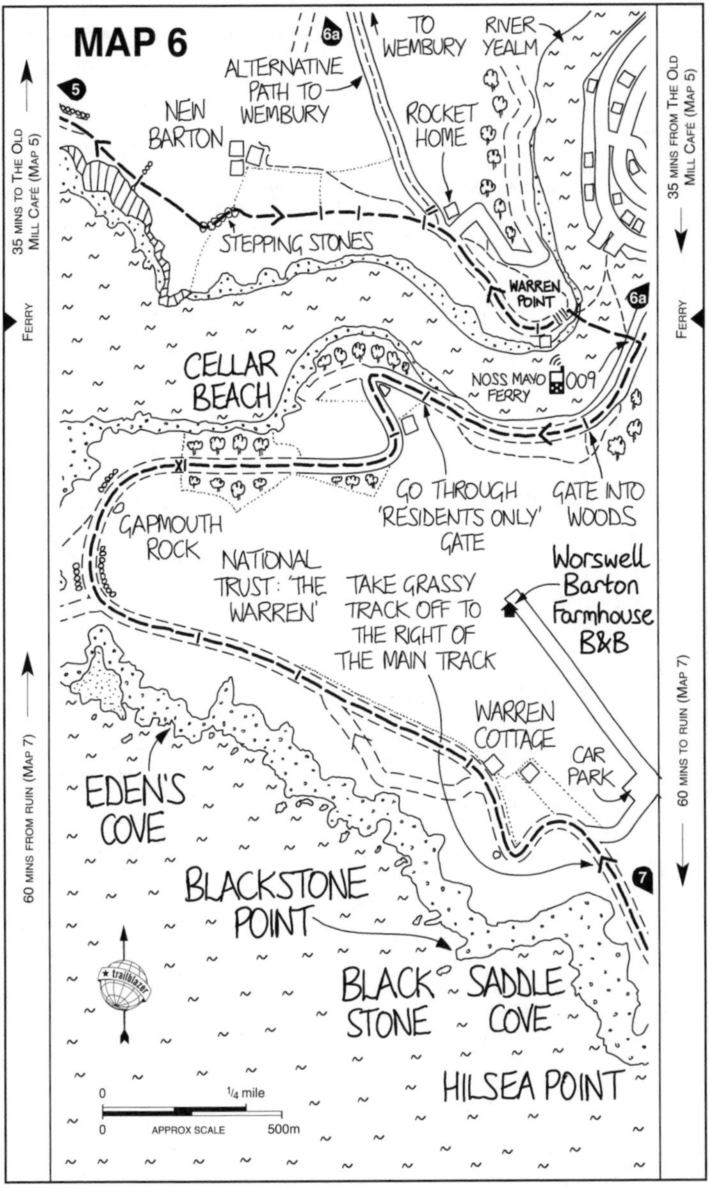

MAP 6

5 35 MINS TO THE OLD MILL CAFÉ (MAP 5)

FERRY

NEW BARTON

STEPPING STONES

6a ALTERNATIVE PATH TO WEMBURY

TO WEMBURY

RIVER YEALM

ROCKET HOME

35 MINS FROM THE OLD MILL CAFÉ (MAP 5)

WARREN POINT

6a FERRY

CELLAR BEACH

NOSS MAYO FERRY 009

GAPMOUTH ROCK

NATIONAL TRUST: 'THE WARREN'

GO THROUGH 'RESIDENTS ONLY' GATE

GATE INTO WOODS

TAKE GRASSY TRACK OFF TO THE RIGHT OF THE MAIN TRACK

Worswell Barton Farmhouse B&B

60 MINS FROM RUIN (MAP 7)

WARREN COTTAGE

CAR PARK

EDEN'S COVE

60 MINS TO RUIN (MAP 7)

7

BLACKSTONE POINT

BLACK STONE

SADDLE COVE

HILSEA POINT

* trailblazer

| 0 | 1/4 mile |
| 0 | APPROX SCALE | 500m |

ROUTE GUIDE AND MAPS

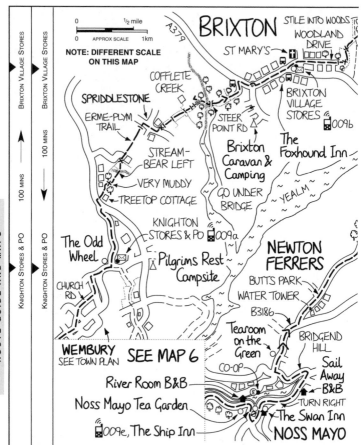

BRIXTON VILLAGE STORES

BRIXTON VILLAGE STORES

100 MINS

100 MINS

KNIGHTON STORES & PO

KNIGHTON STORES & PO

BRIXTON

STILE INTO WOODS

WOODLAND DRIVE

ST MARY'S

COFFLETE CREEK

SPRIDDLESTONE

ERME-PLYM TRAIL

BRIXTON VILLAGE STORES

009b

STREAM-BEAR LEFT

STEER POINT RD

Brixton Caravan & Camping

The Foxhound Inn

YEALM

VERY MUDDY

TREETOP COTTAGE

GO UNDER BRIDGE

The Odd Wheel

KNIGHTON STORES & PO

009a

NEWTON FERRERS

Pilgrims Rest Campsite

CHURCH RD

BUTTS PARK

WATER TOWER

B3186

Tearoom on the Green

BRIDGEND HILL

WEMBURY SEE TOWN PLAN

SEE MAP 6

CO-OP

Sail Away B&B

River Room B&B

TURN RIGHT

Noss Mayo Tea Garden

The Swan Inn

009e, The Ship Inn

NOSS MAYO

NOSS MAYO & NEWTON FERRERS [Map 6a]

Separated by a narrow tidal creek, these tidy twin villages lie on the estuary of the River Yealm. **Newton Ferrers** is the larger of the two. Originally called *Niwetone*, the village was given as a gift to the Norman Ferrers family – hence the name. Here you'll find a Co-op **supermarket** (Mon-Sat 8am-8pm, Sun 9am-7pm) with a free **ATM**, as well as *Tearoom on the Green* (☎ 07902-256539; ⚑ on lead; Wed-Sat

10am-4.30pm, Sun to 4pm), a lovely café that does cream teas (£6), breakfasts, soups and sandwiches, but only accepts cash.

The quieter, and ever-so charming **Noss Mayo**, which clings tightly to the edge of a side creek, is nearer to the coast path, with the ferry across the Yealm calling in at the edge of the village, about 10 minutes' walk from the centre. There's some **accommodation** here, as well as two fine pubs.

Sail Away B&B (☎ 01752-873556, 🖳 sailawaystays.webs.com; 2D; ⬤; WI-FI;

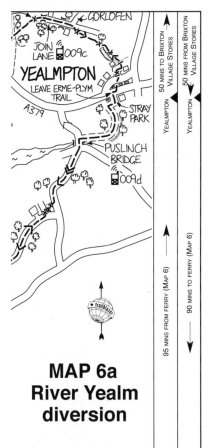

MAP 6a
River Yealm
diversion

£37.75-43.75pp, sgl occ £72.50-82.50), is a smart place on Bridgend Hill. You could also try *River Room B&B* (☎ 01752-872581, 🖥 www.dev onissimo.com; 1D; 🐾; £45pp, sgl occ room rate), a self-contained studio room with a shower room (accessed from across a terrace), a kettle and a microwave, and stunning views of the estuary. They prefer bookings to be made through Airbnb (🖥 airbnb.co .uk), although it's owned by the same people who run *Noss Mayo Tea Garden* (spring–autumn weekends & bank hols noon-5pm; 🐾), so you may be able to contact them there.

A third option is to stay at *The Swan Inn* (☎ 01752-872333, 🖥 theswannossmayo.co.uk; 1S/1D shared facilities; ☕; WI-FI; 🐾; walkers' rate from £45pp, sgl from £55, sgl occ rates on request), one of two great pubs in Noss Mayo, which look out at each other from across the creek. Their **food** (Mar/Apr-end Oct Tue-Fri noon-3pm & 6.30-8pm, Sat noon-8pm, Sun noon-6/7pm, rest of year hours variable) is fairly standard pub fare, but reasonably priced. The other pub, *The Ship Inn* (☎ 01752-872387, 🖥 nossmayo.com; food daily noon-9.30pm; 🐾), also has a smashing location, but is more of a gastro-pub, with pricier (but better quality) food. Both stock real ales.

Target Travel's No 94 **bus service** journeys calls at Newton Ferrers & Noss Mayo and also at Yealmpton (en route to Plymouth) where you connect with Stagecoach's No 3; see pp50-4.

ROUTE GUIDE AND MAPS

WEMBURY TO BIGBURY-ON-SEA   [MAPS 6-11]

This **15¼-mile (24.5km; 5hrs 25mins)** stage is fairly typical of the South Devon section of the SWCP. With a couple of river crossings (including one, uniquely for this stretch of the coast path, that you have to wade across), an excellent café to stop at for lunch, and a quiet village at the end of your hike with a very quirky pub. And with mile after mile of lovely scenery to delight the eyes and lift the soul, this is very much in keeping with this county's ability to inspire and entertain. There are some possible problems on the trail. The first is that this is actually one of the quietest stretches on the entire path, with the café at Mothecombe the only place to eat at before Challaborough and Bigbury. *(cont'd on p108)*

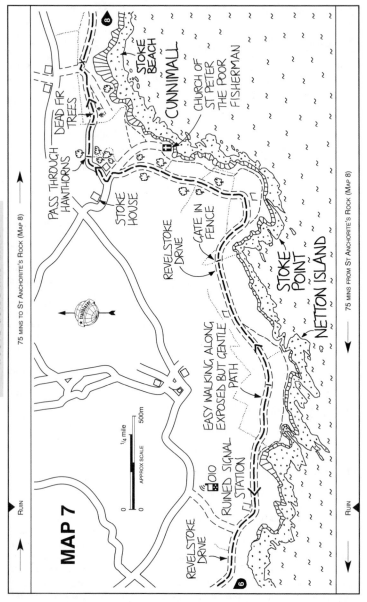

MAP 7

RUIN

75 MINS TO ST ANCHORITE'S ROCK (MAP 8)

PASS THROUGH HAWTHORNS

DEAD FIR TREES

STOKE BEACH

CUNNIMALL

CHURCH OF ST PETER THE POOR FISHERMAN

STOKE HOUSE

REVELSTOKE DRIVE

GATE IN FENCE

STOKE POINT

NETTON ISLAND

75 MINS FROM ST ANCHORITE'S ROCK (MAP 8)

EASY WALKING ALONG, EXPOSED BUT GENTLE PATH

APPROX SCALE

0   500m

0   ¼ mile

REVELSTOKE DRIVE

RUINED SIGNAL STATION

RUIN

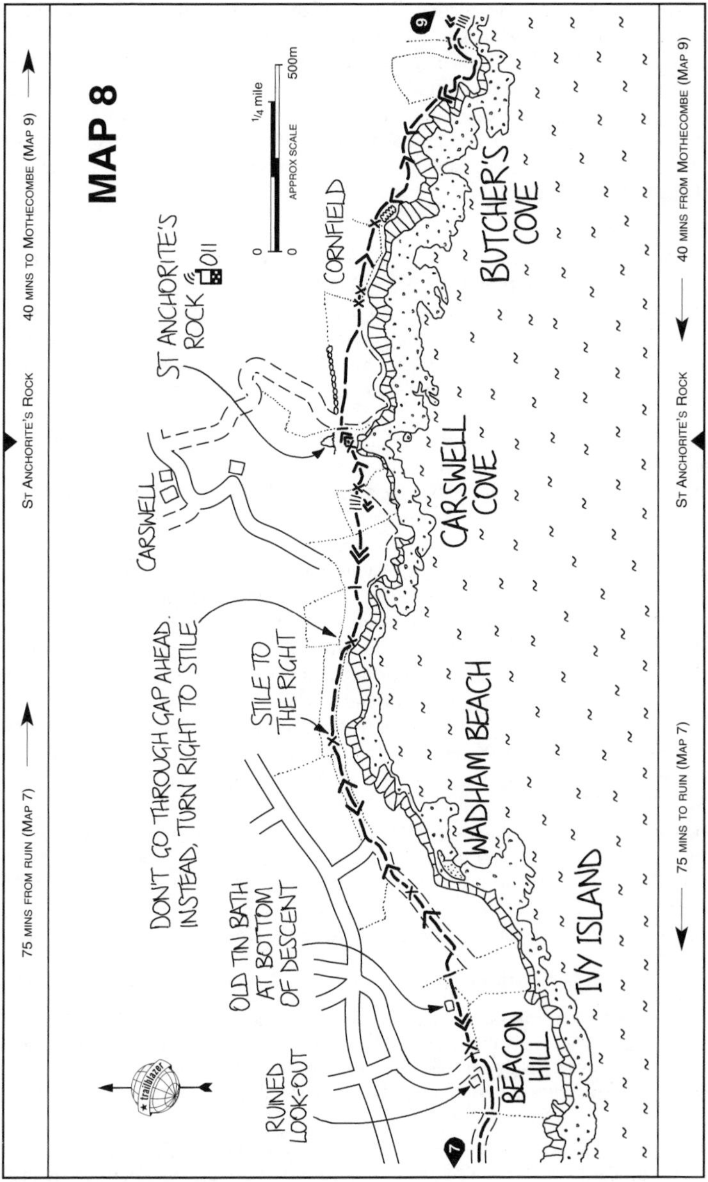
MAP 8
75 MINS FROM RUIN (MAP 7)
ST ANCHORITE'S ROCK
40 MINS TO MOTHECOMBE (MAP 9)
75 MINS TO RUIN (MAP 7)
ST ANCHORITE'S ROCK
40 MINS FROM MOTHECOMBE (MAP 9)
0
0
1/4 mile
500m
APPROX SCALE
trailblazer
RUINED LOOK-OUT
OLD TIN BATH AT BOTTOM OF DESCENT
DON'T GO THROUGH GAP AHEAD. INSTEAD, TURN RIGHT TO STILE
STILE TO THE RIGHT
CARSWELL
ST ANCHORITE'S ROCK
CORNFIELD
BEACON HILL
IVY ISLAND
WADHAM BEACH
CARSWELL COVE
BUTCHER'S COVE
7
9

(Cont'd from p105) The second problem is the crossing of the Erme: with no ferry, the only way to tackle it is to wade across – which, according to the noticeboards dotted about, **is possible only an hour either side of low tide**. It's important, therefore, that you find out when this will be and keep a close eye on your progress against the clock. Mistime your arrival and you'll have to arrange a taxi, or walk around – and given that this walk around the estuary is almost entirely on roads without pavements, this is one estuary diversion you really don't want to have to do.

The route

Having crossed the Yealm, your next task on the trail is to follow an old carriage drive west round **Gapmouth Rock** (Map 6) then east past various old ruins (including a **ruined signal station**) to Stoke Beach. Along the way you'll pass a track leading to a car park from where you can access ***Worswell Barton Farmhouse B&B*** (☎ 01752-872977, 🖳 worswellbarton.co.uk; 4D/1T; limited WI-FI; 🐾 only if sleep in outside kennel; from £45pp, sgl occ £50-60), a working farm with five guest rooms.

Next comes a really lovely stretch; fairly straightforward on gentle, grassy **Revelstoke Drive**, wooded in places, with delicious sea views every now and then on your right. Passing above the **Church of St Peter the Poor Fisherman** – which dates back to the 12th century and is once again, following extensive repairs in the 1970s, used for services occasionally – the path reaches the drive to Stoke House and, soon after, at **Beacon Hill** (note the ruined look-out by the path), becomes even more strenuous – though, if anything, more gorgeous too.

The main feature on this approach to the River Erme is undoubtedly **St Anchorite's Rock**, a huge tor gazing silently out over the sea. (An *anchorite* is an old term for a hermit and it is probable that a hermitage was established near here at some point in the dim and distant past.)

Not long afterwards the mouth at **Mothecombe** is reached, from where you can head inland to wait for low tide at the excellent café, ***Schoolhouse*** (☎ 01752-830552, 🖳 schoolhouse-devon.com; WI-FI; 🐾; Apr-Oct Mon-Tue 9.30am-5pm, Wed-Sun 9.30am-9pm, for the rest of the year check their website). Sit in the garden or at long shared tables inside the rustic barn-like main room, while you gorge on breakfasts (£8.50), gourmet sandwiches (£7.50-10.50), or Italian mains (£12-20). The more affordable takeaway menu includes pasties (£4) and ordinary sandwiches (£4.50). Don't forget to keep an eye on the time and tide, though. It would be a shame to miss your only chance of fording the Erme for the sake of a coffee.

TACKLING THE ERME   [Map 9; Map 9a, p110]

Wading across Assuming you are here an hour either side of low tide you can wade across the river; the best place is clearly signposted. The terrain underfoot is sandy and, on occasion, pebbly too – but it doesn't take more than a few minutes at most to cross. Note, at low tide you're likely to be wading at least up to your knees.

By taxi A taxi will cost £20-30. Since it's quite a way from any of the taxi offices to Mothecombe it is advisable to book a taxi in advance. Be aware that

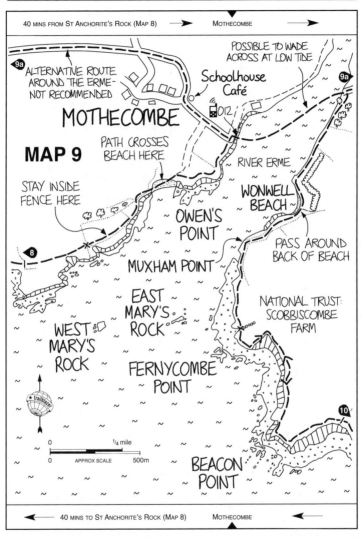

the taxi driver may not know where you are and also may not know the route. **Taxi** firms worth trying include: Clarke Cars (☎ 07976-551532); Eco-Taxi (☎ 07811-385275); Ivy Cabs (☎ 01752-696969); John Edwards (☎ 07967-374502, or ☎ 01548-830859); Steve's Taxi (☎ 07811-150349); and Wembury Cars (☎ 01752-863710).

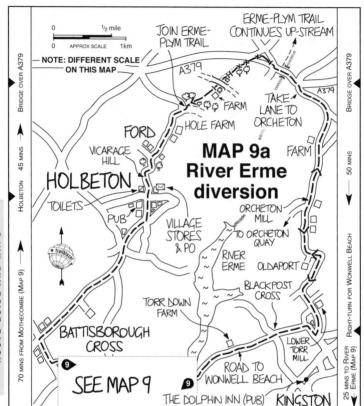

SEE MAP 9

Walking around the Erme

This is the least pleasant of the riverside diversions in the book – so either of the above options is far more preferable.

The walk (**8¾ miles; 3hrs 10 mins**) begins – and largely continues – along roads, both upriver and back down the other side again. Hopefully Maps 9 and 9a make the correct route clear. Don't be tempted by some attractive-looking footpaths leading off the roads in what seems to be the correct direction; trust us when we say that they don't lead to anywhere useful. It goes without saying that you need to be careful as most of these country lanes have no pavements. The OL20 Ordnance Survey map is useful to find your way, though it's not particularly difficult.

Follow the road west out of Mothecombe, turning right at **Battisborough Cross**, continue north for a couple of miles to **Holbeton** before following Vicarage Hill to the left of the Village Stores.

The even tinier village of **Ford** is your next destination, again signposted, north of which is **Hole Farm**. Continuing north, eventually you'll hit the Erme-Plym Trail which you should take right to join the A379. Thankfully, your stay on this road lasts for only a few hundred metres, where a lane to the right is signed to Orcheton.

Follow this for another couple of miles down past **Orcheton Mill** and its nearby quay, then **Oldaport**, Clyng Mill, the turn-off to Waster and Shearlangstone, and so on to Torr Rock and **Lower Torr**. Finally a road to the right is signposted to **Wonwell Beach** (if you reach Kingston you've walked too far), your destination for this walk, and reachable after taking a left where the road forks past the row of pink cottages, passing Blackpost Cross and Torr Down Farm on your way down to the east bank of the Erme.

There's no let-up in the beauty of the walking after the Erme, though there are no major sites – just more miles of magnificence to meander through, including **Muxham Point** and **Beacon Point**, both of which have wonderful panoramic views, and the cliffs of **Westcombe** and **Ayrmer Cove**.

Finally, you find yourself trudging, weary but happy, into **Challaborough** and its neighbour, **Bigbury-on-Sea**.

CHALLABOROUGH & BIGBURY-ON-SEA   [Map 10, p112; Map 11, p113]

These two conjoined settlements probably wouldn't linger in the memory for too long, were it not for the curious Burgh Island that sits just offshore (see box below).

Challaborough, which is dominated by Challaborough Bay Holiday Park (no camping), is home to *The Waterfront* (food served daily 9-11am, noon-3pm & 5-9pm), a restaurant-café run by the holiday park,

Fryer Tucks (☎ 01548-810425; Easter/Apr to end Oct daily noon-10pm), a no-frills fish-&-chips restaurant that's been going for more than 20 years, and a handy Nisa Local **supermarket** (daily 8am-6pm). There's an **ATM** in the holiday park, though it charges for withdrawals.

Facilities in **Bigbury** are pretty much non-existent now that the post office has closed down.   *(continued on p114)*

❏ Burgh Island

Burgh Island is joined to the mainland at low tide by a lovely sand spit. However, if you wish to visit it when the tide's against you, you'll have to take the specially adapted sea tractor. There is good reason to visit, too, for not only does this small lump of grassy rock boast the remains of a chapel (possibly part of an ancient monastery) and an equally venerable pub but also, dominating the whole island, the exclusive and extortionate 1920s' Art Deco *Burgh Island Hotel* (☎ 01548-810514, 🖥 burghisland .com; 10D/15 suites; 🛏; WI-FI), which inspired the setting for Agatha Christie's *And Then There Were None*. Their more celebrated guests – Noel Coward, Josephine Baker, Amy Johnson and Gertie Lawrence – now each lend their names to one of the hotel's suites. With dinner, bed and breakfast from £420 per night, it's out of reach for most trekkers – but that doesn't stop one from being able to admire it, if only from afar.

Frustratingly, because it could be such a wonderful pub, the *Pilchard Inn* is rather disappointing when it comes to serving walkers; much of the bar is given over for the sole use of the island's hotel residents, the service is lukewarm at best, and the only food on offer is overpriced baguettes at lunchtime. Such a shame for a place that's said to have been serving thirsty punters for more than 700 years.

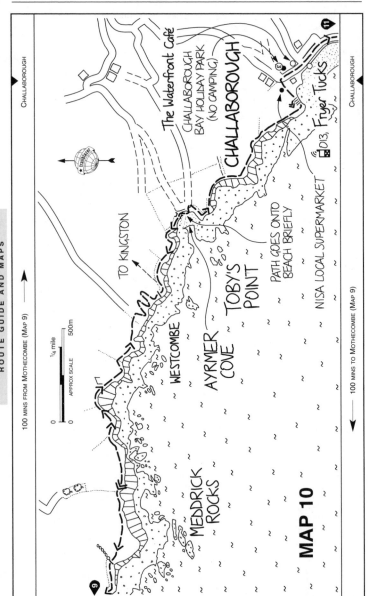

CHALLABOROUGH

100 MINS FROM MOTHECOMBE (MAP 9)

The Waterfront Café

CHALLABOROUGH BAY HOLIDAY PARK (NO CAMPING)

CHALLABOROUGH

Fryer Tucks

D13, NISA LOCAL SUPERMARKET

PATH GOES ONTO BEACH BRIEFLY

TOBY'S POINT

AYRMER COVE

WESTCOMBE

TO KINGSTON

¼ mile

500m

APPROX SCALE

MEDRICK ROCKS

MAP 10

100 MINS TO MOTHECOMBE (MAP 9)

CHALLABOROUGH

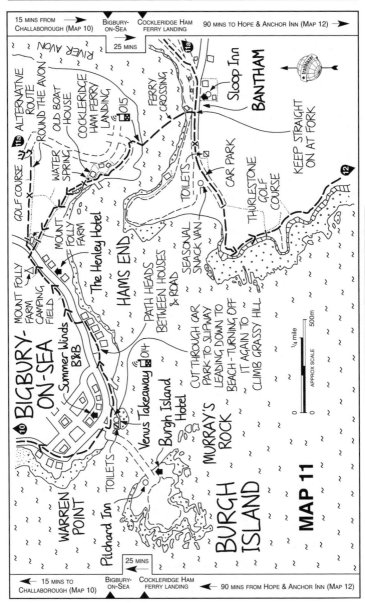

(Cont'd from p111) **Campers** can pitch a tent at the welcoming *Mount Folly Farm* (☎ 01548-810267, 🖥 bigburyholidays.co .uk; 🐾 on lead; walkers £6pp; showers £1), which is right on the coast path, where the path turns down to the ferry crossing.

Unless you're a millionaire and are able to stay on super-expensive Burgh Island (see box on p111), there are only two **B&B** options. *Summer Winds* (☎ 01548-810669, 🖥 pritchard212@btinternet.com; 1D/1T; 🐾; WI-FI; £42.50-45pp, sgl occ £50); note that in general they don't offer B&B during the school summer holidays and they are closed around Christmas. The other is *The Henley Hotel* (☎ 01548-810240, 🖥 thehenleyhotel.co.uk; 2D/3T; 🐾; WI-FI; 🐾; £63.50-80pp, sgl occ from £95; mid Mar-Oct), which was originally built as a smart Edwardian holiday cottage. Advance bookings must be for a minimum of two nights.

For **food**, there is only *Venus Takeaway* (☎ 01548-810141, 🖥 lovingthe beach.co.uk; daily July & Aug 9am-6pm, rest of year 10am-5pm), a takeaway-only café (albeit a pretty decent one) in the car park down towards the beach, facing the island.

BIGBURY-ON-SEA TO SALCOMBE   [MAPS 11-16]

The coast path for this **13-mile (21km; 5hrs 5mins)** stage continues to be fairly remote and wild though there are more places on the way where you can get refreshments than on the previous stage.

The highlight – other than the scenery, of course, particularly during the latter half of the walk which is just unremittingly breathtaking – is the likeable village of **Hope** (or Outer Hope to give it its full title and to distinguish it from neighbouring Inner Hope, to the south). Overall, it's one of those stages where you should pray for fine weather; if your prayers are answered expect to spend a lot of time taking photos. However, before you set off make sure you have checked the ferry times for this section of the path.

The route

As before, the day begins with a crossing of a river, in this case the **Avon** (no, not *that* one). Getting to the ferry launch is a little tricky: from the beach at Bigbury, the path meanders close to – or on – the road out of the village up to **Mount Folly Farm**, which it cuts through on its way, via a sheep field or two, down to the ferry at **Cockleridge Ham**.

TACKLING THE AVON   [Map 11, p113; Map 11a]
Ferry
The short ferry trip (☎ 01548-561196; £3 one-way) across the Avon from Cockleridge Ham in Bigbury to Bantham operates all year, but only between the hours of 10am and 11am, and 3pm and 4pm. The ferry runs by request and if the ferryman happens to be on the opposite bank to you, you have to signal to him by waving that you are waiting for a lift. If you time things wrong for the ferry, and you don't want to tackle the walk around the Avon, you could call a taxi (Arrow Cabs ☎ 01548-856120; Eco-Taxi, see p109).

Avon Estuary Walk – walking around the Avon
This pleasant **8-mile (13km; 3hrs) diversion** is gentle on the eye without being stunning. The scenery is unsurprisingly verdant, there's a village at the

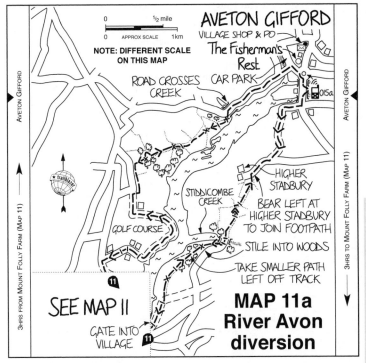

AVETON GIFFORD

MAP 11a
River Avon
diversion

ROUTE GUIDE AND MAPS

halfway point where you can get a bite to eat, and it's very peaceful. Furthermore, though this trail has been officially designated as the Avon Estuary Walk, it's rare to find other people on it, giving you plenty of time to take in the lovely views and contemplate how much further along the coastal path you would be if only you had managed to catch the boat across the Avon.

The trail begins on the road just uphill from **Mount Folly Farm** (see opposite) where a path off right takes you into the fields and across a **golf course**. The climb up the western side of the Avon is a little meandering but never more than a field or two away from the river, the path picked out with the blue 'heron' waymarkers of the Avon Estuary Walk. Undulating at first, towards its northern end the path flattens to cross the mudflats and creeks on its way to the only settlement on the route.

Aveton Gifford (⬚ aveton-gifford.co.uk) is not the prettiest of places but there is a pub here, *The Fisherman's Rest* (☎ 01548-550284, ⬚ thefishermans rest.co.uk; WI-FI; 🐾 bar area only; food served daily noon-2pm & 7-9pm) and, 400 metres further along the road, a community-owned **village shop & post office** (☎ 01548-550996; Mon-Fri 8am-6pm, Sat 8.30am-3pm, Sun 8.30am-1pm, closed for lunch Mon & Thur 1-2pm) which sells groceries, sandwiches, baked goods and ice-creams.

Stagecoach's No 3 **bus** (see pp50-4) passes though on its way to Dartmouth & Kingsbridge from Plymouth.

It's just outside the village that the path changes direction, crosses the Avon, and starts to head back south towards the coast again. A steep climb takes you away from the riverbank, before the path stumbles back down to cross **Stiddicombe Creek**. A lovely stretch follows through the woods and fields leading eventually to the village of **Bantham**, where you'll find food (Mon-Sat noon-2pm & 6.30-9pm, Sun noon-4pm & 6.30-9pm), beer and accommodation at the 14th-century *Sloop Inn* (☎ 01548-560489, 🖳 the sloop.co.uk; 4D/1D or T/1Qd; 🛏; WI-FI; 🐾; £42-49.50pp, sgl occ from £54).

From the inn it's a few steps to the top of the road leading down to the ferry point – and a reunion with the coast path.

From the ferry point the path heads up to a car park, thereafter bending west then south and skirting the edge of **Thurlestone Golf Course**. There's often a **seasonal snack van** in the car park at Bantham, but the first proper eatery on this stage is the slightly pricey, but very good *Beachhouse Café* (☎ 01548-561144, 🖳 beachhousedevon.com; daily school summer holidays 9.30am-7pm, Apr-Jun & Sep-Oct Mon-Thur 9.30am-3pm, Fri-Sun to 4/5pm, Nov-Mar Wed-Sun only but check hours), looking out towards the holed **Thurlestone Rock** which stands, sea-battered but proud, nearby. From here, a relatively straight-forward stroll on low cliffs brings you to **Outer Hope**.

OUTER HOPE
[Map 12 & Map 13, p118]

Given its remote location, it won't surprise you to discover that Hope Cove was once a favourite haunt of smugglers. You perhaps also won't be too shocked to discover that the wild and rugged coast around here has also seen its fair share of shipwrecks; as a result, the village is something of a mecca for divers.

The focus of interest on the cove for trekkers is Outer Hope. Facilities are minimal though there is a **village store** (daily 8am-6pm) that sells pasties and takeaway coffee as well as groceries, and has a **post office** inside it. There's an **ATM** (£1.50) in the Hope & Anchor Inn.

Tally Ho's 162 **bus service** travels between Outer Hope, Inner Hope (p118) and Kingsbridge, where you can connect with other services; see pp50-4.

For **accommodation**, the main place in town is *Cottage Hotel* (☎ 01548-561555, 🖳 hopecove.com; 2S/29D or T/1T; 🛏; WI-FI; 🐾; dinner B&B £60-100pp, sgl from £60, sgl occ rate on request; closed Jan to early Feb), a smart old pile dating back to the 19th century, though the hotel only

opened in the 1920s and its décor certainly harks back more to that era. Note that the rate includes dinner.

Below Cottage Hotel, *Hope & Anchor Inn* (☎ 01548-561294, 🖳 www.hopeand anchor.co.uk; 1T/7D/2Tr/one sleeping up to 5; 🛏; WI-FI; 🐾; £55-70pp, sgl occ £70-140) offers some of the best accommodation in the village though the prices reflect this. *Lantern Lodge B&B* (☎ 01548-561280, 🖳 lantern-lodge.co.uk; 3T/1OD/1Tr; 🛏; WI-FI; 🐾; £45-62.50pp, sgl occ room rate; mid Mar to mid Nov) is on the cliffs above town with some smart bedrooms – three with four-poster beds – that are designed to make the most of the far-reaching views (not all rooms have a view).

Sand Pebbles (☎ 01548-561673; 8D/1T/1Qd; 🛏; WI-FI; 🐾; £35-62.50pp, sgl occ rates on request) is a hotel, bar and restaurant up above the beaches. They offer **food** (daily 8.30am-9pm) to non-residents throughout the day, including breakfasts, lunches, cream teas and evening meals.

The two most popular place to eat, though, and certainly the most convenient for passing walkers, are both side by side,

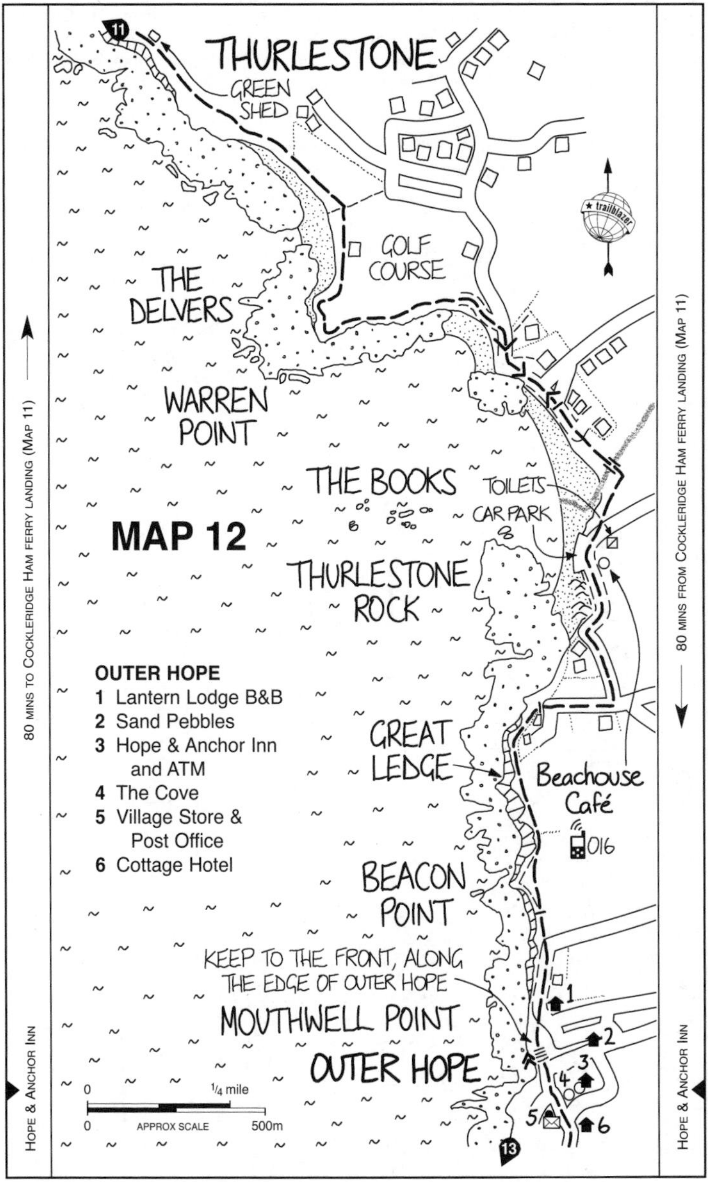

THURLESTONE

GREEN SHED

GOLF COURSE

THE DELVERS

WARREN POINT

THE BOOKS

MAP 12

THURLESTONE ROCK

TOILETS

CAR PARK

OUTER HOPE

1 Lantern Lodge B&B
2 Sand Pebbles
3 Hope & Anchor Inn
  and ATM
4 The Cove
5 Village Store &
  Post Office
6 Cottage Hotel

GREAT LEDGE

Beachouse Café

☎ 016

BEACON POINT

KEEP TO THE FRONT, ALONG THE EDGE OF OUTER HOPE

MOUTHWELL POINT

OUTER HOPE

0   ¼ mile
0   APPROX SCALE   500m

80 MINS TO COCKLERIDGE HAM FERRY LANDING (MAP 11)

80 MINS FROM COCKLERIDGE HAM FERRY LANDING (MAP 11)

ROUTE GUIDE AND MAPS

HOPE & ANCHOR INN

HOPE & ANCHOR INN

down by the village store. ***Hope & Anchor Inn*** (see p116; food daily 8.30-10am & noon-9pm) is a large, smart, gastro-pub; it is open for breakfasts and has plenty of outdoor seating. Next door ***The Cove*** (☎ 01548-561376, ☐ thecovedevon.co.uk; WI-FI; 🐾; food daily 10am-9pm) is a café-bar that knocks out some great burgers.

From Outer Hope the path meanders past seafront residences to its Siamese twin, **Inner Hope**, from where a wooded path once again leads away

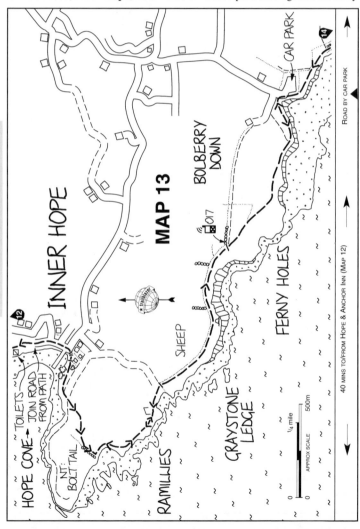

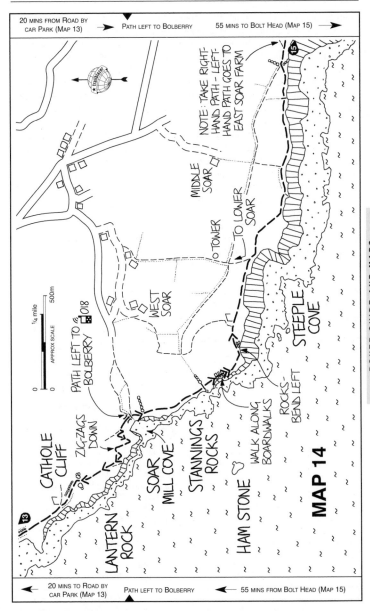

ROUTE GUIDE AND MAPS

20 MINS FROM ROAD BY CAR PARK (MAP 13) → PATH LEFT TO BOLBERRY   55 MINS TO BOLT HEAD (MAP 15) →

NOTE: TAKE RIGHT-HAND PATH – LEFT-HAND PATH GOES TO EAST SOAR FARM

★ trailblazer

¼ mile
500m
APPROX SCALE

MIDDLE SOAR

TO LOWER SOAR

TO TOWER

WEST SOAR

STEEPLE COVE

PATH LEFT TO BOLBERRY   018

CATHOLE CLIFF

ZIG-ZAGS DOWN

ROCKS-BEND LEFT

WALK ALONG BOARDWALKS

SOAR MILL COVE

STANNINGS ROCKS

HAM STONE

LANTERN ROCK

MAP 14

20 MINS TO ROAD BY CAR PARK (MAP 13)   ← PATH LEFT TO BOLBERRY   ← 55 MINS FROM BOLT HEAD (MAP 15)

from civilisation. This stretch from Inner Hope to Salcombe is book-ended by two promontories, **Bolt Tail** (Map 13) and Bolt Head (Map 15). Bolt Tail comes first, a lovely westerly-facing headland which the path contours round before describing a hairpin bend south-east through fields to **Bolberry Down**. The whole stretch is owned by the National Trust and, despite the car park, the path feels quite remote. Indeed, there's nowhere to eat or drink until Salcombe, unless you choose to detour off the path slightly earlier to visit *East Soar Farm* (Map 15; ☎ 01548-561904, 🖥 eastsoaroutdoorexperience.co.uk). This innovative, South African-run farm offers camping-type accommodation (though you can't pitch your own tents here) in the form of six **bell tents** (these sleep up to six and there is a minimum stay of two nights; £40pp inc breakfast & dinner; Easter to end Sep) and a **bunkhouse** (sleeps 20; £45pp inc breakfast & dinner). You sleep on mattresses, but no bedding is provided. They also have a huge *Walker's Hut* (daily Apr-Sep 10.30am-5pm, Feb, Mar & Oct 11am-4pm, closed Nov-Jan; 🐾) which offers hot drinks, snacks and shelter to campers and passing hikers alike.

The approach to **Bolt Head** is marked by increasingly severe gradients, ensuring that by the time you reach civilisation again, at the twin millionaire hamlets of **South Sands** and **North Sands** you'll be ready for a drink again.

The very busy beach café *Winking Prawn* (Map 15; ☎ 01548-842326, 🖥 winkingprawn.co.uk; summer daily 9am-8.30pm, winter hours vary but usually Mon-Fri 9.15am-4pm) does sandwiches, wraps and baguettes (£6-9) as well as main meals (£15-20), and has garden BBQs in good weather. Most people, however, will probably want to continue to Salcombe, where further options await.

SALCOMBE   [map p123]

Sophisticated, seafaring Salcombe sits at the mouth of Kingsbridge Estuary, its condos, penthouses, hotels and holiday homes stretching up the steep surrounding hills. Its written history harks back only as far as 1244, making it a positive youngster compared to some of the settlements around here and, in this respect, it very much sits in the shadow of neighbouring Dartmouth, whose past is indubitably both longer and richer. Salcombe followed the well-trodden path of many villages around here, eking out a living from the industries of fishing, smuggling and piracy. However, in 1764, the first holiday home, 'The Moult', was built by a Mr John Hawkins between Salcombe and North Sands (and still stands there); and Salcombe has been thriving on holidaymakers pretty much ever since.

A second income stream, from shipbuilding, started up at the same time and ensured the town's prosperity for much of the next century. In particular, Salcombe specialised in the building of fruit schooners – light and rapid craft required by traders to hurry their cargo of perishable fruit back from Spain and the Azores before it spoilt. The invention of ships made of iron and steel spelt the end of the industry in Salcombe and while its reputation as a seafaring centre remains to this day, its sailors now tend to come from the retired and wealthy rather than the ambitious and intrepid.

There's a lot to like about the town, not least **Salcombe Maritime Museum** (🖥 salcombemuseum.org.uk; Apr-Oct daily 10.30am-12.30pm & 2.30-4.30pm; £2) below the tourist office, which has a number of displays recounting the town's history; the friendly staff are also a good source of local knowledge.

Services

The **tourist information centre** (☎ 01548-843927, 🖥 salcombeinformation.co.uk; Easter-end Oct Mon-Sat 10am-5pm, Sun

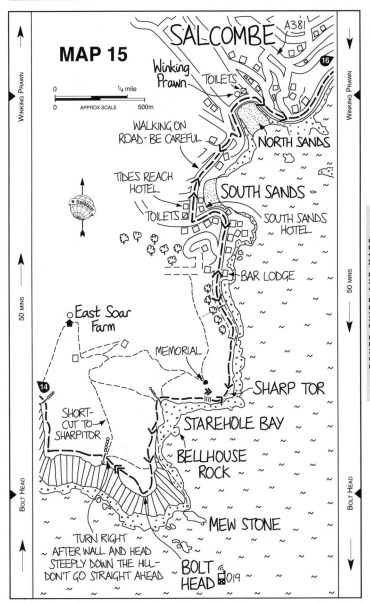

MAP 15

SALCOMBE

A381

16

Winking Prawn

TOILETS

0   ¼ mile

0   APPROX SCALE   500m

WALKING ON
ROAD - BE CAREFUL

NORTH SANDS

TIDES REACH
HOTEL

SOUTH SANDS

TOILETS

SOUTH SANDS
HOTEL

★ trailblazer

BAR LODGE

East Soar
Farm

MEMORIAL

SHARP TOR

14

SHORT-
CUT TO
SHARPITOR

STAREHOLE BAY

BELLHOUSE
ROCK

MEW STONE

TURN RIGHT
AFTER WALL AND HEAD
STEEPLY DOWN THE HILL -
DON'T GO STRAIGHT AHEAD

BOLT
HEAD   019

WINKING PRAWN

WINKING PRAWN

50 MINS

50 MINS

BOLT HEAD

BOLT HEAD

10am-4pm, rest of year Mon-Sat 10am-3pm) is at the Market St end of Fore St.

For **internet** head to the library (☎ 01548-843423; Tue 2-5.30pm, Wed 9.30am-1pm, Thur 11am-5.30pm; WI-FI; internet £1 for 30 mins, £4 for up to 2hrs with guest ticket) at Cliff House, Cliff Rd.

The **post office** is inside the Spar **supermarket** (Mon-Sat 7am-10pm, Sun 8am-10pm) on Loring Rd. There's a free-to-use **ATM** in the car park beside The Kings Arms (see Where to eat) and one that charges for withdrawals inside The Fortescue Inn (see Where to eat). For a **pharmacy** there's a Boots (Mon-Fri 9am-6pm, Sat 9am-5pm, Sun 10am-6pm) on Fore St.

Transport

[See also pp50-4] The town is connected to Kingsbridge via Tally Ho Coaches' regular No 606 **bus** service and on a Sunday via Stagecoach's 164.

For a **taxi**, try Salcombe and District Taxi Company (also known as Taxi Mike; ☎ 0771-451 2516, 🖳 www.salcombeand districttaxico.co.uk), or Clark Cars (☎ 01548-842914).

Where to stay

Campers need to walk about 1½ miles out of town to reach *Ilton Farm Campsite* (☎ 01548-843635, 🖳 iltonfarmcampsite.word press.com; WI-FI; 🐾 on lead) – take the pavement alongside the A381 and you'll eventually see a signpost for the campsite on your right. A basic pitch costs £10-15 for a tent and up to two adults, depending on the season, and there are showers (20p). Tallyho's No 606 bus (see box p54) stops by the junction to the campsite.

Finding a **B&B** that allows you to book in advance for one night only, and

isn't a long trudge from town, is not as easy as you'd hope. One option is the pub, *Victoria Inn* (☎ 01548-842604, 🖳 victoria inn-salcombe.co.uk; 1D/1T; WI-FI; room only £25-45pp, sgl occ full room rate), on Fore St, although it doesn't provide breakfast. The two rooms do have character, though, having been built in the grounds of the pub and together christened 'The Hobbit House' – watch your head as you enter through the front door! Another pub with rooms is *The Fortescue Inn* (☎ 01548-842868, 🖳 thefortsalcombe.co.uk; 6D; 🛁; WI-FI; 🐾; £40-70pp, sgl occ rates on request); rates here include a full English breakfast.

Rocarno (☎ 01548-842732, 🖳 www .rocarno.co.uk; 1T/1D; WI-FI; from £38pp, sgl occ from £50) isn't anything out of the ordinary but they are more central than some, and welcome coast-path walkers. Not far away is *Waverley* (☎ 01548-842633, 🖳 waverleybandb.co.uk; 2D/2D or T/2Tr; WI-FI; 🐾; £35-45pp, sgl occ from £50; Mar-Nov), one of the few that allows dogs to stay.

With a minimum of a two-night stay and a stiff walk up from the centre, is *Little Hill House* (☎ 01548-842530, 🖳 littlehill house.co.uk; 1D private facilities; 🛁; WI-FI; from £37.50pp, sgl occ negotiable), on the road of the same name. *Fo'c'sle* (☎ 01548-843243, 🖳 bedandbreakfastsalcom be.co.uk; 2D or T/1Qd; 🛁; WI-FI; 🐾; from £80pp, sgl occ from £50), on Onslow Rd, offers both self-catering and B&B.

Where to eat and drink

Salcombe is awash with eateries, most of which are on or just off Fore St.

Delis & takeaways If a quick sandwich and a sit down on a bench is what you're

---

❑ **Where to stay: the details**
Unless specified, B&B-style accommodation is either en suite or has private facilities; 🛁 means at least one room has a bath; 🐾 signifies that dogs are welcome in at least one room but always by prior arrangement, an additional charge may also be payable; WI-FI means wi-fi is available in the property, though not always (reliably) in every room.

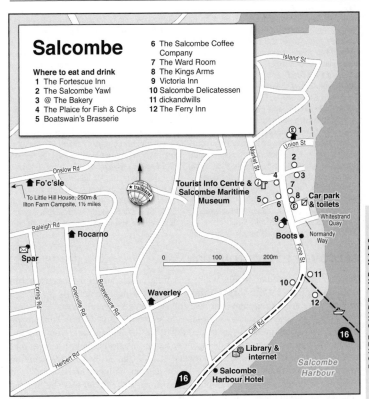

Salcombe

Where to eat and drink
1 The Fortescue Inn
2 The Salcombe Yawl
3 @ The Bakery
4 The Plaice for Fish & Chips
5 Boatswain's Brasserie
6 The Salcombe Coffee Company
7 The Ward Room
8 The Kings Arms
9 Victoria Inn
10 Salcombe Delicatessen
11 dickandwills
12 The Ferry Inn

ROUTE GUIDE AND MAPS

after *Salcombe Delicatessen* (☎ 01548-842332, 🖥 salcombedeli.co.uk; Mon-Sat 9am-5pm, Sun 9am-4pm, winter daily 10am-3pm), at 52 Fore St, is just the ticket. They also do pasties and takeaway tea and coffee. Further on, at 10a Fore St, *The Salcombe Yawl* (☎ 01548-842143; daily 8am-5pm), does sandwiches such as Parma ham, breast of chicken and avocado (£4.95), whilst practically opposite is *@ The Bakery* (☎ 01548-843003; daily June-Aug 8am-5pm, rest of year 8am-3/3.30pm but likely to be closed in Jan), which as well as serving pasties and sandwiches also sells typical deli produce.

The Plaice for Fish & Chips (☎ 01548-843693; Feb half-term to end Oct daily noon-3pm & 4-9/9.30pm, school summer holidays open all day) is a popular takeaway chippy (though they also do pizza) on Fore St, which has a sit-down restaurant section too.

Cafés, pubs & restaurants Breakfasts and **café** lunches are available at *The Salcombe Coffee Company* (☎ 01548-842319; WI-FI; summer Mon-Fri 9am-4pm, Sat & Sun to 5pm, winter hours variable), on Fore St. They do a great bacon or sausage bap (£4.95) as well as crab sandwiches (£9.95). In summer, they also serve bistro-style evening meals (Thur-Mon 6-9.30pm).

At 19 Fore St, through Crew Clothing shop, is *The Ward Room* (☎ 01548-843333;

WI-FI; 🐾 daytime only; Mon-Sat 9am-5pm, Sun 10am-4pm) where drinks, cakes, cream teas and views over the harbour are all on offer. They also do evening meals in summer (Tue-Sat 6-9.30pm).

For **pub food** next to the ferry passenger terminal (and thus the path) *The Ferry Inn* (☎ 01548-844000; WI-FI but not always reliable; 🐾; food Mon-Fri noon-3pm & 6-9pm, Sat & Sun noon-9pm) is hard to beat in terms of location, especially if you take advantage of the waterside back terrace. Mains (£11-17) include mussels and prawns as well as pub classics such as steak and ale pie. Other pubs include the charming *Victoria Inn* (see Where to stay; WI-FI; 🐾; food served daily noon-9pm) which welcomes dogs and has a great beer garden, *The Kings Arms* (☎ 01548-842202; WI-FI; 🐾; food daily noon-2.30pm & 6-9pm but

hours can vary), which also has a garden, and *The Fortescue Inn* (see Where to stay; WI-FI; 🐾; food daily noon-9.30pm), on Union St, which is the place to go for stone-baked pizza and occasionally has live music.

For a **restaurant** meal, head to *dickandwills* (☎ 01548-843408, 🖥 dickand wills.co.uk; food daily noon-1.45pm & 6-8.45pm, Nov-Feb Thur-Sat only), a smart waterside brasserie and bar where you can have lunchtime tapas (from £6) or top-quality evening mains (£16-24). Or else try *Boatswain's Brasserie* (☎ 01548-842189; Feb half-term to Oct half-term daily 6.30-9/10pm but check as the hours can vary), a fine, relaxed establishment tucked away off Fore St down Russell Court. Expect excellent service and a good choice of seafood.

SALCOMBE TO SLAPTON TURN   [MAPS 16-22]

Another stage, another lovely walk; this time consisting of **14¼ reasonably untaxing miles (23km; 4hrs 35mins)**, a few of which are actually iron flat – though there are just enough sharp ascents, too, to keep you honest.

This stage also boasts several places to stop and get some refreshments on the way and some great places to bed down for the night should you come to the justifiable conclusion that the scenery along this stretch is just too good to be hurrying through. These settlements include the idiosyncratic, camping hotspot of East Prawle and the one-street seafront villages of Beesands and Torcross. These places are undoubtedly charming in their own way; but it's the countryside around here that truly makes the heart soar and stays in the memory long after you've finished this walk.

The route
As has become traditional on this trek, before you even begin walking you have to cross a stretch of water, in this case by catching the boat to **East Portlemouth**. The **ferry** (Mon-Fri 8am-6.30pm, Sat, Sun & Bank Hols 8.30am-6.30pm; £1.60; 🐾 free) shuttles back and forth continuously all day (although only half-hourly or hourly during quiet periods). In summer (Apr-Oct) it leaves from beside The Ferry Inn. In winter (Nov-Mar) it leaves from Whitestrand Quay.

Back on *terra firma*, on your left is *The Venus Take Away* (☎ 01548-843558, 🖥 lovingthebeach.co.uk; Jun-Aug daily 9am-6pm, Easter-Jun & Sep 10am-5pm; check website for rest of year), another takeaway-only outlet of The Venus café chain, where you can buy hot drinks, paninis and pasties as well as cakes and ice-creams. Turn right when you step off the ferry, however, and you'll pick up the trail along the tree-shaded tarmac leading to **Mill Bay**.

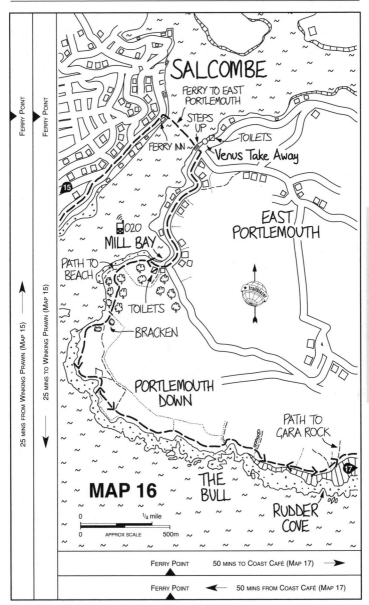

The woods mark the start of a relatively easy, largely flat, very pleasant and pretty spectacular south-easterly amble. The path takes on a decidedly porcine theme, passing **Pig's Nose** and **Ham Stone** before reaching (after one of the larger climbs of the day) **Gammon Head**.

On the way you'll pass, on your left, an empty conical **thatched hut** (a great shelter in rain), behind which you'll find *Coast* (☎ 01548-845946; daily 9.30am-5pm, July & Aug Fri & Sat till 10pm but sometimes also other evenings, check in advance), a clifftop café-restaurant that's part of a small holiday complex known as Gara Rock (🖥 gararock.com).

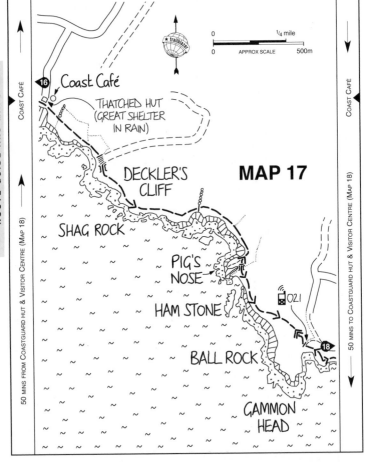

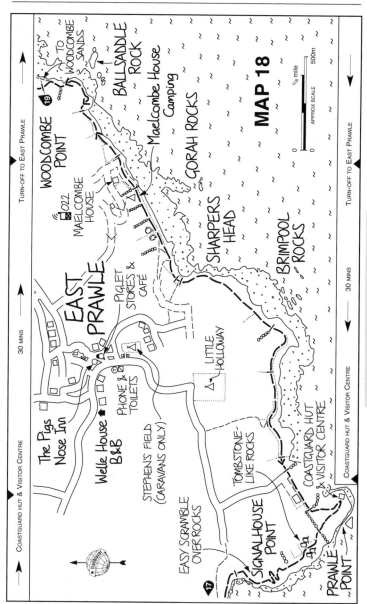

TURN-OFF TO EAST PRAWLE

TURN-OFF TO EAST PRAWLE

TO WOODCOMBE SANDS

19

WOODCOMBE POINT

BALLSADDLE ROCK

Maelcombe House Camping

O22

MAELCOMBE HOUSE

GORAH ROCKS

MAP 18

0 500m

0 ¼ mile

APPROX SCALE

EAST PRAWLE

PIGLET STORES & CAFÉ

SHARPERS HEAD

BRIMPOOL ROCKS

30 MINS

30 MINS

The Pigs Nose Inn

Welle House B&B

PHONE & TOILETS

STEPHEN'S FIELD (CARAVANS ONLY)

LITTLE HOLLOWAY

TOMBSTONE-LIKE ROCKS

COASTGUARD HUT & VISITOR CENTRE

EASY SCRAMBLE OVER ROCKS

SIGNALHOUSE POINT

PRAWLE POINT

17

Trailblazer

COASTGUARD HUT & VISITOR CENTRE

COASTGUARD HUT & VISITOR CENTRE

More largely flat walking follows before a steady ascent leads to the **Coastguard Hut** at **Prawle Point**, complete with its own small **Visitor Centre** (daily 9am-5pm). Descending from here, there is now a very flat section that hugs the coast, contouring round fields, passing the turn-off to **East Prawle**.

EAST PRAWLE   [Map 18, p127]

It's a steep climb up from the path to Devon's southernmost village – but for campers (in July and August at least) and for those who take delight in ancient, isolated and offbeat pubs, the exertions are worth it.

The centre of this idiosyncratic village is the fabulously eccentric pub, *The Pigs Nose Inn* (☎ 01548-511209, 🖳 pigsnose inn.co.uk; bar June-end Aug Mon-Thur noon-3pm & 5-11.30pm, Fri-Sat noon-11.30pm, Sun noon-10.30pm, Sep-Jun Mon-Sat noon-3pm & 6.30-11.30pm, Sun to 10.30pm; food served daily noon-2pm & 6-9pm; WI-FI; 🐾), often voted best pub in south Devon. Overlooking the village green, this 500-year-old establishment used to be a haunt of smugglers who would store their booty here. Complete with board games, live music, a pool room, a knitting corner and piggy paraphernalia galore, it's the kind of quirky place you'll be telling your friends about long after you've returned home. As well as serving a fine choice of local ales (from behind an unusually low bar) they offer an uncomplicated menu of pub-grub mains (fish & chips, chilli con carne, vegetable lasagne etc) plus pub-lunch sandwiches. As if that's not enough, they even have **showers** (£2) and self-service **laundry facilities** (£3 wash, £3 dry) for passing hikers and campers.

Directly opposite is the well-stocked **Piglet Stores** (daily 9am-4pm) and the ever-so-cute *Piglet Café* (same hours), which does bacon baps (£4.50), cream teas

(£5.95) and light lunches (£6.50-8) and has a couple of picnic tables beside the village green.

During July and August East Prawle is something of a Mecca for **campers** with a number of fields opened up informally for basic tent pitches, including two run by *Mollie Tucker* (☎ 01548-511422, 🖳 east prawlefarmholidays.co.uk). Her 'Stephen's Field' is usually for caravans only, but 'Little Hollaway' is for tents (£3 for a hiker and tent; 🐾 if tethered) – simply pitch your tent and Mrs Tucker will come round in the morning to collect your cash. There are portacabin toilets (no toilet paper), a washing-up sink and drinking taps, but no showers. However, you can shower in the pub.

South-east of the village, right down on the coast path, *Maelcombe House Camping* (£7 per tent) offers a wild-camping field within the grand grounds of Maelcombe House. It's a wonderful location, but the only facility here is a single drinking tap; there aren't even any toilets. Owners ask that campers place their pitch fees in an honesty box that's tied to a gate. They then promise to pass on the money to Devon Air Ambulance Trust (🖳 daat.org).

For **B&B**, the only option is *Welle House* (☎ 01548-511151, 🖳 wellehouse.co .uk; 1D/1D or T/1T/1Qd; 🛏; WI-FI; 🐾; from £33pp, sgl occ rates on request); friendly and unfussy. But note, they don't usually take one-night bookings at weekends in high season unless there is some last-minute availability.

Those sticking to the path will continue past Maelcombe House (see above) before emerging at *Lannacombe Farm B&B* (☎ 01548-511158; 1T/1D, shared bathroom; 🛏; 🐾; £30-35pp; Feb-Oct) and its lovely beach. The farm also has a **campsite** (£10 per pitch) but no toilet or shower facilities. Booking is essential in the summer months.

After leaving pretty Lannacombe Beach, a steady ascent through the nature trail of 600-year-old **Down Farm** follows, the trail passing through an area

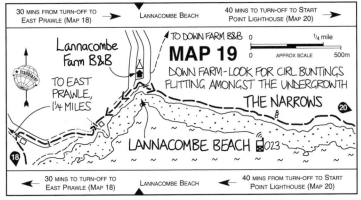

Lannacombe Farm B&B

TO EAST PRAWLE, 1¼ MILES

TO DOWN FARM B&B

MAP 19

0   ¼ mile
0   APPROX SCALE   500m

DOWN FARM - LOOK FOR CIRL BUNTINGS FLITTING AMONGST THE UNDERGROWTH

THE NARROWS

LANNACOMBE BEACH ☐023

ROUTE GUIDE AND MAPS

☐ The Destruction of Old Hallsands

Set precariously between sea and cliff, the existence of Hallsands (or Old Hallsands as we must call now it to distinguish it from the clifftop village that still stands) was always a perilous one. Its eventual demise, however, became the subject of controversy and legal disputes that rumble on even to this day.

Originally founded sometime in the 18th century, by the time of its destruction there were 37 houses in Old Hallsands and, according to the 1891 census, 159 inhabitants living in them, most of whom made their living by fishing. The pebble beach was all that separated the village from the often tempestuous tides that pounded the shoreline of southern Devon.

That beach, however, was largely removed in the 1890s by Sir John Jackson Ltd, a huge engineering firm that had recently received permission to dredge for shingle along the shoreline between Hallsands and Beesands. The locals were very unhappy with the granting of this licence, complaining that the dredging would cause damage to their crab pots, disturb the fish and might also cause damage to their houses.

Little did they know the full extent of that damage. To ameliorate their tempers, Sir John Jackson Ltd agreed to pay the villagers £125 for every year the dredging continued. It wasn't until 1900, however, that it dawned on everyone how slight this reward was. By then, the sea wall had washed away and the locals were complaining to their MP about the damage being caused. By this time the beach had also fallen by an estimated 7-12ft because of the dredging work, and a report concluded that '*in the event of a heavy gale from the East...few houses will not be flooded, if not seriously damaged*'. The work was only stopped in 1902, however, when the villagers decided upon direct action and prevented the dredgers from landing.

Unfortunately, by then, the damage had been done and in 1903 the engineers were forced to compensate the owners of six houses that had been lost to the sea, since the newly lowered beach was no longer an effective barrier against time and tide. Further huge storms in 1917 washed the village away, leaving only one building standing. Miraculously, however, no-one in the village was killed during these storms – though the village itself never recovered.

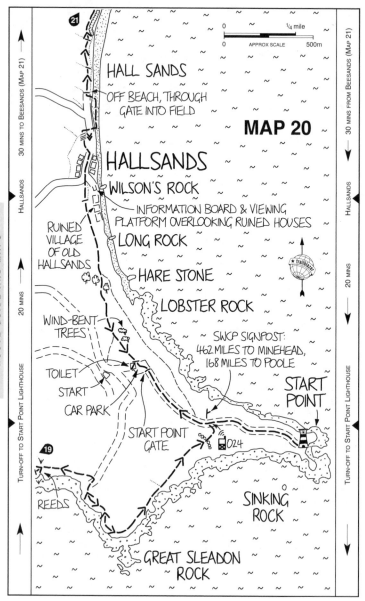

30 MINS TO BEESANDS (MAP 21)

30 MINS FROM BEESANDS (MAP 21)

21

0 .... 1/4 mile

0 .... 500m

APPROX SCALE

HALL SANDS

OFF BEACH, THROUGH
GATE INTO FIELD

MAP 20

HALLSANDS

WILSON'S ROCK

INFORMATION BOARD & VIEWING
PLATFORM OVERLOOKING RUINED HOUSES

RUINED
VILLAGE
OF OLD
HALLSANDS

LONG ROCK

HARE STONE

LOBSTER ROCK

N
trailblazer

WIND-BENT
TREES

SWCP SIGNPOST:
462 MILES TO MINEHEAD,
168 MILES TO POOLE

TOILET

START
CAR PARK

START
POINT

19

START POINT
GATE

024

SINKING
ROCK

REEDS

GREAT SLEADON
ROCK

HALLSANDS   20 MINS

HALLSANDS   20 MINS

ROUTE GUIDE AND MAPS

TURN-OFF TO START POINT LIGHTHOUSE

TURN-OFF TO START POINT LIGHTHOUSE

specifically preserved for the benefit of the declining population of **cirl buntings** (see p71). ***Down Farm B&B*** (☎ 01548-511234, 🖳 downfarm.co.uk; 1D/1D or T/1Qd with double bed and bunk beds; 🛏; WI-FI; 🐾; £37.50-50pp, sgl occ from £45) can be accessed from a signposted path near Lannacombe Beach.

After a few ups and downs, the path soon climbs steadily towards **Start Point Lighthouse** (open sporadically throughout the year, though most days in Jul & Aug; £5), though walkers will probably be more interested in photographing the nearby signpost that states that there are 168 miles left to Poole (or, for those aiming to complete the whole trail and are heading in the other direction, 462 miles to Minehead in Somerset).

The path now heads towards and then through a car park on its way to **Hallsands**; it's worth pausing here awhile to look over the devastated and abandoned village of Old Hallsands (see box p129), standing hard against the cliffs below. There's a fascinating **information board** here, detailing the village's harrowing story. It's a relatively easy stroll from here to Beesands – and its pub.

BEESANDS   [Map 21, p132]

Derived from 'Bay Sands', Beesands is a typically tiny Devonian settlement, consisting of around 50 houses, 100 people, a church, snack shack and a good pub.

There's accommodation at both the pub and in a self-contained garden annex at ***Valseph B&B*** (☎ 01548-580650, 🖳 bee sandsbandb.co.uk; 1D; WI-FI; Easter-Oct/ Nov; from £37.50pp, sgl occ room rate), which overlooks the village green.

The Cricket Inn (☎ 01548-580215, room reservations ☎ 01548-581457, 🖳 the cricketinn.com; 3D/2T/1Tr/1Qd; WI-FI; 🐾 bar only; Feb-Dec; £55-75pp, sgl occ room rate) is the social centre of the village, a fine place that dates back to the 19th century but is thoroughly up to date, with modern rooms named after English cricket grounds or famous English cricketers; they don't, however, take one-night bookings at weekends. The award-winning **food** (daily noon-2.30pm & 6-8.30pm; summer school holidays also 3-5.30pm) focuses on fresh and local seafood.

Just a little way along the seafront is ***Britannia @ The Beach*** (☎ 01548-581168, 🖳 britanniaathebeach.co.uk; Mar-Oct Tue-Sun 10am-8/8.30pm, reduced hours in winter), a friendly **shop-cum-café** specialising in locally caught seafood and shellfish, but also serving breakfasts, sandwiches and the like. There's a takeaway window for those in a hurry, and the small shop sells groceries and toiletries.

A reasonably sharp up-and-downer brings you to the next settlement on the route, **Torcross**, with even more places at which to eat.

TORCROSS   [Map 21, p132]

Tiny Torcross consists of a busy promenade lining the sea wall – but very little behind. Back from the seafront there is a **post office** (Mon-Tue & Thur-Fri 9am-4pm, Sat 9am-1pm) inside the **village store** (Mon-Fri 7am-4.15pm, Sat 7am-1pm, Sun 8am-1pm), a **bus stop** and, incongruously, a **WWII tank** (see box p134) – but it's on the promenade that the action happens.

Stagecoach's No 3 **bus service** (see pp50-4) stops in Torcross on its journey between Plymouth and Dartmouth.

Here you'll find several places to eat including the thatched pub, ***Start Bay Inn*** (☎ 01548-580553, 🖳 startbayinn.co.uk; 🐾 out of food hours only; food Mon-Fri 11.30am-2.15pm & 6-10pm, Sat & Sun 11.30am-10pm) where you can scoff on

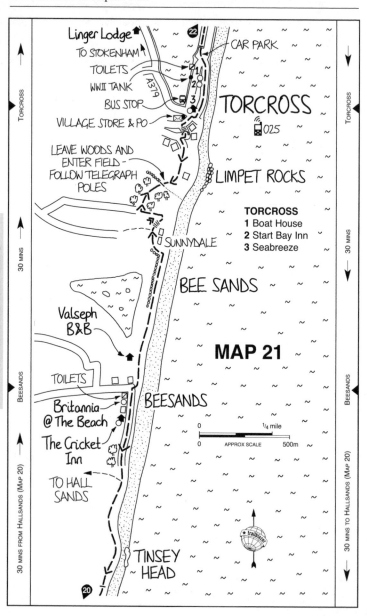

Linger Lodge
TO STOKENHAM
TOILETS
WWII TANK
BUS STOP
VILLAGE STORE & PO

CAR PARK

A379

TORCROSS

025

LEAVE WOODS AND
ENTER FIELD -
FOLLOW TELEGRAPH
POLES

LIMPET ROCKS

TORCROSS
1 Boat House
2 Start Bay Inn
3 Seabreeze

SUNNYDALE

BEE SANDS

Valseph
B&B

MAP 21

TOILETS

BEESANDS

Britannia
@ The Beach

The Cricket
Inn

0   ¼ mile

0   500m
APPROX SCALE

TO HALL
SANDS

TINSEY
HEAD

20

★ trailblazer

TORCROSS

30 MINS

BEESANDS

30 MINS FROM HALLSANDS (MAP 20)

TORCROSS

30 MINS

BEESANDS

30 MINS TO HALLSANDS (MAP 20)

any number of fish specials plus pub-grub favourites such as ham & chips (£8.95). Next door, *Boat House* (☎ 01548-580747, 🖥 torcrossboathouse.com; 🐾; food daily June-Sep noon-8/9pm, coffee from 11am, rest of year 9.30/10am-5pm) is a family-friendly café serving seafood, burgers and pizza. Along the same strip is another nice café, the slightly smarter *Seabreeze* (☎ 01548-580697, 🖥 seabreezebreaks.com; daily summer 9.30am-4.30pm, winter days/hours variable), which does a fine line in cakes, scones and pancakes, as well as a decent cup of coffee. Seabreeze also offers seaview **accommodation** (1D/1T; 🛏; WI-FI; £60-70pp, sgl occ £110-130) though not usually just for one night – but it's always worth calling to see.

Away from the front, is *Linger Lodge* (☎ 01548-580599, 🖥 lingerlodge.co.uk; 2D; 🛏; WI-FI; £44-46.50pp, sgl occ £65-80), occupying an elevated position on the main A379 road that allows it to make the most of the views across Slapton Ley. Note that they only accept advance bookings for a minimum of two nights.

For those who want to push on still further, an entirely horizontal 1½-mile stroll leads to **Slapton Turn**, the name given for the turn-off to the pretty village of **Slapton** (see below), about three-quarters of a mile inland.

SLAPTON   [Map 22, p135]

A quiet little huddle of historic buildings, Slapton (🖥 slapton.org) lies about a mile off the coast path on the other side of the Ley from the beach which both share its name. The village is perhaps most famous for being evacuated to allow American GIs to stay (see box p134). Facilities-wise, there's not much to the place other than the **village shop** (Mon, Tue, Thur & Fri 8am-12.45pm & 2.15-5pm, Wed 8am-12.45pm, Sat 8am-12.45pm & 2.15-4pm, Sun 9-11.45am), but it does boast a couple of fine pubs and a very good campsite, as well as some B&Bs.

Transport-wise, Stagecoach's No 3 **bus service** is easily accessed from Slapton

Turn and also less frequently from the village itself; see pp50-4 for details.

On the way into the village is *Slapton Sands Camping & Caravanning Club Site* (☎ 01548-580538, 🖥 campingandcaravanningclub.co.uk; from £7.50pp; WI-FI; 🐾; Mar/Apr to end Oct/early Nov), a well-run, clean site with a laundry, a small shop and marvellous sea views.

There's **B&B** at the other end of the village at the fascinating *Tower Inn* (☎ 01548-580216, 🖥 www.thetowerinn.com; 3D; WI-FI; 🐾; from £45pp, sgl occ from £70), a 14th-century building which sits under the shadow of a striking, half-ruined tower that was once part of a monastery

---

❑ **Slapton Ley National Nature Reserve**   **Map 22, p135**

Separated from the sea by only the narrowest sliver of beach and tarmac, Slapton Ley can boast of being the largest freshwater lake in the South-West. A national nature reserve (🖥 slnnr.org.uk), the area plays host to badgers, dormice, bats and otters; unsurprisingly, however, it's the birdlife for which the reserve is famous, with the lake a natural staging post for migrants.

One resident of Slapton Ley is **Cetti's warbler** (*Cettia cetti*), which can often be seen from the old stone bridge near Slapton Turn, where two males often nest (one on either side). As an insect-eating non-migrant, the warbler can suffer during very cold winters but at Slapton the population is stable at around 40 singing males. **Greater crested grebes** (*Podiceps cristatus*) and **cirl buntings** (*Emberiza cirlus*; around four pairs) also live near the lake. See also pp68-72.

linked to the nearby church via a bridge spanning the village road. The inn was built to house the workers who built the monastery, so is actually older than the tower itself, which sadly is no longer safe to enter, but still retains a mysterious charm. They serve a number of local ales and some cracking **food** (daily noon-2.30pm & 6.30-9.30pm, winter hours more limited & closed on a Sunday evening).

Also dating back to the 14th century, though less dramatic in appearance, is *The*

Queens Arms (☎ 01548-580800, 🖥 queens armsslapton.co.uk; bar daily noon-3pm & Mon-Sat 5.30-11pm, Sun 6-10.30pm; food served daily noon-2pm & 5.30-9pm; WI-FI; 🐾), a small, old and exceptionally friendly pub – especially to (well-behaved) dogs, who sometimes outnumber the human patrons. The food here is excellent too, though the pub's popularity (and small size) means you sometimes have to wait a while for both a seat and your meal.

SLAPTON TURN TO DARTMOUTH [MAPS 22-25]

This lovely **8¾-mile (14km; 3hrs 25mins)** stage is full of interest and, given the rugged nature of much of this coastline, surprisingly straightforward too. True, there are several climbs – but they are uniformly short and nearly always

---

❏ **Operation Tiger**

As tranquil and picturesque as Slapton Sands and its namesake village may appear today, during World War II this whole area was converted into a 'practice ground' for 30,000 American troops prior to the Normandy landings. The site was chosen because of its similarity to Utah Beach in Normandy – namely a gravel beach followed by a thin ribbon of land and a lake – where the plan was that the troops would land during D-Day. As a result of this likeness, the 3000 residents of Slapton and Torcross – some of whom had never left their village before – were forced to evacuate.

While the landings were, of course, ultimately successful, the rehearsal itself was marred by tragedy on a huge scale. Despite protection from the Royal Navy, a convoy of eight Allied ships heading to this 'rehearsal' was attacked by nine German E-Boats, leading to the loss of 638 servicemen. Worse was to follow: when the remaining boats reached land, a further 308 personnel were killed by – unbelievably – friendly fire, following an order by Dwight Eisenhower to use live ammunition to harden the troops! As a result of the tragedy the landings were almost cancelled altogether. Ten men were unaccounted for following the Battle of Lyme Bay (as it became known) and with the generals afraid that they may have been picked up by the Germans and forced to reveal the plans, the invasion was close to being cancelled until the bodies of each of these 10 men were found.

Those who witnessed the tragic events of April 28th, 1943, were sworn to secrecy and indeed the incident was pretty well covered up by the authorities. Indeed, if it wasn't for local resident Ken Small, who used to find evidence of Operation Tiger while beachcombing in southern Devon in the '70s, it's uncertain whether there would be any memorial to the battle at all. Ken made it his ambition to find out exactly what had happened that day and, having done so, decided to try to commemorate the event. The Sherman DD tank at the eastern end of Torcross was bought by Ken and raised from the seabed in 1984, and now stands as a tribute to the 946 US servicemen who died that day. A second memorial, the obelisk-like **monument** by Slapton Turn, was erected to thank the people of the local area for abandoning their homes whilst the American GIs moved in. In recent times people have placed stones at its base emblazoned with messages and memorials for those serving in contemporary wars.

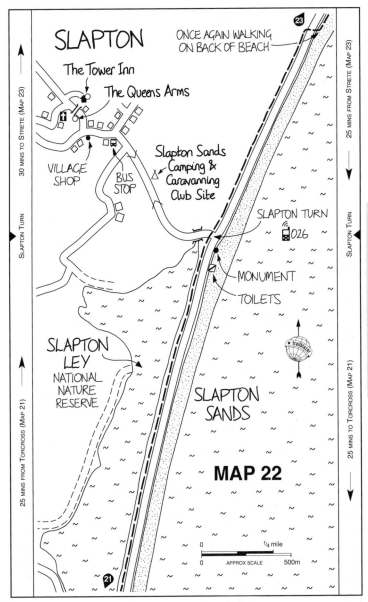

SLAPTON

The Tower Inn

The Queens Arms

ONCE AGAIN WALKING
ON BACK OF BEACH

VILLAGE
SHOP

BUS
STOP

Slapton Sands
Camping &
Caravaning
Club Site

SLAPTON TURN

026

MONUMENT

TOILETS

SLAPTON
LEY
NATIONAL
NATURE
RESERVE

SLAPTON
SANDS

MAP 22

0   1/4 mile
0   APPROX SCALE   500m

30 MINS TO STRETE (MAP 23)   SLAPTON TURN   25 MINS FROM TORCROSS (MAP 21)

25 MINS FROM STRETE (MAP 23)   SLAPTON TURN   25 MINS TO TORCROSS (MAP 21)

ROUTE GUIDE AND MAPS

gentle. Indeed, the only difficulty with this stage is the stretch after the tourist beach at Blackpool Sands, much of which is undertaken on a busy and pavement-less main road. As with the previous stage, there are several places to stop and eat at including the villages of Strete and Stoke Fleming – as well as a beach or two where you can kick off your boots and feel the sand between your toes.

The route

This stage starts with a stroll beside the road at Slapton Sands. With the nature reserve on one side and a lovely pebbled shore on the other, it's hard to know on which side of the road to walk, though the official coast path sticks to the nature reserve side.

At the end, as the road bends left to climb up to **Strete**, the path crosses the road to begin its own climb up to the village by the **Lime Coffee Company van** (🖳 limecoffeeco.com; Easter to end Oct but weather dependent). The gentle climb eventually stiffens into a series of steep switchbacks that brings you up onto the road leading into Strete.

STRETE [Map 23]

Strete was another settlement where the residents were evacuated for Operation Tiger (see box on p134) during WWII and if you walk through here in the low season, it can feel as if they never came back. It's a sleepy place at the best of times, the only activity – save for the occasional inhabitant emerging to mow their lawns or tend to their begonias – focusing around **Strete Post Office and Stores** (☎ 01803-770225; Mon-Sat 7am-5.30pm, Sun 8am-1pm; post office Mon & Wed-Sat 9am-5.30pm, Tue 9am-1pm).

Stagecoach's No 3 **bus service** (see pp50-4) passes through Strete en route between Plymouth and Dartmouth.

Campers need to walk north of the village, past The Laughing Monk (see opposite), to *Manor Farm Campsite* (☎ 01548-511441, 🖳 manorfarmstrete.co.uk; wi-fi; 🐾 under control at all times; minimum charge £10-12 for hiker and tent, if two people or more £7.25pp; Mar-end Oct) which has a lovely six-acre slope of green fields running down in the direction of the sea. Facilities include a full kitchen and washing machine, a TV room and coin-operated showers. Note that the site has a naturist area, which is separated only by a low fence.

For **B&B**, the most central option is *Roxburgh B&B* (☎ 01803-770870, 🖳 roxburghhouse.co.uk; 2D/1T; £40-45pp, sgl occ £55-65; 🛁; wi-fi; 🐾), a lovely Victorian property with two double rooms in the house and a twin room in a converted barn in the walled garden.

Nearby, *Strete Barton House* (☎ 01803-770364, 🖳 stretebarton.co.uk; 4D/1D or T/1D in a self-contained cottage; 🛁; wi-fi; 🐾 allowed in cottage; Feb-Nov; £52.50-85pp, sgl occ room rate) is a 16th-century manor house with a splendid garden in which to relax after a long day's slog. This is a top-end B&B, with prices to match, and unfortunately they usually take one-night bookings only in November and February to March.

A little further along the road that leads from the middle of the village is *Frogwell* (☎ 01803-770273, 🖳 frogwell.net; 3D; 🛁; wi-fi; room only from £45pp, sgl occ room rate). Set in a great location, this is one of Strete's original houses (it dates back to the 1600s) and it backs on to fields which in turn back on to the sea. They don't provide breakfast and advance bookings must be for a two-night minimum stay.

Sadly the charming village pub, the King's Arms, with its ornate first-floor balcony jutting out over the pavement, had closed down at the time of research, with no word on when, or if it might re-open. Fingers crossed it will open soon because the only other place to eat is a restaurant (albeit it a very good one) that's open

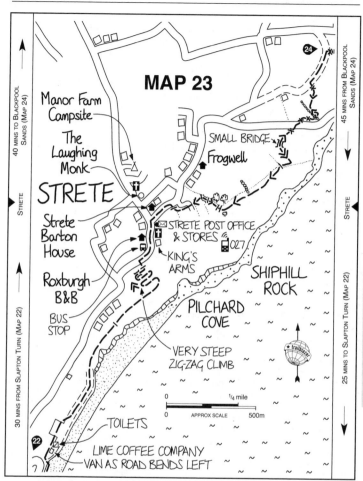

MAP 23

40 MINS TO BLACKPOOL SANDS (MAP 24)

STRETE

30 MINS FROM SLAPTON TURN (MAP 22)

45 MINS FROM BLACKPOOL SANDS (MAP 24)

STRETE

25 MINS TO SLAPTON TURN (MAP 22)

Manor Farm Campsite

The Laughing Monk

STRETE

Strete Barton House

Roxburgh B&B

BUS STOP

SMALL BRIDGE

Frogwell

STRETE POST OFFICE & STORES

027

KING'S ARMS

SHIPHILL ROCK

PILCHARD COVE

VERY STEEP ZIG-ZAG CLIMB

trailblazer

0   ¼ mile
0   APPROX SCALE   500m

TOILETS

22

LIME COFFEE COMPANY
VAN AS ROAD BENDS LEFT

ROUTE GUIDE AND MAPS

evenings only, and only five days a week. **The Laughing Monk** (☎ 01803-770639, 🖥 thelaughingmonkdevon.co.uk; Apr-Sep Tue-Sat 6-9pm, Oct-Nov & Feb-Mar Tue-Sat 6.30-9pm) has won awards for its food, and is housed in an 1839 former school building. Main courses (£16-25) include such delights as slow-roasted Dartmoor pork belly, and pan-fried fillet of south-coast turbot.

❏ **Important note – walking times**
All times in this book refer only to the time spent walking. You will need to add 20-30% to allow for rests, photography, checking the map, drinking water etc.

From Strete the path passes through several fields which may or may not be filled with cows when you visit, before traversing the vertiginous dip in the earth's surface separating you from the road; it's steep but it's also mercifully very short and, having rejoined the road, you cross it then hug it, strolling alongside the tarmac in lush fields of livestock.

The path leaves the line of the road briefly to cut down to **Blackpool Sands**, yet another gorgeous stretch of sand and home to *Venus Café* (☎ 01803-770209, 🖳 lovingthebeach.co.uk; daily 8.30am-7pm, last orders 5pm), a licensed café with an extensive restaurant menu as well as takeaway items which you can enjoy at tables on the decking overlooking the beach.

From here the path continues along the main road before forking off to the left to follow a quieter lane, past the church into **Stoke Fleming** by The Green Dragon pub.

STOKE FLEMING   [Map 24]

Recorded in the Domesday book as 'Stoc', Stoke Fleming is an ancient village dominated by a church, St Peter's, that's almost as old as the village itself, with written references dating back to 1272; George Parker Bidder, the famous engineer who worked with George Stephenson in the early days of steam railways, is buried in the graveyard.

Facilities are limited to the **village shop and post office** (shop Mon, Tue, Thur & Fri 8am-5.30pm, Wed 8am-1pm, Sat 8.30am-3pm, Sun 9am-3pm), and the small **shop** (Apr-May Mon-Sat 8am-5pm, Jun-Sep Mon-Sat 8am-6pm, Sun 8-11am & 3-6pm, Oct-Mar Mon-Fri 8am-5pm, Sat 9am-noon) in reception at the holiday park.

There's **internet** access at the library (Mon & Thur 3-5pm, Tue 10.30am-12.30pm), which is by a sports field that contains, unusually, a **pétanque** piste, home to Dartmouth Club de Pétanque (🖳 dartmouthpetanque.uk).

The only **bus service** to call here is Stagecoach's No 3 (Plymouth to Dartmouth); see also pp50-4.

The local pub, *The Green Dragon* (☎ 01803-770238, 🖳 greendragonsf.co.uk), is a lovely old snug with a stone floor, big fireplace and comfy old sofas to fling your tired frame onto at the end of the day. They stock a selection of west country ales, and their **food** (daily noon-2pm & 6.30-8.30pm) includes locally made venison burger (£10) and a good-value lunchtime cottage pie (£5.50).

Alternatively, you could try *Radius 7* (☎ 01803-770007, 🖳 radius7.co.uk; WI-FI; 🐾 bar only; restaurant Jun-late Aug daily 5-9pm & Sun noon-3pm, May & late Aug-end Oct Mon-Sat 6-9pm & Sun noon-5pm but contact them to check; takeaway also available; bar open all day), a very popular restaurant-bar run by the campsite in high season. It also opens for breakfast (school summer hols daily 8-10.30am, Sep & Oct Fri-Sun). You can also eat at the smart *Stoke Lodge Hotel* (see p140) for lunch (mains £9.45) or dinner (set four-course £32.50).

Accommodation includes a good **campsite** behind Radius 7 restaurant. *Leonard's Cove Holiday Park* (☎ 01803-770206, 🖳 leonardscove.co.uk; WI-FI; May-Sep) charges £15-25 for a tent for up to two people, but in the low season offers hikers a special rate: £10/15 for one/two people. It's well equipped with clean shower blocks, laundry facilities and flat grassy pitches with sea views.

Opposite the campsite, you can get **B&B** at *Channel View* (☎ 01803-770389, 🖳 channelviewguesthouse.com; 2D/2D or T; WI-FI; 🐾; £47.50pp, sgl occ £75), a dog-friendly establishment (they have two dogs themselves) standing opposite the entrance to the campsite. Note that advance bookings for a one-night stay may not be accepted here between April and October.

There is also the smart *Ford's House* (☎ 01803-770105, 🖳 stokefleming.com; 2D; 🛏; WI-FI; Mar-Oct; from £40pp, sgl

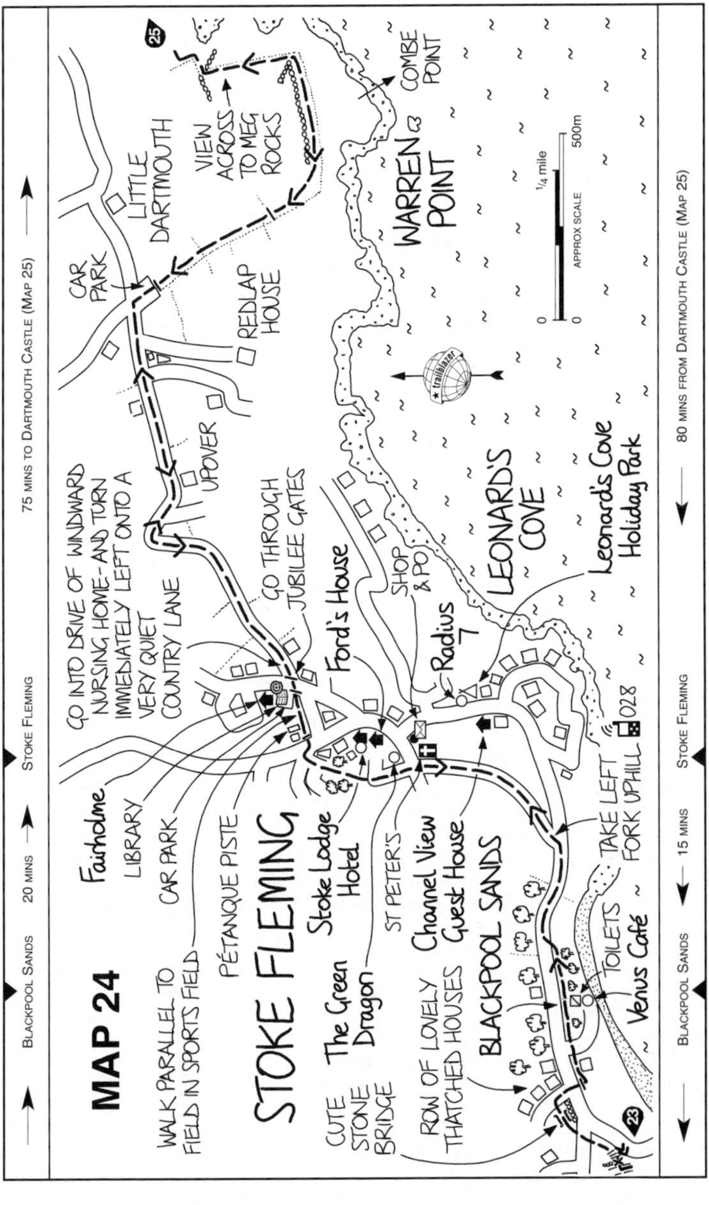
MAP 24
Blackpool Sands
20 mins
Stoke Fleming
75 mins to Dartmouth Castle (Map 25)
Blackpool Sands
15 mins
Stoke Fleming
80 mins from Dartmouth Castle (Map 25)
WALK PARALLEL TO FIELD IN SPORTS FIELD
Fairholme
LIBRARY
CAR PARK
PÉTANQUE PISTE
STOKE FLEMING
Stoke Lodge Hotel
The Green Dragon
CUTE STONE BRIDGE
ROW OF LOVELY THATCHED HOUSES
ST PETER'S
Channel View Guest House
BLACKPOOL SANDS
TOILETS
Venus Café
TAKE LEFT FORK UPHILL
028
GO INTO DRIVE OF WINDWARD NURSING HOME - AND TURN IMMEDIATELY LEFT ONTO A VERY QUIET COUNTRY LANE
GO THROUGH JUBILEE GATES
Ford's House
SHOP & PO
Radius 7
LEONARD'S COVE
Leonard's Cove Holiday Park
UPOVER
REDLAP HOUSE
CAR PARK
LITTLE DARTMOUTH
VIEW ACROSS TO MEG ROCKS
WARREN POINT
COMBE POINT
APPROX SCALE
0
1/4 mile
0
500m
trailblazer
23
25

ROUTE GUIDE AND MAPS

occ from £70), on Dartmouth Rd, while up by the library, *Fairholme* (☎ 01803-770356, 🖳 fairholmedartmouth.co.uk; 2D/1T; WI-FI; from £40pp, sgl occ £60) has smoked salmon and scrambled eggs on the breakfast menu.

Near Ford's House, but a fair way up the price scale, stands *Stoke Lodge Hotel* (☎ 01803-770523, 🖳 www.stokelodge.co.uk; 3S/21D or T; ☜; WI-FI; 🐾 but not in public rooms; £53-69pp, sgl £78-81, sgl occ £91.50-111.50), a smart place set in three acres of gardens, with indoor and outdoor pools and a giant chess set.

The path continues past the pub to a wooded alleyway and then out across the playing fields and their **pétanque piste**. Follow the signposts carefully and you'll eventually leave the village by Windward Nursing Home. The route now follows a very quiet country lane to the National Trust owned **Little Dartmouth** (look out for hares), where you finally get to enjoy a little bit of clifftop walking – once again very gentle – as you stroll round **Blackstone Point** before heading up the Dart via **Dartmouth Castle** and **Warfleet** and on to the lovely town itself.

DARTMOUTH   [map p143]

Dartmouth is a pleasant town; friendly, fascinating and with some lovely medieval streets and a rich history. Its prosperity was founded on the natural deep-water harbour and its accompanying port, the latter having originally been developed by the Normans almost a thousand years ago.

By 1147 that harbour was being used as a muster point for the 164 ships leaving for the Second Crusade – a role it reprised in 1190 during the Third Crusade under King John. (The suburb of Warfleet is said to be so named because of the numerous times fleets have assembled here before heading off to battle.) Home to the Royal Navy since Edward III's reign (1327-77), unsurprisingly the town has often been the target of attacks by foreign foes, a problem exacerbated by the town's secondary reputation as a centre for privateers (officially sanctioned pirates). The twin castles of Dartmouth and Kingswear were built at the end of the 14th century to defend against such assaults, and a chain once stretched

---

❏ **Dartmouth Castle**   [Map 25]
Built in 1388 to protect the town from invasion from the sea, Dartmouth Castle was in use right up to the Second World War. Features include the gun tower – the first, so it is believed, purpose built to carry heavy cannon big enough to sink ships – a Victorian gun battery and, unusually, a church, St Petrox. Doubtless the one aspect of the castle that will linger longest in the memory, however, is the beautiful view it provides of the Dart and the wooded slopes beyond.

The castle (🖳 english-heritage.org.uk; Apr-Sep daily 10am-6pm, Oct daily 10am-5pm, Nov-Mar Sat & Sun only 10am-4pm; £6.60, EH members free) is today owned by English Heritage, which means it's in a fine state of preservation, the displays are interesting and well presented, and the story of the castle is clearly and imaginatively presented.

Outside the castle is *Dartmouth Castle Tearooms* (☎ 01803-833897, 🖳 dartmouthcastletearooms.co.uk; summer daily 9am-5.30pm, winter Fri-Mon 9am-4pm), known as the Castle Light in the mid 19th century when it was built and acted as a form of lighthouse, providing light to ships sailing up the Dart. Now it provides breakfasts (until 11.30am), light lunches (until 3pm) and fabulous views.

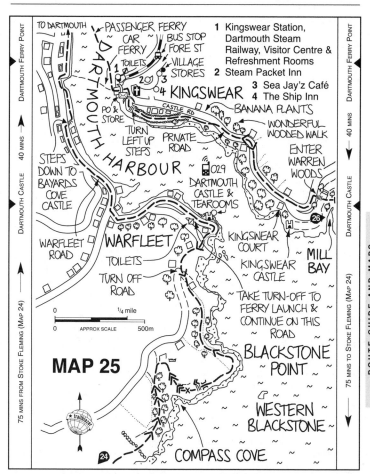

1 Kingswear Station, Dartmouth Steam Railway, Visitor Centre & Refreshment Rooms
2 Steam Packet Inn
3 Sea Jay'z Café
4 The Ship Inn

MAP 25

across the narrow river mouth to prevent invaders sailing straight up to the port.

With such a rich maritime heritage, it's no surprise that the town is home to the only naval college in Britain. **Britannia Royal Naval College** occupies a glorious hilltop building that dates back to the turn of the 19th century; prior to this, the college was based on two large hulks moored in the Dart itself. The college is famous for its royal links: kings George V and VI and the current Prince of Wales and Duke of York all trained here, as did their father, Prince Philip, now the Duke of Edinburgh; indeed, it is said that Prince Philip first met the then Princess Elizabeth (now Queen Elizabeth II), while a student here.

Given its long history and worldwide fame, it comes as something of a surprise to discover just how small the town actually is, with a permanent population of fewer than 6000. Nevertheless, there's enough here, including some great old buildings, to warrant a rest day should time and inclination allow. A significant number of the historic buildings here are listed, including **Butterwalk**, a terrace of rich merchants' houses built in 1640. Their intricately carved wooden fascia is supported on granite columns. Charles II held court here whilst sheltering from storms in 1671 in a room which now forms part of the small but fascinating **Dartmouth Museum** (☎ 01803-832923, 🖥 dartmouthmuseum.org; Easter/Apr-Oct Tue-Sat 10am-4pm, Sun & Mon 1-4pm, rest of year daily noon-3pm; £2).

Dart Music Festival is held here in May and **Dartmouth Food Festival** in October; see p14 for details.

Services

Dartmouth's centre is a compact place and it doesn't take long to get your bearings. Facilities in the centre include a **tourist information centre** (☎ 01803-834224, 🖥 discoverdartmouth.com; Mon-Tue & Thur-Sat 10am-4pm, Wed 10am-2pm, Sun 11am-2pm, winter hours may vary) in the Engine House on Mayor's Ave, and a **post office** inside a Spar **supermarket** (daily 7am-10pm) on Victoria Rd.

There's also a larger Co-op supermarket (daily 7am-10pm) on Fairfax, a Boots **pharmacy** (Mon-Sat 9am-5.30pm, Sun 10am-4pm), a **launderette** (daily 8am-9pm, service wash 9am-1pm only), on Market St, and **internet** and free wi-fi at Dartmouth Library (Mon, Wed, Sat 9am-1pm, Tue & Fri 9am-5pm, Thur 9am-6pm) in Flavel Arts Centre, which doubles as the local **cinema**.

There are also plenty of **banks** with **ATMs**. For **hiking and camping gear**, try Mountain Warehouse (Mon-Sat 9am-5.30pm, Sun 10am-4.30pm) on Duke St.

Transport

[See also pp50-4] Stagecoach's No 3 **bus** service connects the town with Kingsbridge and Plymouth as well as a number of coastal locations along the way. Their X64 goes to Exeter. For destinations to the east it is usually necessary to cross to Kingswear; see p146.

Greenway Ferries operate services from here to Greenway (see box p164) hourly and the journey is shorter than going from Torquay.

Where to stay

There's a decent choice of **B&B** accommodation in Dartmouth (though no campsites or hostels). Unfortunately, by the time you've weeded out those that don't take single-night bookings in advance or are at the upper end of town (and thus quite far for weary walkers), the selection is relatively scant.

On the approach into town, and right by the coast path, *Alf's Rooms* (☎ 01803-835880, 🖥 cafealfresco.co.uk; 3D/one room with bunk beds; WI-FI; 🐾; £37.50-55.50pp, sgl occ room rate but if two-night stay £60-92), is run by the same people behind Café Alf Resco (see Where to Eat) and is accessed either through the café on Lower St, or via 47 Newcomen Rd. They have a room with bunk beds and a double above the café, plus a self-contained studio with river-view terrace on the top floor, and another double in a nearby building. Just round the corner, and right on the coast path on South Embankment, *Eight Bells B&B* (☎ 01803-839506, 🖥 dartmouthbandb .com; 1D/1Qd; 🛏; WI-FI; from £37.50pp, sgl occ £45) naturally has great views of the River Dart.

Very central, *Anzac Street Bistro* (☎ 01803-835515, 🖥 anzacstreetbistro.co.uk; 2D; 🛏; WI-FI; £52.50-55pp, sgl occ from £105), at 2 Anzac St, is another tempting option, especially with the sweet aromas wafting in the air from the restaurant below.

A short walk from here, on Lake St, is *Just B, St Elmo's Cottage* (☎ 01803-834311, 🖥 justbdartmouth.com; 3D; WI-FI; £35-45pp, sgl occ rates on request); an unusual room-only set-up, providing three self-contained doubles, each with its own private access, in a townhouse called St Elmo's Cottage. Rates are room only and although the set-up has a hostel feel to it, the rooms are far from basic and promise a very comfortable stay. Just B also has some self-contained apartments in town; see the website for details.

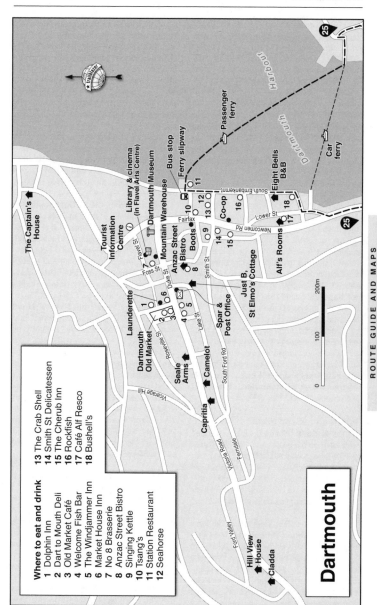

Dartmouth

Where to eat and drink

1 Dolphin Inn
2 Dart to Mouth Deli
3 Old Market Café
4 Welcome Fish Bar
5 The Windjammer Inn
6 Market House Inn
7 No 8 Brasserie
8 Anzac Street Bistro
9 Singing Kettle
10 Tsang's
11 Station Restaurant
12 Seahorse

13 The Crab Shell
14 Smith St Delicatessen
15 The Cherub Inn
16 Rockfish
17 Café Alf Resco
18 Bushell's

ROUTE GUIDE AND MAPS

Most of the rest of the town's B&Bs are centred on nearby Victoria Rd. Closest to the amenities are *Seale Arms* (☎ 01803-832719, 🖥 sealearmsdartmouth.co.uk; 2D/1Tr/one room sleeping up to five; WI-FI; from £40pp, sgl occ from £55), at No 10, *Camelot* (☎ 01803-833805, ☎ 07870-665863, 🖥 jjwright@talktalk.net; 2D/1T; WI-FI; £35-37.50pp, sgl occ £50-75) at No 61; and *Capritia* (☎ 01803-833419, 🖥 capritia.com; 2D/1Tr; WI-FI; £40-47.50pp, sgl occ rates on request), at No 69, although the last two don't usually accept advance bookings for a one-night stay in the main season and at weekends.

As you wander further along Victoria Rd you will also come across *Hill View House* (☎ 01803-839372, 🖥 hillviewdartmouth.co.uk; 1S/3D/1T; ☛; WI-FI; from £35pp, sgl from £47, sgl occ rates on request) at No 76 – whose breakfast may include muffins and banana smoothies; and the delightful and award-winning *Cladda* (☎ 01803-835957, 🖥 cladda-dartmouth.co.uk; 2D/4D or T; ☛; WI-FI; 🐾; £46.50-67.50pp, sgl occ £83-120), at No 90, who welcome four-legged companions.

Just to the north of the centre, meanwhile, *The Captain's House* (☎ 01803-832133, 🖥 captainshouse.co.uk; 1D or T/2D/1Tr; ☛; WI-FI; room only £41-50pp, sgl occ £75-90) is a Grade II listed townhouse offering beautifully furnished rooms but without breakfast.

Where to eat and drink

Cafés & delis Handy for hikers walking into town on the coast path, *Café Alf Resco* (see Where to stay Alf's Rooms; WI-FI; 🐾; daily 7am-2pm) has a slightly Bohemian feel with live music some weekends, graffitied walls and a roadside terrace that's bursting with punters on sunny days. Great coffee too.

Also convenient, right beside the ferry slipway, is *Station Restaurant* (☎ 01803-832125; 🐾; daily 9am-7.30pm, till 5pm in winter) which despite the name is more of a café, offering good-value meals and splendid views down the Dart. It's a pleasant place to while away some time drinking tea and scoffing scones; if something more

substantial is required they also do cod & chips, bangers & mash and the like.

Slightly away from the river, on the old-town streets, *Singing Kettle* (☎ 01803-906068; WI-FI; 🐾; daily Mar-Sep 10am-6pm, contact them for their winter hours) is what one imagines a proper 'tea shoppe' to look like – quaint, old, garlanded with flowers and with a fine selection of cakes and teas.

Hidden further down the lanes, on Foss St, *No 8 Brasserie* (☎ 01803-832999; daily 10am-4.30pm) does breakfasts (from £3), lunches (from £7) and claims to serve the best coffee in town. It also opens some evenings (6-8.30pm).

Dating from 1823, **Dartmouth Old Market** is lovely collection of shops, cafés and stalls, clustered around a large cobblestone square. Its eateries include *Old Market Café* (Mon-Tue & Thur-Sat 7am-4pm, Wed 7am-3pm, Sun 8am-1pm), which does good old fashioned builders' breakfasts, for £7.50, or a more refined smoked mackerel salad, for £6.75. Also in the old market is the wonderful *Dart to Mouth Deli* (☎ 01803-839377; daily summer 7am-4pm, winter hours variable) a family-run place selling jams, cheeses and chutneys, as well as award-winning scones, which you can sit down and sample at the clutch of tables outside.

Other great delis in town include *Smith Street Delicatessen* (Mon-Sat 9am-4.30pm), which also doubles as a café, and *The Crab Shell* (Mon-Sat 10.30am-2.30pm, Sun 11am-2.30pm) a seafood-sandwich specialist on Raleigh St, with crab sandwiches for £5.25.

Pubs Of all the venerable buildings in town, *The Cherub Inn* (☎ 01803-832571, 🖥 the-cherub.co.uk; WI-FI; 🐾; food served in both bar and restaurant daily noon-2pm & 6-9.30pm) is the oldest (c1380) and it retains many of the original features such as old ship timbers. They do a good lunch menu including the renowned 'Cherub smokey' (smoked haddock in a creamy sauce topped with bubbling cheese) for £8.95.

The green-tiled *Dolphin Inn* (☎ 01803-833698; WI-FI; 🐾; food daily noon-2.30pm

& Mon-Sat 6-9pm) is a 19th-century pub now serving beers from its own brewery (Bridgetown). It welcomes walkers and serves hearty pub-grub classics (£13-15) as well as its signature glamburgers (£10). Food hours in the evening vary depending on whether they have a band in.

Nearby, *The Windjammer Inn* (☎ 01803-832228; 🐾; food Mon-Sat noon-2pm, Sun noon-2.30pm, daily 6-9pm) is a lovely flower-festooned pub on Victoria Rd, with local ales and ciders, sandwiches and ploughman's lunches, and tasty seafood mains such as Windjammer fish pie (£12.75) and smoked haddock, mussels & crab chowder (£12.95).

Between Dolphin Inn and Windjammer, *Market House Inn* (☎ 01803-832901; WI-FI; 🐾; food Tue-Sat noon-3pm, Tue-Thur 6-9pm, Fri & Sat to 8pm) is a sports bar that also does food.

Restaurants On the coast path, and right beside the river, *Bushell's* (🖥 bushells .org.uk) is a sophisticated place split into two restaurants: the ground-floor *Riverside Restaurant* (☎ 01803-833540; summer Tue-Sat noon-3pm & 6-9pm, Sun noon-3pm; winter Tue-Sat 6-9pm, Sun noon-3pm) serves locally sourced British food (mains £14-20), including seafood. Above it, *Upper Deck Restaurant* (☎ 01803-839281; Wed-Mon 6-9pm) has a similarly refined menu (mains £13-17) but plainer décor, and better views.

A short walk along the river is *Rockfish* (☎ 01803-832800, 🖥 rockfishde von.co.uk; daily noon-9.30pm), a smart fish restaurant with takeaway attached. More than just a chippy (though they perform that role very well too), they have some unusual items including oysters (£12), soft shell crab rolls (£12.95) and crispy fish tacos (£11.95). Further along South Embankment, and perhaps the smartest place on the waterfront, *Seahorse* (☎ 01803-835147, 🖥 seahorserestaurant.co .uk; Tue-Sat noon-2.30pm & 6-9.30pm), does some lovely fish dishes, but it's pricey. Mains cost £20-30; even a starter will set you back more than a tenner.

If you are all fished out, head a couple of streets inland to *Anzac Street Bistro* (see Where to stay; Tue-Sat 6-9.30pm) which serves Mediterranean mains with a Polish twist, such as fasolka bean stew with sausage & bacon (£15.50) and golden halloumi with sweet potatoes & roasted vegetables (£14.50). They also do a mean goulash.

Tsang's (☎ 01803-832025; Wed-Mon 5.30-11pm), on Fairfax Place, meanwhile, has all your Chinese-food cravings covered.

For an ordinary takeaway chippy, try *Welcome Fish Bar* (Mon-Sat noon-2pm & 5-9pm) on Victoria Rd.

DARTMOUTH TO BRIXHAM   [MAPS 25-29]

Once you've crossed the river, this **11-mile (17.5km; 4hrs)** stage starts and ends with some flat and easy walking which book-end a rather strenuous middle section.

After the simple stroll to Inner Froward Point, a particularly enjoyable wooded amble leads you to Pudcombe Cove and the marvellous views it offers out to sea. The shaded pathways here offer a splendid contrast to the long cliff-top walk that follows, a walk that's interrupted only by the need to descend to two gloriously quiet beaches. Your eventual arrival at Berry Head is an important point on your coastal journey as you now enter the area called the English Riviera (see box on p146) and also the English Riviera Global Geopark (see box p150), an area of international geological importance, and a powerful magnet for tourists.

Note that refreshment options are limited to the towns that sandwich your walk; carrying plenty of water and a picnic to enjoy at one of the many beauty spots en route is highly recommended.

However, before you set off make sure you have checked the ferry times for this section of the path.

The route

To cross the river Dart take **Dartmouth to Kingswear Passenger Ferry** (☎ 01803-555872, 🖳 dartmouthrailriver.co.uk; Mon-Sat 7.30am-11.10pm, Sun 9am-11.10pm; £1.50, 🐾 50p), a shuttle service that departs every 15 minutes year-round from outside Station Restaurant (p144) on the South Embankment.

Kingswear then causes a brief distraction....

KINGSWEAR   **[Map 25, p141]**

Lying on the eastern bank of the River Dart, the peaceful little settlement of Kingswear (🖳 kingswear-devon.co.uk) has historically been – and remains today – a transport hub.

The earliest mention of a ferry crossing the Dart was in 1365; prior to that it had been used as a landing point for pilgrims heading to Canterbury following the death, in 1170, of Thomas à Becket (for whom the village church was built and dedicated).

The arrival of the railway in 1864 further boosted Kingswear's reputation as a transport centre and it became part of the then Great Western Railway in 1876. Though the line was closed in 1968, the tracks were purchased privately and you can still access the national rail network in Paignton and Torquay courtesy of **Dartmouth Steam Railway** (Apr-Oct daily 11.15am-5pm, slightly extended hours at peak times; Paignton return ticket £16.75, inc ferry to and from Dartmouth). There's a small **visitor centre** in the railway station (Apr-Oct 10am-5pm; free), and just outside is a **post office and store** (Mon-Sat 8am-6pm, Sun 8am-5pm).

Stagecoach's 18/18A and 120 **bus services** (see pp50-4) call here.

For a **taxi** contact Kingswear Taxis (☎ 01803-752626).

There's nowhere to stay in Kingswear now, but there are some food options. You can grab sandwiches and hot drinks in the *Refreshments Rooms* (daily 10am-5pm) inside the railway station. For a proper meal, though, turn left out of the ferry to find two pubs and a café.

The Ship Inn (☎ 01803-752348, 🖳 theshipinnkingswear.co.uk; food daily summer noon-2.30pm & 6.30-9.30pm, winter Tue-Sat noon-2.30pm & 7-9.30pm, Sun noon-4.30pm; WI-FI; 🐾) is a 15th-century establishment, nicely tucked away on Higher St. There are two open log fires and the owners point out that their seafood has travelled less than 200 yards from sea to plate.

Further up Fore St, you'll soon reach *Steam Packet Inn* (☎ 01803-752208; WI-FI; 🐾; food summer daily 12.30-3.30pm & 5.30-9.30pm, winter Thur-Sun only), a small friendly pub that does some cracking stone-baked pizzas. Further along still is *Sea Jay'z Café* (Mon 9am-2pm & 6-9pm, Wed-Sat 9am-2pm, Sun 10am-3pm).

If continuing straight on after the ferry crossing, turn immediately right to go underneath an archway (with the post office to your right) before turning left

---

❑ **Torbay, Tor Bay, or the English Riviera?**

'Torbay is an area which endears itself to the patriot, the naturalist and the artist'
                                             Charles Kingsley

The 'English Riviera' is the Victorian nickname given to the Torbay area of South Devon that encompasses the three main towns of Brixham, Paignton and Torquay, the title deriving from the area's plentiful beaches and mild climate. Torbay is the council's name for the area; the actual bay is called Tor Bay.

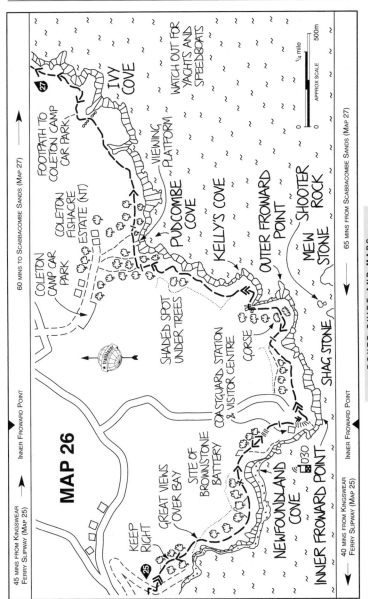

up Alma Steps. A brief jaunt along a wooded road follows before the houses are left behind and you are once again left with just nature for company – banana plants and date palms turn to pine and other coniferous trees, while (with a bit of luck) sun-rays scatter sporadically through the branches. A right turn off the path will take you to **Kingswear Castle**, built in 1502 to complement Dartmouth Castle (see box p140) on the other side of the river. It's now owned by The Landmark Trust (☎ 01628-825925, 🖥 landmarktrust.org.uk) and used as a holiday let (1D/1T; 🍷; 🐾; minimum stay three/four nights weekend/mid week).

As you leave the minor road a sign welcomes you into Warren Woods, whilst below you shelter **Mill Bay** and **Newfoundland coves**.

Eventually, after a strenuous climb or two (looking back there are great views over Dartmouth Castle and the bay), you arrive at the site of **Brownstone Battery**, an extensive WWII coastal defence position that is now managed by the National Trust. Its scattered collection of gun batteries, store huts and observation posts reaches right up to **Inner Froward Point**, from where both Start Point and Stoke Fleming church can still be seen. The site also contains a **coast-guard station** housing a small **visitor centre**. The path now zig-zags steeply down, its route etched along the cliff and hillsides in front of you. There is the occasional tree amongst the gorse but little else for cover should the weather turn against you. The larger of the rocks you see out at sea is **Mew Stone** and its smaller companions are **Shag Stone** and **Shooter Rock**: seals may occasionally be seen resting on these lonely outcrops.

Arriving at picturesque **Pudcombe Cove**, behind you in the woods is **Coleton Fishacre Estate** (☎ 01803-752466, 🖥 www.nationaltrust.org.uk/coleton-fishacre; Mar-Oct daily 10.30am-5pm, Nov & Dec Sat & Sun 11am-4pm; £11, NT members free), the 1920s 'Arts and Crafts' holiday home of the D'Oyly Carte family with a lovely 30-acre garden.

The path again becomes exposed as it tacks its way along the hillside to **Scabbacombe Sands**, a pretty pebble beach worthy of a stop – the crystal-clear water certainly appears inviting on a hot summer's day. Note that the beach is also open to naturists.

The trail now begins on the first of two substantial ascents in this stage, the initial descent presenting a large **lime kiln** on the right at **Man Sands**. The views back over the valley as you clamber away from the beach are wonderful.

Following the edge of **Southdown Cliff** you arrive at **Sharkham Point National Nature Reserve** which, along with the nearby 100-acre Berry Head National Nature Reserve (see p150), plays host to a colony of guillemots, greater horseshoe bats and eight species of orchid. There are more wildlife treats at nearby **St Mary's Bay** where, out at sea, dolphins and porpoises can sometimes be spotted. The path passes close to the campsite, Centry Touring Park (see p153).

❏ **Important note – walking times**
All times in this book refer only to the time spent walking. You will need to add 20-30% to allow for rests, photography, checking the map, drinking water etc.

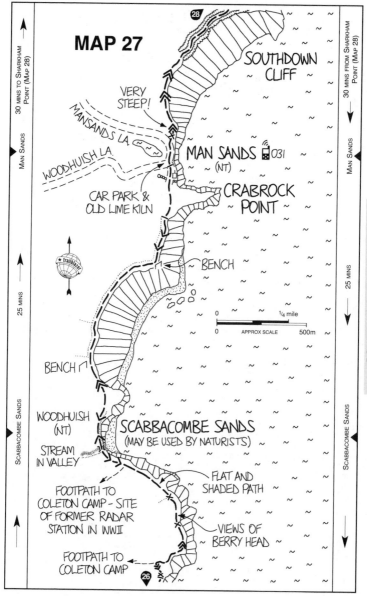

MAP 27

30 MINS TO SHARKHAM POINT (MAP 28)

MAN SANDS

25 MINS

SCABBACOMBE SANDS

VERY STEEP!

MANSANDS LA.

WOODHUISH LA.

CAR PARK & OLD LIME KILN

★ trailblazer

BENCH

BENCH

WOODHUISH (NT)

STREAM IN VALLEY

FOOTPATH TO COLETON CAMP - SITE OF FORMER RADAR STATION IN WWII

FOOTPATH TO COLETON CAMP

SOUTHDOWN CLIFF

MAN SANDS (NT) 031

CRABROCK POINT

0 ¼ mile
APPROX SCALE
0 500m

SCABBACOMBE SANDS (MAY BE USED BY NATURISTS)

FLAT AND SHADED PATH

VIEWS OF BERRY HEAD

30 MINS FROM SHARKHAM POINT (MAP 28)

MAN SANDS

25 MINS

SCABBACOMBE SANDS

ROUTE GUIDE AND MAPS

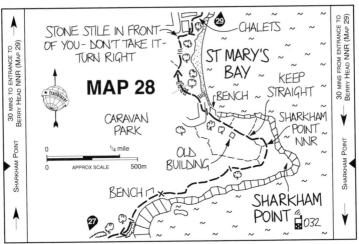

The walking is now easy. Reaching a road, the entrance to **Berry Head** – home to two Napoleonic-era forts – appears to your right. **Berry Head Country Park National Nature Reserve** (NNR; Map 29; ☎ 01803-882619, ☐ country side-trust.org.uk/berryhead; visitor centre Easter-early Oct & October half-term daily 10am-4pm, rest of year Sat & Sun 10am-4pm) is open year-round.

The award-winning *Guardhouse Café* (☎ 01803-855778, ☐ guardhouse cafe.com; intermittent WI-FI; 🐾 on lead; daily 9am-5pm, winter to 4pm) has a

---

❑ **The English Riviera Global Geopark**

The English Riviera Global Geopark straddles the area called The English Riviera (see box p146), its coastal borders being at Sharkham Point (Map 28) and just north of Maidencombe Beach (see Map 36, p173).

A geopark is a site recognised and protected by UNESCO because of its unique geological significance. There are only 127 of these in the entire world, seven of which are in the UK, though the English Riviera is unique in being the only one that is largely urban. In addition to the Riviera's diverse geology, covering a number of periods, and its contribution to our understanding of geology, the area is also a rich source of fossils, wonderful examples being those of a **woolly rhinoceros** and a **cave lion** that were both discovered at Kent's Cavern near Torquay. The **oldest human fossil** (a jawbone) yet to be found in the UK was also discovered in this cavern.

The park includes 32 **geosites** (geological sites of international importance) in total, though not all are open to the public. However, **Berry Head Country Park NNR**, guarding the southern entry to Tor Bay, **Petit Tor** and **Hope's Nose Site of Special Scientific Interest**, the latter at the geopark's northern extremity, are all visitable and on the path. Look out for the information boards that give further details on their geological importance.

The park also has **visitor centres** at Berry Head NNR (see p150) and Kent's Cavern (see p170), near Torquay.

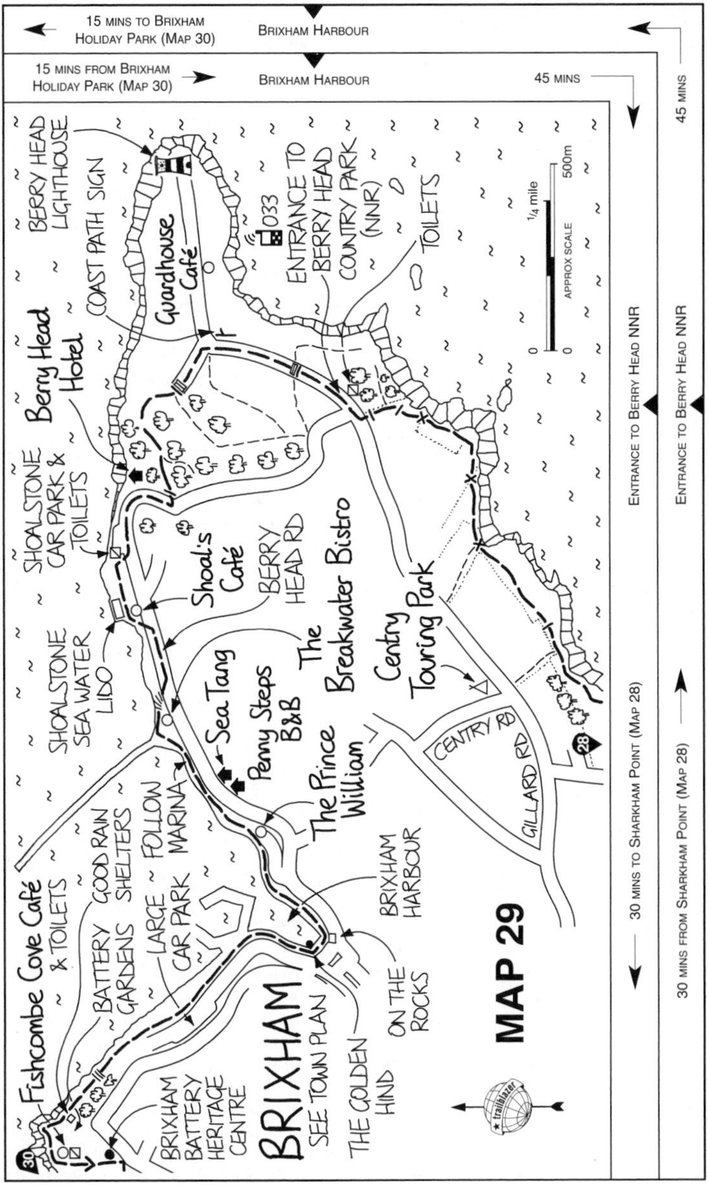

MAP 29

BRIXHAM
SEE TOWN PLAN

15 MINS TO BRIXHAM HOLIDAY PARK (MAP 30)

15 MINS FROM BRIXHAM HOLIDAY PARK (MAP 30)

BRIXHAM HARBOUR

BRIXHAM HARBOUR

45 MINS

45 MINS

BERRY HEAD LIGHTHOUSE

COAST PATH SIGN

Guardhouse Café

☎1033
ENTRANCE TO
BERRY HEAD
COUNTRY PARK
(NNR)

TOILETS

Berry Head Hotel

500m

¼ mile

APPROX SCALE

0

0

SHOALSTONE CAR PARK & TOILETS

Shoal's Café

BERRY HEAD RD

The Breakwater Bistro

SHOALSTONE SEA WATER LIDO

Sea Tang

Penny Steps B&B

Centry Touring Park

ENTRANCE TO BERRY HEAD NNR

ENTRANCE TO BERRY HEAD NNR

The Prince William

CENTRY RD

GILLARD RD

28

Fishcombe Cove Café & TOILETS

GOOD RAIN SHELTERS

BATTERY GARDENS

LARGE FOLLON CAR PARK MARINA

BRIXHAM HARBOUR

30 MINS TO SHARKHAM POINT (MAP 28)

30 MINS FROM SHARKHAM POINT (MAP 28)

BRIXHAM BATTERY HERITAGE CENTRE

THE GOLDEN HIND

ON THE ROCKS

ROUTE GUIDE AND MAPS

fabulous cliff-top location close to the **lighthouse** on Berry Head which, at 58m above sea level, is located at the highest altitude of any British lighthouse. Probably as a result of its lofty location, it is also the smallest lighthouse in Britain, being just 5m high.

Gentle walking continues as you amble to **Berry Head Hotel** (see p154), where the trail leads into Shoalstone car park before reaching the wonderful **Shoalstone Sea Water Pool** (🖳 shoalstonepool.com), a free-to-use, open-all-hours, Art Deco lido with changing rooms beside it and a fine café – *Shoals* (☎ 01803-854874, 🖳 shoalsbrixham.co.uk; WI-FI; 🐾 daytime only; mid Feb to mid Dec daily 10am-9pm) – overlooking it.

The path as you enter Brixham is not wonderfully signed: look out for the steps shortly before the harbour-arm for an easy walk along the marina. You soon pass *The Breakwater Bistro* (☎ 01803-856738, 🖳 brixham-restaurant .co.uk; WI-FI; 🐾 ; summer daily 9am-9.30pm, winter Mon-Thur 10am-4pm, Fri 10am-9pm, Sat 9am-9pm, Sun 9am-4pm) and arrive at Brixham Harbour.

BRIXHAM [map opposite]

Sitting at the southern end of Tor Bay, Brixham, or *Briseham* as it is recorded in the Domesday Book (when it had a population of 39!) is the first of the three main towns of the English Riviera (the other two being Paignton and Torquay). Not quite as busy as Paignton, and far smaller than Torquay, the old harbour area may nevertheless feel a little too crowded for some walkers, particularly after the peace of the previous stage.

Synonymous with fishing, Brixham was the largest fishing port in South-West England during the Middle Ages. By the early 19th century there were over 200 trawlers operating out of the town and by 1850 it had become the largest fishery in England. Even today it remains the nation's foremost fishing port, landing a staggering £20 million worth of fish every year.

The harbour is dominated by an impressive 50-year-old replica of *The Golden Hind* (☎ 01803-856223, 🖳 golden hind.co.uk; Easter to end Oct generally daily 10am-4pm but the opening hours vary and they close some days so check their website before going; £7), the ship with which Francis Drake became the first Englishman (and the second person in the world) to circumnavigate the globe. Behind the replica is the **statue of William, Prince of Orange**. Invited by Protestant English politicians concerned by King James II's

Catholicism, William landed his 20,000-strong Dutch army at Fischcombe Cove, just outside Brixham, in 1688. From there he went on to overthrow James – in what became known as the Glorious Revolution – and become William III of England.

The social and maritime history of the town is celebrated at **Brixham Heritage Museum** (☎ 01803-856267, 🖳 brixham museum.uk; Easter-Oct Tue-Fri & bank hols 10am-4pm, Sat 10am-1pm; free) in the Old Police Station at Bolton Cross, where there are two floors of galleries and displays including one on life at the Berry Head Barracks in Napoleonic times.

Brixham Pirate Festival (see p14), held here in May, features a variety of events including 'record attempts' for the 'Biggest gathering of pirates' (2010 saw the town gain – briefly – the world record).

Services

There's a **tourist information point** inside Hobb Nobs Gift Shop (daily 10am-5pm); just a table with leaflets on it so it is not much use, although shop staff will help you if they can.

Internet is available at Brixham Library (Mon & Thur 9.30am-5pm, Tue 9.30am-6pm, Wed, Fri & Sat 9.30am-1pm). Other services include a Co-op **supermarket** (daily 7am-11pm) near the harbour on Fore St, with an **ATM** outside it, and

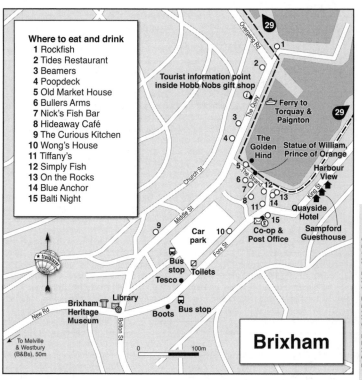

Where to eat and drink
1 Rockfish
2 Tides Restaurant
3 Beamers
4 Poopdeck
5 Old Market House
6 Bullers Arms
7 Nick's Fish Bar
8 Hideaway Café
9 The Curious Kitchen
10 Wong's House
11 Tiffany's
12 Simply Fish
13 On the Rocks
14 Blue Anchor
15 Balti Night

Tourist information point
inside Hobb Nobs gift shop

Ferry to
Torquay &
Paignton

The
Golden
Hind

Statue of William,
Prince of Orange

Harbour
View

Quayside
Hotel

Sampford
Guesthouse

Co-op &
Post Office

Car
park

Bus
stop

Toilets

Tesco

Library

Brixham
Heritage
Museum

Boots

Bus stop

To Melville
& Westbury
(B&Bs), 50m

0   100m

Brixham

Brixham's **post office** (Mon-Sat 9am-5.30pm) within it. There's also a branch of Tesco (daily 7am-10pm) near the top of the same street where you'll also find Boots **pharmacy** (Mon-Sat 9am-5.30pm).

Transport
[See also pp50-4] The town is well connected to the rest of the Riviera (and Kingswear) via Stagecoach's hop12, 18 & 18A **bus** services.

Assuming the weather and tides are OK, Paignton Pleasure Cruises (☎ 01803-529147, or ☎ 07767 622727, boat ☎ 07768 014174, 🖥 www.paigntonpleasurecruises .co.uk; Apr-Oct daily hourly 10.30am-4.30pm; about £2/3 single/return) operate a **ferry** to Torquay and Paignton; see p159.

Where to stay
As you follow the path into Brixham you'll find **camping** available at *Centry Touring Park* (see Map 29; ☎ 01803-856389, 🖥 centrytouring.co.uk; hiker and tent £10; 🐾; Apr-Oct) where Centry Rd meets Gillard Rd. Booking is recommended for August.

The first **B&B** you'll see as you enter town along Berry Head Rd is *Sea Tang* (Map 29; ☎ 01803-854651, 🖥 seatang-guesthouse.com; 2S/2D or T/1D/1Qd; WI-FI; £40-45pp, sgl £45-50, sgl occ from £65), at No 67, from where there are tremendous views over the bay and marina. Next door, at No 65, is *Penny Steps* (Map 29; ☎ 01803-856301, 🖥 bed-breakfast-brixham .co.uk; 1S/3D/1T; 🛏; WI-FI; £37.50-45pp, sgl from £53, sgl occ room rate), but there's a minimum two-night policy for advance booking.

Overlooking the harbour from King St is *Harbour View* (☎ 01803-853052, 🖳 har bourviewbrixhambandb.co.uk; 6D/1T/1Tr; ➍; WI-FI; £37.50-42.50pp, sgl occ £65-75; Feb-Nov), No 65, which was on the market at the time of research so it may have changed hands by the time you are here. Previously it was the residence of the harbourmaster and is grade II listed. Further down King St there is dog-friendly *Sampford Guesthouse* (☎ 01803-857761, 🖳 sampfordhouse.com; 4D/1T; ➍; WI-FI; 🐾; £37-47.50pp, sgl occ £60-70), at Nos 57-59, which unfortunately does not accept advance bookings for one-night stays in the summer.

At the back end of town on New Rd there are other decent options such as *Westbury Guesthouse* (☎ 01803-851684, 🖳 westburyguesthouse.co.uk; 2D/2T/2Tr; ➍; WI-FI; from £37.50pp, sgl occ from £45), at No 51, where breakfast includes fresh fish caught by the owners and items grown on their allotment; and *Melville Guesthouse* (☎ 01803-852033, 🖳 themel villebrixham.co.uk; 1T/6D; WI-FI; £32.50-45pp, sgl occ rates on request; closed Feb) at No 45. They also don't accept advance bookings for a one-night stay.

For **hotel** accommodation, *Berry Head Hotel* (Map 29; ☎ 01803-853225, 🖳 berryheadhotel.com; 2S/29D, some can be T; ➍; WI-FI; 🐾; £68-100pp, sgl occ £84-140) is a splendid – though not cheap – option to consider. Dinner can be provided but beware they do not accept advance bookings for one-night stays at weekends in summer.

Otherwise, *Quayside Hotel* (☎ 01803-855751, 🖳 quaysidehotel.co.uk; 3S/27D or T; ➍; WI-FI; small 🐾; £46.50-92.50pp, sgl £70-85, sgl occ £88-135), overlooking the harbour from King St, is a slightly more economical option. Many of the higher-priced rooms have sea views.

Where to eat and drink

It comes as no surprise, given the fact that the town can boast of one of the largest and

newest fish markets in the UK, that seafood is something of a speciality. You don't have to stray too far from the path to sample it, either, with restaurants standing cheek by gill on the western side of the harbour – paradise for piscivores.

Cafés The best located cafés are on the coast path surrounding Brixham (see Map 29), but in the town itself, there's the intriguing *Hideaway Café* (Wed-Sun 9am-5pm), secreted away in a quiet alley called Beach Approach, just off the harbour. An all-day full English breakfast costs £6.95 including a tea or coffee, and cream teas are just £3.95.

Out on Fore St, *Tiffany's* (Mon-Sat 9.30am-5pm, Sun 10am-5pm) is another no-frills café with a huge menu containing every savoury fancy and sweet treat any café customer could wish for. Breakfasts (£4.95-7.25) all come with tea or coffee, and lunchtime mains cost just £6.95. Despite the name, *Tides Restaurant* (☎ 01803-852195; WI-FI; 🐾; daily 8am-3pm) is really more of a greasy-spoon café; an unfussy place, with good-value lunchtime mains (£4.50-6.50). It's most popular, however, at breakfast (fry-ups from £5.50).

A classier café, which transforms into an informal restaurant on some evenings, is *The Curious Kitchen* (☎ 01803-854816, 🖳 thecuriouskitchen.co.uk; WI-FI; 🐾 daytime only; food daily 9am-3pm & Thur-Sat 7-9pm, winter Fri & Sat 7-9pm), on Middle St. It's a modern place, with a rustic feel, serving healthy food and top-notch coffee. Evenings are by prior booking only.

Pubs On the approach into town, you'll pass *The Prince William* (Map 29; ☎ 01803-854468, 🖳 theprincewilliam.co.uk; food daily noon-2.30pm & 6-9pm) right on the coast path. It's somewhat soulless inside, but everyone sits outside, at tables overlooking the harbour. The Sunday carvery is popular.

In the heart of the harbour, *Blue Anchor* (☎ 01803-469165; WI-FI; 🐾; food served Tue-Sat noon-2.30pm & 5-8.30pm, Sun noon-3pm) is a more traditional, dog-friendly, real-ale pub with a decent pub-grub menu. There's a similar feel to *Bullers Arms* (☎ 01803-850143; WI-FI; 🐾; food daily noon-3pm & 5-9pm, winter hours variable), at 4 The Strand. Opposite this, and overlooking The Golden Hind, *Old Market House* (☎ 01803-856891, 🖥 www .oldmarkethousebrixham.co.uk; WI-FI; 🐾 on ground floor only; food served daily noon-9pm) is a gastro-pub with standard pub mains plus numerous seafood options. There's plenty of outdoor seating, including a first-floor terrace with unmatched views of the famous galleon moored beside it.

Restaurants Dominating the northern end of the harbour is a huge branch of the well-regarded seafood chain, *Rockfish* (☎ 01803-850872, 🖥 therockfish.co.uk; daily noon-9.30pm), with a large terrace looking out over Brixham's fishing fleet.

Nearby, *Beamers* (☎ 01803-854777, 🖥 beamersrestaurant.co.uk; Wed-Mon from 6.30pm) is another fish-centric establishment, though more refined. Seafood mains cost around £20, but there's also some fine cuts of steak here.

A few doors down, *Poopdeck* (☎ 01803-858681, 🖥 poopdeckrestaurant .com; Tue-Sun noon-9.30pm) is similarly stylish (though cheaper), and has some lovely meals including whole Dover sole in a brandy & crab sauce (£18.95) and skate wings topped with leek, fennel, tomato & prawns and finished with a splash of Pernod (£14.95).

For more down-to-earth seafood dining, walk round the harbour to *Nick's Fish Bar* (☎ 01803-853357; Mon-Fri 11am-8pm, Sat to 9pm, takeaway till 9/10pm, winter hours variable), an excellent takeaway chippy with some indoor seating too, or *Simply Fish* (☎ 01803-883858, 🖥 rob ertsfisheries.com; daily noon-9/9.30pm, winter noon-3pm & 5-9pm), which has been opened by one of the fish merchants operating at the market.

For those less fish inclined, *On The Rocks* (☎ 01803-857921, 🖥 ontherocks-brixham.co.uk; 🐾 daytime only; food Apr-end Sep daily noon-3.30pm & 6-9pm, rest of year evening only) is a smokehouse grill and bar overlooking the harbour. There's also *Balti Night* (☎ 01803-882040; Sun-Thur 5.30-11pm, Fri & Sat 5.30pm-12.30am) for Indian cuisine, and *Wong's House* (☎ 01803-856314; summer Mon-Sat 5-11pm, Sun 5.30-11pm, winter closed Tue) for Chinese.

BRIXHAM TO TORQUAY   [Maps 29-33]

For many, this is a stage to endure rather than enjoy. Involving vast stretches where you'll be plodding on pedestrian promenades, this easy (though hard-on-the-ankles) **8½-mile (13.6km; 3hrs 10 mins)** stretch starts with an interesting section of sylvan walking that passes by pretty coves and through ancient woodland. After Broad Sands, however, the walk has little to excite unless beach huts and Brunellian railway lines are your thing.

That said, and in spite of this stage's shortcomings, there are plenty of options for refreshment on the English Riviera. So we advise you not to hurry through. Instead, take your time, spoil yourself with snacks, have your fill of fish & chips and conduct some in-depth research into what flavour ice-cream is your favourite. In doing this, you'll be saving your legs for tomorrow's stage – a stretch which does not allow for such frivolities.

The route

Having left Brixham via the large car park to the east of the harbour, you follow a set of steps that disappear into woodland. Continue on the path through **Battery Gardens** ready to defend England since the 16th century and one of the best-preserved WW2 Emergency coastal defence batteries.

At **Fishcombe Cove** there is a **seasonal** *café* (Easter-Oct daily 10am-6pm, weather permitting), with a lovely perch above the cove, and good-value food, but only outdoor seating. The path climbs up behind the café to reach **Brixham Battery Heritage Centre** (☎ 01803-852449, 🖳 www.brixhambattery.net; Mon, Fri & Sun 2-4pm; free). Note the fierce snout of the 1950s Humver 'pig' and twelve-pounder gun that guard the centre.

Following the Battery you soon leave the road again by **Brixham Holiday Park** and enter **Elberry** and **Marridge** ancient woods (aka **The Grove**). The walk is wonderful and the woods friendly as you pass by the peaceful little **Elberry Cove** (look out for wild campers) before climbing over **Churston Point** to arrive by the multicoloured beach huts at **Broad Sands**. Note the rich red colour of the earth (an indication of iron-rich soil) and watch the trains as they chug along the railway line on the approaching cliffs. It is that railway line you now follow, first passing underneath it – where you can join the road to get to *Beverley Park campsite* (p159) – and later passing **Saltern Cove** – an SSSI and nature reserve that's unique in Britain as its boundaries extend underwater for 376 metres further than the low-water mark due to its unusual geology.

Goodrington Sands is the next stop, essentially a larger version of the previous beach and the home of *South Sands Café* (Mar-Sep daily 10am-4pm weather permitting). The beach at Goodrington Sands is partitioned by the rocky spit of **Middle Stone** where, nearby, you'll find the popular *Inn on the Quay* (☎ 01803-559754; breakfast served Mon-Fri 6.30-10.30am, Sat & Sun 7-11am, daily noon-10pm; WI-FI), part of the Brewers Fayre chain. Dogs are not allowed in the restaurant but there is an area where they can be left.

Off to the left of the path is the UK's biggest outdoor waterpark, **Splashdown Quaywest** (☎ 01803-555550, 🖳 splashdownwaterparks.co .uk/quaywest; Mar-Aug daily 10am-5pm, till 7.30pm in peak times; £12-15), but the coast path passes in front of the pub and more beach huts to another seasonal café, *North Sands Kiosk*. It then climbs away from the beach to skirt the edge of **Roundham Head** where, as well as the possibility of spotting peregrine falcons and bottlenose dolphins, there is also the opportunity to play pitch 'n' putt. From here it's a road walk into **Paignton** via the harbour, where there are various eateries.

PAIGNTON [map p161]

Paignton is, it must be said, a rather run-down seaside town, though it's not entirely without its charms, boasting a fine pier, a pleasant harbour area and a massive promenade where the pavement is separated from the traffic by a large empty sward of grass. What's more, the B&Bs nearer the centre offer some of the cheapest accommodation along the whole of the South-West Coast Path.

Originally a Celtic settlement and first mentioned in the Domesday Book of 1086, 'Peynton' or 'Paington' (note the spelling)

was a small fishing village until the Paington Harbour Act of 1837 initiated the construction of a safe haven for craft in the village; the modern-day spelling, 'Paignton', arrived simultaneously. The town boomed with the construction of the railway in 1859 that linked the Riviera with London. The national rail network no longer goes as far as Brixham or Kingswear, though **Dartmouth Steam Railway** (☎ 01803-555872, 🖳 dartmouth railriver.co.uk) provides a fun substitute. The ticket office is beside the main railway

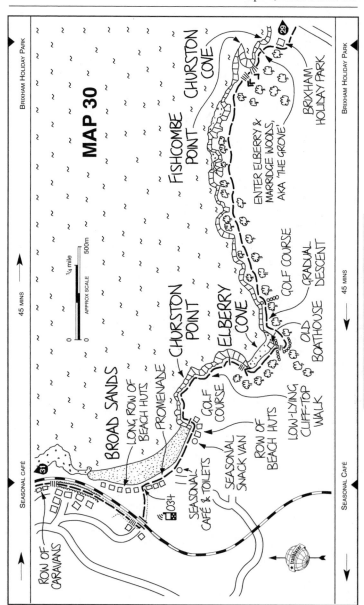

MAP 30

BROAD SANDS

CHURSTON POINT

FISHCOMBE POINT ~ CHURSTON COVE

ELBERRY COVE

45 MINS

¼ mile   500m
APPROX SCALE
0

BRIXHAM HOLIDAY PARK

SEASONAL CAFÉ

LONG ROW OF BEACH HUTS

PROMENADE

GOLF COURSE

ROW OF BEACH HUTS

LOW-LYING CLIFF-TOP WALK

OLD BOATHOUSE

GOLF COURSE

GRADUAL DESCENT

ENTER ELBERRY & MARRIDGE WOODS, AKA 'THE GROVE'

BRIXHAM HOLIDAY PARK

ROW OF CARAVANS

SEASONAL CAFÉ & TOILETS

SEASONAL SNACK VAN

45 MINS

SEASONAL CAFÉ

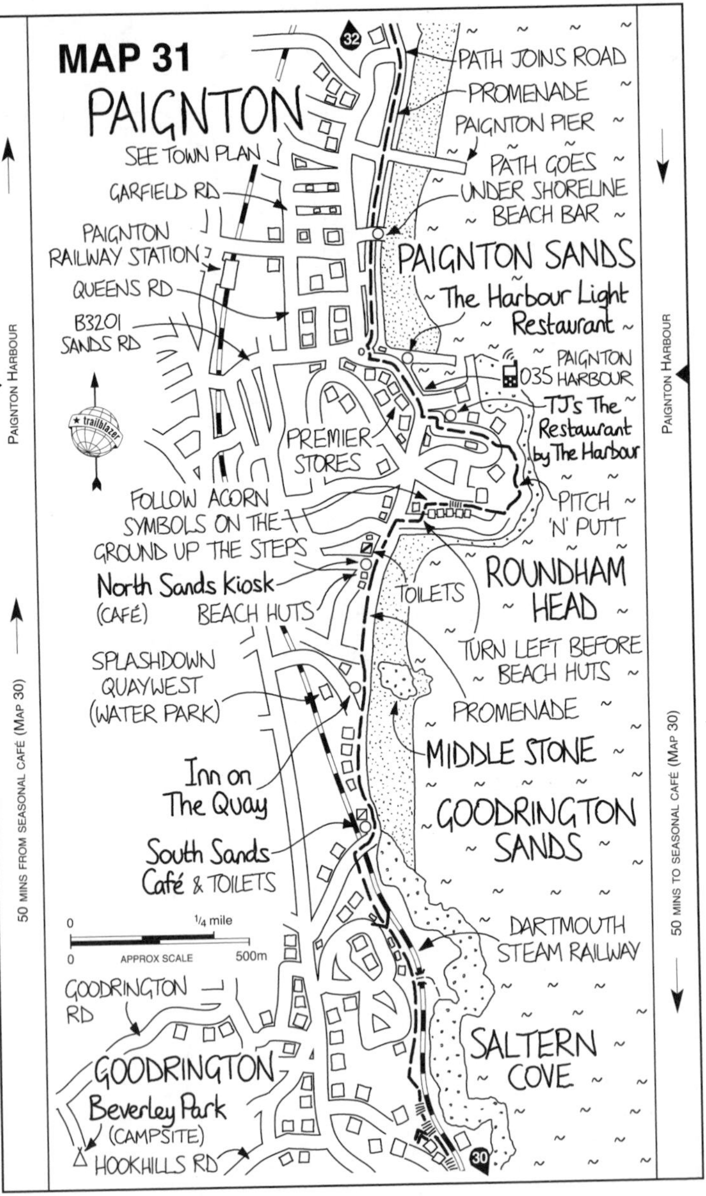

MAP 31
PAIGNTON

SEE TOWN PLAN

GARFIELD RD

PAIGNTON RAILWAY STATION

QUEENS RD

B3201 SANDS RD

trailblazer

PATH JOINS ROAD

PROMENADE

PAIGNTON PIER

PATH GOES UNDER SHORELINE BEACH BAR

PAIGNTON SANDS

The Harbour Light Restaurant

035 PAIGNTON HARBOUR

TJ's The Restaurant by The Harbour

PREMIER STORES

FOLLOW ACORN SYMBOLS ON THE GROUND UP THE STEPS

North Sands kiosk (CAFÉ)

BEACH HUTS

TOILETS

PITCH 'N' PUTT

ROUNDHAM HEAD

TURN LEFT BEFORE BEACH HUTS

SPLASHDOWN QUAYWEST (WATER PARK)

PROMENADE

MIDDLE STONE

GOODRINGTON SANDS

Inn on The Quay

South Sands Café & TOILETS

DARTMOUTH STEAM RAILWAY

0   1/4 mile
0   APPROX SCALE   500m

GOODRINGTON RD

GOODRINGTON
Beverley Park (CAMPSITE)
HOOKHILLS RD

SALTERN COVE

PAIGNTON HARBOUR

PAIGNTON HARBOUR

50 MINS FROM SEASONAL CAFÉ (MAP 30)

50 MINS TO SEASONAL CAFÉ (MAP 30)

station and it has a gift shop and *café*. A return ticket to Kingswear costs £16.75.

Paignton Pier (🖥 paigntonpier.co.uk; pier free, charges for the attractions) was built in 1879 and was a popular attraction for holidaying Victorians until a fire all but destroyed it in 1919. A major redevelopment in 1980 brought it back to life and these days it houses the usual collection of arcade games, ice-cream stalls and children's fairground rides, as well as its own *café* (see Where to Eat p160).

If you fancy a spot of **sea fishing** while you're here, head to the harbour to find Paignton Pleasure Cruises (see Transport opposite) who also run a ferry service to Torquay and Brixham.

Torbay Carnival Paignton (see p14) is held here in July.

Services

Paignton Library & Information Centre (☎ 01803-208321) includes a **library** (Mon & Fri 9.30am-5pm, Tue & Thur to 6pm, Wed to 1pm, Sat to 4pm) with **internet** (£1 for 30mins, or free if you join the library on the spot) and free wi-fi, and a **tourist information point** with attached café (Mon-Fri 9am-5pm). There are **banks** with **ATMs** around town – try Victoria St – and there is a **post office** (Mon-Sat 9am-5.30pm) on Torquay Rd.

For **provisions** there is a Premier Stores (Mon-Sat 7am-9pm, Sun 8am-8pm), by the harbour; a Spar (daily 8am-8pm) on Torbay Rd, and a Lidl supermarket (Mon-Sat 8am-8pm, Sun 10am-4pm) a little further into town on Parkside Rd. A **chemist**, Superdrug (Mon-Sat 8.30am-6pm, Sun 10am-5pm) is on Victoria St while there's a fairly decent **bookshop**, Parkside Books (Mon-Sat 9am-5pm, Sun 10.30am-4.30pm), on the road of the same name.

Outdoor and camping gear can be bought at Field & Trek, inside Sports Direct (Mon-Sat 9am-6pm, Sun 10am-5pm), near the railway station.

The most convenient **launderette**, Preston Laundry (☎ 01803-552526; Mon-Fri 8.30am-8pm, Sat-Sun 8.30am-6pm), 27-29 Seaway Rd, is about a mile north of the town, just off the coast path (see Map 32).

Transport

[See also pp50-4] Stagecoach's No 120 **bus** connects the town to Kingswear; Kingswear and Dartmouth are connected by ferry. To access Brixham or Torquay you will need to catch their hop12 service and for Dawlish Warren and St Marychurch their hop22. First's The Stagecoach Gold service (Plymouth to Torquay) also calls here. All services call at the bus station as does National Express's NX501 **coach** service (see box p49).

Paignton is a stop on both Great Western Railway's (see box p54) and Dartmouth Steam Railway's (see p156) **train** services.

Paignton Pleasure Cruises (see p153; boat ☎ 07768-014174; Apr-Oct hourly 10.30am-4.30pm, about £3 single, £5-6 return) operate a regular **ferry** service from the harbour to both Torquay and Brixham, though it is dependent on the weather, the sea and the tides. It is best to call the boat to check if the service is operating.

Where to stay

For **camping**, you need to come off the coast path before you reach Paignton, to find *Beverley Park* (Map 31; ☎ 01803-843887, 🖥 beverley-holidays.co.uk; WI-FI; late Mar to early Oct), a large, well-equipped holiday park with pitches for around £14-18 for a tent and up two people. Note that prices rocket to £25 or even £35 per tent during peak holiday weeks. The main entrance is off Goodrington Rd.

Paignton is almost overrun with **B&B** accommodation, particularly along the three parallel streets of Kernou Rd, Beach Rd and Garfield Rd. However, as with most places on the Riviera (and beyond) the main issue facing walkers will be a reluctance to take one-night bookings in advance.

Near to the harbour on Sands Rd there are a few decent options. *Seaways* (☎ 01803-551093, 🖥 seawayshotel.com; 1S/6D/2T/1D or T; WI-FI; £35-40pp, sgl/sgl occ from £40), No 30, has a licensed bar.

Both *The Sands* (☎ 01803-551282, 🖥 sandshotelpaignton.co.uk; 2S/7D or T/2Tr; WI-FI; £35-37.50pp, sgl £35-45, sgl occ from £40), No 32, and **The Briars** (☎ 01803-557729, 🖳 briarshotel.co.uk; 1S/ 10D/1T; 🐾; WI-FI; £37.50-45pp, sgl from £45, sgl occ room rate; Mar-Oct), No 26, also have a licensed bar.

The town centre is surrounded by swinging 'vacancy' boards. To the north of Torbay Rd along Garfield Rd you'll find **Blueberry Guesthouse** (☎ 01803-552211, 🖳 blueberryhouse.co.uk; 2S/1T/5D; 🐾; WI-FI; 🐾; £28-30pp, sgl occ £36-38) at No 34.

Also on this road and all just as reasonable are: **Kingswinford** (☎ 01803-558358, 🖳 thekingswinford.com; 3D/2Tr/ 1Qd; WI-FI; £27-34pp, sgl occ room rate), No 32; **Beach House** (☎ 01803-525742, 🖳 beachhouse-paignton.co.uk; 4D/1Qd; WI-FI; £27.50-31pp, sgl occ £38-50) at No 39; and **Rosemead** (☎ 01803-557944, 🖳 rosemead paignton.co.uk; 2S/4D/1D or T/1Tr; 🐾; WI-FI; Jan-early Nov; £29-35pp, sgl occ from £40) at No 22, which has one room with a four-poster bed as well as a lounge for guests. There's also **Belle Dene** (☎ 01803-559645, 🖳 belledeneguesthouse.co.uk; 1S/1T/3D/1Tr; WI-FI; £26.50-32.50pp, sgl from £35, sgl occ rates on request), at No 25, which has a great sun-trap front garden.

Further good-value places are available on Beach Rd, where you'll find: **Bay Cottage** (☎ 01803-525729, 🖳 baycottage paignton.co.uk; 1S/6D/1T; 🐾; WI-FI; Mar-Dec; £26.50-32pp, sgl 29-34, sgl occ from £54) at No 4; **Barbican Hotel** (☎ 01803-551332, 🖳 barbicanhotelpaignton.co.uk; 5D/2T/2Qd; WI-FI; from £26pp, sgl occ from £30) at No 5; and **Brampton Guest House** (☎ 01803-665389, 🖳 thebramp ton.co.uk; 2S/4D/1Tr; some share facilities; WI-FI; £25-33pp, sgl £22-25, sgl occ room rate), at No 11, but they only accept advance bookings for a minimum three-night stay in July and August plus some bank holidays.

Nearby there's also **Dalehurst Guest House** (☎ 01803-557628, 🖳 dalehurst.co .uk;1S/2D share facilities; 1T/2D en suite; WI-FI; Easter-end Oct; £25-30pp, sgl/sgl occ £30-40), at 4 Berry Square, whose new owners have redecorated the property with flair, flamboyance and furniture from around the world. The rooms are smallish, but the prices are very reasonable and the breakfast substantial.

Where to eat and drink

Paignton's residents are nicknamed 'Puddin' Eaters', a moniker that comes from the huge Paignton Pudding, which originated in the 13th century and is historically baked to celebrate local events. Thousands turning up for a piece of the one baked in celebration of the railway's arrival almost caused a riot, such was the desire for a chunk! You'll struggle to find any on a Paignton menu today, at least when there aren't any special occasions being celebrated; but if you do find some for sale somewhere, you'd be foolish to miss the chance.

Cafés   Near the railway station, **Urban Edge** (☎ 01803-521700, 🖳 theurbanedge coffeecompany.co.uk; WI-FI; Mon-Sat 8.30am-5/6pm, Sun 10am-4pm) is the most stylish café in town, and the best for food, although nearby **Coffee #1** (☎ 01803-663795, 🖳 coffee1.co.uk; WI-FI; Mon-Fri 8am-5pm, Sat to 6pm, Sun 9am-5pm) also does an excellent brew.

As cute as the name suggests, **Cupcake** (☎ 01803-431506, 🖳 cupcake cafepaignton.co.uk; WI-FI; 🐾; daily 9.15am-5pm) is perfect for a quick pit stop. It does soups and sandwiches as well as its signature homemade cupcakes.

For something more traditional, consider popping into **The Paignton Club** (☎ 01803-559682, 🖳 thepaigntonclub.co.uk) for afternoon cream teas (from £3.95; Tue-Sat 2-4.30pm).

If you're just passing through Paignton, **Pier Café** (daily 9am-9pm, winter 9am-3pm), at the entrance to the pier, could hardly be more convenient and, naturally, has unmatched sea views, plus fish & chips.

Restaurants & pubs   Up near Urban Edge and Coffee #1, the charming café-bistro **The Lions Monocle** (☎ 01803-445886, 🖳 thelionsmonocle.co.uk; WI-FI; 🐾; food daily 10am-2.30pm, Wed-Sat 5.30-8/8.30pm) is a joy to eat at. Staff are welcoming, food is sourced locally wherever

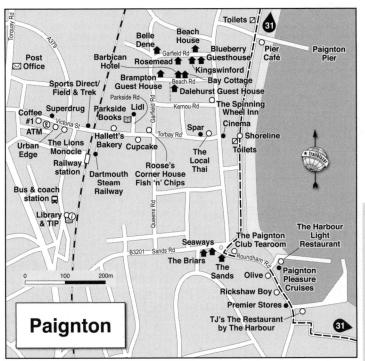

Paignton

possible, and there are numerous vegetarian and vegan options. It's a great place for breakfast or a light lunch as well as for evening meals, and it stays open late as a wine bar on Fridays and Saturdays. Further down Torbay Rd, *The Local Thai* (☎ 01803-559938, 🖥 thelocalthai.co.uk; Thur-Tue 2-10pm) is a decent-value, reasonably authentic Thai restaurant where you can get 'som tam' papaya salad for £6 or chicken 'pad thai' noodles for £7.90.

Overlooking the harbour, the awkwardly named, but excellent *TJ's The Restaurant by The Harbour* (☎ 01803-527389, 🖥 tjsrestaurant.co.uk; Wed-Sat 6-9pm, Sun 6-8pm; school summer hols daily 6-9pm; occasional summer lunchtimes) offers a full tapas menu (£2.95-7.95), a specials board (mains £9.95-£15.95) and occasional music nights. Nearby, the seafood-led

menu at *The Harbour Light Restaurant* (☎ 01803-666500, 🖥 theharbourlight.co.uk; May-Oct daily from 6pm, Nov-Dec & Mar/Apr Fri & Sat only) includes rainbow trout and various other fish dishes as well as steaks, pork tenderloin and coq au vin. Mains cost £12.50 to £22.95. Close by, but less classy, *Olive* (☎ 01803-411642, 🖥 en joytapas.com; daily noon-9pm, winter noon-3pm & 6-9pm) is a Mediterranean-style restaurant with a rooftop terrace, above the Harbour Inn pub.

The best pub at the seaside end of town, though, is *The Spinning Wheel Inn* (☎ 01803-555000, 🖥 spinningwheelinn.co .uk; WI-FI; 🐾; food daily noon-9pm) with an oak-beam interior, a large front garden, good-value pub grub (mains from £8) and a strong selection of real ales on tap. They also have live music most nights.

Snacks & takeaways For fish & chips, try *Roose's Corner House* (☎ 01803-558126; Mon-Fri 9.30am-7pm, Sat-Sun 9.30am-9pm), at 49 Torbay Rd. Nearby *Hallett's Bakery* (summer Mon-Sat 8am-6pm, winter 8.30am-5pm, Sun 9am-5pm) has baked goods and pastries covered. For a Chinese takeaway, head to the harbour where you'll find *Rickshaw Boy* (☎ 01803-559901; summer daily 5-11pm, rest of year Tue-Sun only) at 55 Roundham Rd.

The path through Paignton pursues the promenade, passing the pier and then the pretty, pastel-coloured beach huts at **Preston Sands**.

A brief dalliance with tranquil **Hollicombe Park** – a refreshing respite from the roads and promenades – leads, eventually, to **Corbyn's Head**, where (if local folklore is to be believed) the pirate Samuel Corbyn was hanged for his swashbuckling crimes.

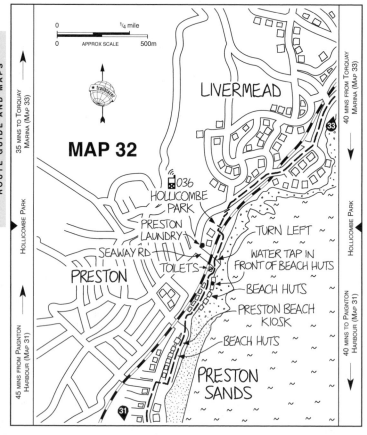

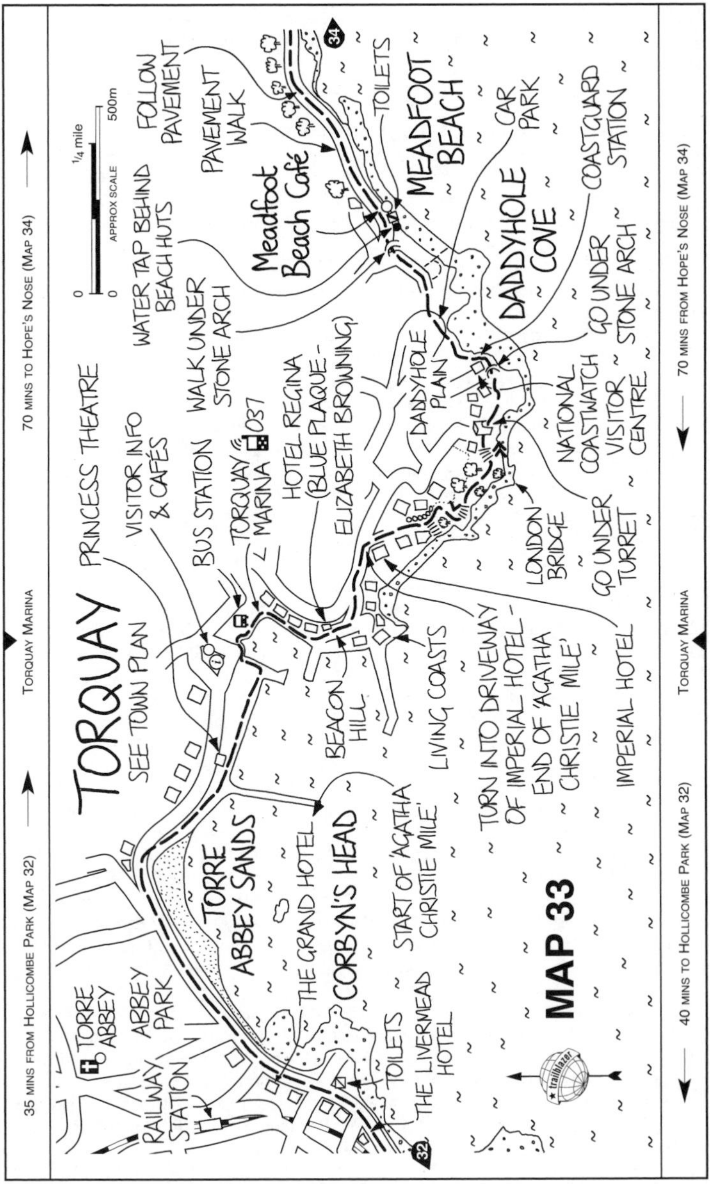
35 MINS FROM HOLLICOMBE PARK (MAP 32)
TORQUAY MARINA
70 MINS TO HOPE'S NOSE (MAP 34)
40 MINS TO HOLLICOMBE PARK (MAP 32)
TORQUAY MARINA
70 MINS FROM HOPE'S NOSE (MAP 34)
0 ¼ mile
0 500m
APPROX SCALE
MAP 33
TORQUAY
SEE TOWN PLAN
TORRE ABBEY
ABBEY PARK
RAILWAY STATION
TORRE ABBEY SANDS
THE GRAND HOTEL
CORBYN'S HEAD
START OF 'AGATHA CHRISTIE MILE'
TOILETS
THE LIVERMEAD HOTEL
PRINCESS THEATRE
VISITOR INFO & CAFÉS
BUS STATION
TORQUAY MARINA
WALK UNDER STONE ARCH
HOTEL REGINA (BLUE PLAQUE – ELIZABETH BROWNING)
BEACON HILL
LIVING COASTS
TURN INTO DRIVEWAY OF IMPERIAL HOTEL – END OF 'AGATHA CHRISTIE MILE'
IMPERIAL HOTEL
LONDON BRIDGE
GO UNDER TURRET
DADDYHOLE PLAIN
NATIONAL COASTWATCH VISITOR CENTRE
GO UNDER STONE ARCH
DADDYHOLE COVE
COASTGUARD STATION
CAR PARK
WATER TAP BEHIND BEACH HUTS
Meadfoot Beach Café
MEADFOOT BEACH
TOILETS
PAVEMENT WALK
FOLLOW PAVEMENT
32
34
trailblazer

ROUTE GUIDE AND MAPS

Passing **Abbey Park**, the beach at **Torre Abbey Sands** and **Princess Theatre** (🖥 atgtickets.com/venues/princess-theatre-torquay), you soon arrive at Torquay Marina.

❏ **Torquay's most famous daughter: Agatha Christie**

No-one can accuse Torquay of under-exploiting the legacy of its most famous daughter. In addition to The Agatha Christie Literary Trail and the Agatha Christie Mile (see below), the town also hosts an annual Agatha Christie Festival (see opposite) every September. But who exactly was Agatha Christie, anyway – and what precisely was her connection with the town?

Ms Christie's biography is, of course, fairly well documented. Born on 15th September, 1890, Agatha Christie during a spectacularly successful career tried her hand at a variety of formats and genres, from short stories to plays and even romances (under the pseudonym Mary Westmacott). But it is, of course, her crime fiction, and particularly those stories involving the detectives Miss Marple and Hercule Poirot, that gave her worldwide fame and even earned her the sobriquet the 'Queen of Crime'. Her novels have sold a staggering four billion copies, a figure that puts her joint-first with William Shakespeare on the world's all-time bestsellers' list. What's more, her play *The Mousetrap*, having opened in November 1952, is still running in London's West End to this day, and having ratcheted up more than 26,000 performances is by far the longest-running West End show in history.

There is no doubt that Agatha's Christie's links with Torquay are numerous. Born in the town in 1890, she also honeymooned here in 1914, worked as a nurse in the local hospital during the First World War and – though she travelled widely between the wars – in 1938 she and her second husband, the archaeologist Max Mallowan, purchased a holiday home on the nearby River Dart. Perhaps more importantly, however, Christie was greatly inspired by the rugged moors, cliffs, beaches, villages and islands of South Devon, many of which are recognisable (albeit under different names) in much of her work. Indeed the best-selling mystery novel of all time, *And Then There Were None* (1939), takes place on fictional Soldier Island which Agatha Christie based on Burgh Island (see box on p111) in Bigbury Bay. The island also features (though this time it's called Smugglers' Island) as Poirot's holiday destination in *Evil Under the Sun* (1941), the super sleuth's vacation being rather rudely interrupted by the discovery of an actress's strangled body in a nearby cove.

Today, Christie-philes – of which, to judge by the crowds that swarm in summer around all things Agatha, there are many – have plenty of ways of indulging their passion in her hometown. The holiday home she bought with her second husband, **The Greenway Estate** (☎ 01803-842382, 🖥 nationaltrust.org.uk/greenway; mid Feb-end Oct daily 10.30am-5pm, Nov-Dec weekends only; £11.60), is open to the public. You can reach the estate by ferry from Dartmouth (☎ 01803-882811, 🖥 greenwayferry.co .uk; Mar-Oct daily 11am-3.30pm, extra ferries at peak times; £8.50 return), or by steam train from Paignton (see p156; get off at Greenway Halt from where the estate is a 30-minute woodland walk away).

There's also the **Agatha Christie Literary Trail**, stretching from Greenway on the River Dart to Babbacombe (north of Torquay), that links 20 of the writer's novels with locations that are believed to have influenced or inspired them. And the **Agatha Christie Mile** (see Map 33, p163) which begins at The Grand Hotel – where she honeymooned – and continues along Torquay seafront to The Imperial Hotel, which features in a number of her novels. For more details, the English Riviera Tourist Board produces a leaflet on both trails.

TORQUAY [map p167]

The largest and most central of the three Riviera towns, Torquay's population swells from somewhere around the 65,000 mark to nearer 200,000 at the height of summer. At these times you'll either have to embrace it or continue to the far more peaceful suburb of St Marychurch – or even, if stamina allows, the blink-and-you'll-miss-it village of Maidencombe.

As with Brixham, Torquay has its origins as a fishing village (though one with an important abbey – see below) but secured an advantage in the tourism stakes during the Napoleonic Wars. With the Royal Navy spending a lot of time anchored in Tor Bay, it became a chic (if rather exclusive) seaside resort, where the relatives of the boats' officers would visit. It was during the Victorian era that Torquay and its environs earned the nickname of the English Riviera, with its mild and healthy climate being part of the attraction for holidaymakers as well as those wishing to convalesce. The opening of the town's railway stations (in 1848 and 1859) further accelerated Torquay's popularity.

Torre Abbey (☎ 01803-293593, ☐ torre-abbey.org.uk; Tue-Sun 10am-5pm; £8, under-18s free, garden-only ticket £2.50), the first building of note in the town, was a Premonstratensian (a Catholic order of canons founded at Premontre) monastery founded in 1196. Today it houses an art collection, runs tours and invites you to explore its exotic gardens. The *tea room* (daily 9.30am-5pm) is a lovely spot for a light lunch or cream teas.

Living Coasts (☎ 01803-202470, ☐ livingcoasts.org.uk; daily 10am-5pm, winter to 4pm; £11.80) is Torquay's very own coastal zoo where penguins play and fur seals frolic. As you leave town, look for the nets on the right as you head up Beacon Hill and you can't miss it.

The area's most famous discovery, a prehistoric jawbone found at Kent's Cavern (see box p170), can be seen in **Torquay Museum** (☎ 01803-293975, ☐ torquaymuseum.org; Mon-Sat 10am-4pm, Sun too during summer school hols; £6.45), which also tells the story of the caves and houses an Agatha Christie gallery (see box opposite).

The **International Agatha Christie Festival** (see p14) is held in and around the town during September. Some of the events in Torbay's **Festival of Poetry** (see p14) are also held here in October.

Services

The **English Riviera Visitor Information Centre** (☎ 01803-211211, ☐ www.englishriviera.co.uk; Jun-end Sep plus Easter hols daily 10am-1pm & 1.30-5pm, Oct-end Dec & mid Feb-May Mon-Wed & Fri-Sat 10am-1pm & 1.30-5pm) is conveniently placed in the marina.

For **internet** (30 mins £1, or free with any UK library card), Torquay Central **Library** (Mon, Wed & Fri 9.30am-6pm, Tue & Thur 9.30am-1pm, Sat 9.30am-4pm) is the place to head to. There are plenty of **banks** with **ATMs** around town.

For **trekking and camping gear**, Mountain Warehouse (Mon-Sat 9am-5.30pm, Sun 10am-5pm) is on Union St, the main thoroughfare, and Trespass (Mon-Sat 9am-5.30pm, Sun 10.30am-4.30pm) is lower down on Fleet St.

Opposite Mountain Warehouse is the **pharmacy**, Boots (Mon-Sat 9am-5.30pm, Sun 10.30am-4.30pm), while further down the road is the **post office** (Mon-Sat 8.30am-5.30pm), hidden away in the local branch of WH Smith, and the **supermarket** Tesco (Mon-Sat 7am-11pm, Sun 11am-5pm). There is also a **convenience store**, McColl's (Mon-Sat 7am-11pm, Sun to 10pm), nearer the Marina.

Transport

[See also pp50-4] Stagecoach's hop12, hop22, 46 & X80 **buses** call at the bus station and travel as far west as Brixham and east as Shaldon and Teignmouth.

Frequent **trains** connect Torquay with Exeter.

For a **taxi** try 1st Class Cars (☎ 01803-299305), or Torbay Taxis (☎ 01803-211611, ☐ torbaytaxis.co.uk).

Where to stay

It will be no surprise that Torquay is full of accommodation aimed at the holidaying masses, though there are no campsites or hostels. Behind Abbey Park and along Belgrave Road there are numerous B&Bs and hotels; once again, however, finding one willing to accept an advance booking for a one-night stop, particularly in July and August and at weekends, can be problematic though most will if they have availability near the time.

Options on Belgrave Rd include the remarkably cheap *The Wayfarer* (☎ 01803-299138, 🖳 wayfarertorquay.co.uk; 4D/1D or T; WI-FI; £24-32.50pp, sgl occ £32-50), at No 37; *Kethla House* (☎ 01803-473767, 🖳 kethlahouse.co.uk; 6D/1Tr; WI-FI; £27.50-37.50pp, sgl occ room rate), No 33, who will cater for any special dietary requirements if requested in advance; and *Cranborne* (☎ 01803-211660, 🖳 cranborne torquay.co.uk; 1S/6D/1T; ➸; WI-FI; £31.25-40pp, sgl £35-40, sgl occ room rate), at No 58, which has a guest lounge.

On Scarborough Rd, just off Belgrave Rd, you'll come across *South View* (☎ 01803-296029, 🖳 thesouthview.com; 4D/1T; WI-FI; £27.50-32.50pp, sgl occ £30-45), at No 12, and *The Southbank Hotel* (☎ 01803-296701, 🖳 southbankhotel.co.uk; 2S/2D or T/7D/1Tr/2Qd; ➸; WI-FI; £37-62pp, sgl £42, sgl occ by negotiation), Nos 15-17; neither, unfortunately, takes advance bookings for a one-night stay in July and August. The Southbank is licensed (bar open from 7pm).

Nearer to the town centre, on Babbacombe Rd, are *Tusker Lodge* (☎ 01803-292668, 🖳 tuskerlodge.co.uk; 4S shared facilities/7D all en suite; WI-FI; 🐾; £25-31pp, sgl from £30, sgl occ £38-46; Feb to mid Dec), at No 533, and *Ravenswood* (☎ 01803-292900, 🖳 ravens woodhotel.co.uk; 6D/1T, all en suite; WI-FI; £29.50-44.50pp, sgl occ £49-79), at No 535.

Others worth considering on this stretch of road include *The Palms Hotel* (☎ 01803-293970, 🖳 palmshoteltorquay.co .uk; 1S/6D/2T; WI-FI; £25-40pp, sgl £39-49, sgl £50-60), No 537.

Still on Babbacombe Rd, are: *Kingsholm* (☎ 01803-297794, 🖳 www .kingsholmhotel.co.uk; 1S/5D/3T; WI-FI; £30-40pp, sgl £40-45, sgl occ £50-70; Mar-Nov) at No 539; *Hotel Peppers* (☎ 01803-293856, 🖳 hotel-peppers.co.uk; 2S/4D/2D or T; WI-FI; £31-40pp, sgl £40-48, sgl occ room rate), at No 551, which has an honesty bar and is more than willing to put walkers up for a solitary night; and *Hotel Hudson* (☎ 01803-203407, 🖳 hotelhudson .co.uk; 2S/7D; WI-FI; £25-45pp, sgl £35-50, sgl occ £40-80), No 545, which does not take advance bookings for a one-night stay at the weekend.

At the top of the hill (74 Braddons Hill Rd East) is the dog-friendly *Robin Hill Hotel* (☎ 01803-214518, 🖳 robinhillhotel .co.uk; 5D/5T/2Qd; WI-FI; 🐾; £35-60pp, sgl occ £55-70). It's a great place to stop although it's a fair old march from the path itself (however, Stagecoach's No 32 bus service (Mon-Sat 6/hr, Sun 2/hr) stops near the top of Babbacombe Rd and leaves from The Strand).

Larger **hotels** available in Torquay include *The Grosvenor* (☎ 01803-294373, 🖳 grosvenorhoteltorquay.co.uk; 23D/15D or T/6T/2Qd; ➸; WI-FI; 🐾; £39-67pp, sgl occ £78-114), on Belgrave Rd. The restaurant here is open daily (12.30-2.30pm & 6.30-9pm).

Opposite is a branch of the *Premier Inn* (☎ 0871-527 9102, 🖳 premierinn .com/gb/en/hotels/england/devon/torquay/ torquay.html; 143D or T; ➸; WI-FI) chain; it is just a short distance from the seafront and path at the bottom of Belgrave Rd. Saver/Flex rates start from £41/58 for a

---

❏ **Where to stay: the details**
Unless specified, B&B-style accommodation is either en suite or has private facilities; ➸ means at least one room has a bath; 🐾 signifies that dogs are welcome in at least one room but always by prior arrangement, an additional charge may also be payable (see also pp315-17); WI-FI means wi-fi is available in the property, though not always reliably in every room.

Torquay

Where to eat and drink
1 Green Leaf Café
2 The Bay Bakery
3 Prezzo
4 Shiraz
5 Offshore
6 Harbour Fish & Chips
7 Man Friday's Lobster
   House

8 Burridges
9 The Devon Arms
10 Hole in the Wall
11 Amici
12 Jingles
13 Bianco's
14 Ephesus
15 Maha-Bharat
16 Cotton-eyed Joe's

room, but can be up to double that; for the best rate book online and well in advance. Most rooms can also sleep additional children but not more than two adults. An all-you-can-eat cooked breakfast costs £8.99 (continental £6.99).

Where to eat and drink

Cafés One of the loveliest aspects of a stay in Torquay is the smell of coffee that wafts across parts of the town from **Costa Rica coffee roasters** (🖥 costa-rica.co.uk; Mon-Fri 9am-5pm), a family firm at 49 Abbey Rd that's been going for over 50 years. It's not a café itself, but you can buy a cup made from the fruits of their labours at nearby *Green Leaf Café* (☎ 01803-293207, 🖥 greenleafcafe.co.uk; Mon-Sat 10am-2.30pm), a small, friendly, health-conscious café that's located at the bottom of a flight of steps leading down from Abbey Rd, but which is also accessed from Union St.

Close to the coast path you can get sandwiches and pastries, or sit down for a coffee, at *The Bay Bakery* (☎ 01803-411361; Mon-Sat 9.30am-4.30pm, Sun 10am-3.30pm), while further around the marina, you'll find *Burridge's* (☎ 01803-213964; WI-FI; 🐾; summer Mon-Fri 10am-6pm, Sat-Sun 10am-5.30pm, closes earlier in winter), a smart café-tearoom with a very tempting line in cream teas (from £6), and pavement seating overlooking the harbour. For a Devon cream tea with a dash of history, try *Torre Abbey Tea Rooms* (☎ 01803-215948, 🖥 torre-abbey.org.uk; 🐾; daily 9.30am-5pm, winter Tue-Sun 10am-4pm). You don't have to pay to get into the abbey to visit the tea room.

Pubs Hugely popular, thanks largely to its prime location overlooking the harbour, *Offshore* (☎ 01803-292108, 🖥 offshore torquay.co.uk; food served daily 9am-9pm) is a bar-restaurant that's great for a pint of ice-cold lager on a sunny summer's evening, but also does very good food, including seafood.

Nearby *Shiraz* (☎ 01803-200002; food summer daily 9am-9pm, winter to 6pm) is a gastro-pub with a similar location, although the food (standard pub grub including fish & chips) isn't of the same standard. Both places are also open for breakfast.

Torquay's best traditional pub is also its oldest; the discreet *Hole in the Wall* (☎ 01803-200755, 🖥 holeinthewalltorquay.co .uk; WI-FI; 🐾 bar area only; food daily noon-2.30pm & 5.30-9pm), a 16th-century inn (c1540) located up a dead-end alley called Park Lane. They have as many as seven real ales on tap at any one time and also do decent pub grub. Practically next door, is *The Devon Arms* (☎ 01803-361671; WI-FI; 🐾; food daily noon-9pm), which has been going since the 18th century, but has lost much of its charm in modern renovations. It is, though, a very welcoming place, and the food (standard pub fare) is exceptionally affordable (mains £5-8). Has Sharp's Doom Bar on tap.

Restaurants There's an eclectic mix of restaurants to choose from here, many of which are on or close to the marina. *Prezzo* (☎ 01803-389525, 🖥 prezzorestaurants.co .uk; Mon-Sat noon-11pm, Sun noon-10.30pm) is a branch of a reasonably smart nationwide pizza chain (pasta and pizza mains from £10) at the northern end of the marina.

On the other side of the marina, on Victoria Parade, *Man Friday's Lobster House* (☎ 01803-296416, 🖥 manfridays.co .uk; summer daily 7pm to late, closed Mon & Tue in winter) is a lovely, intriguing little fish restaurant with first-floor terrace seating and a menu (mains from £15.50) that includes sea bass, roasted monkfish and lemon sole as well as mussels and lobster. For more traditional British seaside fare, head to the nearby chippy *Harbour Fish & Chips* (daily 10am-7pm, till 10/11pm during summer school hols), which has indoor seating as well as tables and chairs scattered around the pavement outside. A small cod & chips costs £4.95.

Leading off the marina, up Torwood St, you'll find *Jingles* (☎ 01803-293340, 🖥 jinglesrestaurant.com; daily 6pm to late), a typically exuberant Mexican restaurant, where you can eat enchiladas to your heart's content.

Next door, *Bianco's* (☎ 01803-293430, 💻 biancos.co.uk; daily 6-11pm) is arguably the best Italian restaurant in town. Across the road is *Amici* (☎ 01803-201770, 💻 amicitorquay.co.uk; summer daily noon-11pm, rest of year may close earlier), another Italian with an outside eating area. Further up you'll find *Ephesus* (☎ 01803-294466, 💻 ephesustorquay.co.uk; daily 4.30pm-late), which specialises in Turkish and Greek cuisine, *Maha-Bharat* (☎ 01803-215541, 💻 maha-bharat-torquay.co .uk; daily 5pm to midnight), an Indian restaurant with an emphasis on Bengali cuisine and some excellent Balti dishes, and *Cotton-eyed Joe's* (☎ 01803-214444, 💻 cottoneyedjoes.co.uk; Tue-Thur 4.30-9.30pm, Fri-Sat 4.30-10pm, Sun 4.30-9pm), an American bar and grill with plenty of burgers and steaks.

TORQUAY TO TEIGNMOUTH   [MAPS 33-37]

This is a strenuous **11¼-mile (18km; 4hrs 35mins plus 10 mins for the ferry crossing to Teignmouth)** walk: after the concrete monotony of the previous stage it's time to open your lungs again and get back out into the wilds. Having passed Hope's Nose, Torbay is finally left behind and although you'll be sucked back into civilisation briefly at St Marychurch, for most of this stage you'll find yourself enjoying some beautiful walking and mesmerising views interrupted only by the occasional and pleasantly isolated public house or seasonal café. With a ferry crossing (before you set off make sure you have checked the ferry times) from Shaldon to Teignmouth at the end of the day and numerous twists and turns, ascents and descents along the way, this stage should not be underestimated. Planning for rest-stops would be wise as well as carrying ample food and water.

The route
Leaving Torquay can take a little concentration: look for acorns on the ground and stickers on lamp posts – as well as more orthodox signage – and you should be fine. Eventually, after turning right at **The Imperial Hotel** (the path actually enters the car park of the hotel before skirting the hotel's grounds), the path finally finds some space and freedom from humanity through a stone archway leading to **Daddyhole Plain**, where you'll also find a small, un-manned **National Coastwatch Visitor Centre** with displays on the history of Torbay, CCTV footage of the coastline, and a pair of binoculars for visitors to use. Due to its Devonian limestone, the accompanying cove here is one of the Riviera's geosites (see box on p150).

The path now passes through woodland overlooking **Meadfoot Beach** where there is *Meadfoot Beach Café* (☎ 01803-213988; Mar/Apr-Oct/Nov daily 9am-5pm depending on the weather) with toasties, soups, jacket potatoes and wonderful sea views. Note, you can fill up your water bottle from the **water tap** behind the beach huts beside the café.

A short climb and some road rambling soon sees you rounding **Thatcher Point** and brings you to a junction where, officially at least, the coast path turns right down to **Hope's Nose** – an SSSI (note that because it is an SSSI you can't hammer the rock in search of fossils or take specimens; you can only photograph any fossils you see) and the northern promontory of Tor Bay – before following a path above the road to continue. Wonderful woodland walking now follows as you continue along **Black Head** past **Anstey's Cove**.

Kent's Cavern (☎ 01803-215136, 🖳 kents-cavern.co.uk; daily 9.30am-4pm, Jul & Aug till 4.30pm, tours from 10am, café 10am-4pm; entrance ticket £10), a prehistoric cave system where in 1927 the oldest human fossil – an upper jawbone – yet to be discovered in the UK was unearthed, can be accessed by turning left and heading inland here; it is about a 10-minute walk.

The coast path, however, continues above **Redgate Beach** to **Long Quarry Point**. The signage is particularly poor here but look out for a wooden signpost leading off into the trees shortly after the mock-Roman shelter. Descending steep wooded steps you eventually arrive at the charming *Cary Arms* (☎ 01803-327110, 🖳 caryarms.co.uk; 7D/1Qd; ☞; WI-FI; 🐾; £85-135pp, sgl occ £120-220), where the Devon steak mushroom & Otter Ale pie (£15.50) may well

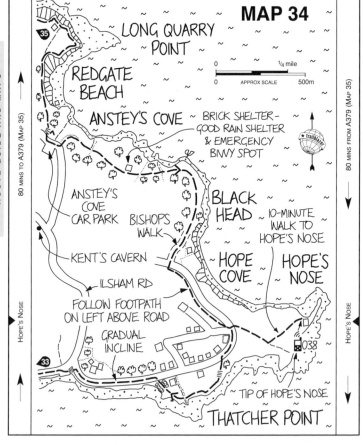

ROUTE GUIDE AND MAPS

80 MINS TO A379 (MAP 35)

HOPE'S NOSE

MAP 34

LONG QUARRY POINT

REDGATE BEACH

ANSTEY'S COVE ~ BRICK SHELTER – GOOD RAIN SHELTER & EMERGENCY BIVVY SPOT

ANSTEY'S COVE CAR PARK   BISHOPS WALK

KENT'S CAVERN

ILSHAM RD

FOLLOW FOOTPATH ON LEFT ABOVE ROAD

GRADUAL INCLINE

BLACK HEAD ~ 10-MINUTE WALK TO HOPE'S NOSE

HOPE COVE

HOPE'S NOSE

☎038

~ TIP OF HOPE'S NOSE

THATCHER POINT

0 ___ 1/4 mile
0 ___ APPROX SCALE ___ 500m

★ trailblazer

80 MINS FROM A379 (MAP 35)

HOPE'S NOSE

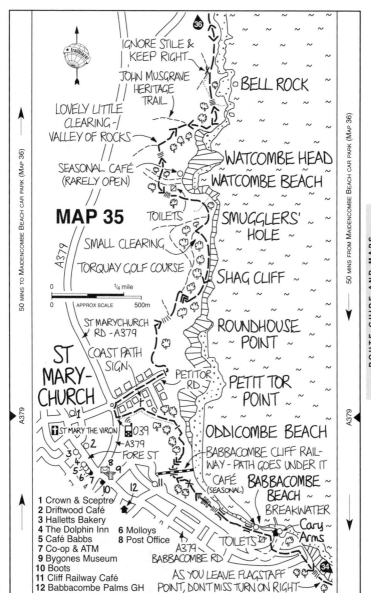

IGNORE STILE & KEEP RIGHT

JOHN MUSGRAVE HERITAGE TRAIL

BELL ROCK

LOVELY LITTLE CLEARING - VALLEY OF ROCKS

SEASONAL CAFÉ (RARELY OPEN)

WATCOMBE HEAD

WATCOMBE BEACH

MAP 35

TOILETS

SMUGGLERS' HOLE

SMALL CLEARING

TORQUAY GOLF COURSE

SHAG CLIFF

0 ¼ mile
0 APPROX SCALE 500m

ST MARYCHURCH RD - A379

ROUNDHOUSE POINT

COAST PATH SIGN

ST MARY-CHURCH

PETITOR RD

PETIT TOR POINT

ST MARY THE VIRGIN

039

A379 FORE ST

ODDICOMBE BEACH

BABBACOMBE CLIFF RAILWAY - PATH GOES UNDER IT

CAFÉ (SEASONAL)

BABBACOMBE BEACH

BREAKWATER

Cary Arms

1 Crown & Sceptre
2 Driftwood Café
3 Halletts Bakery
4 The Dolphin Inn
5 Café Babbs
6 Molloys
7 Co-op & ATM
8 Post Office
9 Bygones Museum
10 Boots
11 Cliff Railway Café
12 Babbacombe Palms GH

TOILETS

A379 BABBACOMBE RD

AS YOU LEAVE FLAGSTAFF POINT, DON'T MISS TURN ON RIGHT

50 MINS TO MAIDENCOMBE BEACH CAR PARK (MAP 36)

A379

50 MINS FROM MAIDENCOMBE BEACH CAR PARK (MAP 36)

A379

ROUTE GUIDE AND MAPS

prove too tempting to resist; **food** is served daily noon-3pm & 6.30-9pm. From the pub you can see where, in 2010, a 5000-tonne rockfall occurred at the northern end of **Oddicombe Beach** near **Petit Tor Point**. The path avoids this by climbing steeply beside the fabulously fun, 90-year-old **Babbacombe Cliff Railway** (☎ 01803-328750, 🖥 babbacombecliffrailway.co.uk; Jun-Sep daily 9am-5.55pm, Feb-May & Oct 9.30am-5pm, Nov & Dec weekends only; sgl/return £2/2.50) and on, eventually, to the A379. Here you can either turn right to continue along the coastal path, or left to St Marychurch.

ST MARYCHURCH   [Map 35, p171]

Strictly speaking an outer suburb of Torquay, St Marychurch has a village-like vibe and is one of the oldest settlements in south Devon, dating back to around AD1050. The Saxon font at the **church of St Mary the Virgin** dates from AD1110, although the main part of the church was destroyed on May 30, 1943, by a German WWII bomb that killed 26 people, including 21 children who were attending a Sunday School service at the church. A simple plaque above the door commemorates the tragic event.

Fore St is home to **Bygones Museum** (☎ 01803-326108, 🖥 bygones.co.uk; daily Nov-Mar 10am-4pm, Apr-Jun & Oct 10am-5pm, Jul-Sep 10am-6pm; £9.50), where there are numerous displays relating to the Victorian era as well as a life-size Victorian street.

There is also a Co-op **supermarket** (daily 7am-11pm) with an **ATM** outside it, a **pharmacy**, Boots (Mon-Fri 8.30am-5.30pm, Sat 9am-1pm), and a **post office** (Mon-Fri 8.30am-5.30pm, Sat 9am-1pm).

Stagecoach's hop22 (Dudlish Warren to Paignton) **bus** (see pp50-4) calls here.

For a **B&B** you could try *Babbacombe Palms Guest House* (☎ 01803-327087, 🖥 babbacombepalms.com; 1S/5D/1D or T/1Qd; wi-fi; £27.50-35pp, sgl from £45, sgl occ from £55), a small hotel with a licensed bar at 2 York Rd.

Food-wise, at the top of the railway is *Cliff Railway Café* (☎ 01803-324025, 🖥 yellands.com; wi-fi; daily 9.30am-4.30pm, to 5pm in summer, food served till 4/4.30pm), with ice-cream, scones, paninis and cold beer, as well as fabulous views. On Fore St, *Café Babbs* (☎ 01803-312619; wi-fi; Mon-Sat 9am-4pm) serves breakfasts (from £3.60), jacket potatoes (from £4) and sandwiches and baguettes (from £3.20) as well as cream teas (£4.20).

At No 55, *Driftwood Café* (☎ 01803-314057; wi-fi; 🐾; Mon-Sat 9am-4pm) does similar fare at slightly higher prices. Opposite, *Halletts Bakery* (Mon 9am-5pm, Tue-Fri 8.30am-5pm, Sat 8.30am-4pm) does pastries, pasties and the like.

There are two pubs on Fore St too: *Molloys* (☎ 01803-311825) doesn't do food, but has real ales on tap; *The Dolphin Inn* (☎ 01803-311670, 🖥 thedolphintorquay.co.uk; food Mon-Sat 12.30-8pm, Sun 12.30-6pm; mains £8-10) does decent food but is a bit soulless.

The best pub in town, though, is round the corner, back towards the coast path: the *Crown & Sceptre* (☎ 01803-328290; food daily noon-2.30pm, plus 6-9pm in high season) is a proper spit-and-sawdust locals pub with a strong selection of real ales and good pub grub, although food is only served at lunchtime for most of the year.

You stay with the A379 only until the roundabout, where Petitor Rd takes you to the back of the tor. Passing through the woods that decorate **Shag Cliff** you cross the track leading to **Watcombe Beach** where you'll find a *seasonal café* (that's rarely open these days) and a public **toilet**. More woodland wandering brings you to Maidencombe via a beautiful little glade called **Valley of Rocks** and a junction with the John Musgrave Heritage Trail (see p37).

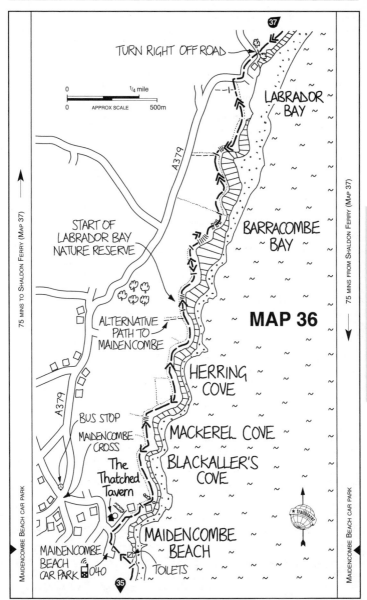

TURN RIGHT OFF ROAD

0   1/4 mile
0   APPROX SCALE   500m

A379

LABRADOR BAY

START OF
LABRADOR BAY
NATURE RESERVE

BARRACOMBE BAY

MAP 36

ALTERNATIVE
PATH TO
MAIDENCOMBE

HERRING COVE

A379

BUS STOP

MAIDENCOMBE CROSS

MACKEREL COVE

The Thatched Tavern

BLACKALLER'S COVE

MAIDENCOMBE BEACH

MAIDENCOMBE BEACH CAR PARK

040

TOILETS

75 MINS TO SHALDON FERRY (MAP 37)

75 MINS FROM SHALDON FERRY (MAP 37)

ROUTE GUIDE AND MAPS

MAIDENCOMBE BEACH CAR PARK

MAIDENCOMBE BEACH CAR PARK

★ trailblazer

37

35

MAIDENCOMBE   [Map 36, p173]

A quiet and remote cluster of houses, the centre of focus here is the delightful *Thatched Tavern* (☎ 01803-329155, 🖳 the thatchedtaverndevon.co.uk), a pretty, thatched-roofed country pub that offers **B&B** (2D; ✆; WI-FI; 🐾; £60-65pp, sgl occ £100) as well as excellent **food** (Oct-Jun

Mon-Fri noon-2.30pm & 6-9pm, Sat noon-9pm, Sun noon-4pm; Jul-Sep Mon-Sat noon-9pm, Sun noon-8pm), and also has a delightful garden.

You need to walk up to Maidencombe Cross to catch Stagecoach's hop22 **bus** (Dawlish Warren to Paignton), see pp50-4.

A gravel path takes you away from Maidencombe; following the copper-coloured cliffs it careens its way past **Blackaller's** and **Mackerel coves**, never seeming to find a straight (or horizontal) line until arriving at **Labrador Bay Nature Reserve** (🖳 rspb.org.uk, click on Reserves and events). Purchased by the RSPB in 2008 the reserve's aim is to help protect the **cirl bunting** (see also p71 and p133), a rare bird which is almost unique to South Devon. Other species regularly spotted include buzzards, peregrines and yellowhammers.

The path continues to dip and rise steeply via several combes, rejoining the A379 briefly before heading back into the fields. As you climb over **Bundle Head**, Teignmouth comes into full view – as does Shaldon Golf Course below you. Exmouth can also be seen – just – in the distance. A flat amble by the golf course brings you to a pleasant walk through woods. A bench offers a tremendous view across Teignmouth Pier as well as the delights that await you over the next few days.

Dropping down through the woods you arrive at a pub, *The Ness* (see p176 and p177), on the outskirts of the charming village of Shaldon.

SHALDON   [map p177]

The quiet Georgian village of Shaldon offers a peaceful alternative to staying over the water in Teignmouth (not that it's especially boisterous there either!).

It's a pity that most people hurry over the Teign as Shaldon is much more than just a commuter village. For a start, it has a few decent accommodation options, including campsites, as well as a couple of very likeable boozers serving hearty food in an amiable atmosphere. It also boasts a **botanical garden** (**Homeyards**; built by the late widow of William Homeyard, the inventor of Liqufruta cough medicine; open all year, free) with its own ruined castle, a **limekiln** (Map 37; behind The Ness pub) and even a small zoo: **Shaldon Zoo**

(Map 37; ☎ 01626-872234, 🖳 shaldon wildlifetrust.org.uk; daily Apr-Sep 10am-5pm, Oct-Mar 10am-4pm; £6.70) is set in one acre of woodland on Ness Drive and plays host to several endangered animals including the smallest monkey in the world, the South American pygmy marmoset.

The village also has its own **classical music festival** (see p14) in June and a **water carnival day** (🖳 www.shaldonwater carnival.co.uk) in August. Furthermore, when visiting in summer do not be surprised to see local people dressed in Georgian costume: Wednesdays between early June and mid September are known as **1785 day** with celebrations including a farmer's market and craft fair (10am-4pm),

---

❏ **Important note – walking times**
All times in this book refer only to the time spent walking. You will need to add 20-30% to allow for rests, photography, checking the map, drinking water etc.

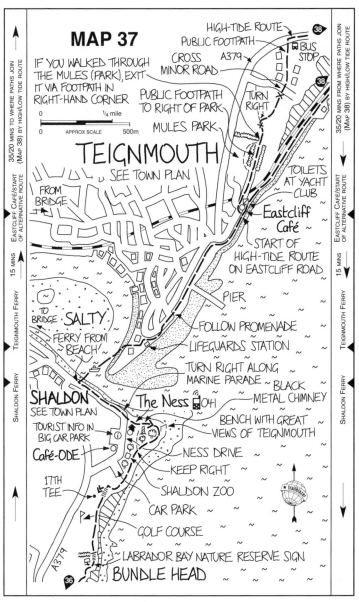

MAP 37

IF YOU WALKED THROUGH THE MULES (PARK), EXIT IT VIA FOOTPATH IN RIGHT-HAND CORNER

HIGH-TIDE ROUTE
PUBLIC FOOTPATH
CROSS MINOR ROAD
A379
BUS STOP
38
38

PUBLIC FOOTPATH TO RIGHT OF PARK
TURN RIGHT

MULES PARK

0   ¼ mile
0   APPROX SCALE   500m

TEIGNMOUTH

SEE TOWN PLAN

FROM BRIDGE

TOILETS AT YACHT CLUB

~ Eastcliff Café ~

START OF HIGH-TIDE ROUTE ON EASTCLIFF ROAD

TO BRIDGE   SALTY

FERRY FROM BEACH

PIER

FOLLOW PROMENADE

LIFEGUARDS STATION

TURN RIGHT ALONG MARINE PARADE ~ BLACK METAL CHIMNEY

SHALDON
SEE TOWN PLAN

TOURIST INFO IN BIG CAR PARK

Café-ODE

17TH TEE

The Ness

BENCH WITH GREAT VIEWS OF TEIGNMOUTH

NESS DRIVE

KEEP RIGHT

SHALDON ZOO

CAR PARK

GOLF COURSE

~ LABRADOR BAY NATURE RESERVE SIGN

A379

36

BUNDLE HEAD

trailblazer

35/20 MINS FROM WHERE PATHS JOIN (MAP 38) BY HIGH-TIDE ROUTE
EASTCLIFF Café/START OF ALTERNATIVE ROUTE
15 MINS
TEIGNMOUTH FERRY
SHALDON FERRY
ROUTE GUIDE AND MAPS

as well as maypole dancing and Punch 'n' Judy shows in the evenings.

Services
The **tourist information centre** (Map 37; ☎ 07546-995623, 🖳 shaldon-village.co.uk; late May to late Sep daily 10.30am-4.30pm) stands in its own building in the car park opposite The Ness pub.

Everything else is down by the water in the village centre, including the well-stocked **village store** (Mon-Sat 8am-6pm, Sun 9am-4pm), an **ATM**, a **post office** (Mon-Wed & Fri 9am-5.30pm, Thur 9am-1pm, Sat 9am-12.30pm) and a **pharmacy** (Mon-Wed & Fri 9am-1pm & 2-6pm, Thur & Sat 9am-1pm).

Transport
[See also pp50-4] Stagecoach's hop22 **bus** calls here en route between Dawlish Warren and Paignton.

For a **taxi** try any of the Teignmouth taxi firms. See opposite for details about the **ferry** to Teignmouth.

Where to stay
For **camping**, you need to walk about a mile (1.2km) beyond the village to *Long Meadow Farm* (☎ 01626-872732, 🖳 longmeadowfarm.co.uk; 🐾; £10-13 for a hiker & tent plus £2 for each extra person; Easter to end Sep), a very welcoming family-run campsite with five flat grassy pitches, a large barn known as the 'farm hub' where campers can read, eat their meals and charge mobile phones, and various farm animals (chickens, pigs, goats and ponies) to keep young campers amused. If you don't fancy the walk back into Shaldon, you can eat at the large holiday park opposite the farm entrance, which has a restaurant and a pub with a riverside terrace. To get to Long Meadow Farm, walk past the Shipwrights Arms on Ringmore Rd (which becomes Coombe Rd) and you'll see the farm entrance on your left.

For **B&B**, it's possible to stay at the super-smart pub *The Ness* (Map 37; ☎ 01626-873480, 🖳 theness.co.uk; 7D/2D or T; 🐾; WI-FI; 🐾; £52.50-70pp, sgl occ room rate), right on the coast path. All the rooms

have balconies, but not all have clear views over the estuary. Rates are higher for sea-view rooms.

Away from the shoreline and facing onto the picturesque village green is the dog-friendly *Potters Mooring* (☎ 01626-873225, 🖳 pottersmooring.co.uk; 4D/1T/1Tr plus two cottages – one with D & T, the other with 1T); 🐾; WI-FI; 🐾; £42.50-60pp, sgl occ £65-95), at No 30. Unfortunately, they are unlikely to be able to accept advance bookings for one-night stays at weekends in July and August.

Maybe, instead, you'd like to rent a **beach hut**! *Shaldon Beach Huts* (☎ 01803-213814, 🖳 shaldonbeachhuts.co.uk; WI-FI; £165-175 per hut per night for a single-night stay; rates reduced for longer stays) have two self-catered beach huts; one sleeps two, the other sleeps two to four. There is underfloor heating and they all have terraces which lead out on to the beach, as well as showers and their own little kitchens.

Where to eat and drink
Cafés   The award-winning *Shaldon Bakery* (☎ 01626-872401; summer Mon-Sat 8am-4/4.30pm, low season to 3pm, winter to 2pm) sells breads and cakes as well as local preserves for souvenirs and hot drinks to take away. Look out for their speciality 'uglibun'; an oversized, oddly-shaped, but ever-so-tasty currant bun that's so popular it has its own Twitter account.

With a prime location overlooking the estuary, *Clipper Café* (☎ 01626-873747, 🖳 theclippershaldon.co.uk; WI-FI; 🐾 ground floor only; daily 8am-9pm) is a popular, modern café with good coffee, a riverside terrace out the back, and a separate evening menu (from 6pm; mains £10-15). Across the road, *The Strand Café* (☎ 01626-872624, 🖳 thestrandcafebistro.co.uk; well-behaved 🐾; school summer holidays daily 9.30am-4pm, rest of year Wed-Fri 10am-4pm, Sat-Sun 9.30am-4pm) is a café-bistro that specialises in brunches (£7-10).

Along Fore St, *Coffee Rush* is a café-tearoom (cakes, pastries, cream tea), which is housed inside The Clifford Arms pub (see opposite).

Up near the zoo, *Café ODE* (Map 37; ☎ 01626-873427, 🖥 odetruefood.com; WI-FI; daily 10am-5pm, summer Fri & Sat to 7pm) is an award-winning café-restaurant that brews its own beer. Its ever-changing menu includes delights such as pulled pork burgers, speckled lentil dhal, and fish chowder.

Pubs & restaurants Shaldon is blessed with numerous pubs of distinction. The largest and swishest of these is *The Ness* (see Where to stay; food served daily noon-9pm), a Hall & Woodhouse property – so more of a restaurant than a traditional pub – but the food is good value and top quality, and the sea views from the tables on the terrace are superb.

A close rival to The Ness, *Ferry Boat Inn* (☎ 01626-872340; food served daily noon-3pm, Mon-Sat 6-9pm; 🐾; WI-FI) is an atmospheric place which hosts a barbecue in summer on their lovely patio across the road overlooking the water.

There are three more pubs for your consideration. Overlooking the pleasant village green, *The London Inn* (☎ 01626-872453, 🖥 londoninnshaldon.co.uk; WI-FI; 🐾 bar area only; food Mon-Sat noon-2.30pm & 6-9pm, Sun noon-5pm) serves real ales and plenty of decent walker-sized meals such as Devon beef burger (£12.95) and pie & mash (£13.95).

The Clifford Arms (☎ 01626-872311; WI-FI; 🐾; food daily 9am-4pm, Fri & Sat 6-8pm also food on jazz Mondays) converts into a jazz café on Mondays, while a band honks out some jazz tunes. They've got a nice beer garden out the back too.

A little further from Shaldon's centre, on Ringmore Rd, *The Shipwrights Arms* (☎ 01626-873232, 🖥 shipwrightsshaldon.co.uk; 🐾; food daily noon-10pm) is less popular, but welcoming nonetheless, and serves good-value pub grub (mains £8.50-12) as well as a selection of real ales.

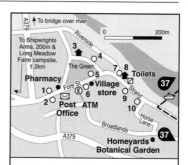

Shaldon

Where to stay, eat and drink
1 The Clifford Arms & Coffee Rush
2 ODE-dining
3 Potters Mooring
4 The London Inn
5 Village Fish & Chips
6 Shaldon Bakery
7 Clipper Café
8 Shaldon Beach Huts
9 Ferry Boat Inn
10 The Strand Café

Away from the pubs, *ODE-dining* (☎ 01626-873977, 🖥 odetruefood.com/dining; Fri-Sat 7-9pm) was once voted one of the top 100 restaurants in the UK. It's certainly a treat, but is usually only open on Friday and Saturday evenings. Their regionally inspired tasting menu costs £55 per person with a wine flight an extra £25pp.

Back down to earth, a cod & chips at nearby *Village Fish & Chips* (☎ 01626-873213, 🖥 thevillagefishandchips.co.uk; summer Tue, Wed, Fri & Sat noon-2.30pm & 5.30-9pm, Thur 5.30-9pm, Sun 5.30-8.30pm, winter days/hours variable) will set you back just £6. It's a takeaway really, but they do have a couple of tables inside too.

The cute **ferry to Teignmouth** (☎ 07896-711822, 🖥 teignmouthshaldonferry.co.uk; daily Apr to mid July, Sep & Oct 8am-6pm, mid July to end Aug 8am to dusk, Nov-Jan 8am-4.30pm, Feb & Mar 8am-5pm; note that at the weekends in summer/winter the service starts from 9/10am; £1.50, 🐾 free) leaves from the beach itself. If you happen to arrive when there's no ferry, the alternative is to walk up to the road bridge and cross there (about 30 mins in total).

Note that, having arrived in Teignmouth, the coast path is less well signed, but if you walk up to the road from the ferry drop-off and keep following Teignmouth's promenade you can't go wrong.

TEIGNMOUTH

The last place in mainland England to have been successfully invaded by a foreign foe (in this instance the French in 1690), Teignmouth (pronounced 'Tinmouth') is a fun, friendly and compact place and one that's mercifully less hectic than its cousins down the coast. Lively cafés and proper pubs abound but sadly these days there's a dearth of tourist accommodation.

Visitors started to frequent the town in great numbers during the Georgian era (1714-1837) and many of the streets are adorned with architecture from this time. **Teignmouth & Shaldon Museum** (☎ 01626-777041, ☐ teignheritage.org.uk; Tue-Sat Apr-Sep 10am-5pm, Mar & Oct to 4.30pm; £2.20), at 29 French St, houses a number of collections celebrating the area's maritime links, and the **Victorian pier** is charming. The octagonal **St James Parish Church**, at the junction of Exeter Rd and Bitton Park Rd, has a 13th-century sandstone tower.

Hot hikers can cool off with an outdoor swim in **Teignmouth Lido** (☐ teign bridgeleisure.co.uk/swim; May-early Sep daily; £4.50), right by the coast path as you leave the town.

Teignmouth Folk Festival (see p14) is held here in June and the **Jazz Festival** (see p14) in November. Details of other local events can also be found on ☐ love teignmouth.co.uk.

Services

There's a **tourist information point** (☎ 01626-215665; Mon-Sat 10am-3pm) with leaflets inside the reception area of the theatre, Pavilions Teignmouth. Theatre box office staff are also usually on hand to help with local information queries but it is also worth looking at ☐ loveteignmouth.co.uk.

On Den Rd is the **post office** (Mon-Fri 9am-5.30pm, Sat 9am-12.30pm), while the

Co-op **supermarket** (daily 7am-10pm) is close by on Bank St where, unsurprisingly, you'll find **banks** with **ATMs**.

Internet access (Mon & Wed 9am-6pm, Tue & Fri 9am-5pm, Sat 9am-1pm) is available at the library on the A379, just outside the town centre. Quayside **Bookshop** (Mon-Sat 10am-5pm) is in the old part of town on Northumberland Place, as is the local **pharmacy**, Maunder (Mon-Fri 9am-5.30pm, Sat 9am-1pm), at 4 Somerset Place. For a larger pharmacy, open on Sunday too, try Superdrug (Mon-Sat 8.30am-6pm, Sun 10am-5.30pm) on Bank St.

There's a **launderette** (daily 7am-6pm) on Brunswick St.

Transport

[See also pp50-4] Stagecoach's 2 **bus** (Newton Abbot to Exeter) calls here and as does their hop22 (Dawlish Warren to Paignton) service.

Trains call here regularly en route between Exmouth and Paignton.

For a **cab** try Alpha Taxis (☎ 01626-773030) or Bryan's Taxis (☎ 01626-776011).

Where to stay

No more than a few hundred metres from the path and great value for money is the dog-friendly *Seaway* (☎ 01626-879024, ☐ seawayteignmouth.co.uk; 2S/3D/1T/1Tr; ☞; WI-FI; ✼; £35-42.50pp, sgl £38-43, sgl occ from £60), at 27 Northumberland Place.

Slightly more expensive is *Lynton House* (☎ 01626-774349, ☐ lyntonhouse teignmouth.com; 2S/3D/3T/3Qd, one room sleeping up to five; ☞; WI-FI; ✼; B&B from £40pp, sgl/sgl occ from £34/60; Mar-mid Nov), at 7 Powderham Terrace. Most of the rooms have great views over either

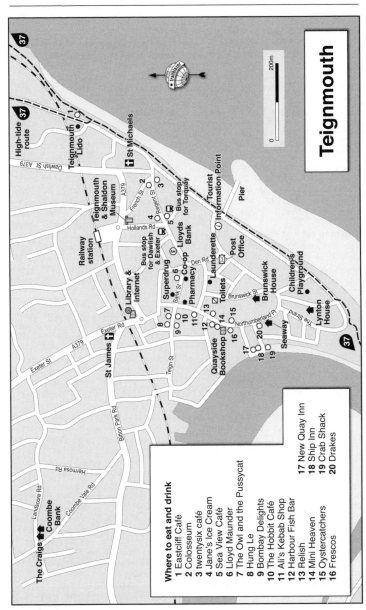

Teignmouth

High-tide route

200m

0

Where to eat and drink
1 Eastcliff Café
2 Colosseum
3 twentysix café
4 Jane's Ice Cream
5 Sea View Café
6 Lloyd Maunder
7 The Owl and the Pussycat
8 Hung Le
9 Bombay Delights
10 The Hobbit Café
11 Ali's Kebab Shop
12 Harbour Fish Bar
13 Relish
14 Mini Heaven
15 Oystercatchers
16 Frescos

17 New Quay Inn
18 Ship Inn
19 Crab Shack
20 Drakes

the sea or river but they do not take one-night bookings in advance between June and August.

Centrally, at 5 Brunswick St, is the dog-friendly **Brunswick House** (☎ 01626-774102, ☐ brunswick-house.com; 1S/4D/3Tr; WI-FI; ✹; £33.50-37pp, sgl/sgl occ from £39/49).

Further away from town there are two other decent options for walkers. Approximately 15 minutes from the centre, on Landscore Rd, **Coombe Bank** (☎ 01626-772369, ☐ coombe3.webs.com; 6D/3T/1Tr; ✎; WI-FI; from £32.50pp, sgl occ from £45) and **The Craigs** (☎ 01626-778003, ☐ thecraigsbandb.co.uk; 3D; ✎; WI-FI; from £35pp, sgl occ from £45); both offer rooms at competitive rates.

Where to eat and drink

The oldest part of town near the mouth of the river is undoubtedly the best place to search for food, with some idiosyncratic cafés as well as several characterful old pubs that have watched over the comings and goings on the Teign for centuries.

Cafés

Our favourite café is **Oystercatchers** (☎ 01626-774652; WI-FI; ✹; daily 8am-3pm, sometimes till 4pm), 12 Northumberland Place, a fully licensed place with a mellow vibe and some terrific food; breakfasts or paninis cost around £5. Just along the way, **Relish** (☎ 07770 938204; Mon-Fri 9.30am-2.30pm, Sat 10am-2.30pm) is an unassuming burger café with some whopping great burgers at very reasonable prices.

The small but delightful **Crab Shack** (☎ 01626-777956, ☐ crabshackonthebeach .co.uk; WI-FI; mid Feb to Dec Wed-Sun noon-3pm & 6-9pm) is a licensed café-restaurant tucked away on the waterfront beside Ship Inn and has its own fishing boats. The menu changes according to the catch, though you can usually rely on there being some delicious crab sandwiches. The views towards Shaldon are lovely too.

The Hobbit Café (Mon-Sat 10am-4pm, Sun 12.30-3pm), on Teign St, is another quirky little place; pleasant enough and with a huge selection of homemade cakes alongside the usual sandwiches and paninis.

Over on Regent St, near the coast path, **twentysix café** (☎ 01626-879000, ☐ twen tysixcafe.co.uk; ✹; Sun-Fri 10am-3pm, Sat 9.30am-3pm) feels a bit too smart for this corner of town – it's more of a café-bistro than a straight café – and has equally sophisticated dishes such as *coq au vin*, for £13.75, and *tartine avocat* (crispy smoked bacon, avocado and poached egg baguette; £8.25). Kids-at-heart hikers will no doubt enjoy the soft-boiled egg and soldiers (£3.25) on the breakfast menu. Nearby, but more down to earth, **Sea View** (☎ 01626-777888; WI-FI; ✹; summer daily 7.30am-7.30pm, may close earlier in winter) has cheap treats, such as beans on toast (£1.70) and spag bol (£3.95) and is friendly, central and has long opening hours in the summer; in fact, it has everything except a sea view.

As you leave town, and right on the trail, **Eastcliff Café** (☎ 01626-777621; ✹; daily 10am-4.30pm) has hot drinks and snacks, but only outdoor seating.

Pubs & restaurants

As good as some of the cafés are here, it's the pubs that really bring in the crowds. **Ship Inn** (☎ 01626-772674, ☐ theshipinnteignmouth.co.uk; WI-FI; ✹; food served Mon-Sat noon-2.30pm & 6-9.30pm, Sun noon-3pm, no food Mon & Tue in winter), an historical establishment built in the 1830s, is arguably the most popular. The food is just what you want from pub grub, being hearty and tasty, and with fish specials to boot, and there are four or five cask ales on tap. Also has patio seating overlooking the harbour. Note the list of 14 men who served in the Battle of Trafalgar on the exterior wall facing the sea.

Virtually next door is **New Quay Inn** (☎ 01626-774145, ☐ newquayinn.co.uk; WI-FI; ✹ bar area only; food Tue & Sun noon-3pm, Wed-Sat noon-3pm & 5-8.30pm), established way back in 1661. It also does food and has real ales, and has some harbour-side seating on its own little beach outside.

Back from the harbour slightly, **Drakes** (☎ 01626-772777; ✹; food served

Fri-Wed 11.30am-9pm, closed on Thur) is a no-nonsense pub-restaurant with an extensive, inexpensive menu, including toasted sandwiches (£4-5) and cream teas (£4) as well as pub-grub favourites such as steak & ale pie (£7.95). Great value.

For Italian cuisine, *Frescos* (☎ 01626-777181, 🖥 frescorestaurant.co.uk; July & Aug Wed-Mon 6pm to late, Sep-June Wed-Sun from 6pm) is a classy, authentic restaurant with mains (£14-28) including oven-baked ricotta and butterfly chicken breast, and pizza costing between £10 and £12. Up on Regent St, *Colosseum* (☎ 01626-870000; summer Mon-Sat 6.30-9.30pm, rest of year days and hours vary) is another fine Italian establishment with mains for £10-24, and pizza from £8.50. Both have an extensive wine list.

The Owl and the Pussycat (☎ 01626-775321, 🖥 theowlandpussycat.co.uk; Mon-Fri 6-9pm, Sat noon-2pm & 5.30-9.30pm), at 3 Teign St, is a great little place; sophisticated and yet still willing to serve decent-sized portions of lovely, local food, all of which is sourced responsibly. Mains are priced from around £15 to £25, and include delights such as loin of south Devon pork with Dauphiniose potatoes, crispy bacon and honey-glazed apple (£18.95).

Snacks & takeaways For Chinese, head to *Hung Le* (☎ 01626-773495; daily noon-2pm & 5-11pm) on Teign St. For Indian, try *Bombay Delights* (☎ 01626-773824; daily 5.30-11pm) at No 38. *Ali's* (☎ 01626-777911; Sun-Thur 4pm to midnight, Fri-Sat 4pm-2am) is a kebab house at 11 Somerset Place, while *Harbour Fish Bar* (☎ 01626-775906; Mon-Sat noon-2pm & 5-9.30pm) is Teignmouth's best chippy.

For quick snacks on-the-go, the local butcher, *Lloyd Maunder* (Mon-Sat 8.30am-5pm), does carvery baguettes (£2.95), while the bakery *Mini Heaven* (daily 8.30am-4pm) is good for pastries, pasties and cakes. *Jane's Ice Cream* (daily 10am-6pm in summer, Mon-Sat 9.30am-5pm, Sun 10am-4.30pm in winter) should have all your ice-cream cravings covered.

TEIGNMOUTH TO EXMOUTH [MAPS 37-41]

This short and easy **8-mile (13km; low-tide route 3hrs, high-tide route 3¼hrs; times include the ferry journey)** section will likely be welcome following yesterday's exertions. For this stage you need to consult a **tide-timetable**, though, as there is the possibility of having to follow two high-tide routes. Neither results in a lengthy detour, but both are inferior routes compared to the official coast-hugging path. You will also need to get to Starcross in time for the last ferry (before you set off make sure you have checked the ferry times) across to Exmouth. Otherwise you certainly will have a lengthy detour to negotiate (an extra 14 miles!).

The terrain on this section is generally flat as you follow Brunel's railway along the sea-walls. Refreshments are also in ample supply, both in Dawlish and Dawlish Warren, and there are two really cracking pubs in Cockwood. Once at Starcross, if the ferry's not running you need to consider your options: Exmouth can be reached by public transport from Starcross (see p190), though ambling addicts will probably prefer to tighten their bootlaces and stroll along the attractive Exe Estuary Trail (see pp192-4). Doing so will add another eight miles to your walk if you're able to connect with the small ferry at Topsham, or another 14 miles to your walk if you miss all the ferries and have to walk all the way up to the nearest pedestrian bridge at Bridge Road.

The route

There are two alternative trails leaving Teignmouth which divide near Eastcliff Café (see Map 37, p175) at the eastern end of the seafront. If the tide is in your favour you can walk straight along the sea wall with the railway to your left, towards the two giant rock stacks that loom in front of you. These are the **Parson** and the **Clerk**, said to have once been human until the devil turned them into stone (see box below). Just out to sea another rock formation, the finger-like rock that appears like Neptune's digit poking out of the waves, is **Shag**

ROUTE GUIDE AND MAPS

❏ **The legend of the Parson and the Clerk**

East of Teignmouth stand two huge rock stacks – and as you probably would expect from such prominent features, there are various legends surrounding the formation of these outcrops. The best known is this gothic morality tale:

Once upon a time the Bishop of Exeter was lying in bed in Dawlish, severely ill and close to death. An ambitious local parson, spying an opportunity to succeed the bishop, contrived to visit him on a regular basis to try to persuade him of his suitability for the promotion. Accompanying him on these visits was his clerk, who was tasked with guiding the parson across the local moor to Dawlish.

One evening, having received news that the bishop's health had rapidly declined, the parson decided to leave for Dawlish immediately despite the lateness of the hour. The two men galloped as fast as they were able, whipping their horses and stabbing them with their spurred heels in their attempt to get to the bishop's deathbed. The weather, however, turned against them, and a huge storm rose as the sun descended. The rain lashed down so heavily that the two men became lost in the gloom. The parson, furious that he could miss the bishop's demise, turned on his clerk and sneered the ominous words: 'May Satan take us to Dawlish for we shall never get there ourselves.'

Strangely enough (or maybe not, for those who are familiar with such legends), it was shortly after this that the two men were surprised by the sound of galloping hooves and a peasant on a moor pony approached and offered to be the two men's guide. In desperation, the two men paid little attention to the fact that both pony and rider were as black as the darkest night and followed the man to Dawlish. On the way they came to a well-lit mansion that neither the parson nor the clerk had noticed before. With the weather still against them, their guide, claiming to be the mansion's owner, invited them in, promising that he would guide them to Dawlish first thing in the morning instead.

Once inside, the pair were greeted by the sight of a large group of wild-looking folk indulging in an orgy of gorging and drinking and partying – a scene of unfettered hedonism to which the parson and the clerk were soon willing participants.

The next morning it was reported that the bishop had died, news that caused the two men to dash out of the mansion and mount their horses with the intention of continuing on their journey, realising that the parson's chances of promotion were slipping away. Their horses, however, would not move. To the backdrop of peals of laughter coming from the party within, the parson cursed 'Devil take the brutes'. It was at this point that their peasant guide appeared and thanked them – before ordering the horses to gallop into the sea, their cruel masters rooted in the saddles.

The following morning, when the god-fearing population of Dawlish left their homes to survey the damage caused by the storm, they saw that the red cliffs had been broken into two halves; and that on one half lay the lifeless body of the parson – while on the other lay that of his faithful clerk.

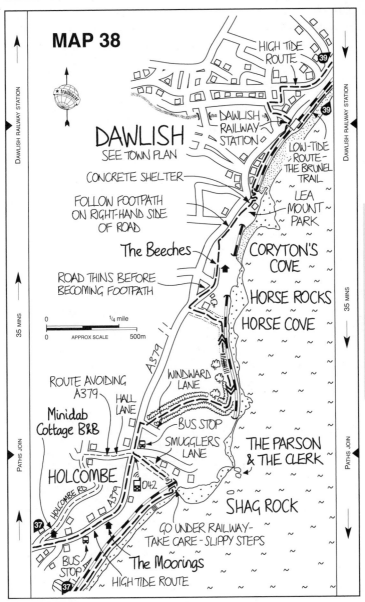

MAP 38

DAWLISH
SEE TOWN PLAN

HIGH TIDE ROUTE

39

DAWLISH RAILWAY STATION

LOW-TIDE ROUTE - THE BRUNEL TRAIL

LEA MOUNT PARK

CONCRETE SHELTER

FOLLOW FOOTPATH ON RIGHT-HAND SIDE OF ROAD

The Beeches

CORYTON'S COVE

ROAD THINS BEFORE BECOMING FOOTPATH

HORSE ROCKS

HORSE COVE

0   ¼ mile
0   APPROX SCALE   500m

A379

WINDWARD LANE

ROUTE AVOIDING A379

HALL LANE

Minidab Cottage B&B

BUS STOP

SMUGGLERS LANE

THE PARSON & THE CLERK

HOLCOMBE

042

SHAG ROCK

HOLCOMBE RD

A379

37

GO UNDER RAILWAY - TAKE CARE - SLIPPY STEPS

BUS STOP

37

The Moorings

HIGH TIDE ROUTE

DAWLISH RAILWAY STATION

35 MINS

PATHS JOIN

39

DAWLISH RAILWAY STATION

35 MINS

PATHS JOIN

ROUTE GUIDE AND MAPS

Rock. At the end, and having dipped underneath the railway line to ascend **Smugglers Lane**, the path meets up with the high-tide route on the busy A379.

High-tide route: Teignmouth–Smugglers Lane (35 minutes)

Just before Eastcliff Café take the road on the left – Eastcliff Rd – to **Mules Park** (which you can either walk through or follow the public footpath that runs to the right). At the top of the park you cross a field and minor road, continuing down the footpath until you reach the A379.

The official high-tide route continues on this busy A-road, passing *The Moorings* (☎ 01626-770400, 🖳 themooringsteignmouth.co.uk; 2D; 🍴; WI-FI; from £45pp, sgl occ from £60; Apr-Oct), at 33 Teignmouth Rd, and so on down the hill.

For a more pleasant walking experience, however, turn left at the **Holcombe** sign and head down Holcombe Rd, with the pink, crenellated and thatched *Minadab Cottage* (☎ 01626-772044, 🖳 minadab.co.uk; 2D/1D or T; WI-FI; 🐾; £40-45pp, sgl occ room rate), on your right. They don't accept advance bookings for a single-night stay in June to September but nearer the time it is worth calling them.

Follow Holcombe Rd, a quiet country lane surrounded by hedgerows, until you walk down into a dip, coming to a minor crossroads. Take Hall Lane on your right and this will reacquaint you with the A-road, the official high-tide route – and indeed the low-tide route too.

With all the paths reunited, a short walk up a hill brings you to **Windward Lane**, from where a path leads back to the railway, though it's not long before you're back on the A379 again. Don't follow this but instead take Old Teignmouth Rd on the right that leads past *The Beeches* (☎ 01626-866345, 🖳 thebeechesbandb.co.uk; 2D/1T; 🍴; WI-FI; £37-42pp, sgl occ £64-74), at No 15A.

Another encounter with the A379 follows before the path heads through **Lea Mount Park**, sandwiched between the noisy A-road and **Coryton's Cove**, with its wonderful little beach (off the path). The path descends sharply now, zig-zagging its way down to the railway and Dawlish.

ROUTE GUIDE AND MAPS

DAWLISH

Dawlish is a pleasant-enough place though the crowds in summer can be suffocating. Originally a little fishing community, Dawlish's name is thought to come from the Celtic 'Deawlisc', meaning 'Devil Water' – possibly because torrential rains are thought to have saturated the area's red cliffs, turning Dawlish Water – the stream which runs through the town's centre – a satanic red (see box p182). Another hypothesis suggests that it comes from the Welsh 'du(g)lais', meaning 'black stream' as today the brook is known for its black swans that paddle happily in the very heart of the town.

Dawlish is famous in fiction as the birthplace of Charles Dickens' *Nicholas Nickleby*, and if you're interested in the town's history you may wish to visit **Dawlish Museum** (☎ 01626-888557; May to end Sep Wed-Fri 10.30am-5pm, Sat & Sun 2-5pm, but open daily in August; £2) at the top of Brunswick Place.

Attached to the Old Mill Tearoom, **Strand Mill** is one of the country's largest mill wheels (15m in diameter). Originally built in 1717, when it would have stood alone, beside a brook in the middle of a meadow, it was rebuilt in 1825 after being destroyed in a fire, and continued to be in use until 1959.

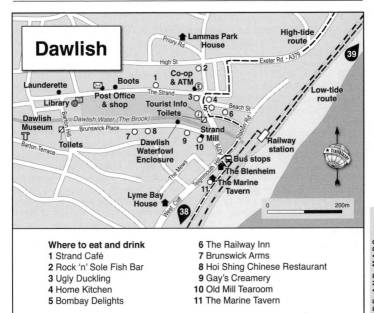

Where to eat and drink
1 Strand Café
2 Rock 'n' Sole Fish Bar
3 Ugly Duckling
4 Home Kitchen
5 Bombay Delights
6 The Railway Inn
7 Brunswick Arms
8 Hoi Shing Chinese Restaurant
9 Gay's Creamery
10 Old Mill Tearoom
11 The Marine Tavern

Dawlish Arts Festival (see p14) is held here in June. It started in 1953 and is thought to be the longest-running arts festival in the South-West.

Services
The **tourist information office** (☎ 01626-215665; Easter to end Oct Mon-Sat 10am-5pm, rest of year Thur-Sat 10-4pm) is behind the public toilets beside Dawlish Water. Also check out 🖥 www.dawlish.com. Most of the other services lie along The Strand that runs parallel and east of the stream. They include a Co-op **supermarket** (Mon-Sat 7am-10pm, Sun 10am-4pm), a **post office** (daily 7am-10pm), which is inside One Stop convenience store, and a branch of Boots the **pharmacy** (Mon-Sat 9am-6pm, Sun 10am-4pm) between them.

There are **banks** with **ATMs** dotted around, including an ATM inside the Co-op. For **internet** (15 mins free) and free wi-fi, head to the **library** (Mon & Sat 9am-1pm, Tue & Fri 9am-5pm, Thur 9am-6pm) at the top of The Strand, just beyond which is a **launderette** (daily 7am-7pm).

Transport
[See also pp50-4] Stagecoach's 2 **bus** connects the village with Teignmouth, Dawlish Warren, Starcross and Exeter. **Trains** call here regularly en route between Exmouth and Paignton via Exeter.

For a **taxi** try Jim's Taxis (☎ 0775-930 5093, ☎ 01626-779079) or Dawlish Taxi (☎ 01626-888111).

Where to stay
Rooms are thin on the ground in Dawlish. On the walk into town, **B&B** is available at *The Marine Tavern* (☎ 01626-865245, 🖥 marinetaverndawlish.com; 2D/2Tr; 🛇; WI-FI; £25-32.50pp, sgl occ £50-65), 2 Marine Parade.

Close by, on the corner of Marine Parade and Teignmouth Hill, is *The Blenheim* (☎ 01626-862372, 🖥 www.the blenheim.uk.net; 2S/4D/3T/2Tr; WI-FI; 🐾;

£34-44pp, sgl/sgl occ from £50/60), 1 Marine Parade, from which there are great views out to sea and along the immediate stretch of coastline.

On West Cliff, the dog-friendly *Lyme Bay House* (☎ 01626-864211, 🖥 lymebay dawlish.co.uk; 5D/3T/1D or T; ✆; WI-FI; 🐾; £43-47.50pp, sgl occ from £79), No 34, is a short walk up the hill from the centre of town.

For top-notch B&B accommodation, try the wonderfully elegant *Lammas Park House* (☎ 01626-888064, 🖥 lammaspark house.co.uk; 2D/1T/1Qd; ✆; WI-FI; £42.50-52.50pp, sgl occ £75-100), at 3 Priory Rd. The rooms are spacious, beautifully appointed and come with sea views; the 'quad' is a suite with a sitting room in between.

Where to eat and drink

Cafés The trickling brook known as **Dawlish Water** makes the perfect café setting. *Old Mill Tearoom* (Thur-Tue 10.30am-4pm, winter hours dependent on weather) is right beside it, and dates back to 1717 when it used to be a flour mill. Cream teas are a speciality here as is their savoury tea – homemade cheese scones and butter with mature cheddar cheese; £6.25. Just up the road is *Gay's Creamery* (Mon-Sat 7.30am-6pm, Sun 8.30am-6pm), a gift shop really, but one that also does takeaway coffee, tea, pastries and ice-creams, as well as delicious cream teas. Best of all, customers can use their picnic tables over the road to sit right by the brook.

On the other side of Dawlish Water is *Strand Café* (daily 7.30am-3pm) which does all-day breakfasts for as little as £3.75

and has some pavement seating. At the bottom end of The Strand are two more upmarket cafés: *Ugly Duckling* (☎ 01626-437343; WI-FI; 🐾; Tue-Thur 8am-3pm, Fri-Sat 8am-7.30pm, Sun 10am-3pm) is a café-bistro that does good breakfasts and a decent carvery, while *Home Kitchen* (☎ 01626-895192, 🖥 homekitchendawlish.co .uk; WI-FI; 🐾; Thur-Tue 9am-4pm, closed Jan) specialises in gluten-free products.

Pubs *Brunswick Arms* (☎ 01626-862181, 🖥 thebrunswickarms.co.uk; WI-FI; 🐾; food daily noon-3pm, also Mon-Fri 6-8pm in school summer holidays) is probably the best pub in town, with local ales on tap, decent pub grub and even a skittles alley. *The Railway Inn* (☎ 01626-863226) is another traditional real-ale pub, but was looking a bit tired when we visited, and no longer does food. Handiest for the coast path, and with sea-facing terrace seating (albeit beside a road), *The Marine Tavern* (see Where to stay; summer food daily noon-3pm & 6-9pm, Sun noon-3pm, winter Thur-Sun only; WI-FI; 🐾) provides fairly standard pub grub and three or four real ales on tap.

Restaurants & takeaways For Chinese, head to *Hoi Shing* (☎ 01626-865351; daily 5.30-11pm, Sat lunch noon-2pm), a licensed restaurant and takeaway. For Indian, try the takeaway-only *Bombay Delights* (☎ 01626-863316; daily 5-11pm), while up the hill to the north *Rock 'n' Sole Fish Bar* (Mon-Thur 5-8pm, Fri noon-1.45pm & 5-9pm, Sat 5-9pm) is the local takeaway chippy.

Dawlish to Dawlish Warren (35 mins)

If you're sure that the tide is sufficiently low, begin this stretch by heading under the railway bridge to follow the path, also known as **The Brunel Trail** (Map 38), alongside the railway. It's a straightforward stroll that leads, eventually, to **Langstone Rock**. Cross the next pedestrian railway bridge and follow the path towards the road and into Dawlish Warren (see p188).

High-tide route: Dawlish to Dawlish Warren (35 mins)

At Dawlish Railway Station turn left to follow the A379 – Exeter Rd – as it winds its way out of town. The road has a pavement but it regularly switches sides – take care. Rather tediously, you remain on the road for half a mile,

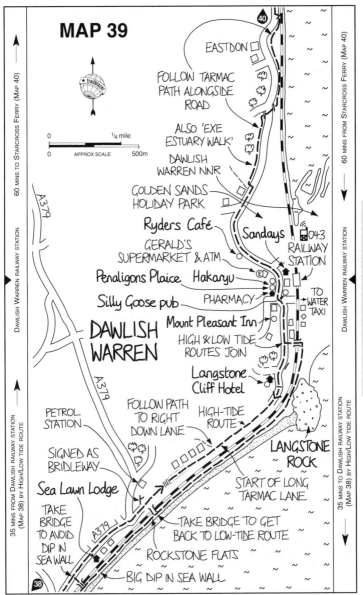

MAP 39

★ trailblazer

0 ¼ mile
0 500m
APPROX SCALE

EASTDON

FOLLOW TARMAC PATH ALONGSIDE ROAD

ALSO 'EXE ESTUARY WALK'

DAWLISH WARREN NNR

GOLDEN SANDS HOLIDAY PARK

Ryders Café

Sandays

RAILWAY STATION

GERALD'S SUPERMARKET & ATM

Penaligons Plaice

Hakaryu

Silly Goose pub

PHARMACY

DAWLISH WARREN

Mount Pleasant Inn

HIGH & LOW TIDE ROUTES JOIN

TO WATER TAXI

Langstone Cliff Hotel

PETROL STATION

FOLLOW PATH TO RIGHT DOWN LANE

HIGH-TIDE ROUTE

SIGNED AS BRIDLEWAY

LANGSTONE ROCK

START OF LONG TARMAC LANE

Sea Lawn Lodge

TAKE BRIDGE TO AVOID DIP IN SEA WALL

TAKE BRIDGE TO GET BACK TO LOW-TIDE ROUTE

ROCKSTONE FLATS

BIG DIP IN SEA WALL

A379

60 MINS TO STARCROSS FERRY (MAP 40)

DAWLISH WARREN RAILWAY STATION

35 MINS FROM DAWLISH RAILWAY STATION (MAP 38) BY HIGH/LOW TIDE ROUTE

60 MINS FROM STARCROSS FERRY (MAP 40)

DAWLISH WARREN RAILWAY STATION

35 MINS TO DAWLISH RAILWAY STATION (MAP 38) BY HIGH/LOW TIDE ROUTE

ROUTE GUIDE AND MAPS

passing *Sea Lawn Lodge* (☎ 01626-865998, 🖥 sealawnlodge.com; 2Tr; 🐾; WI-FI; 🐕; from £42pp, sgl occ room rate), before turning right and entering a grassy area called **Rockstone Flats** (if you reach the petrol station you have gone too far). Keep to the left and follow what is signed as a bridleway. Passing some bungalows on your left you join a tarmac path that seems to roll out endlessly in front of you.

The path gradually descends past *Langstone Cliff Hotel* (☎ 01626-221329, 🖥 langstone-hotel.co.uk; 1S/12D/1T/48Qd, one room sleeps up to six; 🐾; WI-FI; 🐕; B&B £63-117pp, sgl £81-100, sgl occ rates on request; dinner bed & breakfast rates also available), where passing walkers are welcome to stop for a coffee, some lunch or a cream tea, before eventually arriving in Dawlish Warren.

DAWLISH WARREN   [Map 39, p187]

Essentially a railway station – with a few amenities dotted here and there to service the area's numerous holiday parks – Dawlish Warren has little to warrant a lengthy stop.

Dawlish Warren National Nature Reserve is absorbing and sometimes plays host to rare vagrant birds including the greater sand plover, elegant tern and great spotted cuckoo. However, it's located on the sand-spit on the opposite side of the railway tracks and thus a walk away from the trail, which will deter all but the most determined twitcher.

Refreshments are available in the village, as is limited accommodation. There is a **pharmacy** (Mon-Fri 9am-6pm, Sat 9am-noon) and a **supermarket**, Gerald's (daily 8am-10pm), with an **ATM** (£1.50).

Note that there is the option of a (seasonal) **water taxi** between Dawlish Warren and Exmouth Docks: ExePlorer Water Taxis Ltd (☎ 07970-918418, 🖥 explorer watertaxis.co.uk; Apr-early Sep daily on the hour 8am-5pm, later in peak periods, no dogs as they are not allowed on the beach!) will come and collect you from the beach. The taxi leaves from near the end of the sand spit that juts out from Dawlish Warren. From the railway station, walk to the end of the amusements past the Visitor Centre; keeping on the left-hand side (ie on the opposite side to the sea), continue past the golf course and through the dunes until you see the sign stating: 'Pick Up Point'. The walk will take approximately half an hour.

Stagecoach's 2 and hop22 **bus** services call here as do Riviera line **trains** (Exmouth to Paignton via Exeter); see pp50-4.

Sandays B&B (☎ 01626-888973, 🖥 sandays-devon.co.uk; 2D/1T; WI-FI; £32.50-38.50pp, sgl occ £44-50), on Warren Rd, accepts single-night bookings but the rate is higher; the twin room is nice, however, and has its own sitting room overlooking the garden.

Mount Pleasant Inn (☎ 01626-863151, 🖥 mountpleasantinn.com; 🐕) is a pub that's a short walk up the hill but means it has great views overlooking the bay. It's the best spot in town (as far as it goes in Dawlish). It does **food** (daily noon-2pm & 6-9.30pm, school summer hols daily noon-9.30pm), with mains at lunch costing £9-12 and £10-20 on the more extensive evening menu, which includes tapas, seafood, curries and steaks. There is a separate afternoon menu for the school summer holidays.

The *Silly Goose* (☎ 01626-438781; WI-FI; 🐕; food Mon-Sat 10am-9pm, Sun noon-9pm) is a cheaper, family-friendly pub right on the path. They do food every day, including breakfasts every day except Sundays.

Also right on the trail, *Ryders* (daily 8am-5pm) is a bakery-café that's convenient for a quick coffee and pastry. Takeaway options include Chinese food at *Hakaryu* (☎ 01626-888388; daily 5-11pm), 3 Warren Rd, and fish & chips at *Penaligon's Plaice* (Mon-Tue & Thur-Sat 5-8pm) next door.

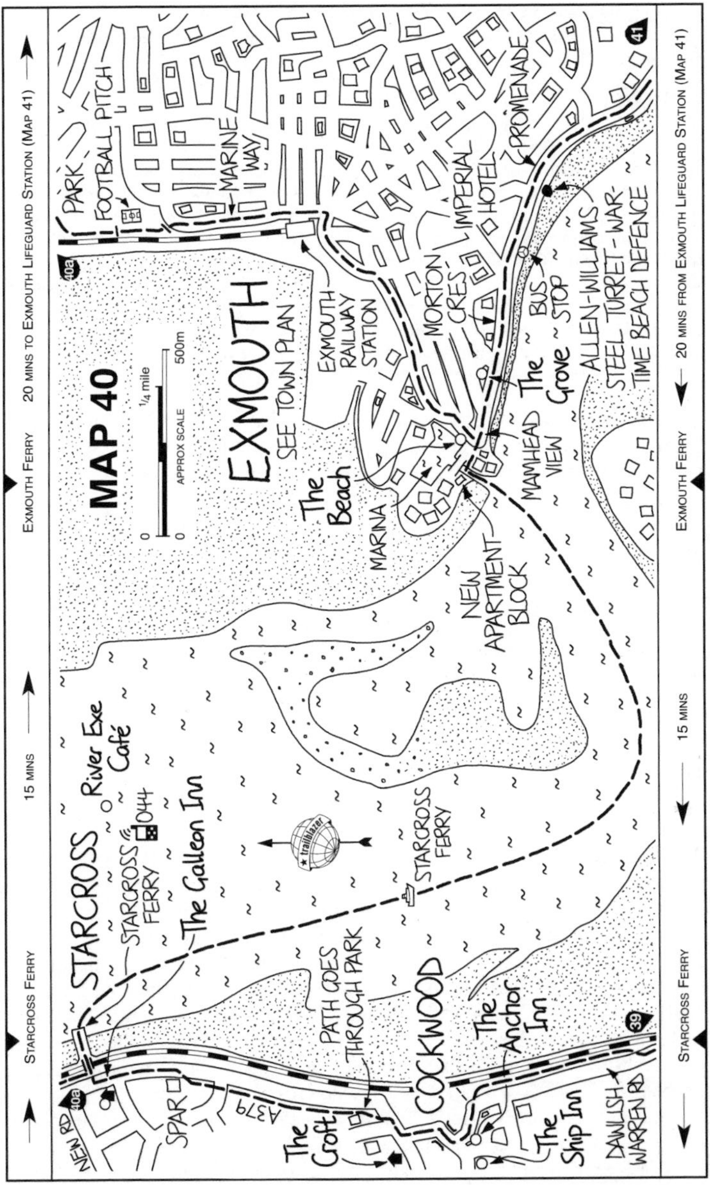

MAP 40

APPROX SCALE

0 — ¼ mile
0 — 500m

EXMOUTH
SEE TOWN PLAN

PARK
FOOTBALL PITCH
MARINE WAY
103
EXMOUTH RAILWAY STATION
MORTON CRES'
IMPERIAL HOTEL
PROMENADE
41
BUS STOP
The Grove
MANHEAD VIEW
ALLEN-WILLIAMS STEEL TURRET - WAR-TIME BEACH DEFENCE
The Beach
MARINA
NEW APARTMENT BLOCK

STARCROSS
STARCROSS FERRY
River Exe Café
1044
The Galleon Inn
STARCROSS FERRY

COCKWOOD
PATH GOES THROUGH PARK
The Anchor Inn
The Croft
SPAR
A379
103
NEW RD
The Ship Inn
DAWLISH WARREN RD
69

STARCROSS FERRY | 15 MINS | EXMOUTH FERRY | 20 MINS TO EXMOUTH LIFEGUARD STATION (MAP 41)
STARCROSS FERRY | 15 MINS | EXMOUTH FERRY | 20 MINS FROM EXMOUTH LIFEGUARD STATION (MAP 41)

ROUTE GUIDE AND MAPS

The path leaves Dawlish Warren along the road, bypassing holiday parks and chippies. Joining the Exe Estuary Walk, aka Cycle Track 2, you soon arrive in Cockwood.

COCKWOOD   [Map 40, p189]

This small harbour village is blessed with two great pubs. The warm and friendly *Ship Inn* (☎ 01626-890373, 💻 shipinn cockwood.co.uk; WI-FI; 🐾 if well-behaved and on lead; Mon-Sat noon-2.30pm & 6-9pm, Sun noon-9pm), on Church Rd, serves up delicious food (mains £9-15) and cask ales.

Close by, and right on the harbour-front on Dawlish Warren Rd, *The Anchor Inn* (☎ 01626-890203, 💻 anchorinncock wood.com; 🐾; food summer Mon-Sat noon-9.30pm, Sun to 9pm, winter hours variable) is over 450 years old and specialises in seafood, particularly mussels.

For **bed and breakfast** there is just *The Croft* (☎ 01626-890282, 💻 thecroft cockwood.com; 5D/3T; WI-FI; 🐾; £40-42.50pp, sgl occ from £56), on Exeter Rd; it is a large house set in an acre of secluded gardens. The owner offers massage and reflexology (if prebooked), will dry clothes, and guests get a 10% discount in the two local pubs.

Follow the road over the bridge and out of the village. A brief interlude in a park follows before, in short order, you arrive in Starcross, from where you can board the Starcross to Exmouth **ferry**; for details, see below.

STARCROSS
          [Map 40, p189; Map 40a]

This is the main departure point for the ferry across the Exe, but there are a few amenities in the village.

On The Strand you will find a Spar **supermarket** (daily 7am-10pm) and Boots **pharmacy** (Map 40a; Mon-Fri 9am-6pm, Sat 9am-1pm).

The Galleon Inn (☎ 01626-890412, 💻 galleoninnstarcross.co.uk) offers **B&B** (3D/1Tr; WI-FI; from £35pp, sgl occ rates on request), as well as **food** (Mon-Sat noon-3pm & 6-9pm, Sun noon-4pm).

Pub food is also available opposite the railway station at *The Atmospheric Railway Inn* (Map 40a; ☎ 01626-890335, 💻 atmosphericrailwaystarcross.co.uk; WI-FI; 🐾; Tue-Sat noon-8pm, Sun noon-4pm), where you can enjoy one of their jacket potatoes (from £6.50) whilst supping an ale in their beer garden.

Stagecoach's 2 **bus** connects the village with Teignmouth, Dawlish, Dawlish Warren and Exeter. **Trains** call here regularly en route between Exeter and Paignton. See pp50-4 for more details.

Tackling the Exe   [Map 40, p189]

● **The Starcross to Exmouth Ferry** For a river that is crossed by no fewer than three ferry services, it can be surprisingly difficult crossing the Exe sometimes. The easiest way – and which is on the official coast path route – is the main Starcross to Exmouth Ferry (☎ 07779-157280, ☎ 07974-022536; Apr-end Oct daily, leaves Starcross hourly from 10.10am to 4.10pm & Exmouth 10.40am to 3.40pm, plus until 5.10pm & 5.40pm mid May-mid Sep; 15-20 mins; single £4.50, day return £6; well-behaved 🐾); the ferry no longer has its own website, but you can find up-to-date news about the ferry on its official Facebook page (💻 www.facebook.com/StarcrossExmouthFerry).

As you cross the Exe look for out for avocets and ospreys in the skies above and grey seals from the waves below you.

For Exmouth and the continuation of the route see p194.

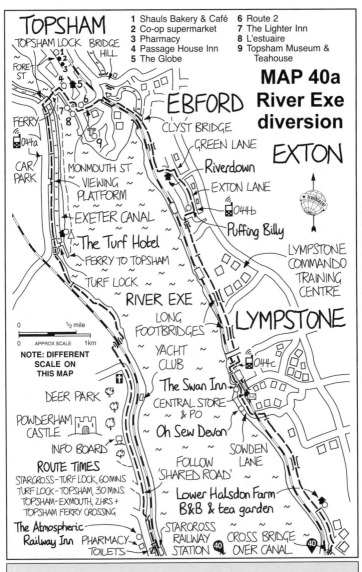

TOPSHAM

1 Shauls Bakery & Café
2 Co-op supermarket
3 Pharmacy
4 Passage House Inn
5 The Globe
6 Route 2
7 The Lighter Inn
8 L'estuaire
9 Topsham Museum & Teahouse

MAP 40a
River Exe
diversion

TOPSHAM LOCK   BRIDGE HILL

FORE ST

FERRY

☐044a

CAR PARK

MONMOUTH ST VIEWING PLATFORM

EBFORD

CLYST BRIDGE

GREEN LANE

Riverdown

EXTON LANE

☐044b

Puffing Billy

EXTON

★ trailblazer

EXETER CANAL

The Turf Hotel

FERRY TO TOPSHAM

TURF LOCK

RIVER EXE

LONG FOOTBRIDGES

YACHT CLUB

LYMPSTONE COMMANDO TRAINING CENTRE

LYMPSTONE

☐044c

The Swan Inn

CENTRAL STORE & PO

Oh Sew Devon

0   ½ mile
0   APPROX SCALE   1km

NOTE: DIFFERENT SCALE ON THIS MAP

DEER PARK

POWDERHAM CASTLE

INFO BOARD

ROUTE TIMES
STARCROSS-TURF LOCK, 60MINS
TURF LOCK-TOPSHAM, 30 MINS
TOPSHAM-EXMOUTH, 2HRS +
TOPSHAM FERRY CROSSING

The Atmospheric Railway Inn   PHARMACY
TOILETS

STARCROSS RAILWAY STATION 40

FOLLOW 'SHARED ROAD'

Lower Halsdon Farm B&B & tea garden

SOWDEN LANE

CROSS BRIDGE OVER CANAL   40

ROUTE GUIDE AND MAPS

Symbols in text (see also p83)
● Bathtub in at least one room

🐾 Dogs allowed subject to prior arrangement
Ⓛ Packed lunch available if requested in advance

● **Ferries further upstream** If you can't take the Starcross ferry you'll have to head inland to get across the Exe. There are **two further ferry services** that operate upstream of Starcross and Exmouth: the first leaves from **Turf Lock** (2½ miles from Starcross), the second from **Topsham Lock** (4 miles from Starcross), with both heading to the launch at **Topsham**; details of these services can be found below. Taking either of these will save you having to walk all the way up to Bridge Rd and back again. **Note with either service it is recommended that you phone beforehand to make sure they're operating and at what times.** To get to either, you need to follow the **Exe Estuary Trail**, which heads north inland from Starcross round the pretty estuary, an SSSI with an abundance of wildlife including avocets and curlew. This is the route described below.

● **Public transport** Should there not be any ferries running when you plan to cross the Exe, there is a strong case to be made for taking public transport rather than walking all the way towards Exeter and back. Stagecoach's No 2 **bus** service (see pp50-4) heads to Exeter from Starcross; from Exeter you can get Stagecoach's No 56 back south to Exmouth.

● **Walking** (14 miles; 4½hrs) If you really do want to walk it, you'll have to follow the Exe Estuary Trail a further three miles beyond Topsham Lock, pass under the M5 motorway bridge (which you can't cross on foot) and **cross the bridge at Bridge St**, before walking south to Exmouth.

Exe Estuary Trail

The way (**8 miles, 12.8km; 3½ hours plus 10 mins for Topsham ferry crossing**) is well-signed from Starcross Railway Station. The path soon says a welcome farewell to the A379 as you follow a very quiet lane along the river and railway, your attention eventually being diverted away from the water by the estimated 600 fallow deer residing in the grounds of impressive **Powderham Castle** – the historic home of the Earl of Devon – on your left.

Passing **Starcross Yacht Club** to your right and a church on your left, you cross the railway line to follow the edge of the estuary to **Turf Lock** and *The Turf Hotel* (☎ 01392-833128, 🖳 turfpub.net; Mar-Oct), a very popular pub with cracking **food** (Mon-Fri noon-2.30pm, Sat-Sun noon-3pm, Mon-Sat 6-8.30pm), fine local ales and a huge riverside beer garden. As well having two lovely **B&B** rooms (1D/1T shared bathroom; ☛; 🐾; from £50pp, sgl occ from £50), they also allow you to **camp** (£5pp; breakfast available for £7.50 from 9.30am) in the garden here. There is also a **yurt** (Apr-Sep; sleeps up to nine people; £95/117 for two/three sharing; see website for further details) and a **shepherd's hut** (sleeps two; £95). The rate for the yurt and shepherd's hut includes a simple breakfast. Toilet and shower facilities are available.

Running from the back of the pub, **Turf Lock Ferry** (☎ 07778-370582, 🖳 topshamtoturfferry.co.uk; single £4, return £5, 🐾 50p) runs daily from late May to mid September and at weekends only over Easter and in April. Ferries depart Turf Lock at 11.45am, 12.30pm, 2pm & 3pm. There's also a 1.15pm and a 4pm ferry at weekends in July and August. Note that times are subject to tides and weather conditions.

If you wish to (or have to) continue to the next ferry, keep to the left-hand side of Exeter Canal for just over a mile to **Topsham Lock** where **Topsham**

Lock Ferry (☎ 07801-203338; Apr-Sep Wed-Mon 9.30am-5.30pm, Oct-Mar weekends & bank hols only 10am-5pm or dusk; £1.20, 🐾 60p) – basically a man and his boat – takes about two minutes to cross to Topsham. Note that the ferry doesn't operate in bad weather conditions, or at low tide; for the latter check the tide times (🖳 easytide.ukho.gov.uk). It also doesn't run for one month a year for the boat to be repaired and the ferryman to have a holiday, though this is likely to be in winter so won't affect many walkers.

Remember that you need to phone either ferry beforehand to make sure it's running.

Topsham On Fore St you'll find a Co-op **supermarket** (daily 7am-10pm) and a **pharmacy** (Mon-Fri 9am-6pm, Sat 9am-5pm). Stagecoach's 57 **bus** service (see pp50-4) calls here as does the **train** between Exmouth and Exeter.

Should Topsham's considerable charms compel you to stay longer, hotel-style accommodation can be found at *The Globe* (☎ 01392-873471, 🖳 www .theglobetopsham.co.uk; 19D or T; 🛏; WI-FI; 🐾; room only £37.50-70pp, sgl occ full room rate), at 34 Fore St. Breakfast is available (continental/full English £6.50/8.50).

Topsham has some great pubs and eateries. Shortly after the ferry slipway you will come to *Passage House Inn* (☎ 01392-873653, 🖳 passagehouseinn topsham.co.uk; WI-FI; 🐾; food served daily noon-9pm) with terrace seating overlooking the quay. Also doing pub meals is *The Lighter Inn* (☎ 01392-875439, 🖳 lighterinn.co.uk; WI-FI; 🐾; food daily noon-9pm), while nearby *L'estuaire* (☎ 01392-876801, 🖳 lestuaire.co.uk; WI-FI; 🐾; food served daily 9.30-11am, noon-3pm & 6-9pm) is a smart café-bistro-bar with plenty of quayside seating for sunny days.

Close to L'estuaire is the excellent café, *Route 2* (☎ 01392-875085, 🖳 route2topsham.co.uk; WI-FI; 🐾; daily 8am-5pm, hot food to 3pm), on the corner of Monmouth Hill; a friendly, comfortable place, with newspapers for customers to read, and some of the best breakfasts you'll taste anywhere on the trail – the scrambled eggs are to die for.

There's also a small *teahouse* inside the grounds of the charming **Topsham Museum** (Apr-Oct Mon, Wed, Sat & Sun 2-5pm; free). Up on Fore St (the main shopping strip) is *Shauls Bakery & Café* (Mon-Sat 8.30am-5pm, café till 4.30pm), a good-value coffee stop.

Having disembarked from either ferry in Topsham, turn right and walk along Ferry Rd until you meet Fore St where you turn right. Crossing a mini roundabout, follow the thin lane up Monmouth Hill and after just over 100 metres turn left along **Monmouth St**; having followed this for approximately a quarter-of-a-mile you arrive on Bowling Green Rd. Turn right here, then after 200 metres turn left over the railway line and follow the long, sweeping Clyst Bridge over the marshy expanses surrounding the River Clyst. Coming off the bridge, continue straight along the footpath-cycle lane until it turns left, bringing you out onto Green Lane. Turn right here and follow this and then Exton Lane as far as the junction with Station Rd where, turning right, you pass *The Puffing Billy* (☎ 01392-877888, 🖳 thepuffingbilly.co.uk; WI-FI; 🐾; food daily noon-3pm & 6-9pm), an upmarket gastro-pub.

For **B&B**, *Riverdown* (☎ 01392-873852, 🖳 riverdownbedandbreakfast .co.uk; 1D/1T; 🛏; WI-FI; from £37.50pp, sgl occ rates on request) is on your right, just before you turn right onto Green Lane. They don't accept advance bookings for a single-night stay other than in the winter months.

Having followed Station Rd for approximately 200 metres you pass through a gate on your left and arrive at the railway line. Gigantic wooden boardwalks now become your pathway and you follow them to **Lympstone** where, having crossed the railway line, you arrive opposite Central **convenience store & post office** (daily 7am-9pm). The pub to your right is *The Swan Inn* (☎ 01395-272644, 🖥 theswaninn-lympstone.co.uk; WI-FI; 🐾; food Mon-Fri 9.30-11.30am, noon-2.30pm & 6-9/9.30pm, Sat-Sun 9.30am-9pm), which serves food throughout the day, including breakfasts.

Turn right at the road here, and you'll soon reach *Oh Sew Devon* (☎ 01395-488338; WI-FI; Mon-Fri 9am-5pm, Sat-Sun 10am-5pm), a cute little tea-room that does toasties, cream teas and ice-creams. Follow the road through the village, with Exmouth finally appearing on the horizon. Follow **Sowden Lane**, turning sharp left to pass under the railway line before taking a footpath on your right, which is then followed for a further two miles into **Exmouth**.

Just before you reach Exmouth, you'll pass the beautiful grounds of the dog-friendly *Lower Halsdon Farm* (☎ 01395-267744, 🖥 lowerhalsdon.com; 1D; 🛏; WI-FI; 🐾; £35-50pp, sgl occ rates on request), which has an en suite double room for **B&B** and a rustic **tea garden** (Easter-end Sep weekends & bank hols only 11am-4.30pm).

EXMOUTH

Exmouth is a decent-sized town with all the amenities required and a good supply of accommodation, all (apart from the camp-site) within easy walking distance of the ferry terminal and coastal path. Called Lydwicnaesse, or 'The point of the Bretons' in the 11th century, the town's name today is somewhat more self-explanatory, with 'Exe' a Celtic word for 'fish'. The town grew with the construction of permanent docks in the 19th century, its popularity as a destination for holidaymakers increasing exponentially as a result.

If you are interested in the town's history and social development **Exmouth Museum** (☎ 07768-184127, 🖥 devonmuseums.net/exmouth; Apr-Oct Mon, Fri, Sat 10.30am-12.30pm, Tue & Thur 10.30am-4.30pm, Wed 10.30am-4pm; £1.50) is on Sheppards Row.

Exmouth Festival (see p14) is held here in May or June.

Services

Bizarrely, the **tourist information centre** (☎ 01395-830550, 🖥 exmouth-guide.co.uk; Apr-Oct Mon-Sat 10am-4pm, Oct-Apr Mon-Sat to 2pm, but subject to the availability of volunteers) is located inside the premises of AJ's Taxis at 42 The Strand.

For **internet access** head to the **library** (Mon, Tue, Thur & Fri 9am-6pm, Sat 9am-4pm) on Exeter Rd.

The pedestrianised centre is not the most becoming of places but just about everything you need can be found within it. There's a **post office** (Mon & Wed-Fri 9am-5.30pm, Tue 9.30am-5.30pm, Sat 9am-12.30pm) in Magnolia Walk (the pedestrianised road that runs through Magnolia Centre, a shopping precinct), as well as a **pharmacy**, Boots (Mon-Sat 8.30am-5.30pm, Sun 10am-4pm), the **trekking/camping shop** Mountain Warehouse (Mon-Sat 9am-5.30pm, Sun 10am-4pm) and a Co-op **supermarket** (Mon-Sat 6am-11pm, Sun 10am-4pm). There's also a Tesco (daily 6am-11pm) on Rolle St and a large M&S supermarket (Mon-Sat 8am-8pm, Sun 10am-4pm) beside the railway station.

There's a **launderette** (daily 8am-8pm) at 6 High St.

There are plenty of **banks** with **ATMs** around town. Indoor **Exmouth Market** (Mon-Sat 9am-5.30pm) is good for souvenirs.

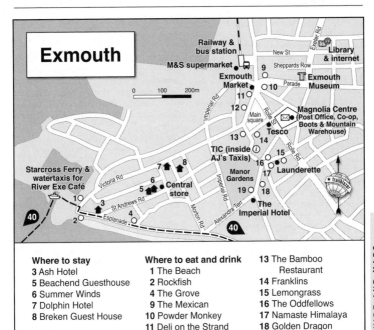

Where to stay
3 Ash Hotel
5 Beachend Guesthouse
6 Summer Winds
7 Dolphin Hotel
8 Breken Guest House

Where to eat and drink
1 The Beach
2 Rockfish
4 The Grove
9 The Mexican
10 Powder Monkey
11 Deli on the Strand
12 Crusty Cob

13 The Bamboo
   Restaurant
14 Franklins
15 Lemongrass
16 The Oddfellows
17 Namaste Himalaya
18 Golden Dragon
19 Bumble & Bee

Transport

[See also pp50-4] Stagecoach's No 57 **bus** connects the town with Exeter via Topsham and Lympstone; their No 56 service goes to Exeter via Lympstone. Meanwhile, their No 157 goes to Sidmouth via Budleigh Salterton and their No 357 to Budleigh Salterton.

Trains run regularly to Exeter.

For a **cab** try AJ's Taxis (☎ 01395-222655). See p190 for details of the Starcross to Exmouth Ferry.

Where to stay

Camping is an option, but the nearest site, *Prattshayes National Trust Campsite* (Map 41; ☎ 01395-276626, 🖳 exmouth-countrylodge.com/campsite; WI-FI in Cow Shed; 🐾 on a lead; £9 for a tent and up to two hikers; Apr-end Oct) is a two-mile walk from the town centre and one mile

from the path; either turn off the path at Maer Lane, just as you leave Exmouth, or you can continue on the coastal trail past Orcombe Point to a small path signposted to Gore Lane, which in turn leads to Maer Lane. This is a decent campsite, though, with good showers, a small shop and even a bar (the 'Cow Shed') in a large barn that sometimes also opens for breakfasts and evening BBQs. They also have two **bell tents** (sleeping up to four people from £50). In the lodge there is **bunk-bed accommodation** (1 x 2-, 2 x 6-bed, shared facilities, from £39 per room), which can be booked by individuals for a single-night stay though is also let out for sole occupancy. Bedding is provided and there is a kitchen area.

The number of **bed and breakfasts** in Exmouth seems to be diminishing, but there are still a few that are well located for both the trail and town centre.

On Morton Rd is *Dolphin Hotel* (☎ 01395-263832, 🖵 dolphinhotelexmouth.co .uk; 6S share facilities, 7T/10D/1Tr/2Qd, all en suite; ➡; WI-FI; 🐾; £35-55pp, sgl £35-50, sgl occ £50-70), which has its own bar (daily from 6pm) but they don't serve food.

Close by is *Breken Guest House* (☎ 01395-269800, 🖵 brekenguesthouse.co.uk; 1S/2D/2T/1Tr; ➡; WI-FI; £35-40pp, sgl from £35, sgl occ from £50), at No 13.

St Andrews Rd is home to some establishments, such as: *Ash Hotel* (☎ 01395-224983, 🖵 ashbedandbreakfast.com; 1S/8D/1T; ➡; WI-FI; from £30pp, sgl £35), by the junction with Esplanade; *Summer Winds* (☎ 01395-489043, or 07786-375317, 🖵 summerwindguesthouse.co.uk; 2D/1T; WI-FI; room only from £30pp, sgl occ room rate), at No 64, which doesn't provide breakfast; and *Beachend Guest House* (☎ 01395-222732, 🖵 enquiries @beachend.co.uk; 2D/1T; ➡; WI-FI; room only £27.50-35pp, sgl occ from £45) at No 68. Whilst not taking one-night bookings over the summer months unless they fit in with their diary, Beachend is a popular stop for walkers. One of their double rooms has a roll-top bath and the bathroom itself is almost the same size as the bedroom! However, note that the rate doesn't include breakfast.

Where to eat and drink
For most of Exmouth's eating options you have to walk five minutes from the path into the town centre. This is dominated by the main square, around which are dotted numerous eateries.

Cafés The most pleasant café is nestled into one corner of Manor Gardens. *Bumble and Bee* (☎ 07791-229741, 🖵 bumblean dbee.co.uk; Apr-Oct daily 9am-5pm, Feb-Mar Tue-Sun 9am-4pm) does healthy breakfasts, light lunches, and unusual honey and lavender scones. It's good value and is licensed too.

Of the places on the main square, *Deli On The Strand* (☎ 01395-279977; daily 9am-4pm, closed Sundays off-season) is a good choice, with seating spilling out onto the pavement. It does well-made and delicious sandwiches and paninis, plus pies, soups and cream teas. Nearby, and cheaper, *The Crusty Cob* (☎ 01395-267634; Mon-Fri 7am-5pm, Sat 7am-4pm, also Sun in summer school holidays) is a bakery with some good-value sandwiches.

Across the square, *Franklins* (☎ 01395-263086; WI-FI; 🐾; food daily 8am-9.30pm) is a café by day, tapas bar by night.

Pubs Almost as soon as you step off the Starcross Ferry you come to *The Beach* (☎ 01395-272090; WI-FI; 🐾; food daily 7-11am & noon-9pm), a vibrant place with some good food (including breakfasts) and a great atmosphere. Dogs are welcome too.

Continuing along the Esplanade, *The Grove* (☎ 01395-272101; WI-FI; 🐾; food summer daily noon-9.30pm, winter Mon-Thur noon-2.30pm & 5.30-9.30pm, Fri & Sat noon-9.30pm, Sun to 8.30pm), part of

---

❏ Dining out on the waves
A rundown of the eating options in Exmouth wouldn't be complete without mention of the multi award-winning *River Exe Café* (Map 40; ☎ 07761-116103, 🖵 riverexe cafe.com; Tue-Sat noon-8pm, Sun noon-6pm), the town's most unusual eatery. Situated on a barge floating on the River Exe, you have to get a water taxi to get to it; bookings for a meal are essential and include a booking for the water taxi – they allow two hours for a meal.

The water taxi leaves on the hour (£5 return from the Marina) and takes 20 minutes. Mains cost £15-18, while two-person seafood-sharing platters are £50-80. The mussels (£15.95 for a main dish including crusty bread) are a delicious speciality, while some of the fish is delivered from local fishing boats directly to the café – it doesn't get much fresher than that!

the Young's chain, offers a similar menu (mains £11-20, sandwiches from £5), and has a large beer garden plus a first-floor terrace with sea views. Dogs are very welcome here too.

Further towards the centre, *The Oddfellows* (☎ 01395-277030; WI-FI; 🐾; food Mon-Sat noon-3pm & 6-9pm, Sun noon-5pm) is a gastro-pub with plenty of space, including some patio seating, but little in the way of atmosphere.

Near the railway station is the Wetherspoon's pub, *Powder Monkey* (☎ 01395-280090; food daily 8am-11pm), a hugely popular place with a large front patio. The food is cheap, but again it lacks a genuine pub atmosphere, and doesn't welcome dogs. The name, incidentally, commemorates the career of local girl Nancy Perriam who, unusually for a woman, worked on the naval ships as a powder monkey (ie someone who filled shells and cartridges with powder – a task usually done by boys). Nancy lived nearby in Tower St where she died in 1865 aged 98.

Restaurants Right on the coast path, *Rockfish* (☎ 01395-272100, 🖥 therockfish .co.uk; daily noon-9.30pm) is a modern seafood restaurant with ceiling-to-floor windows and terrace seating overlooking the sea. Mains, including traditional fish & chips (£12.95), cost between £10 and £20, and they have an ever-changing local-fish menu too.

Inland a bit, *The Bamboo Restaurant* (☎ 01395-267253, 🖥 www.bambooex mouth.com; Sun-Wed 5.30-10.30pm, Thur-Sat 5.30-11pm) is a large but discreet place by the main square, with some tantalising Chinese dishes including sliced duck with fresh ginger & spring onions. For more bog-standard Chinese cuisine, try *Golden Dragon* (☎ 01395-264027; daily 6-11.30pm) on The Beacon, with a menu including crispy seaweed (£3.70) and chicken in oyster sauce (£5.40).

Near Golden Dragon you'll find *Lemongrass* (☎ 01395-269306; Tue-Sat 5.30-9.30pm), an OK Thai restaurant, and *Namaste Himalaya* (☎ 01395-222831, 🖥 namastehimalayaexmouth.co.uk; Tue-Thur & Sun 5-11pm, Fri-Sat noon-3pm & 5-11.30pm), serving Nepalese and Indian cuisine, while up by the railway station is *The Mexican* (☎ 01395-223388, 🖥 eatmexican .co.uk; Mon-Thur 11am-2pm & 6-10pm, Fri & Sat 11am-2pm & 6-10.30pm, Sun 6-9.30pm; winter hours may vary) where evening mains cost around £12.

EXMOUTH TO SIDMOUTH   [MAPS 40-46]

Today's **12½-mile (20km; 4hrs 25 mins)** stage begins with a saunter through Exmouth on what, at approximately two miles, is said to be the longest seafront in Devon, and within the borders of a World Heritage Site (see box p198).

The cliff-top-walking involved in this stage is pretty relentless at times and there are a couple of moderately strenuous climbs. However, the views from West Down Beacon and Brandy Head more than make up for any aches and pains, while Otter Estuary Nature Reserve and the spectacular sea-stacks at Ladram Bay add plenty of wonder and variation to the day.

Budleigh Salterton makes a pleasant lunch stop. There are also a few cafés on the coast path (albeit some are linked to monstrous caravan parks) and of course, plenty of options for a cream tea or evening meal once you arrive in the elegant Regency town of Sidmouth.

❏ **Important note – walking times**
All times in this book refer only to the time spent walking. You will need to add 20-30% to allow for rests, photography, checking the map, drinking water etc.

ROUTE GUIDE AND MAPS

The route

Disembarking from the ferry in Exmouth, follow the promenade (Esplanade) parallel with the road all the way along the seafront. It's quite a pleasant stretch, with seawall, beach, windsurfers and volleyballers to your right and **The Maer**, a nature reserve, on the opposite side of the road. If it's windy beware the gusts blowing sand off the beach and directly into your eyes. On your way look out for the **Allen Williams turret**, like a dalek's 'head', a relic not of time-travel but of WWII.

At **Exmouth Lifeguard Station** you have two options: turn left up to the roundabout then right to walk above the beach; or continue along the seafront to virtually the end of the tarmac and **Foxholes Beach**, where a steep path zig-zags upwards to rejoin the other path.

The trail is easy as it crosses the pastures of the National Trust-owned **High Land of Orcombe** and the views of the sea and back along the coast are occasionally magnificent. The strange **Geoneedle monument** marks the beginning of the **Jurassic Coast** which now spreads out, daunting and yet inviting in equal measure, in front of you. The path hugs the coast through **Devon Cliffs Holiday Park** (caravans only), where you can stop at *South Beach Café* (Mar-Oct daily 10am-9pm), before reaching **Straight Point Rifle Range**. Below to your right as you pass along the edge of the park is **Littleham Cove** – home to swallows, falcons, kittiwakes and grey seals.

Eventually leaving the caravan park, the trail clambers over the spectacular terracotta cliffs to reach **West Down Beacon** (129m/423ft), from where you descend along foliage-enveloped trails through **Jubilee Park** (keep your eyes open for linnets, falcons and clouded yellow butterflies) to the Promenade in Budleigh Salterton.

❑ The UNESCO Jurassic Coast World Heritage Site

The Jurassic Coast World Heritage Site (aka the Dorset and East Devon Coast World Heritage Site) stretches for 95 miles (155km) from Orcombe Point, just outside Exmouth in East Devon, to Studland Bay and the chalk stacks of Old Harry Rocks in Purbeck, Dorset.

In order to get some sort of handle on the complicated geology (see also pp57-68) of this region, it's useful to remember that, if walking from west to east along the coast path, the rocks on which you tread are getting ever younger the further you go. Starting with the red rocks of the **Triassic Period** (from 250 million years old) between Exmouth and Lyme Regis, the coast path then clambers over the younger stones of the **Jurassic Period** (from 200 million years old) between Pinhay Bay and White Nothe, before finally entering the **Cretaceous Period** (from 145 to 65 million years old) as you climb round Ringstead Bay. (As you probably expect, the division isn't quite as neat as this – many of the cliffs between Durdle Door and Studland, for example, are often still Jurassic due to various geological folds and the land tilting in the mid Cretaceous Period (see p61) – but for non-geologists this simple rule is a good place to begin.

It is due to this incredible and – unusually – very visible geology that the coastline was designated England's first UNESCO World Heritage Site in 2001, thereby placing it alongside sites such as the Great Barrier Reef and the Grand Canyon.

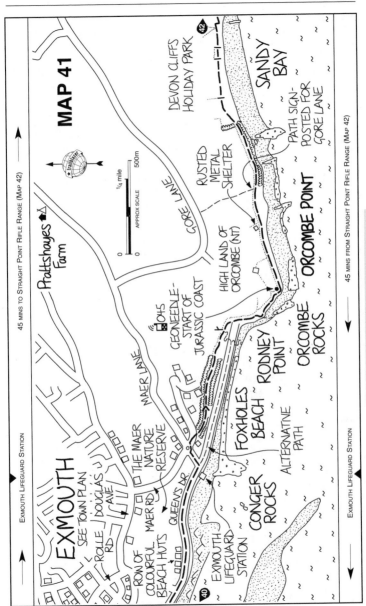

MAP 41

1/4 mile

APPROX SCALE

0   500m

Prattshayes Farm

DEVON CLIFFS HOLIDAY PARK

SANDY BAY

42

GORE LANE

PATH SIGN-POSTED FOR GORE LANE

RUSTED METAL SHELTER

HIGH LAND OF ORCOMBE (NT)

GEONEEDLE-START OF JURASSIC COAST

ORCOMBE POINT

EXMOUTH
SEE TOWN PLAN

THE MAER NATURE RESERVE

MAER LANE

ROLLE RD

DOUGLAS AVE

MAER RD

QUEEN'S DR

ROW OF COLOURFUL BEACH HUTS

EXMOUTH LIFEGUARD STATION

CONGER ROCKS

FOXHOLES BEACH

ALTERNATIVE PATH

RODNEY POINT

ORCOMBE ROCKS

40

ROUTE GUIDE AND MAPS

BUDLEIGH SALTERTON

[map p203]

Situated at the mouth of the River Otter, the genteel town of Budleigh Salterton was appropriately called Ottermouth until the name was changed to reflect what, at the time, was the town's primary industry: salt-panning.

Apart from picking up a sandwich – there are some nice cafés here – or resting on the town's quiet little seafront there is little to keep you in Budleigh Salterton, though the thatched **Fairlynch Museum** (☎ 01395-442666, 🖳 fairlynchmuseum.uk;

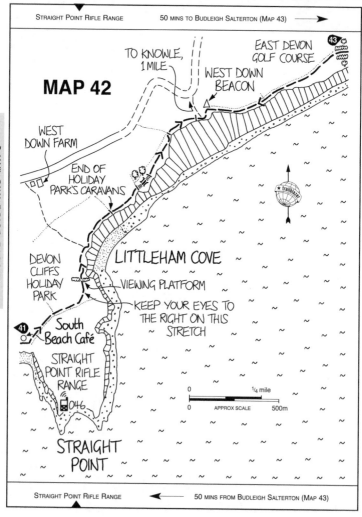

STRAIGHT POINT RIFLE RANGE 50 MINS TO BUDLEIGH SALTERTON (MAP 43) ⟶

TO KNOWLE, 1 MILE

EAST DEVON GOLF COURSE

WEST DOWN BEACON

MAP 42

WEST DOWN FARM

END OF HOLIDAY PARK'S CARAVANS

LITTLEHAM COVE

DEVON CLIFFS HOLIDAY PARK

VIEWING PLATFORM

KEEP YOUR EYES TO THE RIGHT ON THIS STRETCH

South Beach Café

STRAIGHT POINT RIFLE RANGE

0 ¼ mile
0 APPROX SCALE 500m

STRAIGHT POINT

STRAIGHT POINT RIFLE RANGE ⟵ 50 MINS FROM BUDLEIGH SALTERTON (MAP 43)

ROUTE GUIDE AND MAPS

50 MINS FROM STRAIGHT POINT RIFLE RANGE (MAP 42) ← | ← BUDLEIGH SALTERTON | 70 MINS TO BRANDY HEAD OBSERVATION HUT (MAP 44) →

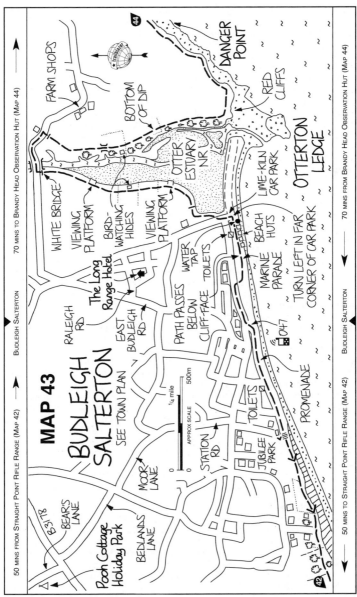

50 MINS TO STRAIGHT POINT RIFLE RANGE (MAP 42) | BUDLEIGH SALTERTON | 70 MINS FROM BRANDY HEAD OBSERVATION HUT (MAP 44) →

Easter-Oct Tue-Sun & bank hols 2-4.30pm; free) is a nice distraction, with Bronze Age and geological displays and an impressive collection of some 4000 items of clothing, some dating back to the early 18th century. Perhaps its most curious possession, however, actually lies chained up outside: a log apparently gnawed by a beaver that washed up on the banks of the River Otter, which is a mystery as there are no beavers in this river, nor indeed supposedly in England. (The most plausible explanation is that one of the Otter's tributaries, the Tale, runs through the private Escot Estate where apparently they do keep beavers – and it must have washed down from there.)

Just past the museum, look for the **blue plaque** on the whitewashed walls of a house known as The Octagon. It celebrates the fact that John Everett Millias was staying in the house in 1870 when he painted his famous *The Boyhood of Raleigh*. The great adventurer Sir Walter Raleigh, the subject of the painting, was actually born a couple of miles inland in East Budleigh. The very keen eyed might be able to spot a **smaller blue plaque** slightly further on, fastened to the low **sea wall** on the opposite side of the road. It claims that this is the wall that features in the painting itself.

Budleigh Salterton Jazz Festival (see p14) is held here in April, while its classical-music cousin, **Budleigh Music Festival** (🖳 budleighmusicfestival.co.uk) runs for a week in July. **Budleigh Salterton Literary Festival** (see p14) is in September.

Services
Though the town makes a good lunch stop and has several services, there is little accommodation here; as a result, most trekkers continue to Sidmouth where more

beds are available. The friendly **tourist information office** (☎ 01395-445275, 🖳 visitbudleigh.com; Easter-Sep Mon-Sat 10am-4pm, Oct-Easter Mon-Sat 10am-1pm), on Fore St, however, can help with accommodation.

There's a Co-op **supermarket** (daily 7am-10pm) in the middle of the High St, which has a **post office** (Mon-Sat 9am-5.30pm) housed within it. Nearby is a Lloyds **pharmacy** (Mon-Fri 9am-6pm, Sat 9am-4pm). There are **ATMs** on the High St.

Transport
[See also pp50-4] For **buses**, Stagecoach's 157 and 357 connect the town with Exmouth and Sidmouth.

For a **taxi** contact Andrew Pelosi ☎ 01395-443122, or Justin Batten ☎ 07949-689912 or ☎ 01392-879503.

Where to stay
Camping is available relatively nearby at the small but well-equipped *Pooh Cottage Holiday Park* (Map 43; ☎ 07875-685595, 🖳 poohcottage.co.uk; £10/15 for tent and one/two hikers; WI-FI; 🐾; mid Mar to Oct), just one mile from the High St.

B&Bs are rather thin on the ground. Next to the tourist office, *Pebbles* (☎ 01395-442417, 🖳 bedandbreakfastbythe beach.com; 3D or T; ✑; WI-FI; £52.50-72.50pp, sgl occ £95-135), at 16 Fore St, has marvellous rooms with tremendous views, but it's expensive. Breakfast is taken in the conservatory overlooking the rear garden; the garden backs onto the path itself.

The Long Range Hotel (☎ 01395-443321, 🖳 thelongrangehotel.co.uk; 2S/4D/3T; ✑; WI-FI; £47.50-72.50pp, sgl £75-79.75, sgl occ rates on request) is away

---

❏ **A pebble's tale**
Budleigh Salterton is known for its Lower Triassic pebble beds. For thousands of years the predominantly oval shaped and extremely hard pebbles have been spilling out from the local cliffs as sea and time take their toll. Four hundred million years old, they are identical to rocks found in Northern France, both being made of hard quartzite. They are thought to have been transported to their two respective homes via one of the giant rivers that flowed through the Triassic period's arid and scorching red deserts (see Geology pp57-62).

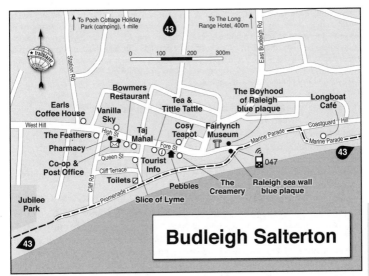

Budleigh Salterton

from the centre on Vales Rd, but only a few hundred metres from the coast path. It's a friendly and efficiently run place with a lovely conservatory looking over the Otter Valley.

Where to eat and drink

If you're just after a **café**, you could do a lot worse than *Earls Coffee House* (☎ 01395-445445; WI-FI; Mon-Thur 8.30am-5pm, Fri & Sat to 8pm, Sun 9.30am-4pm), a modern, friendly place at the corner of High St and Station Rd that does excellent coffee as well as filled croissants, flatbreads and baguettes. Their toasted Devon fruitbread (£1.95) is delicious.

Further down High St, at No 44, is *Vanilla Sky* (☎ 01395-443182; WI-FI; Mon-Sat 9am-5pm), a wonderfully cute, award-winning café-cum-deli – try their Devonshire rarebit (£5.75-7.50), a cheese-toast speciality.

Further still, at 4 Fore St, is *Tea and Tittle Tattle* (☎ 01395-443203, 🖳 www.tea andtittletattle.co.uk; Tue-Sat 10am-4.30pm, Sun noon-4.30pm) a pretty teahouse with hearty home-cooked lunches (£7.50-11.50) as well as breakfasts and cream teas.

Nearby, *Cosy Teapot* (☎ 01395-444016; 🐾; summer daily 10am-4.30pm, winter Fri-Mon only), at No 13, is a very traditional lace-and-doily affair that sells the odd antique as well as a varied selection of cakes and teas.

For a more substantial **restaurant** meal, there's a bistro, a couple of restaurants and a pub. The pub, *The Feathers* (☎ 01395-708852; WI-FI; 🐾; food Mon-Sat noon-3pm & 6-8pm, Sun lunchtimes only), which originally dates back to the 16th century but has been heavily worked on since, offers a fairly standard pub-grub menu but has a specials board. For something more sophisticated, try *Bowmers Restaurant* (☎ 01395-442676, 🖳 bowmers.com; food Wed-Fri 6-9pm, Sat noon-2.30pm & 6-9pm, Sun noon-2.30pm), at 7 High St, which specialises in Mediterranean cuisine.

For Indian food, head to nearby *Taj Mahal* (☎ 01395-446093, 🖳 tajmahal budleigh.co.uk; daily noon-2pm & 5.30-11pm), at 1B High St.

The bistro, *Slice of Lyme* (☎ 01395-442628, 🖳 sliceoflyme.co.uk; Mon 10am-3pm, Tue-Fri 10am-3pm & 6-9pm, Sat 10am-4.30pm & 6-9pm, Sun noon-4pm) serves filling mains such as chicken, ham & mushroom pie, lamb tagine and homemade burgers. It also has an ice-cream kiosk next door, which is handy, though true ice-cream afficionados will head to *The Creamery*, on Fore St, which boasts over 30 ice-cream flavours and is a clotted-cream specialist.

As you leave the town on the coast path, *Longboat Café* (☎ 01395-445619; Easter-end Oct daily 10am-5pm, winter weekends only and weather permitting) is a cheery beachside establishment with a scattering of tables outside.

Leaving Budleigh Salterton along the Promenade, past seemingly endless commemorative benches, eventually you hit the River Otter and there is a brief but pleasant sojourn round **Otter Estuary Nature Reserve**. Don't get too excited by the name, however, for mink are more common than otters and any paw prints you come across are more likely to belong to a Jack Russell. As compensation, however, in the skies above soar merlins and red kites, and kingfishers sometimes work the riverbanks.

Having left the reserve and rejoined the coast, you are now confronted by the ominously named cliffs **Danger Point** and **Black Head**, the trail here making for a majestic stroll on a sun-soaked summer's afternoon. **Brandy Head**, named after the contraband that was smuggled here, is topped by an **Observation Hut** that was used to test weapons and gun sights during WW2.

Continuing past **Chiselbury Bay** and **Smallstone Point**, you soon come to **Ladram Bay** with its impressive display of red sandstone sea stacks and the gigantic *Ladram Bay Holiday Park* (☎ 01395-568398, 🖳 ladrambay.co.uk; WI-FI; 🐾 but restricted areas; mid Mar-end Oct), home to *Pebbles Restaurant & Bar* (daily 9-11am & noon-9.30pm), *Coast Fish & Chips* (Sun-Thur 5-9pm, Fri-Sat 5-10pm), and the very well-stocked **Ladram Bay Stores** (Sun-Thur 8am-6pm, Fri-Sat 8am-7pm), which has an **ATM** (£1.99). They do allow some *camping* here but, particularly for advance bookings, there's a two-night minimum stay (three nights in peak season); rates vary so contact them for details.

Following Ladram Bay you arrive at what initially appears to be a daunting climb. This is **High Peak** (157m) and the haul begins quite leniently, but becomes tough, once you enter the woods.

Once at the top take a deep breath; the reward for your efforts is a gradual descent through the trees and a dramatic view of the coastal cliffs ahead before you need to climb again, this time up the steeper slopes of **Peak Hill**. Descending through woodland once more (look out for the rabbits and mice carved into tree stumps) you arrive with some relief at **Peak Hill Rd**. Leaving it to inspect the ranks of **commemorative benches**, you soon come to a right turn leading down to **Jacob's Ladder Beach**.

As you round the cliff, *Clock Tower Café* (☎ 01395-515319, 🖳 clocktower sidmouth.co.uk; 🐾 in conservatory; daily 9.30am-5pm) stands above you, a restored 17th-century lime kiln and pseudo-fort that serves gourmet sandwiches (£6-8), homemade cakes and other treats, and has a lovely flower-filled garden.

Clifton Walkway and its rockfalls are now all that separate you from the end of the stage. Survive and you'll soon be strolling on Sidmouth seafront with all the other sunkissed sightseers.

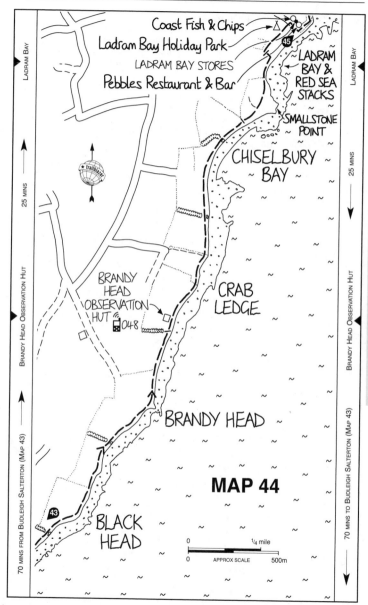

Coast Fish & Chips
Ladram Bay Holiday Park
LADRAM BAY STORES
Pebbles Restaurant & Bar

45

LADRAM
BAY &
RED SEA
STACKS

SMALLSTONE
POINT

CHISELBURY
BAY

BRANDY
HEAD
OBSERVATION
HUT
048

CRAB
LEDGE

BRANDY HEAD

43

BLACK
HEAD

MAP 44

0 .... 1/4 mile
0 .... 500m
APPROX SCALE

LADRAM BAY

LADRAM BAY

25 MINS

25 MINS

BRANDY HEAD OBSERVATION HUT

BRANDY HEAD OBSERVATION HUT

70 MINS FROM BUDLEIGH SALTERTON (MAP 43)

70 MINS TO BUDLEIGH SALTERTON (MAP 43)

ROUTE GUIDE AND MAPS

SIDMOUTH   [map p209]

'A town caught still in a timeless charm'
John Betjeman
Nestling quietly in the Sid Valley, with red
cliffs soaring on either side, Sidmouth is, as
the former poet laureate suggests, a lovely
place. Winner of numerous awards for its
gardens, floral displays abound throughout
the town centre. A touch too old-fashioned
and genteel for some, Sidmouth is ideal for
the average walker who simply seeks shelter and sustenance without too much
razzmatazz.

Featuring in the Domesday Book as
'Sedemuda', Sidmouth began life as a
small fishing community. Its geographical

location prevented the town from successfully constructing a decent harbour, as a
result of which Sidmouth didn't really grow
in earnest until tourism took off during the
Georgian and Regency eras (1714-1837);
much of the town's architecture still dates
from this time. The young Queen Victoria
holidayed in the town as a baby in 1819
(Royal Glen Hotel bears a plaque celebrating the visit) and the town's growth and
popularity as a resort continued throughout
her reign.

Sidmouth Museum (☐ sidvaleassoci
ation.org.uk/museum; Apr-Oct Mon 1-
4pm, Tue-Sat 10am-4pm; free), on Church

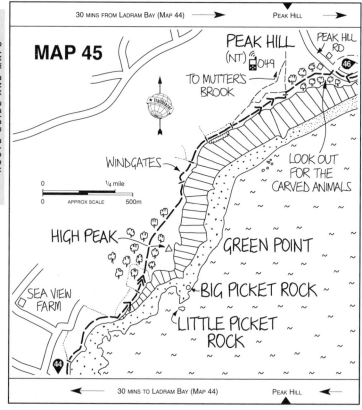

MAP 45

30 MINS FROM LADRAM BAY (MAP 44) ⟶   PEAK HILL ⟶

PEAK HILL
(NT) ☐049

PEAK HILL
RD

46

TO MUTTER'S
BROOK

★ trailblazer

WINDGATES

LOOK OUT
FOR THE
CARVED ANIMALS

0   ¼ mile
0   APPROX SCALE   500m

HIGH PEAK

GREEN POINT

BIG PICKET ROCK

SEA VIEW
FARM

LITTLE PICKET
ROCK

44

⟵ 30 MINS TO LADRAM BAY (MAP 44)   PEAK HILL ⟵

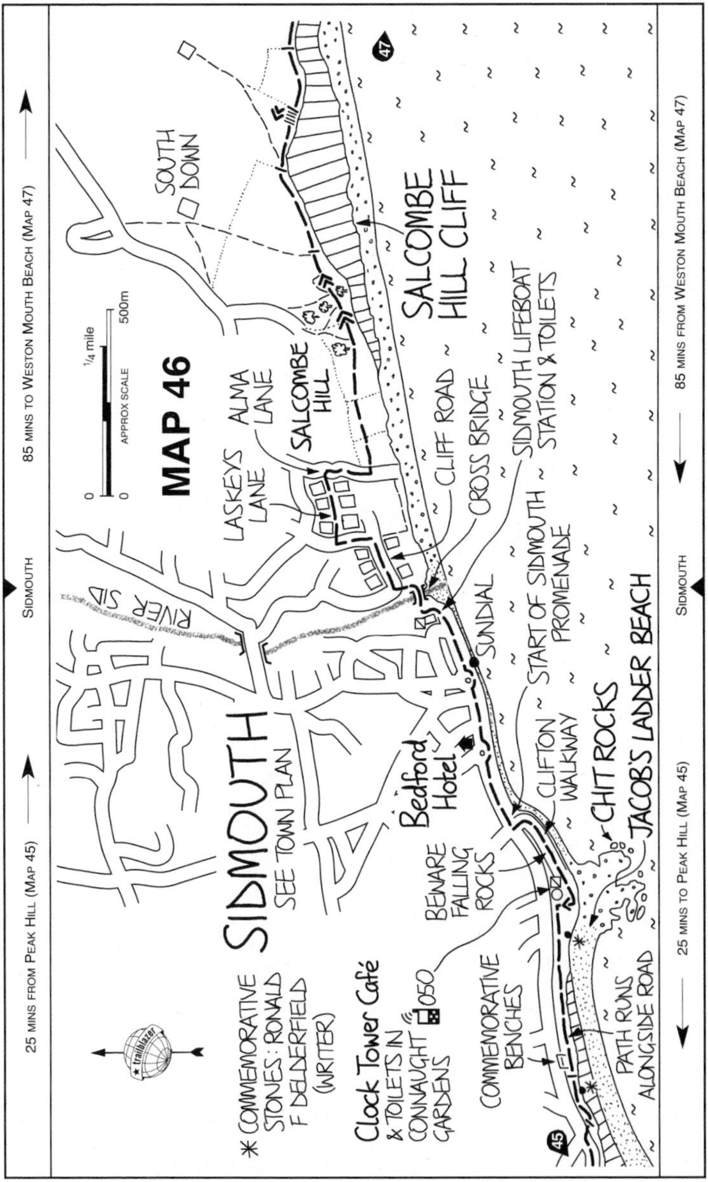
85 MINS TO WESTON MOUTH BEACH (MAP 47)
SIDMOUTH
25 MINS FROM PEAK HILL (MAP 45)
85 MINS FROM WESTON MOUTH BEACH (MAP 47)
SIDMOUTH
25 MINS TO PEAK HILL (MAP 45)
MAP 46
APPROX SCALE
0
1/4 mile
0
500m
SOUTH DOWN
SALCOMBE HILL CLIFF
SALCOMBE HILL
ALMA LANE
LASKEYS LANE
CLIFF ROAD
CROSS BRIDGE
SIDMOUTH LIFEBOAT STATION & TOILETS
RIVER SID
SUNDIAL
START OF SIDMOUTH PROMENADE
SIDMOUTH
SEE TOWN PLAN
Bedford Hotel
CLIFTON WALKWAY
CHIT ROCKS
JACOB'S LADDER BEACH
BEWARE FALLING ROCKS
COMMEMORATIVE BENCHES
PATH RUNS ALONGSIDE ROAD
* COMMEMORATIVE STONES: RONALD F DELDERFIELD (WRITER)
Clock Tower Café
& TOILETS IN CONNAUGHT GARDENS
050
47
45
trailblazer

St, houses exhibitions describing the town's development from a fishing village through to Regency and Victorian times as well as an exhibition on the Jurassic Coast. They also offer free guided walks to various parts of the town, each informative amble lasting approximately two hours.

Sidmouth Folk Week (see p14) is held here in August.

Services

The **tourist information centre** (☎ 01395-516441, 🖳 visitsidmouth.co.uk; Apr-Oct Mon-Sat 10am-5pm, Sun 10am-4pm, Oct-Apr Mon-Sat 10am-1pm) stands at the eastern end of town on Ham Lane. For **internet** go to the **library** (Mon & Fri 9am-6pm, Wed & Thur 9am-5pm, Sat 9am-1pm) on Blackmore Drive, just west of the High St.

There are two **trekking/camping shops** on Fore St, one that's a national chain – Mountain Warehouse (Mon-Sat 9am-5.30pm, Sun 10am-4pm) – and one that's not: Sidmouth Outdoor Co (☎ 01395-513747; Mon-Sat 10am-4.30pm). Nearby there's a **pharmacy**, Boots (Mon-Sat 9am-5.30pm, Sun 10am-4pm).

Much of what a trekker traditionally needs lies in from the seafront at the top end of Fore St (by which point it's actually called High St), including a Co-op **supermarket** (daily 7am-10pm) and the **post office** (Mon-Sat 9am-5.30pm). There are also some **banks** with **ATMs**.

Transport

[See also pp50-4] Stagecoach's No 157 **bus** travels east to Budleigh Salterton and Exmouth; the No 9A meanwhile connects the town with Seaton, Lyme Regis and Exeter, and the No 9 with Honiton and Exeter; their 56B also calls here on Sundays (May-Sep). First's X52 (Exeter to Lyme Regis) calls here and Axe Valley's 899 journeys between Sidmouth and Seaton.

For a **taxi** try Peak Taxis (☎ 01395-513322).

Where to stay

Though there are numerous hotels on the seafront, annoyingly all of Sidmouth's

B&Bs are a short jaunt from the centre. The closest, on Salcombe Rd, are *Canterbury House* (☎ 01395-513373, 🖳 canterburyhouse.com; 1S/4D/1D or T/2T; WI-FI; mid Feb to mid Nov; £39-45pp, sgl £44-48, sgl occ £48-90), and *Berwick House* (☎ 01395-513621, 🖳 www.berwick-house.co.uk; 5D/1T; WI-FI; 🐾; £40-44pp, sgl occ £70-78) where the standard full English is available for breakfast as well as some daily specials.

A little further from the centre and all in a row along Vicarage Rd are: *The Groveside* (☎ 01395-513406, 🖳 thegroveside.com; 1S/5D/3T; WI-FI; £36-40pp, sgl £45-55, sgl occ £60-80), an Edwardian boutique guest-house that serves locally purchased and organic food on its breakfast plates; *Southcombe* (☎ 01395-513861, 🖳 southcombeguesthouse.co.uk; 5D/2T/1Tr; WI-FI; from £38.50pp, sgl occ from £40); and *Lynstead* (☎ 01395-512244, 🖳 www.lynsteadguesthouse.co.uk; 1T/4D; WI-FI; 🐾; £42.50-45pp, sgl occ rates on request), which is dog friendly and also has a pleasant garden in which to relax.

Fifteen minutes from the town centre on Cotmaton Rd, *Glendevon* (☎ 01395-514028, 🖳 glendevon-hotel.co.uk; 4S/3D/1T; WI-FI; £42-47pp, sgl occ rates on request) has lovely big airy rooms.

The seafront is lined with **hotels**. Two of the first that you come to are *Bedford Hotel* (☎ 01395-513047, 🖳 bedfordhotelsidmouth.co.uk; 11S/27D or T/2Qd; WI-FI; 🐾; £72-99.50pp, sgl £70-99.50pp for dinner, bed and breakfast), where £10pp will be deducted if you don't want an evening meal; and *Hotel Riviera* (☎ 01395-515201, 🖳 hotelriviera.co.uk; 7S/3D/16D or T; ☛; WI-FI; small 🐾; mid Feb-end Dec; £112-246pp, sgl occ rates on request), where food is available all day but the restaurant is only open for lunch and in the evening (daily 12.30-2pm & 7-9pm). The top rates are for rooms with sea views.

Also on The Esplanade, there are three hotels owned by the same company, Sidmouth Hotels (toll free ☎ 0800-048 1731, 🖳 www.hotels-sidmouth.co.uk). Both *The Kingswood & Devoran Hotel* (☎ 01395-516367; 11S/17D/17T/3Tr; ☛; 🐾;

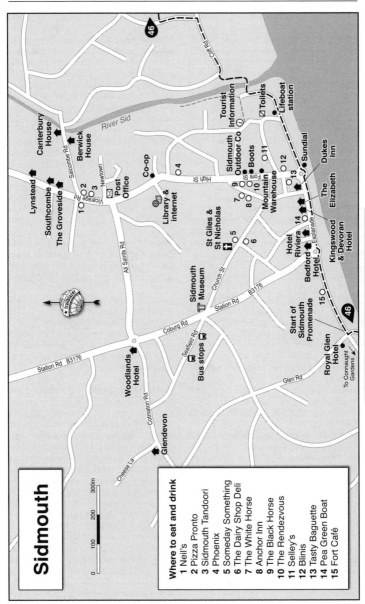

Sidmouth

0 100 200 300m

ROUTE GUIDE AND MAPS

Where to eat and drink
1 Neil's
2 Pizza Pronto
3 Sidmouth Tandoori
4 Phoenix
5 Someday Something
6 The Dairy Shop Deli
7 The White Horse
8 Anchor Inn
9 The Black Horse
10 The Rendezvous
11 Selley's
12 Blinis
13 Tasty Baguette
14 Pea Green Boat
15 Fort Café

WI-FI; closed Jan; B&B £59-90pp, sgl £59-83, sgl occ rates on request) and *The Elizabeth* (☎ 01395-513503; 1S/11D/16T; ✆; WI-FI; B&B £68-84.50pp, sgl £68-73, sgl occ £91-108) also offer dinner, bed and breakfast rates. The cheapest of the three is *Dukes Inn* (☎ 01395-513320, 🖳 dukessidmouth.co.uk; 3S/1T/4D/5Tr; WI-FI; B&B £49.50-70pp, sgl £50-73, sgl occ £99-120).

Away from the seafront is *Woodlands Hotel* (☎ 01395-513120, 🖳 woodlandshotel.com; 3S/2D/13D or T/1Qd; ✆; WI-FI; 🐾; £100-170pp, sgl from £120, sgl occ rates on request), on the corner of Station Rd and Cotmaton Rd, is a 10-minute walk inland.

Where to eat and drink
It's surprising more people in Sidmouth don't suffer from obesity, given the temptation placed before them every day by the huge range of eateries on offer.

Cafés & delis
The first café you come on the seafront is also one of the best: *Fort Café* (☎ 01395-512200; WI-FI; 🐾; summer daily 9.30am-5pm, winter hours variable) is welcoming, dog-friendly, and does toasties, all-day breakfasts and homemade ice-cream. Another dog-friendly café is tiny *Selley's* (Mon-Sat 9am-4.30pm; 🐾), tucked away discreetly in **Libra Court** (🖳 libracourt.com). Most of the seating is in the pleasant courtyard, though there are a couple of cosy tables inside.

On the other side of Fore St, beside St Giles & Nicholas Church, is the narrow corner café *Someday Something* (☎ 01395-515829, 🖳 somedaysomething.co.uk; WI-FI; 🐾; Feb-Dec Mon-Sat 9.30am-5pm, lunch to 2.30pm). Again it's a bit of a squeeze inside, but tables spill out onto the pavements, making this a nice spot for a cream tea.

Opposite is *The Dairy Shop Deli* (☎ 01395-513018; WI-FI; 🐾; summer Mon-Sat 9/10am-5pm, winter to 4pm), a deli-cum-café serving lovely meals and snacks – most made with the local produce they sell in the shop – including Devon ham sandwiches as well as plenty of vegetarian and gluten-free options.

Round the corner, on Old Fore St, *The White Horse* (☎ 01395-514271; summer Mon-Sat 10am-6.30pm, Sun till 5pm, winter hours variable), sounds like a pub but is more of a no-frills licensed café serving fish & chips, jacket potatoes and burgers.

Another licensed place, though far more swish, is *Blinis* (☎ 01395-572920, 🖳 blinis-cafe-bar.co.uk; WI-FI; Mon-Sat 10am-6pm; closed Jan), a stylish bar-café on Fore St that does a lovely crab pâté on hot buttered toast (£8.25). The speciality, naturally, are blinis – a type of pancake; try the scrambled egg, smoked salmon & chives blini (£7).

For made-to-order takeaway sandwiches, try *Tasty Baguette* (☎ 01395-577575; Mon-Sat 8am-2.30pm), on Dove Lane.

Pubs
The only dog-friendly pub is *The Black Horse* (☎ 01395-513676, 🖳 blackhorseinn-sidmouth.co.uk; food daily 9am-9.30pm; WI-FI; 🐾), on Fore St. It serves food every day including breakfasts; lunchtime and evening menus include stone-baked pizzas.

Nearby *Anchor Inn* (☎ 01395-514129; WI-FI; food Mon-Sat 10am-9.30pm, Sun noon-9pm), on Old Fore St, does a fair fish pie (£11.95) as well as cheaper cod & chips (£6.25).

Restaurants
Down on the seafront, *Pea Green Boat* (☎ 01395-514152, 🖳 thepeagreenboat.com; food summer Mon-Fri noon-2.30pm & 5-8.30pm, Sat noon-3pm & 5-9pm, Sun noon-3pm & 5-8.30pm, winter hours variable), is a small but smart place with terrace seating looking out to sea. Food is Mediterranean meets West Country, with Exmouth mussels (£16.50 for a main) and Lyme Bay fish & chips (£14) on the menu alongside Parma ham pizza (£12.50) and Caprese salad (£7.50).

Up on Fore St, *The Rendezvous* (☎ 01395-516724, 🖳 therendezvoussidmouth.co.uk; Mon-Sat 11am-3pm & 6-9pm, but hours depend on demand) is a bistro that does tasty lunchtime sandwiches (£6-7) as well as mains such as portobello mushrooms & mascarpone pie (£12.95).

The best seafood place in town – in fact, probably the best restaurant in town – is *Neil's* (☎ 01395-519494, 🖥 neilsrestaurant.com; Tue-Sat from 6.30pm) on Radway Place (Vicarage Rd). As they justifiably put it, they turn seafood into great food (though other, non-fishy dishes are also available). Mains include pan-roasted John Dory with lemon sautéed prawns & asparagus (£18.25) and Brixham monkfish curry (£18.50).

Also up this end of town are *Pizza Pronto* (☎ 01395-516319; Sun-Thur 5-11pm, Fri 5pm-1am, Sat 5pm-2.30am) and *Sidmouth Tandoori* (☎ 01395-579944; Sun-Thur 5-10.30pm, Fri & Sat 5pm to midnight), where you can bring your own booze. Down the road slightly is the Chinese restaurant, *Phoenix* (☎ 01395-514720; July & Aug daily noon-2pm & 5-10pm, rest of year closed on Tue).

SIDMOUTH TO SEATON [MAPS 46-50]

Today's **10¼-mile (16.5km; 4hrs 10 mins)** stage is tough, but rewarding. As far as Branscombe Mouth it is a trail of very steep and largely wooded pathways, but one where the lucky walker gets to cross pretty combes on the way to barren and sparsely populated beaches. Only the occasional periods of level clifftop walking show any mercy to the knees today, but the scenery, particularly gorgeous Lincombe, offers ample consolation.

There is also a decent café at Branscombe Mouth (note, this is the only place to get refreshments before Beer, unless you detour to The Fountain Head), whereafter the terrain changes drastically as you begin a spectacular walk below Hooken Cliffs, formed by a landslip in 1790. At windy Beer Head there are great views over Seaton Bay, where one finds both the friendly, photogenic fishing village of Beer, offering plentiful food and accommodation, and Seaton, this stage's destination. With the distance between Beer and Seaton being only 1½ miles, the former is a viable overnight stop, especially as the next stage is relatively short.

The route

Your first task, having left Sidmouth, is to climb up steep **Salcombe Hill Cliff**, an ascent that bears more than a passing similarity to a couple of yesterday's climbs: the path begins gently in a field before winding up the steep slope to some woods that sit on the summit like a toupee.

Following the path along the cliff-tops, you then drop sharply into **Salcombe Mouth** and skirt round **Combe Wood** before climbing the immense **Maynard's Cliff** and the even steeper **Higher Dunscombe Cliff**. Note the colours of the cliffs with the pastel reds and dirty oranges of the Triassic era topped, on occasion, with the lighter-hued Cretaceous Upper Greensand – the Jurassic-era rock having been eroded away entirely (a phenomenon that geologists call an 'unconformity').

Afterwards, the path flirts with **Lincombe**, the calf muscles enjoying a lucky escape as the trail for once passes around the back of the combe rather than dropping into it. Keep your eyes peeled for green woodpeckers, painted lady butterflies and the rare marsh helleborine (*Epipactis palustris*) orchid as the trail continues to tackle the undulations before descending through **Dunscombe Coppice** to **Weston Mouth**'s undisturbed pebble beach.

(cont'd on p214)

ROUTE GUIDE AND MAPS

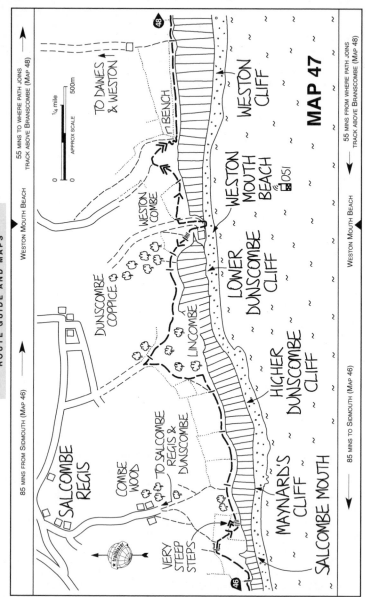

ROUTE GUIDE AND MAPS

MAP 47

85 MINS FROM SIDMOUTH (MAP 46) ▶ WESTON MOUTH BEACH ▶ 55 MINS TO WHERE PATH JOINS TRACK ABOVE BRANSCOMBE (MAP 48) ▲

85 MINS TO SIDMOUTH (MAP 46) ◀ WESTON MOUTH BEACH ◀ 55 MINS FROM WHERE PATH JOINS TRACK ABOVE BRANSCOMBE (MAP 48) ◀

48

TO DANES & WESTON

BENCH

WESTON CLIFF

WESTON MOUTH BEACH

051

LOWER DUNSCOMBE CLIFF

WESTON COMBE

DUNSCOMBE COPPICE

LINCOMBE

HIGHER DUNSCOMBE CLIFF

SALCOMBE REGIS

COMBE WOOD

TO SALCOMBE REGIS & DUNSCOMBE

MAYNARD'S CLIFF

SALCOMBE MOUTH

VERY STEEP STEPS

46

¼ mile
APPROX SCALE
500m

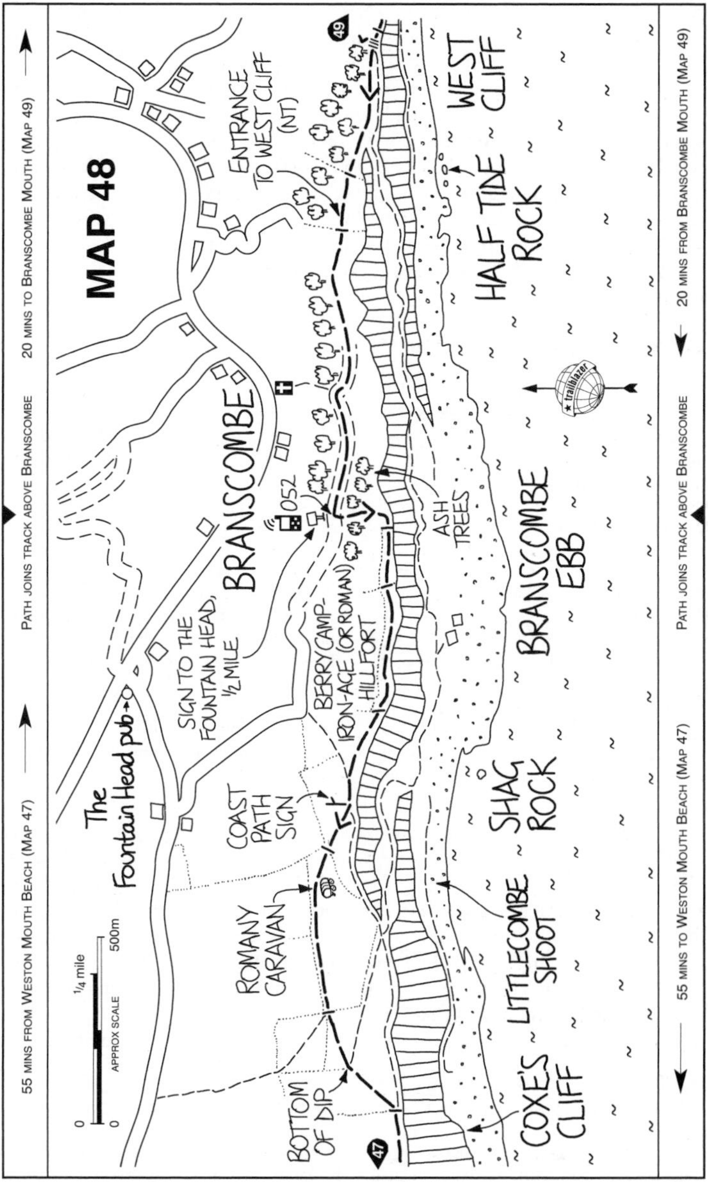
MAP 48
55 MINS FROM WESTON MOUTH BEACH (MAP 47)
PATH JOINS TRACK ABOVE BRANSCOMBE
20 MINS TO BRANSCOMBE MOUTH (MAP 49)
55 MINS TO WESTON MOUTH BEACH (MAP 47)
PATH JOINS TRACK ABOVE BRANSCOMBE
20 MINS FROM BRANSCOMBE MOUTH (MAP 49)
0 1/4 mile
0 500m
APPROX SCALE
The Fountain Head pub
SIGN TO THE FOUNTAIN HEAD, 1/2 MILE
BRANSCOMBE
052
ENTRANCE TO WEST CLIFF (NT)
BERRY CAMP IRON-AGE (OR ROMAN) HILLFORT
COAST PATH SIGN
ROMANY CARAVAN
BOTTOM OF DIP
ASH TREES
WEST CLIFF
HALF TIDE ROCK
BRANSCOMBE EBB
SHAG ROCK
LITTLECOMBE SHOOT
COXE'S CLIFF
trailblazer
47
49

(Cont'd from p211) Climbing out – and it is some climb! – you soon find your-self amongst the wild flowers on the rim of **Weston Cliff**, the way sticking to the cliff edge before heading inland across farmland on **Coxe's Cliff**.

Passing the site of **Berry Camp**, an Iron-age (or possibly Roman) hill-fort, you now follow a wooded path with ash trees to your right heading above the small village of **Branscombe** where, if you need a break, you'll find a wonder-ful, dog-friendly, real-ale pub, *The Fountain Head* (☎ 01297-680359, 🖥 foun tainheadinn.com; food daily noon-2pm & 6.30-9pm; 🐾) that does great food and serves ales (and ciders) from the local Branscombe Vale Brewery, and is signposted half a mile from the path. The path itself carries on to the National Trust owned **West Cliff**, from where you continue through the steep woods to Branscombe Mouth.

BRANSCOMBE MOUTH   [Map 49]

Branscombe Mouth reached the headlines back in 2007 when a container ship, *MSC Napoli*, ran aground offshore while being towed to Portland, having been badly dam-aged in a storm off Lizard Point. The cargo that was subsequently washed ashore – including brand-new BMW motorbikes, perfumes, nappies and car parts – was gratefully (and illegally, as it turned out) taken by scavengers, who had collected on the beach, until the police intervened a few days later.

Though there aren't any motorbikes on offer these days, there's just enough to Branscombe Mouth to keep walkers happy. For **food**, there's *Sea Shanty Beach Café* (☎ 01297-680577, 🖥 theseashanty.co.uk; 🐾; Apr-Oct daily 9am-5pm, winter week-ends only) with some great outdoor seating.

They do breakfasts (£8), sandwiches (£5.50-7.50) and substantial lunchtime mains (£9-13), and stock beer from the local micro-brewery. The attached **shop** (same hours) sells basics such as newspa-pers and pasties.

Less than 200 metres (about 180 yards) up the road from Branscombe Mouth, **B&B** is provided at *Great Seaside* (☎ 01297-680470, 🖥 greatseaside.co.uk; 1D/1Qd; 🍺; WI-FI; £47.50-60pp, sgl occ rates on request). It is a 16th-century farm-house, the first written evidence of which dates from 1339 (!), and is now surrounded by National Trust land.

Axe Valley's 899 **bus service** (from Branscombe Village Hall) travels between Sidmouth, Beer and Seaton; see pp50-4 for details.

From Branscombe Mouth head up **East Cliff** to follow the path through Sea Shanty Caravan Park. (Alternatively, you can climb up over the top of **Hooken Cliffs**, the two paths reconvening shortly before Beer Head.) The time spent amongst the caravans is brief and you're soon back on a pleasant if rugged path that twists and turns its way through foliage sandwiched between Hooken Cliffs and Hooken Beach. A steep climb presents marvellous views back over a col-lection of chalk pinnacles before a field takes you to **Beer Head** – and the most westerly chalk cliffs in England. From here you then skip down to and over **Arratt's Hill** before a short road walk into the pretty fishing village of Beer.

BEER   [map p217]

Devon villages don't come much more quintessential than cosy Beer, an ancient thatched village nestled on the county's south coast. Along with the village called

Hope, Beer seems to be one of those places that was named after something that most trekkers need to function properly. However, the name actually derives from

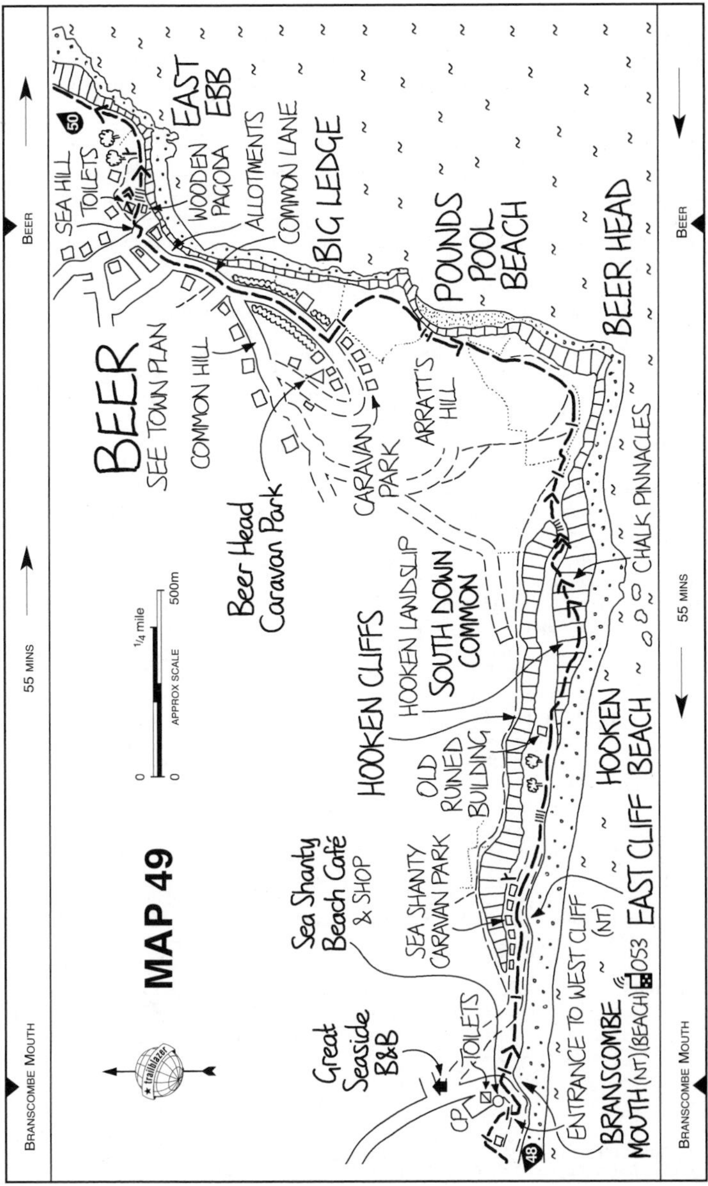

MAP 49

¼ mile

APPROX SCALE

0   500m

BRANSCOMBE MOUTH

55 MINS

BEER

Great Seaside B&B

Sea Shanty Beach Café & Shop

Sea Shanty Caravan Park

Beer Head Caravan Park

BEER

SEE TOWN PLAN

COMMON HILL

HOOKEN CLIFFS

HOOKEN LANDSLIP

SOUTH DOWN COMMON

CARAVAN PARK

ARRATT'S HILL

OLD RUINED BUILDING

CP TOILETS

ENTRANCE TO WEST CLIFF (NT)

BRANSCOMBE MOUTH (NT)(BEACH) 053 EAST CLIFF BEACH

HOOKEN BEACH

CHALK PINNACLES

BRANSCOMBE MOUTH

55 MINS

BEER

SEA HILL

TOILETS

50

WOODEN PAGODA

ALLOTMENTS

COMMON LANE

BIG LEDGE

POUNDS POOL BEACH

BEER HEAD

EAST EBB

48

the Anglo-Saxon word 'Bearu', meaning 'Grove', referring to the woodlands that originally cloaked the area.

The main joy of Beer can be had simply by strolling along its lovely main street, which follows a trickling brook down to the harbour, but the village also has some quirky sights. Behind Jimmy Green's clothes shop you'll find the **Bomb Shelter** (Mon-Fri 10am-5pm, Sat 10am-5.30pm, Sun 10.30am-4.30pm; free), which rather than being an underground wartime bunker, is actually an exhibition room which displays and recounts the story of an unexploded 500kg WWII German bomb that landed safely in a field nearby, rather than destroying the village, thanks to the selfless heroics of Luftwaffe pilot Gunther Blaffert.

Down by the harbour, **Beer Heritage Centre** (🖳 beervillageheritage.org.uk; free) stands opposite an old World War II **gun-position**, and continues the military theme. The 16th-century **Starre House**, meanwhile, is the village's oldest building and was built from local stone. Speaking of which, at the top end of town, half a mile beyond the turning to the YHA (turn left up Quarry Lane), are **Beer Quarry Caves** (☎ 01297-680282, 🖳 beerquarrycaves.co.uk; Easter to Sep daily 10am-5pm, Oct 11am-4pm; £8) which have a history stretching back over two millennia. 'Beer stone' was used in the construction of Exeter and Winchester cathedrals as well as Westminster Abbey and the Tower of London – where no doubt some of those smugglers who hid contraband in this vast underground complex feared they may end up. Beer Quarry Caves are also a stop on Axe Valley's 899 bus service; see box p51.

Beer Rhythm & Blues Festival (see p14) is held here in October.

Services

Assuming you have an account accepted by the post office you can withdraw money for free at the **post office** (Mon-Thur 9am-1pm & 2-6pm, Fri-Sat 9am-1pm & 2-7pm), which is inside a village shop called Rock Villa, which also sells some cracking craft beers. If not, there are **ATMs** at both The Anchor Inn and Dolphin Hotel (both charge

around £1.85 to withdraw cash), too. There's also a **pharmacy** (Mon-Wed & Fri 9am-1pm & 2-5.30pm, Thur & Sat 9am-1pm) and **Beer Village Stores** (Mon-Sat 7am-7pm, Sun 7.30am-5pm).

Transport

[See pp50-4] First's (Jurassic Coaster: Exeter to Lyme Regis) X52 **bus** service stops here; Axe Valley's No 899 calls here en route between Sidmouth and Seaton.

Where to stay

Budget travellers are well catered for here. There's **camping** available at the excellent *Beer Head Caravan Park* (Map 49; ☎ 01297-21107, 🖳 beer-head.com; WI-FI; 🐾; end Mar-end Oct; from £8pp), with great sea views from its flat grassy pitches and its own shop and bistro.

There's also a **hostel** (which offers camping as well): *YHA Beer* (☎ 0345-371 9502, 🖳 yha.org.uk/hostel/beer; 3 x 4-/3 x 5-/2 x 6-bed rooms; dorm beds from £13pp, private rooms from £39; WI-FI social areas only) provides meals and has 24hr access. There are spacious **dorms** as well as private **rooms**; one of the 6-bed rooms is en suite. **Camping** (from £11pp; 🐾) is allowed in the garden with full use of the hostel's facilities, which includes a laundry and drying room, and a self-catering kitchen. The hostel is a short walk out of town; follow Causeway until it bends sharply round to the right at which point you should go straight on before turning right down Bovey Lane.

There are also some particularly impressive **B&Bs** in the village.

On Fore St you'll find both the delightful *Colebrooke House* (☎ 01297-20308, 🖳 colebrookehouse.com; 4D/2Tr; WI-FI; £37-42.50pp, sgl occ from £55), and *Durham House* (☎ 07710-631721, 🖳 durhamhouse .co.uk; 7D/1T; WI-FI; £32.50-42.50pp; sgl occ £60-75), where breakfast options may include crêpes and eggs Benedict.

Just off Fore St, at 6 Gordon Terrace, is *Ashdale House* (☎ 01297-20683, 🖳 ash dalehouse.co.uk; 3D; WI-FI; from £35pp, sgl occ from £40). Next door – though with an address on Dolphin Rd – is the more

ROUTE GUIDE AND MAPS

upmarket ***Belmont House*** (☎ 01297-24415, 🖳 www.beer-devon.com; 5D; ▼; WI-FI; room only £32.50-55pp, sgl occ from £65); they don't serve breakfast but they do operate their own walking company (Jurassic Coast Walking; see p29).

Closest to the beach, and with sea views from most of its eight rooms, ***Bay View Guest House*** (☎ 01297-20489, 🖳 bayviewguesthousebeer.com; 1S/6D/1T, all en suite; WI-FI; Apr-end Oct £44.50-46.50pp, sgl £60-65, sgl occ £79-86) is right on the coast path and has its own tea room (see Where to Eat).

Both pubs also do B&B. ***The Anchor Inn*** (☎ 01297-20386, 🖳 anchorinn-beer.com; 4D/2T; ▼; WI-FI; 🐕; £37.50-57.50pp, sgl occ room rate) has six rooms, all of which have a sea view, though they don't accept advance one-night bookings at weekends in the main season. ***Dolphin Hotel*** (☎ 01297-20068, 🖳 dolphinhotelbeer.co.uk; 3S/14D/5T/1Tr; one room sleeping up to five; ▼; WI-FI; 🐕; £37.50-50pp, sgl occ £55-80), meanwhile, has rooms ranging from singles to a room that sleeps up to five though that is over the bar so may be noisy. Again, advance bookings for one-night stays are not accepted for summer weekends.

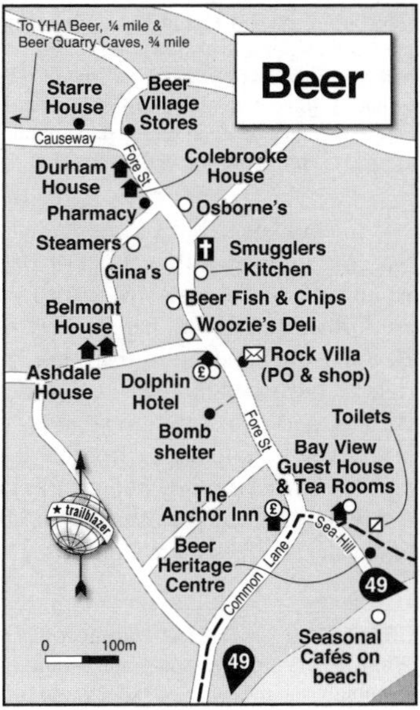

Where to eat and drink

Almost everything is on Fore St, where you'll find a surprisingly wide choice of cuisines to cater for all budgets. For lunch-box fillers, ***Woozie's Deli*** (Mon & Wed-Sat 9am-5.30pm, Sun 10am-5pm) does a good line in pasties. Next door, ***Beer Fish & Chips*** (☎ 01297-625774; Mon-Thur noon-8.30pm, Fri-Sat noon-9pm, Sun noon-8pm, winter Tue-Sat only) is the local chippy, where you can eat in (cod & chips £9.50) as well as take away.

Cafés are thin on the ground, though there is ***Bay View Tea Rooms*** (see Where to stay; summer daily 10am-5pm) overlooking the harbour, and there are ***seasonal cafés*** down on the beach.

The smartest **restaurant** in town (though still fairly informal) is ***Smugglers Kitchen*** (☎ 01297-22104, 🖳 thesmugglerskitchen.co.uk; Wed-Sat noon-2pm, plus Tue-Sat 6-9.30pm, to 9pm in winter), which focuses on West Country cuisine and stocks some fine wines and ales. Slightly further up Fore St, ***Osborne's*** (☎ 01297-24989; food daily 10am-11pm) is an equally popular tapas and wine bar.

Just around the corner, ***Steamers*** (☎ 01297-22922, 🖳 steamersrestaurant.co.uk; 🐕 lunchtime only; Tue-Sat coffee 10.30am-noon, lunch noon-1.30pm, dinner 6.45-8.45pm), on New Cut, gets its name from the building's original use as a steam bakery. The food is inventive and tasty (evening mains £12-19), with such treats as baked veg & goat's cheese in filo pastry with tomato & basil concasse (£12).

Opposite Smugglers Kitchen is the more affordable ***Gina's*** (☎ 01297-21121; Thur-Sun 6.30-9pm), an Italian restaurant with good-value pizza and pasta, but also some Thai dishes.

Disappointingly, given the name of the village, Beer doesn't have any decent **pubs**. The two it does have are ok, but are outclassed by many other pubs you'll have come across on your walk. There's a good selection of bottled ales in Rock Villa (the post office-cum-off-licence), however, so perhaps grab a bottle to sip down on the beach? Of the two pubs, *Dolphin Hotel* (see Where to stay; food served daily noon-2pm & 6-9pm) does the better food, but is less popular for a drink, probably on account of not being so close to the harbour. *The Anchor Inn* (see Where to stay; food daily noon-9.30pm; WI-FI; ⚫) has a nice sea-view beer garden which is separated from the main building by the coast path.

To continue to Seaton, there are two routes – one with steps, one without – that lead up **East Ebb** and out of Beer. The path takes you around East Ebb's white cliffs and along a minor road which ends at the base of **Beer Hill**. There are further alternatives here: at low tide turn right to walk along **Seaton Hole Beach**. At high tide, turn sharp left, along Old Beer Rd. After about 200m turn right up a wooded footpath (signposted), and then right again onto Beer Rd (the B3172), and right a third time along a footpath opposite Wessiter's Rd, which brings you back to the seafront by the seasonal café, *The Hideaway* (Mar-Oct daily 9.30am-4.30pm). Follow the beach past another seasonal café, *Jane's Kiosk* (where there are some toilets), some beach huts and old-style lampposts, to the sleepy seaside town of Seaton.

SEATON [map p221]

While lacking the Regency splendour of Sidmouth or the olde-worlde charm of Beer, Seaton's plentiful amenities and accommodation make it a good option for a stop. Known as Fleet ('Creek') in Saxon times, its location near the mouth of the River Axe once made it an important port, and so it remained up until about the 14th century, when fierce storms caused parts of Haven Cliff to subside into the estuary and a shingle bank to form. The town has also dabbled in shipbuilding and salt-panning down the years, the latter having been practised since the Iron Age.

The banks and flood plains that flank the Axe Estuary now host a number of nature reserves. **Seaton Tramway** (☎ 01297-20375, ▢ tram.co.uk; daily Easter-Oct 10am-4/5pm, check website for other times of the year; Seaton to Colyton £7/10 single/return, all-day explorer £10, ⚫ £1 each way; allow at least two hours) is a good way to see them as it meanders for three miles through the Axe Valley to Colyton, following the old Seaton & Beer Railway line that closed in 1967.

Just beyond the tramway station is **Seaton Jurassic** (☎ 01297-300390, ▢ seatonjurassic.org; daily 10am-5pm but on some Tue and Wed mornings school groups take over the place; £10), a fully interactive, multi-million pound museum complex, complete with café, gift shop and tourist information centre.

Other sites in town include **Seaton Labyrinth** (Map 50) in **Cliff Field Gardens** – a 60ft diameter spiral. Its half-a-mile turf pathways are lined with stones taken from different areas of the Jurassic coast to help explain the region's fascinating 185-million-year-old geological history. Residing on the top floor of the Town Hall in Fore St, **Seaton Museum** (▢ seaton museum.co.uk; late May to Oct Mon-Fri 10.30am-12.30pm & 2.15-5pm; free) has an interactive display on the Jurassic coastline as well as an old smuggler's shawl from the mid 19th century.

Services

The **tourist information centre** (see Seaton Jurassic; open same hours but the TIC staff are volunteers so there is no guarantee someone will be there) is inside Seaton Jurassic (see above).

For **internet access**, head to the **library** (Mon-Thur 9am-5pm, Wed 9am-6pm, Fri-Sat 9am-1pm).

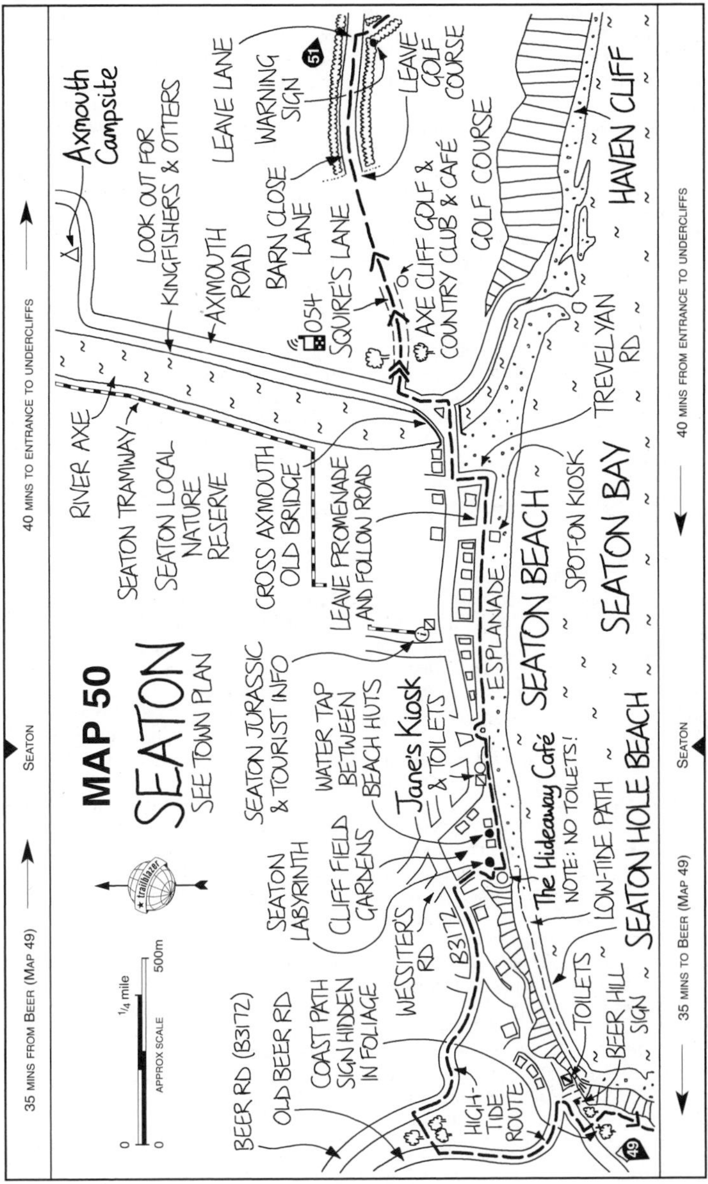

MAP 50
SEATON
SEE TOWN PLAN

¼ mile
APPROX SCALE
0   500m

35 MINS FROM BEER (MAP 49)

40 MINS FROM ENTRANCE TO UNDERCLIFFS

SEATON

40 MINS FROM ENTRANCE TO UNDERCLIFFS

SEATON

35 MINS TO BEER (MAP 49)

BEER RD (B3172)
OLD BEER RD
COAST PATH SIGN HIDDEN IN FOLIAGE
WESSITER'S RD
B3172
HIGH-TIDE ROUTE
BEER HILL SIGN
SEATON LABYRINTH
CLIFF FIELD GARDENS
Jane's Kiosk & TOILETS
WATER TAP BETWEEN BEACH HUTS
SEATON JURASSIC & TOURIST INFO
The Hideaway Café
NOTE: NO TOILETS!
LOW-TIDE PATH
TOILETS
SEATON HOLE BEACH
ESPLANADE
SEATON BEACH
SPOT-ON KIOSK
SEATON BAY
TREVELYAN RD
RIVER AXE
SEATON TRAMWAY
SEATON LOCAL NATURE RESERVE
CROSS AXMOUTH OLD BRIDGE
LEAVE PROMENADE AND FOLLOW ROAD
Axmouth Campsite
LOOK OUT FOR KINGFISHERS & OTTERS
AXMOUTH ROAD
BARN CLOSE LANE
SQUIRE'S LANE
AXE CLIFF GOLF & COUNTRY CLUB & CAFÉ
GOLF COURSE
LEAVE LANE
WARNING SIGN
LEAVE GOLF COURSE
HAVEN CLIFF

ROUTE GUIDE AND MAPS

Other facilities in town include the **post office**, inside Spar supermarket (Mon-Fri 9am-5.30pm, Sat 9am-12.30pm), two **pharmacies** – Lloyds (Mon-Sat 9am-5.30pm) on Queen St, and Boots (Mon-Sat 9am-5pm) on Fore St – a **launderette**, Launderama (daily 7am-7pm), at the top of Fore St, and two huge **supermarkets** – Tesco (Mon-Sat 7am-midnight, Sun 10am-4pm) and Co-op (Mon-Sat 7am-10pm, Sun 10am-4pm) – both set back off Harbour Rd. Both supermarkets have **ATMs** outside them. There are also some **banks**.

Transport

[See pp50-4] For **buses**, Stagecoach's No 9A connects the town with Sidmouth and Exeter while First's X52 (Jurassic Coaster) stops here en route between Exeter, Sidmouth and Lyme Regis. Axe Valley's 899 service also goes to Sidmouth.

For a **taxi** try Pete's Taxis (☎ 01297-20999), or Seaton Taxis (☎ 01297-24666).

Where to stay

Campers should head to the very friendly **Axmouth Campsite** (Map 50; ☎ 01297-24707; tent and one/two hikers from £7/13; ✻; mid Mar-mid Oct), less than three-quarters of a mile from the path. There is a **shop** and **launderette** plus lovely flat pitches, great views and two pubs by the entrance.

Seaton has plentiful **B&B** accommodation, all of which is within a few hundred metres of the path.

Dotted about by Jubilee Gardens and the Clock Tower, you will find: *Baytree* (☎ 01297-21966, ⌨ baytreedevon.co.uk; 1S/1T/3D; ☛; WI-FI; £44-49pp, sgl £45-50, sgl occ £60-65; note they only accept advance bookings for a minimum of two nights), at 11 Seafield Rd; *Holmleigh House* (☎ 01297-625671, ⌨ holmleighhouse.com; 2D/1T; ☛; WI-FI; £42.50-47.50pp, sgl occ £75-85), on Sea Hill; and *Beaumont* (☎ 01297-20832, ⌨ smoothhound.co.uk/hotels/beaumon1; 2D/2T/1Tr; WI-FI; Feb-Nov; £42.50-50pp, sgl occ from £65), on Castle Hill, which is right on the seafront with the park to its rear.

Just across The Esplanade from the path, *Pebbles B&B* (☎ 01297-22678, ⌨ pebbleshouse.co.uk; 2D/1Tr/1Qd; WI-FI; £42.50-47.50pp, sgl occ room rate; Feb to mid Dec), at 2 Sea Hill, doesn't generally accept one-night bookings in advance. Nor does *Mariners* (☎ 01297-20560, ⌨ marinershotelseaton.co.uk; 3D/2D or T; ☛; WI-FI; Mar-Oct; £42.50-47.5pp, sgl occ from £77) on the seafront's eastern side.

In the same vicinity you will find *Redcliffs* (☎ 01297-20926 ⌨ redcliffs-seaton.co.uk; 1D/2T; WI-FI; £40-42.50pp, sgl occ £65-70), at 3 Beach Rd, where they don't accept advance bookings for a single-night stay in the main season and the double room can never be booked for a single-night stay, and *Blue Waters* (☎ 01297-23245, ⌨ bluewatersseaton.co.uk; 4D; WI-FI; from £37.50pp, sgl occ from £55), at 52-54 Harbour Rd.

For pub-based B&B consider *Eyre Court Hotel* (☎ 01297-21455, ⌨ eyrecourthotel.co.uk; 4D/1T/2Tr/1Qd; WI-FI; £32.50-42.50pp, sgl occ £50-85) on Queen St.

Where to eat and drink

Cafés The best-located eateries, and the most convenient for the coast path, are the four cafés strung out along the seafront: *Terrace Arts Café* (☎ 01297-20225, ⌨ art annapola.com; WI-FI; ✻; Tue-Sat 10am-3pm, Sun 11.30am-3pm) is a dog-friendly place with a good selection of teas and smoothies as well as some decent food. There is also local art for sale. It does, however, have the road between it and the sea. The same problem affects nearby *Pebbles Café* (☎ 01297-23400; WI-FI; ✻; daily 9am-5pm), which is good for all-day breakfasts and more substantial lunchtime mains, but doesn't have sea views. For those, step up onto the Esplanade to either *Coast* (☎ 01297-598160; WI-FI; daily 8.30am-5pm, later on sunny days), a café-cum-bar with a popular sea-view terrace, or *The Galley Café* (daily 8.30am-5pm, to 4pm in winter depending on weather), a small but friendly café that also has terrace seating.

A short stroll from the seafront, *Trotters* (☎ 01297-21411; ✻; Mon-Sat

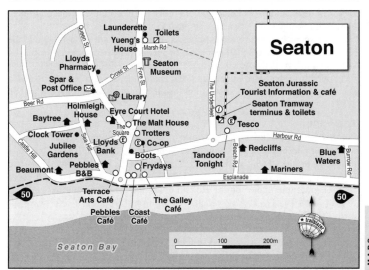

Seaton

Launderette
Yeung's House
Toilets
Marsh Rd
Queen St
Lloyds Pharmacy
Cross St
Fore St
Seaton Museum
Spar & Post Office
Beer Rd
Library
Seaton Jurassic Tourist Information & café
Seaton Tramway terminus & toilets
The Underfleet
Tesco
Holmleigh House
Eyre Court Hotel
Baytree
The Malt House
The Square
Trotters
Harbour Rd
Clock Tower
Sea Hill
Lloyds Bank
Co-op
Castle Hill
Jubilee Gardens
Boots
Redcliffs
Beach Rd
Blue Waters
Burrow Rd
Beaumont
Pebbles B&B
Frydays
Tandoori Tonight
Mariners
Esplanade
50
Terrace Arts Café
The Galley Café
50
Pebbles Café
Coast Café
Seaton Bay
0   100   200m
trailblazer

ROUTE GUIDE AND MAPS

8am-3pm, Sun 9am-3pm, winter days/ hours may vary) is a no-frills greasy-spoon café with a vague *Only Fools And Horses* theme and some big breakfasts (eg workman's breakfast, containing all the usual components, for £6.50).

Restaurants, takeaways & pubs Just back from the seafront, *Frydays* (☎ 01297-23911, 💻 frydays.eu; Easter to end Oct Sun-Thur 11.30am-8.30pm, Fri-Sat 11.30am-9.30pm, rest of year same but Sun to 4pm) is your best bet for fish & chips. They do takeaway and have a comfortable restaurant area.

There's Chinese cuisine (takeaway only) at *Yeung's House* (☎ 01297-625559; Mon & Tue 5-10pm, Wed-Sat noon-1.30pm & 5-10pm), on Fore St, while *Tandoori Tonight* (☎ 01297-22333, 💻 tandoori tonight.co.uk; Sun-Thur 5-11pm, Fri-Sat 5-11.30pm), on Harbour Rd, should satisfy any curry cravings.

For **pub** food, try *The Malt House* (☎ 01297-22695, 💻 themalthouseseaton.co .uk; WI-FI; 🐾; food Mon-Sat noon-10pm, Sun noon-9pm), on The Square, or head up Queen's St to *Eyre Court Hotel* (see Where to Stay; food Mon-Sat noon-2pm & 6-9pm, Sun noon-2pm).

SEATON TO LYME REGIS   [MAPS 50-53]

This **7-mile (11.5km; 3hrs)** section of the coastal path is like no other and will be, without any doubt, one of the highlights of your walk.

The day mainly comprises walking through the remarkable Axmouth to Lyme Regis Undercliffs National Nature Reserve (see box p226), shaped and moulded by landslides then left to its own devices to create that most unique and wonderful of landscapes: an English jungle. However, as with all jungles the terrain underfoot may cause problems, added to which there are some steep ascents to be tackled. Furthermore, the trail winds constantly up and down and back and forth, and is pockmarked with roots and interrupted by the odd fallen tree, so it is a day to be wary of your ankles.

It's also a day for carrying supplies as refreshments are not available in the reserve. Despite the tribulations, though, for most people this day is one of unfettered joy. And should you struggle against all the difficulties, at least comfort yourself in the knowledge that at the end of this stage lies Lyme Regis, a smashing town that's used to catering – from royalty downwards – to those in need of a well-earned rest.

The route

Leaving Seaton via the Esplanade – where, once upon a time, both a Tudor fort and a Martello tower stood – you make your way to **Axmouth Old Bridge**, a pedestrian bridge which was built in 1877 and is thought to be the oldest concrete bridge in Britain. Lying one mile inland, the village of Axmouth and the harbour were of great importance during Roman times and are situated at the end of a Roman road, The Fosse Way, which, running from Lincoln to Exeter was, following the Roman invasion in AD43, the western frontier of the Roman Empire.

A bit of tarmac-treading follows as you make your way to – and then up – Squire's Lane before bisecting **Axe Cliff Golf Club** (☎ 01297-21754, 🖥 axe cliffgolfclub.com), where there is a walker-friendly *café* (WI-FI; 🐾 on lead; daily 8am-5.30pm-ish but closed to non members during events, matches and tournaments), to join **Barn Close Lane**. The turn-off to the nature reserve is marked by a notice warning visitors of the strenuous and remote nature of the path; approach the cliff-edge by negotiating your way along hedgerows and across fields.

After an unspectacular stroll over the fields atop **Haven Cliff**, what follows next is nothing short of extraordinary as you enter an area where nature, as a rule, is definitely in charge: welcome to **Axmouth to Lyme Regis Undercliffs** (see box p226). Apart from the occasional information board and the odd ruined building camouflaged amongst the leaves and vines – such as **Landslip Cottage** near **Downlands Cliff**, from which the Victorian owners used to sell afternoon teas to tourists, or the **old chimney** (part of a 19th-century freshwater pumping station) at the approximate halfway point – there is nothing to distract you away from the natural beauty of the forest. *(cont'd on p226)*

❏ **Landslides**

The geology of the Jurassic coast makes the cliffs and beaches along this stretch particularly susceptible to landslides, especially after periods of prolonged rainfall. Remember to tread carefully when walking on top of the cliffs and **always avoid walking and sitting directly below them where possible**. Remain aware of the edges, particularly in conditions that may leave you vulnerable to sudden gusts of wind and keep your dog on a lead at all times on clifftops. Despite being relatively rare, landslides are occasionally responsible for fatalities, most recently in July 2012 when 400 tonnes of rock slid from the cliffs on to Hive Beach, near Burton Bradstock. In 2017, a huge landslide by West Bay saw more than 1500 tonnes of East Cliff fall into the sea. Thankfully it happened at night and nobody was hurt.

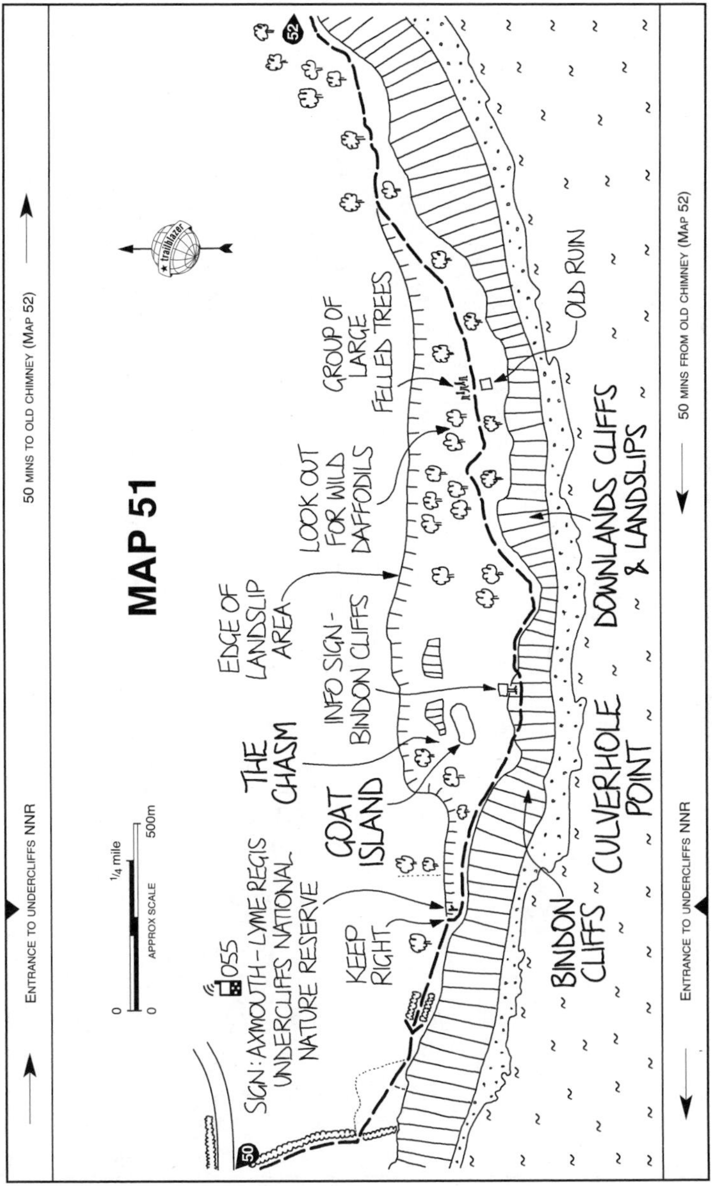

MAP 51

ENTRANCE TO UNDERCLIFFS NNR

← 50 MINS TO OLD CHIMNEY (MAP 52)

0 ¼ mile

0 500m
APPROX SCALE

SIGN: AXMOUTH – LYME REGIS UNDERCLIFFS NATIONAL NATURE RESERVE

KEEP RIGHT

GOAT ISLAND

THE CHASM

EDGE OF LANDSLIP AREA

INFO SIGN – BINDON CLIFFS

LOOK OUT FOR WILD DAFFODILS

GROUP OF LARGE FELLED TREES

OLD RUIN

50 MINS FROM OLD CHIMNEY (MAP 52)

ENTRANCE TO UNDERCLIFFS NNR

BINDON CLIFFS

CULVERHOLE POINT

DOWNLANDS CLIFFS & LANDSLIPS

ROUTE GUIDE AND MAPS

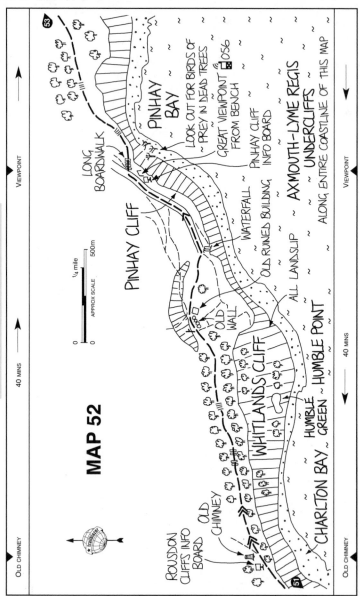

MAP 52

OLD CHIMNEY   40 MINS   VIEWPOINT   40 MINS   OLD CHIMNEY

¼ mile
500m
APPROX SCALE

53

ROUSDON CLIFFS INFO BOARD

OLD CHIMNEY

CHARTON BAY ~ HUMBLE POINT

HUMBLE GREEN ~

WHITLANDS CLIFF

OLD WALL

ALL LANDSLIP

AXMOUTH-LYME REGIS UNDERCLIFFS
ALONG ENTIRE COASTLINE OF THIS MAP

OLD RUINED BUILDING

WATERFALL

PINHAY CLIFF

LONG BOARDWALK

PINHAY BAY

LOOK OUT FOR BIRDS OF PREY IN DEAD TREES

GREAT VIEWPOINT 1056 FROM BENCH

PINHAY CLIFF INFO BOARD

VIEWPOINT

51

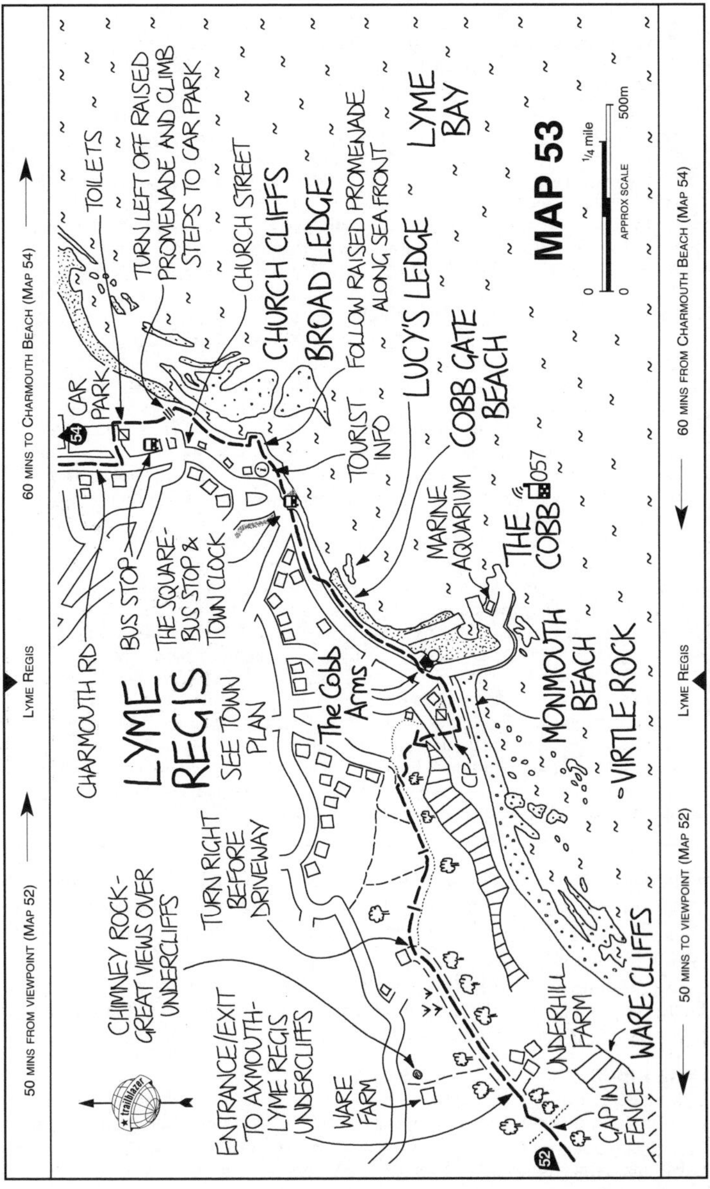

50 MINS FROM VIEWPOINT (MAP 52)

LYME REGIS

60 MINS TO CHARMOUTH BEACH (MAP 54)

CHARMOUTH RD

TOILETS

TURN LEFT OFF RAISED PROMENADE AND CLIMB STEPS TO CAR PARK

CHURCH STREET

CHURCH CLIFFS

BROAD LEDGE

FOLLOW RAISED PROMENADE ALONG SEA FRONT

LUCY'S LEDGE

LYME BAY

COBB GATE BEACH

MAP 53

CAR PARK

BUS STOP

THE SQUARE- BUS STOP & TOWN CLOCK

SEE TOWN PLAN

LYME REGIS

TOURIST INFO

MARINE AQUARIUM

THE COBB ☎057

The Cobb Arms

CP

MONMOUTH BEACH

VIRTLE ROCK

CHIMNEY ROCK- GREAT VIEWS OVER UNDERCLIFFS

TURN RIGHT BEFORE DRIVEWAY

ENTRANCE/EXIT TO AXMOUTH- LYME REGIS UNDERCLIFFS

WARE FARM

UNDERHILL FARM

GAP IN FENCE

WARE CLIFFS

0   ¼ mile

APPROX SCALE

0   500m

50 MINS TO VIEWPOINT (MAP 52)

LYME REGIS

60 MINS FROM CHARMOUTH BEACH (MAP 54)

❏ Axmouth to Lyme Regis Undercliffs National Nature Reserve

Designated a National Nature Reserve in 1955, the Axmouth to Lyme Regis Undercliffs are the result of numerous landslips. They are just one of many areas along the south coast to have suffered from this natural phenomenon, which occurs when long spells of wet weather saturate permeable Cretaceous rocks. As these rocks lie on impermeable clay, they eventually give way to the pressure exerted on them by the sheer volume of water and break away from the cliffs, leading to great scars in the landscape called undercliffs.

The 750-metre-wide **Whitlands Undercliff** (Map 52, p224) is actually the result of two landslips, in 1765 and 1840. However, the vicinity's most spectacular geological collapse happened at **Bindon Cliffs** (Map 51, p223), to the west of Whitlands, on Christmas Eve 1839, when what became known as 'The Great Landslip' occurred. The first landslide ever to be scientifically documented – having been witnessed by the vicar of Axminster, William Conybeare, and William Buckland, a professor of geology at Oxford – where once there had been pasture there was now a gigantic chasm, 100m wide, 50m deep and 1km long. In the process, **Goat Island**, a piece of land forced off the top of the cliffs, formed a new plateau closer to the sea – the wheat and turnips that were grown on it surviving to produce another crop the following year which became popular souvenirs. Following such a remarkable event, the Undercliffs became a Victorian tourist attraction, regularly visited by paddle steamer; they even inspired a piece of music, *Landslide Quadrille*, which would be played on the boats as they passed.

What makes the Undercliffs so special is the fact that the land was left to its own devices during the 20th century, having been deemed too dangerous to graze sheep. Myxomatosis, too, has lent a hand, culling most of the local rabbits. As a result, the Lyme Regis Undercliffs are now one of the most significant wilderness areas in Britain, protected as part of the West Bay Special Area of Conservation and the East Devon AONB. A safe habitat for much **flora and fauna**, the Undercliffs provide sanctuary to green woodpeckers, bullfinches and Dartford warblers amongst many other birds. Many variations of flower thrive here too, including the pink pyramidical and the autumn ladies tresses orchid. Shrews and mice, lizards, grass snakes and newts scurry and slither in the undergrowth, whilst butterflies such as the wood white, silver-washed fritillary and chalk-hill blue flit from plant to plant. And all the while, flying high above you, ravens and peregrine falcons menacingly eye the ground. It's a magical place – and a splendid arena for the walker.

(cont'd from p222) At **Pinhay Cliff** things get a little more civilised as you join a sealed track; but the moment is brief and soon the wilds embrace you once more. From the viewpoint below Pinhay Cliff, Portland Bill can be seen as – on occasion – can peregrine falcons.

Continuing on, and having left the convoluted pathways near **Underhill Farm**, you eventually arrive at **Ware Cliffs**, from where a wide grass path is followed that leads, eventually, to **The Cobb** – Lyme Regis's harbour.

LYME REGIS   [map p231]

Following the granting of a royal charter by King Edward I in 1284, the port-town that had previously simply been known as Lyme added the term 'Regis' in celebration ('regis' merely signifying that it has some sort of royal connection or endorsement). 'The Pearl of Dorset', as Lyme likes to be known, sits just inside the county border and has all that the walker could desire including several sights and attractions.

The town's main landmark is its harbour-wall, **The Cobb**, built in a curved shape in the 13th century to protect the resident boats. It famously features in Jane Austen's *Persuasion* and the book (and, subsequently, film) of John Fowles' *The French Lieutenant's Woman*. Austen and the crooked harbour aside, what Lyme Regis is best known for is fossils, with famed local palaeontologist Mary Anning making numerous discoveries of great importance hereabouts in the early 19th century (see box pp228-9).

Boosted by its £1.5m Mary Anning Wing extension in 2017, **Lyme Regis Museum** (☎ 01297-443370, 🖳 lymeregis museum.co.uk; Apr-Oct Mon-Sat 10am-5pm, Sun 10am-4pm, Nov-Mar Wed-Sun 11am-4pm; £4.95) is now more modern and more accessible than ever. The museum, which organises expert-led **fossil walks** most days (see website for schedules), is built on the site of Anning's birthplace and includes exhibits and displays explaining the local geological and paleontological finds. The town celebrates Mary Anning Day in September each year when there are talks and displays of recently discovered

fossils. Her grave, within the grounds of **St Michael the Archangel Church** (to the left of the church as you face it), can also be visited. The church itself is of considerable antiquity, with its tower dating from Saxon times.

Fossils are also a major component of **Dinosaurland** (☎ 01297-443541, 🖳 dino saurland.co.uk; mid Feb to end Oct daily 10am-5pm, opening hours vary in winter; £5), a small, privately run natural history museum on Coombe St. The museum has more than 12,000 specimens on display and is housed in a Grade I listed building in what was once a church.

For more animated exhibits, **Lyme Regis Marine Aquarium** (☎ 07903 955300, 🖳 lymeregismarineaquarium.co .uk; Mar-end Oct daily 10am-5pm, check website for winter hours; £6) has starfish and sea scorpion as well as a display on the history of The Cobb on which it is situated.

Lyme Regis's **Town Mill** (☎ 01297-444042, 🖳 townmill.org.uk; galleries daily 10.30am-4.30pm, miller-guided tours 11am-4pm subject to volunteer availability; free entrance but donation requested for a guided tour), just off the main strip at the bottom of the hill, is mentioned in the Domesday Book (1086) and can be visited.

❏ The Lassie of Lyme Regis

Most people are familiar with Lassie, the collie dog who, in a succession of hugely popular films and TV series from the '40s right up to the '70s (and there was even a remake as recently as 2006), saved various hapless humans from the bottom of wells/cliff-faces/disused mine shafts, usually by barking at her owner who, somehow, managed to understand exactly what the problem was and help Lassie to effect a rescue. What is less well-known, however, is that the fictional bitch who first appeared in a novel in 1940 called *Lassie Come Home* by Eric Knight, was based on a real-life rough-haired crossbreed whose owner was the landlord of the Pilot Boat Inn in Lyme Regis. Though the breed may have been different, the heroic qualities that made the fictional Lassie so endearing were very much in evidence. According to popular legend, in the First World War the Royal Navy battleship *HMS Formidable* was struck by a torpedo off the coast of South Devon with the loss of over 300 men. One of the life rafts was eventually washed up on the coast off Lyme Regis. Having been brought ashore, it was found that everybody within had seemingly perished too, and the corpses of the sailors were laid on the tables of the Pilot Boat Inn.

Lassie, curious to see what was going on, started to lick at the feet of one of the cadavers – and the landlord noticed that the body responded! The man was revived, his life was saved – and thus a legend was born.

The water mill closed down in 1926, but was restored in 2001 and is once again producing flour for the local community. The cobbled courtyard area around the mill is pleasant to visit, with a tearoom, a restaurant, a bakery and even a local brewery.

Both **Lyme Regis Fossil Festival** (see p14; mostly free) and **Lyme Regis Jazz Festival** (see p14) are held here in April or May.

Services

The helpful **tourist information centre** (☎ 01297-442138, 🖥 www.visit-dorset.com; Apr-Oct Mon-Sat 10am-5pm, Sun 10am-4pm, Nov-Mar Mon-Sat 10am-3pm) is on Bridge St, the eastern extension of Broad St. Contact them for help with booking accommodation, to get advice on fossil

hunting in the area, and for the latest news about any possible changes to the path due to landslips. They also have local tide times posted in their window. Also worth looking at is: 🖥 www.lymeregis.org.

Internet access is available (Mon-Fri 10am-5pm, Sat 9.30am-12.30pm) in the **library** (☎ 01297-443151; free for one hour; wi-fi also available); when the library is closed it is available at Lymenet, in the same building (15 mins £1).

Just about everything else is at the top of Broad St including the **post office** (Mon-Sat 8.30am-5.30pm), Co-op (daily 7am-10pm) and Tesco Express (daily 7am-11pm) **supermarkets** and a branch of Boots the **Chemist** (Mon-Sat 9am-5.30pm, Sun 10am-4pm). There are a couple of banks with **ATMs** on Broad St. The street

❑ Mary Anning and the fossil coast

Born in Lyme Regis in 1799, Mary Anning rose from a poor and uneducated background to become one of the world's leading and most revered fossil collectors and palaeontologists. She was introduced to fossil-hunting by her father, who sold his locally collected curios to tourists to supplement his income as a cabinetmaker, but his early death in 1810 at the age of 44 forced Mary and the rest of her large family to continue his work just to put food on their plates.

Mary's extraordinary ability to make significant discoveries, however, and her increasing knowledge on the subject coincided with the 19th-century's fledgling obsession with geology and evolution. In fact, Charles Darwin was a student of one of her earliest customers and some of her discoveries assisted in proving the extinction of some species – an idea previously given little credence as it suggested that God's Creation was somehow imperfect.

Mary collected her fossils along the coastal cliffs that surround Lyme Bay and some of her finds remain some of the most significant in the palaeontological field. She made the first of several important discoveries with her brother Joseph in 1811 at the tender age of 12, unearthing a

Ichthyosaurus

17ft-long ichthyosaurus ('fish lizard') under the cliffs between Lyme and Charmouth. The family sold it for £23 and it was soon exhibited in London, the skull remaining the property of the Natural History Museum to this day. Down the years, Anning's reputation grew with each spectacular new find: in 1823 she discovered a complete

Plesiosaurus

plesiosaurus ('near lizard') and in 1828 a pterodactyl skeleton, the first of its type to be found outside Germany. By the age of 27 she had opened Anning's Fossil Depot in which she exhibited and sold her finds. Visiting geologists from all over Europe and America flocked also plays host to Sanctuary (☎ 01297-445815, 💻 lyme-regis.com; daily 10.30am-5.30pm), a secondhand **bookshop** that is full of character.

Transport

[See also pp50-4] The most useful **bus** services throughout the Dorset section of the coast path are First's X51 (Aminster to Dorchester), X52 (Exeter to Lyme Regis) & X53 (Axminster to Weymouth) as they stop at numerous locations useful to walkers, including of course Lyme Regis. Stagecoach's 9A bus service also calls here.

Where to stay

Although it's not possible to camp within Lyme Regis itself, *Wood Farm Caravan & Camping Park* (Map 54; ☎ 01297-560697,

💻 woodfarm.co.uk; pitch £6 plus £5-10 per adult; 🐾; WI-FI £3 for two hours; Easter to end Oct) is only a short distance off the path (though approximately two miles from Lyme Regis, between the town and Charmouth). There is a good *café* (daily 9am-6.30pm; WI-FI free for 15 mins) and a well-stocked **shop** (daily 8.30am-7pm) on site, as well as an indoor swimming **pool** (£2.50; daily 10am-7pm).

A night above one of the local **pubs**, all of which are dog friendly, is also an option. The first you arrive at on your way into town is *The Cobb Arms* (☎ 01297-443242, 💻 thecobbarms.co.uk; 1D/1Tr/one room sleeping up to five; WI-FI; 🐾; £45-55pp, sgl occ room rate), Marine Parade, which also serves food (see Where to eat). Meanwhile, high up on Silver St and at the

---

to the shop. Unfortunately, the great social inequality of the time meant that a woman of her background was never going to be given the plaudits she deserved; indeed, many of her finds were credited to (male) palaeontologists who had purchased the items from her. However, in 2010 she was included in a list of the 10 British women to have most influenced the history of science and she is also thought to have been the inspiration for the tongue twister 'She sells seashells on the seashore'.

Mary is buried with her brother Joseph in the grounds of St Michael the Archangel Church (p227). Visitors sometimes leave fossils beside her gravestone.

Fossil hunting today Although a few ichthyosaur skeletons are still discovered each year, it seems rather unlikely that you will find one whilst strolling along the coastal path. However, the Jurassic coast is still a treasure trove for fossil-hunters and there are many great sites for hunting and collecting along the way. Most accessible are the beaches at Seatown and Charmouth but there are several other great spots including Church Cliffs (accessed from Lyme Regis harbour), Thorncombe Beacon, Burton Bradstock, Kimmeridge Bay and Eype. Note that **you must always be wary of the tides**. You should also always **be aware of the stability of any cliffs and do your hunting from the beach**; do not hammer into the cliffs themselves. (Anning herself lost her faithful dog Tray in a landslip in 1833.)

The most common finds are **ammonites** – the spiral-shaped shells of extinct marine molluscs (some of which can be up to a metre in diameter) – and **belemnites** – once called 'Devil's thunderbolts' due to their shape but in reality part of an internal shell in what was a squid-like animal. Occasionally hunters do discover more significant finds including the brown or black bones of an extinct marine reptile.

A good website to consult, particularly if you want to know where to look and whether there is any specific safety advice, is 💻 ukfossils.co.uk; you can also pick up free pamphlets in local tourist offices. Charmouth Heritage Coast Centre (see p234), Lyme Regis Museum (see p227) and the new museum at Kimmeridge (The Etches Collection, see p298) also have good displays on the fossils unearthed nearby.

ROUTE GUIDE AND MAPS

back of the town is *The Nag's Head* (☎ 01297-442312, 🖳 nagsheadlymeregis.co .uk; 1S/1T/1D/1Qd; wi-fi; 🐾; £40pp, sgl occ rates on request), No 32. There is live music most Saturday nights and if there's an event on Sky Sports that brings in a crowd. New owners take over at the end of 2018.

A more central option is *Ship Inn* (☎ 01297-443681, 🖳 palmersbrewery.com/ 2013/01/ship-inn; 2D; wi-fi; 🐾; £25-35pp, sgl occ room rate), on Coombe St, opposite Lyme's Fish Bar. The rate includes a continental-style (help yourself) breakfast.

The most centrally located **B&B** is *The Old Monmouth* (☎ 01297-444124, 🖳 oldmonmouth.com; 4D; ☛; wi-fi; £47.50-70pp, sgl occ rates on request), a charming 16th-century house at 12 Church St. One of the rooms has a four-poster bed; another its own sitting room. Note that B&B is only available some of the year as they let the house out at peak periods. Nearby is the 17th-century *Old Lyme Guest House* (☎ 01297-442929, 🖳 oldlymeguesthouse.co .uk; 4D/1Tr; ☛; wi-fi; mid Feb to early Nov; £45-47.50pp, sgl occ £80-88), at 29 Coombe St. Built from local blue lias limestone, this was the town's post office from 1799 to 1853. Note the wooden posting box, still in its original place in the front wall of the building.

Others that are also close to the amenities can be found on Pound St, including the swish *Lyme Townhouse* (☎ 01929-400252, 🖳 www.lyme-townhouse.co.uk; 6D/1D or T; wi-fi; £45-70pp; sgl occ rates on request), at No 8.

Further uphill, though still within a short stroll of the centre, are: *Lucerne* (☎ 01297-443752, 🖳 lucernelyme.co.uk; 1S/ 2D/1D or T; wi-fi; £40-46.50pp, sgl £48-55, sgl occ rates on request) on View Rd; the very smart *Dorset House B&B* (☎ 01297-442055, 🖳 dorsethouselyme.com; 5D; wi-fi; from £47.50pp, sgl occ from £85), at the junction of Silver St and Pound Rd; and *Lewesdon* (☎ 01297-792469, 🖳 lewesdon.co.uk; 2D/1T; ☛; wi-fi; Feb-Nov; £50-65pp, sgl occ rates on request) on Silver St. They only accept advance bookings for a minimum of two-nights (three nights over bank holiday weekends).

On the eastern edge of town – and actually on the path – is *Albany* (☎ 01297-443066, 🖳 albanylymeregis.co.uk; 1S/3D/ 1T; wi-fi; Mar to mid Nov; £46-57.50pp, sgl £50-60, sgl occ rates on request) on Charmouth Rd, with magnificent views out to sea.

Those wishing to add a little style to their stay may like to opt to go a **hotel**. Centrally located and hard to miss as you walk up Broad St is *Royal Lion Hotel* (☎ 01297-445622, 🖳 royallionhotel.com; 4S/ 17D/12Tr; wi-fi; 🐾 in patio rooms only; B&B £68-90pp, sgl/sgl occ from £75/100); this old coaching inn, built in 1601, is so regal it even has a swimming pool!

Nearby is upmarket *Alexandra Hotel* (☎ 01297-442010, 🖳 hotelalexandra.co.uk; 1S/3D/19D or T; wi-fi; 🐾; from £90-172.50pp, sgl from £95, sgl occ room rate), while further up the hill, on Silver St, is *Mariners Hotel* (☎ 01297-442753, 🖳 hotel lymeregis.co.uk; 1S/10D/2T/1Qd; ☛; wi-fi; 🐾; £57.50-72.50pp, sgl/sgl occ from £65/105), which was also built in the 17th century as a coaching inn. The rates vary so look at their website for special offers.

Where to eat and drink
Always a pretty genteel and civilised place, over the past couple of decades Lyme Regis has also become rather trendy and sophisticated. As a result, the town now boasts several cute cafés, some good delis for takeaway food and a wide variety of cuisines offering food from all over the world.

Cafés One of the most popular cafés is *Town Mill Bakery* (☎ 01297-444754, 🖳 townmillbakery.wordpress.com; wi-fi; daily 8.30am-4pm, may also open later in Aug). It's an informal, atmospheric, family-friendly place where customers sit at long wooden tables and shared benches after placing their main orders at the open kitchen, and helping themselves to extras such as pastries and pieces of fruit, which are on display in bowls and baskets. When you leave it's up to you to be honest about what you ordered and ate before you pay as you go. The food is excellent and sourced locally wherever possible.

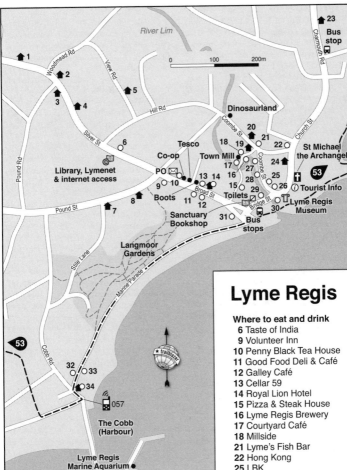

Lyme Regis

Where to eat and drink
6 Taste of India
9 Volunteer Inn
10 Penny Black Tea House
11 Good Food Deli & Café
12 Galley Café
13 Cellar 59
14 Royal Lion Hotel
15 Pizza & Steak House
16 Lyme Regis Brewery
17 Courtyard Café
18 Millside
21 Lyme's Fish Bar
22 Hong Kong
25 LBK
26 Aroma
27 Town Mill Bakery
28 Tierra Kitchen
29 Pilot Boat Inn
30 French Lieutenant's Bistro
31 Bell Cliff
32 Lyme Bay Sandwich Co
33 Royal Standard
34 The Cobb Arms

Where to stay
1 Lewesdon
2 Mariners Hotel
3 Dorset House B&B
4 The Nag's Head
5 Lucerne
7 Lyme Townhouse
8 Alexandra Hotel
14 Royal Lion Hotel
19 Ship Inn
20 Old Lyme Guest House
23 Albany
24 The Old Monmouth
34 The Cobb Arms

ROUTE GUIDE AND MAPS

Even closer to The Town Mill is *Courtyard Café* (☎ 01297-445757, 🖳 court yardcafelyme.co.uk; WI-FI; 🐾; Feb-Dec daily 9.30am-4pm, last food orders 2.45pm), which shares space with an art gallery and faces Lyme Regis Brewery from across a cobbled courtyard.

Another popular spot is *Galley Café* (☎ 01297-445008, 🖳 galleycafe.co.uk; WI-FI; 🐾; daily 9am-5pm), a comfortable, fully licensed, dog-friendly café on Broad St.

Also dog-friendly is *Bell Cliff* (☎ 01297-442459; 🐾; daily 9am-6pm, June-Sep to 8.30 or 9pm), a pleasant place with some lovely outdoor seating, while nearby *Aroma* (☎ 01297-445914, 🖳 aromacafe.co .uk; WI-FI; daily 10am-4pm, Wed-Mon during term time) is also popular despite its location on a busy corner. It offers a good selection of light bites, including bagels (£6.95) and bacon rolls (£4.50), and is caressed by the deeply satisfying aroma of freshly ground coffee beans.

For a quirky option, sneak in behind the post office to find the very friendly *Penny Black Tea House* (Tue-Sat 9am-5pm), which has cheap food, an entrance surrounded by antique stalls and a small back garden.

Pubs The centrally located *Pilot Boat Inn* (☎ 01297-443157, 🖳 thepilotboatinn.co .uk; food daily noon-9.30pm) is the original home of Lassie the wonder dog (see box p227). The pub, which always served a decent selection of real ales, and used to specialise in seafood, was being renovated by new owners at the time of research and was due to re-open, with B&B rooms, in the summer of 2018.

Royal Lion Hotel (see Where to stay; daily breakfast 8-10am, bar food noon-2.30pm & 6-9pm, restaurant 6.45-9pm) exudes venerability with its wood-panelled walls, oak beams and log fire. Alongside their pub grub, they offer some good evening set menus (£25-30) from a menu that changes daily.

The Volunteer Inn (☎ 01297-442214, 🖳 thevolunteerlymeregis.com; WI-FI; 🐾; food Mon-Sat noon-2.30pm & 6-9pm, Sun

lunch only) is a cracking Irish pub, with a good selection of real ales and ciders served alongside their Guinness. This is a drinkers' pub, but they do still serve good food, including locally caught seafood and a Sunday roast.

Championing locally brewed ales are *Lyme Regis Brewery* (see box p23; ☎ 01297-444354, 🖳 lymeregisbrewery.com; Mon-Fri 10am-5pm, Sat-Sun 11am-5pm, winter hours variable, closed Jan; no food), a small brewery-bar beside The Town Mill, and *Cellar 59* (☎ 01297-445086, 🖳 cellar 59.co.uk; WI-FI; 🐾; bar summer Mon 5-11pm, Tue-Sat noon-11pm, Sun noon-10pm, winter Tue-Sun only), which sells bottled and cask ales from Gyle 59 Brewery (🖳 gyle59.co.uk) in Thorncombe, about 10 miles north of Lyme Regis.

Drinkers have a few choices down at The Cobb too. *The Cobb Arms* (see Where to stay; food daily 11.45am-9pm, may stop earlier in winter) has a good menu – fish stew (£9.95); beef stroganoff (£10.95) – that includes some gluten-free options. Nearby, *Royal Standard* (☎ 01297-442637, 🖳 theroyalstandardlymeregis.co.uk; WI-FI; 🐾; food Apr-Sep daily noon-9pm, Oct-Mar daily noon-3pm & 5.30-9pm) is a 400-year-old-plus establishment with a relaxed attitude to dogs and a menu (mains £9-13) that includes shellfish, grilled fish, steaks and burgers.

Restaurants Lyme Regis also boasts some decent restaurants.

Millside (☎ 01297-445999, 🖳 themill side.co.uk; Tue-Sat coffee 10.30am-noon, lunch noon-2.30pm, dinner 6.30-9pm, Sun lunch noon-2.30pm) makes a fine choice and is a great place to sit outside on a sunny afternoon with a beer. The evening menu includes dishes such as roasted quail (£18) and Portland crab linguine (£19).

Not far away, *LBK* (☎ 01297-445816, 🖳 lbkgourmetburgerbar.co.uk; summer Mon-Fri 5-9/10pm, Sat noon-9pm, Sun noon-4pm; rest of year days/hours variable), aka **Lyme Bay Kitchen**, is a fully licensed gourmet burger bar on Coombe St, offering beef, chicken and vegetarian burgers as well as Sunday roasts. Almost directly opposite,

Tierra Kitchen (☎ 01297-445189, 🖳 tier-rakitchen.co.uk; Tue 6-9pm, Wed-Sat noon-2pm & 6-9pm) is a very cute vegetarian restaurant with streamside seating and a modern, Mediterranean-influenced menu.

Nearby on Bridge St *French Lieutenant's Bistro* (☎ 01297-442961, 🖳 frenchbistro.co.uk; Tue-Fri noon-2.30pm & 6-8pm, Sat noon-8.30pm, Sun noon-4pm) has sea views from its back terrace. Most evening mains are less than £20.

For a sit-down Indian meal, try *Taste of India* (☎ 01297-444224; daily noon-2pm & 5.30-11pm), at the top of Broad St. It's BYO (bring-your-own alcohol) so works out cheaper than most.

Delis and takeaways On Broad St is the excellent *Good Food Deli & Café* (Mon-Sat 8.30am-5pm, Sun 10am-4pm)

with great-value breakfasts, pastries and baguettes, as well as loads of lunch-box fillers.

For a takeaway supper there's a Chinese, *Hong Kong* (☎ 01297-445182; Wed, Thur, Sun 5.30-10pm, Fri-Sat 5-11pm), on Church St, a pizza joint, *Pizza & Steak House* (☎ 01297-444788, Mon-Sat from 5.30/6pm) tucked away between Broad St and The Town Mill, and *Lyme's Fish Bar* (☎ 01297-442375; Mon-Fri noon-2.30pm & 5-9pm, Sat & Sun noon-8.30/9pm), the best of several chippies in town.

Down on The Cobb, *Lyme Bay Sandwich Co* (☎ 01297-444299; Easter-Oct daily 11am-3.30pm) does sarnies from £2.95, including local crab sandwiches for £4.70 (as a baguette, £5.70).

LYME REGIS TO SEATOWN (& CHIDEOCK)   [MAPS 53-56]

Very different from yesterday – but just as dramatic – today's 7¼-mile **(11.75km; 3hrs)** stage has much to offer including some wonderful cliff-top walking and an ascent to the highest point of the UK's southern coast: Golden Cap (191m/627ft). Landslides just after Lyme Regis have forced the official trail to divert inland, only rejoining the coast at Charmouth (which is also the last place to pick up any supplies that you may need). A very steep lane-walk leads away from the village but once back on the cliffs and out in the elements the scenery is mesmerising, the views from the summit of Golden Cap and the long descent from it rounding off a fantastic day's walk. Seatown has limited accommodation so it may be worth planning for a night in Chideock, three-quarters of a mile inland.

Note that it is possible to walk to Charmouth from Lyme Regis straight along the beach, which may appeal to fossil hunters. However, this is not the official route and a **tide-timetable must be closely consulted** before embarking on such an adventure. It is also imperative not to walk too close to the cliffs due to the danger of falling rocks.

The route
Continue from the centre of Lyme Regis along the seawall past the theatre and museum until you come to a flight of steps (from where you get a great view of the Black Ven landslip). Follow these steps uphill to Charmouth Road car park, and cross the car park to reach Charmouth Rd. Turn right (north), and walk past Lyme Regis Football Club. Just beyond the club a gate on the right takes you into the first of a series of fields, on the edge of **Timber Hill,** that you cut across to arrive at a patch of woodland. Continue through the woods, climbing steeply

upwards to a diversion (caused by further landslips). The path now goes left to continue amongst the trees, descending leisurely to a B-road where you turn right to pass the entrance to Lyme Regis Golf Club, before arriving at the A3052. It's a road you flirt with a couple of times, deserting it on the first occasion to follow the **white markers** through the golf course and the rhododendron wood at **Fern Hill**; and, secondly, by walking down the driveway that leads past Fernhill Hotel on the way down to the roundabout.

If camping, *Wood Farm Caravan & Camping Park* (see p229) is signed to your left. Should a night under the tarp not be in your itinerary, carry straight on, following the pavement past the blue Charmouth sign. Soon enough the village will rise to greet you. Turn right down **Higher Sea Lane**, which eventually arrives at **Charmouth Beach** and **Charmouth Heritage Coast Centre** (see below).

CHARMOUTH   [map p236]

For those not wanting a night in Lyme Regis, the village of Charmouth has the necessary amenities to make a stop possible and also provides an ample head-start for those wishing to get to Seatown (not to be confused with Seaton), or beyond, the next day.

The centre of interest for tourists in the village – and on the coast path – is the excellent **Charmouth Heritage Coast Centre** (☎ 01297-560772, 🖥 charmouth .org; Apr-Oct daily 10.30am-4.30pm, winter hours variable, see website for details), which displays recent fossil finds from local beaches and organises 'fossil' and rockpooling events. It also has a *café* (Beach Café; see p236).

Most **services** in the village can be found on The Street, the main road running along the back of Charmouth. **Provisions** are available from Charmouth Stores (Mon-Sat 7am-9pm, Sun 8am-9pm), and there is also a **pharmacy** (Mon-Fri 9am-1pm & 2-5.30pm, Sat 9am-1pm) and **post office** (Mon-Wed & Fri 9am-1pm & 2-5.30pm, Thur 9am-1pm, Sat 9am-12.30pm) with **ATM** (not free). You can get camping equipment from a large **camping store** (Map 54; Mon-Sat 9am-5pm, Sun 10am-4pm) as you leave the village on The Street.

Internet access and **wi-fi** are available (donation appreciated) at the community-run library (☎ 01297-560640; Mon-Wed 2-5pm, Thur-Fri 10am-1pm, Sat 10.30am-12.30pm).

Transport

[See pp50-4] First's X51 (Dorchester to Axminster) and X53 (Axminster to Weymouth) **bus services** stop here.

Where to stay

As well as nearby Wood Farm Caravan & Camping Park (see p229), **campers** can pitch tents at *Manor Farm Holiday Centre* (☎ 01297-560226, 🖥 manorfarmholiday centre.co.uk; WI-FI; 🐾; £15-28 per tent and up to two adults), a pricey, but well-equipped holiday park right on the coast path and accessed from The Street.

There are also a few **B&Bs** scattered about the village although finding one willing to do a one-night stop during peak times can be an issue. Close to the beach, in Hammonds Mead, which is off Lower Sea Lane, you'll find *The Beach Rooms* (☎ 01297-560030, 🖥 thebeachrooms.co.uk; 1Qd; 🛏; WI-FI; from £70pp, sgl occ rates on request) which offers a self-contained double suite with its own living room and an extra sofa bed. Although they don't accept one-night bookings in advance, call a few days before and you may land on your feet.

Also off Lower Sea Lane, but in the opposite direction along River Way, is *Swansmead* (☎ 01297-560465, 🖥 swans mead.co.uk; 1D/1Qd; 🛏; WI-FI; Easter to Sep; £42.50pp, sgl occ from £78). There are great views and airy and clean rooms but unfortunately for the walker there is a

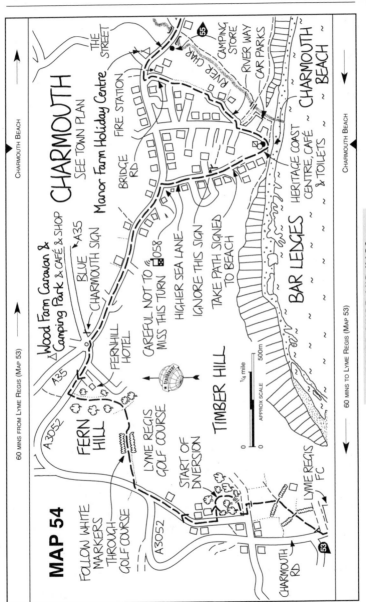

MAP 54

FOLLOW WHITE MARKERS THROUGH GOLF COURSE

CHARMOUTH BEACH

60 MINS FROM LYME REGIS (MAP 53)

Wood Farm Caravan & Camping Park & Café & Shop

A35

BLUE CHARMOUTH SIGN

Manor Farm Holiday Centre

THE STREET

CHARMOUTH

SEE TOWN PLAN

55

CAMPING STORE

RIVER WAY

CAR PARKS

RIVER CHAR

FIRE STATION

BRIDGE RD

FERNHILL HOTEL

CAREFUL NOT TO MISS THIS TURN 058

HIGHER SEA LANE

IGNORE THIS SIGN

TAKE PATH SIGNED TO BEACH

CHARMOUTH BEACH

HERITAGE COAST CENTRE, CAFÉ & TOILETS

BAR LEDGES

FERN HILL

A3052

LYME REGIS GOLF COURSE

START OF DIVERSION

TIMBER HILL

¼ mile

APPROX SCALE

500m

0

LYME REGIS FC

A3052

CHARMOUTH RD

53

60 MINS TO LYME REGIS (MAP 53)

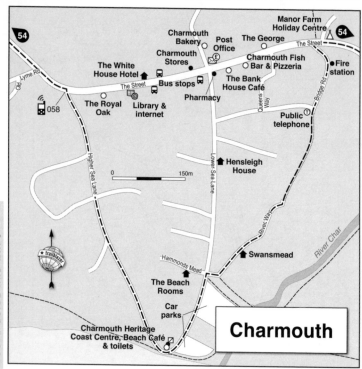

Charmouth

two-night minimum stay policy. Further up Lower Sea Lane is *Hensleigh House* (☎ 01297-560830, 🖳 hensleighhotel.co.uk; 1S/2T/3D; 🍴; WI-FI; £45-65pp, sgl £80-95, sgl occ from £80), while in the village centre, you'll find *The White House Hotel* (☎ 01297-560411, 🖳 whitehousehotel.com; 1D/2D or T/1Tr; 🍴; WI-FI; Mar-Oct; £65-72.50pp, sgl occ from £90) at 2 Hillside, The Street. It's is a fine establishment with decent rooms and wonderful food and all within a Regency-era building. One-night bookings are not always possible at the weekend but a speculative call may discover a gap in the diary.

Where to eat and drink
Charmouth Bakery (☎ 01297-560213; Mon-Fri 8am-3pm, Sat 8am-1pm), on a

lane off The Street, is worth popping into if you're after lunchbox fillers. There's been a bakery on this site since the 1830s and they do bacon rolls (£2.50) and crab sandwiches (£5) as well as other freshly baked goodies and takeaway tea and coffee.

For a proper sit-down café, *The Bank House* (☎ 01297-561600; WI-FI; Apr-Sep daily 9am-5pm & 6-8pm, Sep-Apr Thur-Tue 10am-4pm), on The Street, is a pleasant place (with some roadside patio seating) that serves up jacket potatoes (£6.50), paninis (£5.50), cream teas (£5.25) and the like. There's also *Beach Café* (end Mar to end Oct daily 9.30am-5pm, hours may vary according to the weather) down at Charmouth Heritage Coast Centre.

Next door to The Bank House, fish 'n' chips are available at *Charmouth Fish Bar*

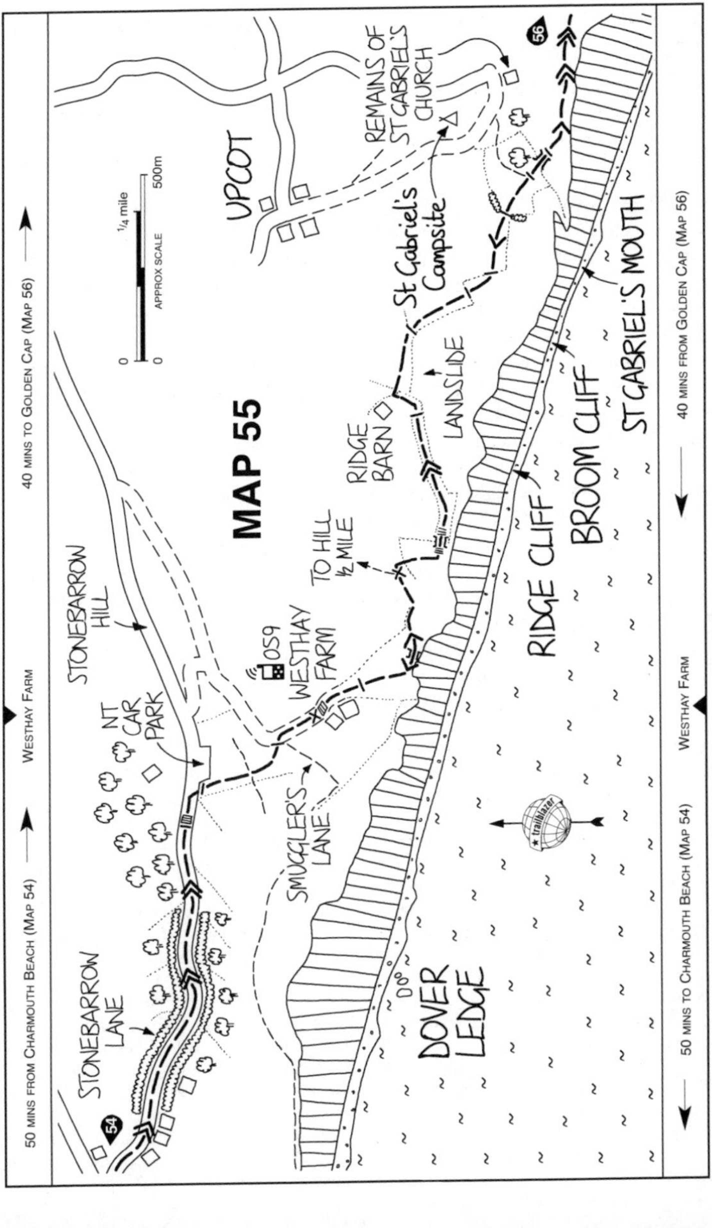

MAP 55

UPCOT

REMAINS OF ST GABRIEL'S CHURCH

St Gabriel's Campsite

LANDSLIDE

RIDGE BARN

TO HILL ½ MILE

STONEBARRON HILL

NT CAR PARK

OS9

WESTHAY FARM

SMUGGLER'S LANE

STONEBARRON LANE

RIDGE CLIFF

BROOM CLIFF

ST GABRIEL'S MOUTH

DOVER LEDGE

APPROX SCALE

0   500m
0   ¼ mile

50 MINS FROM CHARMOUTH BEACH (MAP 54) — WESTHAY FARM — 40 MINS TO GOLDEN CAP (MAP 56)

40 MINS FROM GOLDEN CAP (MAP 56)

WESTHAY FARM

50 MINS TO CHARMOUTH BEACH (MAP 54)

*trailblazer

ROUTE GUIDE AND MAPS

& Pizzeria (☎ 01297-560220, 💻 char mouthfishbar.co.uk; school holidays daily noon-2pm & 5-9pm, summer generally Mon-Tue 5-9pm, Wed-Sat noon-2pm & 5-9pm but days/hours vary so check before going). They also have patio seating out front and do takeaways. For **pub grub** head to *The George* (☎ 01297-560280, 💻 thege orgecharmouth.com; WI-FI; 🐾 on lead; food daily noon-2pm & 6-9pm) or *The Royal Oak* (☎ 01297-560277; WI-FI; 🐾 lower bar; food Mon-Sat noon-2pm & 5.30-8.30pm, Sun noon-2pm), both of which have a selection of real ales on tap.

From Charmouth Heritage Coast Centre, with Portland Bill in the distance – you can clearly make out a path that leads off up the next cliff. However, due to landslips, this has been closed, thus necessitating a further diversion via Lower Sea Lane, River Way, Bridge Rd and The Street, past the **fire station** to **Stonebarrow Lane** and the **hill** of the same name, surmounted by a National Trust car park. Take the footpath on the right, signed 'Golden Cap: 2¼ miles'; a grassy path now leads, via the National Trust's **Westhay Farm**, back to the cliffs.

The path undulates dramatically, at times perilously close to the cliff-edge, before you ascend the mighty **Broom Cliff**, with the ruins of 13th-century **St Gabriel's Church** (which lies on The Monarch's Way – see p38) lying to your left. Near here you'll find *St Gabriel's Campsite* (☎ 01297-489481, 💻 national trust.org.uk; 🐾 on leads; £5pp), an extremely basic camping field (no toilets or showers; just a few water taps) overseen by the National Trust.

Back on the path, a few hundred calf-popping paces further will bring you atop that star of book covers and photoshoots, **Golden Cap** (191m/627ft) – the south coast's highest point. With Portland Bill to the east and the cliffs of Devon to your west, you now descend. Should you do this at dusk, the waning sun will turn the eastward cliffs a brilliant orange – it's just marvellous.

A brief dalliance with both woods and farmland eventually brings you to a road that bends down to **Seatown**.

SEATOWN   [Map 56]

Regarded as one of Dorset's prime fossil-collecting spots, Seatown has little to offer save for a pub, a campsite and some precious tranquillity. However, Chideock (see p240) is only a 15- to 20-minute stroll inland, where there is slightly more on offer. To walk there either take the bridle-way, Mill Lane, to the east of Golden Cap Holiday Park, or follow Sea Hill Lane to the site's west. Details on both places can be found at 💻 chideockandseatown.co.uk.

Campers can find accommodation at *Golden Cap Holiday Park* (☎ 01308-426947, 💻 goldencapholidaypark.co.uk; £17-24 per pitch inc two adults; WI-FI; 🐾; camping mid Mar-Oct), right by the beach. It has a **shop** (summer daily 8.30am-9pm, winter 8.30am-6pm) that is well stocked and sells camping gas as well as hot drinks, snacks and even takeaway pizza. The showers are tremendous. They don't have that many grass pitches for most of the year and can sometimes fill up (be sure to call ahead to check they have space), but they open up a large camping field in late July and August to meet the extra demand.

For **B&B** and **food**, you're even closer to the beach at *The Anchor Inn* (☎ 01297-489215, 💻 theanchorinnseatown.co.uk; WI-FI; 🐾 bar only; food daily noon-9pm), a lovely old smugglers' haunt with a great menu (mains £12-16) and a good selection of local ales. They have three very smart double rooms (3D; 💧; WI-FI; £75-85pp, sgl occ room rate), but online bookings can only be for two nights (as that is what they prefer). However, if you call they may be able to accept a single-night stay.

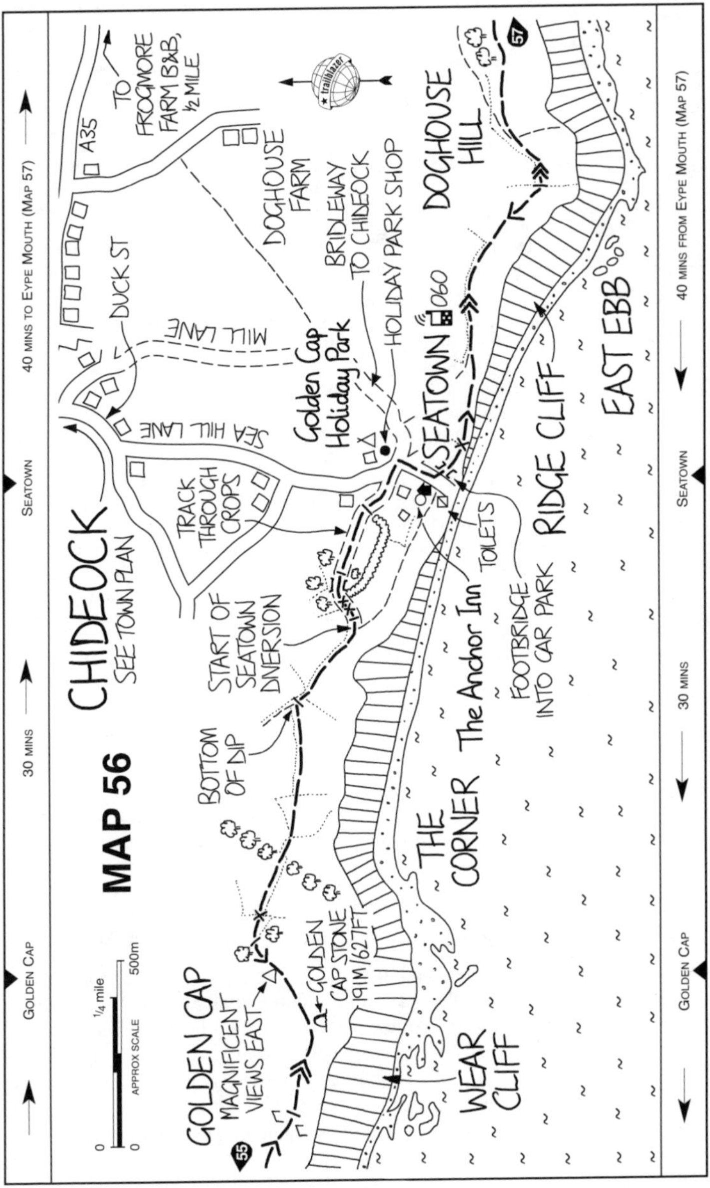
MAP 56
GOLDEN CAP
30 MINS
SEATOWN
40 MINS TO EYPE MOUTH (MAP 57)
GOLDEN CAP
30 MINS
SEATOWN
40 MINS FROM EYPE MOUTH (MAP 57)
0
1/4 mile
APPROX SCALE
0
500m
CHIDEOCK
SEE TOWN PLAN
GOLDEN CAP
MAGNIFICENT VIEWS EAST
GOLDEN CAP STONE 191M/627FT
BOTTOM OF DIP
START OF SEATOWN DIVERSION
TRACK THROUGH CROPS
SEA HILL LANE
MILL LANE
DUCK ST
A35
TO FROGMORE FARM B&B, ½ MILE
DOGHOUSE FARM
BRIDLEWAY TO CHIDEOCK
HOLIDAY PARK SHOP
Golden Cap Holiday Park
SEATOWN
060
DOGHOUSE HILL
The Anchor Inn
TOILETS
FOOTBRIDGE INTO CAR PARK
RIDGE CLIFF
EAST EBB
THE CORNER
WEAR CLIFF
55
57

ROUTE GUIDE AND MAPS

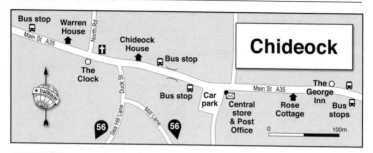

CHIDEOCK   **[map above]**

Up in Chideock (pronounced Chidock) there's a well-stocked Central **store** (Mon-Fri 7am-8pm, Sat & Sun 8am-8pm) which also has a **post office** (same hours).

For **buses**, First's X51 and X53 (see pp50-4) services stop here, connecting the village with places such as Lyme Regis, Abbotsbury and Weymouth.

Chideock has more **B&B** options. On Main St, there's *Warren House* (☎ 01297-489996, ☐ www.warrenhousechideock.co.uk; 2D/1T/1Qd; ♥; WI-FI; Apr-mid Nov; £47.50-50pp, sgl occ from £70), a 17th-century Grade-II Dorset Longhouse (a longhouse is a long thatched cottage), *Chideock House* (☎ 01297-489242, ☐ chideockhouse.co.uk; 2D/1T; ♥; WI-FI; ✱; £37.50-40pp, sgl occ from £65), and the lovely *Rose Cottage* (☎ 01297-489994, ☐ rosecottage-chideock.co.uk; 1T/1D; WI-FI; from £40pp, sgl occ from £65), which offers baggage transfer as far as either Abbotsbury or Seaton (£16-18).

If these are all full, set in a beautiful location (albeit around half a mile along the A35) is *Frogmore Farm* (off Map 56; ☎ 01308-456159, ☐ frogmorefarm.com; 2D/1T; ♥; WI-FI; ✱; £36pp, sgl occ from £42). The next morning you can walk across paths to Thorncombe Beacon (see Map 57, p243) rather than going back along the road.

For **food**, the two local pubs won't disappoint: Home to more than 150 clocks, *The Clock* (☎ 01297-489423, ☐ clockchideock.co.uk; food daily noon-2.30pm & 6-9pm; WI-FI; ✱ welcome in the bar) is a quirky, thatched 16th-century village freehouse that suffered a devastating fire in 2015 but has since reopened. They serve good-value pub grub (with regular and large portions) and have a selection of real ales.

Also thatched, *The George Inn* (☎ 01297-489419, ☐ georgeinnchideock.co.uk; ✱ on a lead and in the bar/on the terrace; WI-FI; food daily noon-2.30pm & 6-9.30pm) is a more upmarket traditional Dorset pub, serving good-quality food (mains £12-20) as well as Palmers' ales. Thursday night is pizza night (from £9).

SEATOWN TO ABBOTSBURY   [MAPS 56-62]

This is a stage of two halves: initially consisting of undulating cliff-top walking (with some steep climbs), this **12½-mile (20km; 4hrs 10 mins)** stage passes through several small coastal hamlets on its way to Burton Freshwater and the outer extremities of Chesil Beach. From here, however, things get much flatter and easier as you pass by nature reserve, mere and common before turning inland to circle Chapel Hill and arrive at one of Dorset's many highlights: the village of Abbotsbury. Refreshments are available every couple of miles or so, as is accommodation should it become required.

(Note that those who are either running out of time to complete their trek, don't fancy walking through Weymouth, or just want a change of scenery from all this seaside, should consider taking the South Dorset Ridgeway. This leaves the main coast path at West Bexington; details can be found on pp251-4.)

The route

The first ascent of the day occurs on leaving Seatown and the climb up **Ridge Cliff**. This is quickly followed by an even more strenuous one which takes you up the interestingly named **Doghouse Hill**, where the path leads along the top of a ridge, traversing rolling cliffs until arriving at **Thorncombe Beacon**.

From the beacon the official path initially turns left and heads inland briefly. However, many people go straight down from the beacon as it is more direct. If you follow the official route you will see signs for *Downhouse Farm Garden Café* (☎ 01308-421232, 🖳 downhousefarm.org; Mar-end Oct Tue-Sun and bank hol Mons 10am-5.30pm, to 6pm in peak season; 🐾, water bowl provided), a hidden gem that's only a five-minute detour from the path. They do breakfasts, sandwiches and delicious cream teas (£6.45) in a cosy garden courtyard. For **B&B**, they also have two simple but comfortable **shepherd's huts** (1D; £27.50-37.50pp, sgl occ rates on request) with a small double bed and a single solar-powered light, but no electricity. A shower and toilet are available behind the farmhouse.

The official path turns back towards the cliffs at **Hope Corner**. There's a spring here, situated in a giant dip and surrounded by a stone wall. The path then descends to **Eype Mouth**.

EYPE MOUTH   [Map 57, p243]

Situated in the dip between two cliffs ('Eype' meaning 'A Steep Place' in Old English) at the mouth of the River Eype, there are limited amenities for walkers here. **Boathouse Visitor Centre**, by the entrance to the car park, is unmanned (and rarely open) but it has some leaflets regarding local tourist attractions as well as panels with information about the geology and flora and fauna in the area.

Camping can be arranged just off Mount Lane at the friendly *Eype House Caravan & Camping Park* (☎ 01308-424903, 🖳 eypehouse.co.uk; £12-24/17-29 for tent and one/two hikers; WI-FI but not free; 🐾; campsite Easter to mid Oct). They have a *tea garden* and **shop** (both peak season daily 9am-5pm, rest of season hours variable also depending on the weather) stocking basic necessities (including camping gas) and serving cream teas, ice-creams and snacks. They also have a **log pod** which sleeps up to four people; bedding is not provided and there is a minimum two-night booking (£35-50 per night).

Hotel rooms can be had a little further up the lane at *Eype's Mouth Country Hotel* (☎ 01308-423300, 🖳 eypesmouthhotel.co .uk; 3S/10D/3T; 🛏; WI-FI; 🐾; £60-70pp, sgl from £90, sgl occ from £105). Note that the hotel is unlikely to accept advance bookings for one-night stays at weekends between March and October but nearer the time it is worth calling. If going here it is nicest to walk along the path heading inland from the eastern side of the stream at Eype Mouth.

Pub-grub **food** is available at the hotel's bar, *The Smuggler's Bar* (food Apr-Oct daily noon-2pm & 6.30-8.30pm). In the winter months (Nov-Mar same hours) food is served in the hotel itself.

Crossing a stream by the beach, you again take off upwards to conquer **West Cliff** (another strenuous climb), at the top of which to the left is *Highlands End Holiday Park* (☎ 01308-426947, ☐ highlandsendholiday park.co.uk; pitch and up to two people £18-37; WI-FI but not free; 🐾; mid Mar-Nov). There is a **shop** (daily 8.30am-8.30pm) on site which stocks a good range of basic foods and has a **tourist information point**. There's also a restaurant, a bar and a leisure club with swimming pool.

The path then goes downhill to **West Bay** – an unprepossessing town that resembles, from this aspect, something out of the old Soviet Union. Continue towards it, however, and you'll find it is an amiable place with a decent harbour.

WEST BAY   [map p245]

At the furthest western point of Chesil Beach, West Bay (☐ westbay.co.uk) is a working harbour but one that also thrives on the passing tourist trade, with several places to stay and eat. The town used to be known as Bridport Harbour and actually falls within the boundaries of Bridport, a couple of miles away. The arrival of the railway in Bridport caused the name change when, in an early example of rebranding, the harbour was renamed West Bay to make it sound more attractive to tourists.

Fans of classic television comedies may want to stand on the beach, remove all their clothes and walk into the sea in homage to the memorable opening scene of *The Life and Times of Reginald Perrin*, which was shot here. More recently scenes from the ITV drama *Broadchurch* were also filmed on the beach here and in parts of the town.

Services

Although there are more services in Bridport, a couple of miles up the road, there is enough for most passing walkers here in West Bay, including a **launderette** (daily 9am-9pm) and a small **supermarket**: Nisa Local (Mon, Fri & Sat 8am-7pm, Tue-Thur & Sun to 6pm). There is an **ATM** (£1.85 per transaction) inside Harbour Amusements.

Transport

[See pp50-4] First's X53 **bus** service stops off en route between Axminster and Weymouth; its SLOWcoaster 510 (Bridport to Weymouth) service also calls here.

Where to stay

Much of the accommodation in West Bay can be found on West Bay Rd, the lengthy thoroughfare which runs all the way to Bridport.

In July and August only **campers** are in luck as *Britt Valley Campground* (off Map 58; ☎ 01308-897232, ☐ brittvalley.co .uk; £12/18 for a tent and one/two hikers inc use of shower; 🐾; open for eight weeks around the school summer holidays) occupies two of the local fields. Follow the West Bay Rd out of town for about 300m, and the site will soon appear on your left.

One of the nearest **B&Bs** to the path is *Durbeyfield House* (☎ 01308-423307, ☐ durbeyfieldguesthouse.com; 1T/6D en suite, 1T/1D share facilities; 🛏; WI-FI; 🐾; £35-42.50pp, sgl occ £40-50, deduct £5pp if breakfast not required), at 10 West Bay Rd. Happy to take one-night bookings and with their own licensed restaurant (Quarterdeck; see Where to eat), this place could hardly be more convenient.

On the other side of the harbour, *Heatherbell Cottage* (☎ 01308-422998, ☐ cu4bnb.com; 2D; from £35pp, sgl occ room rate), in Hill Close, is also conveniently placed for the path. Walk about 100m past Seasider (see Where to eat) and turn right.

The other centrally located options are rooms above a pub, *The George* (☎ 01308-423191, ☐ georgewestbay.com; 1T/4D/ 1Tr, one room with four poster bed; 🛏; WI-FI; £45-70pp, sgl occ rates on request), and in a hotel, *Bridport Arms Hotel* (☎ 01308-422994, ☐ bridportarms.co.uk; 2T/8D/1Tr; 🛏; WI-FI; 🐾; £70-82.50pp, sgl occ rates on

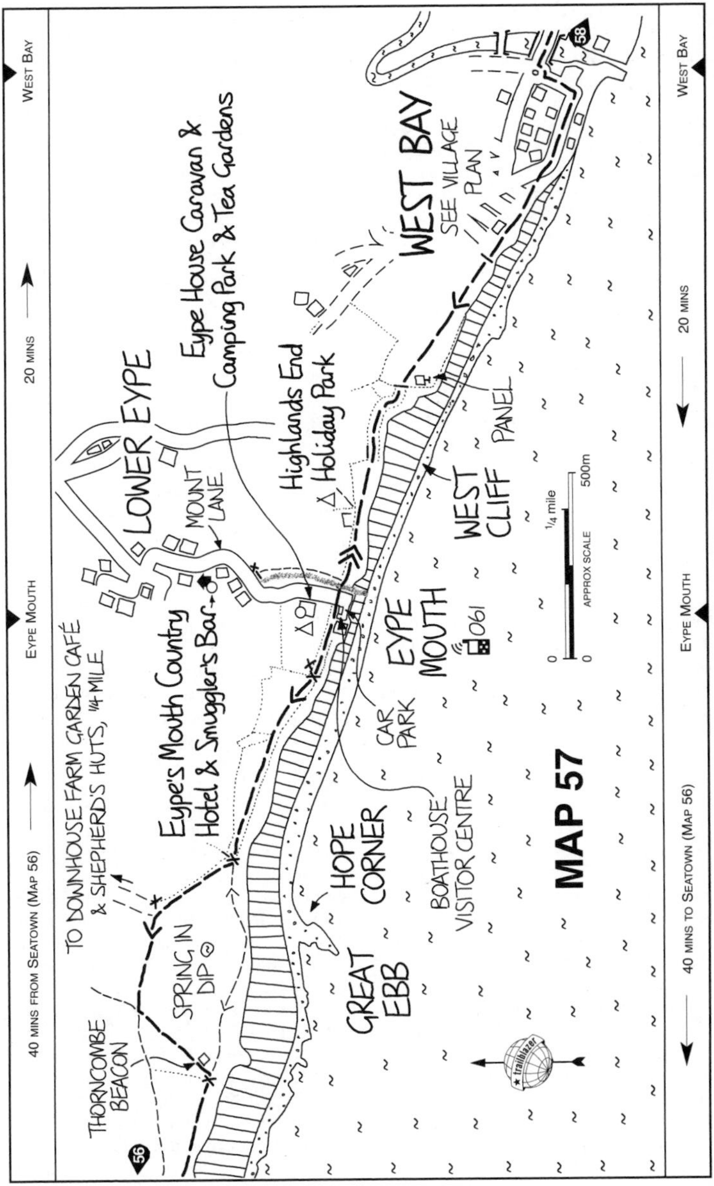

MAP 57

WEST BAY
SEE VILLAGE PLAN

Eype House Caravan & Camping Park & Tea Gardens

LOWER EYPE

MOUNT LANE

Highlands End ∆ Holiday Park

WEST CLIFF PANEL

Eype's Mouth Country Hotel & Smuggler's Bar

TO DOWNHOUSE FARM GARDEN CAFÉ & SHEPHERDS HUTS, ¼ MILE

∆

EYPE MOUTH

CAR PARK

061

BOATHOUSE VISITOR CENTRE

HOPE CORNER

GREAT EBB

SPRING IN DIP

THORNCOMBE BEACON

56

¼ mile

0   500m
0
APPROX SCALE

40 MINS FROM SEATOWN (MAP 56)

EYPE MOUTH

20 MINS

WEST BAY

40 MINS TO SEATOWN (MAP 56)

EYPE MOUTH

20 MINS

WEST BAY

58

ROUTE GUIDE AND MAPS

request), which is a 16th-century flower-fronted inn right on the harbour with smart rooms, some with four-poster beds.

The remaining options are all strung out along West Bay Rd. *Haddon House Hotel* (☎ 01308-423626, 🖥 hotelsbridport. co.uk; 6T/7D; 🐾; WI-FI; from £82.50pp, sgl occ from £110) is the first place you come to, just 100m or so out of town, and one of the most charming and smartest places you'll find. They may accept an advance booking for a one-night stay except on a Saturday night in summer.

Further along, at No 117, *Eypeleaze* (☎ 01308-423363, 🖥 eypeleaze.co.uk; 1D/1T; 🐾; WI-FI; £34-37pp, sgl occ rates on request) is willing to accept one-night stops depending on other bookings. Nearby, at No 154, *Britmead House* (☎ 01308-422941, 🖥 britmeadhouse.co.uk; 3D/1T; 🐾; WI-FI; Easter to end Oct; £40-45pp, sgl occ from £65) is a professionally run establishment that is popular with walkers. Note that they don't accept bookings for a one-night stay at any time; the minimum is two nights.

Where to eat and drink

For those just passing through, the harbour is dotted with **food stalls** selling fish & chips, ice-cream and takeaway coffees, especially in high season.

On the way into the village, on the west side of the harbour, is the modern, glass-fronted *Windy Corner Café* (☎ 01308-459221; WI-FI; 🐾; daily July & Aug 9am-5pm, Sep-Oct & Apr-June 9.30am-4pm, Nov-Mar 10am-3pm), with reasonably priced food and sea views. Round the corner from here is *Seasider* (☎ 01308-427787; summer Mon-Thur 5-9pm, Fri-Sat noon-2pm & 5-9pm, winter hours variable), a decent local chippy with both a restaurant and a takeaway.

Most of the best places to eat, though, are on the other side of the harbour, including several good **cafés**: Right on the sand, *Watch House Café* (☎ 01308-459330, 🖥 www.hivebeachcafe.co.uk, click on Watch House Café; WI-FI; 🐾; summer daily 10am-5pm & Tue-Sat 6-9pm, winter daily 10am-5pm & Thur-Sat 6-8pm), sister to

Hive Beach Café (see p248), has extensive outdoor seating and a menu (breakfasts £6-10, lunch mains £12-16) that includes numerous seafood options.

Inland slightly, is the tranquil *Sladers Yard Art Café* (☎ 01308-459511, 🖥 sladers yard.wordpress.com; 🐾; summer daily 10am-5pm, winter hours vary), which uses local produce and organic ingredients as much as possible, with sandwiches (£8-11) and salads, as well as mains such as Goan fish curry (£15) and Italian bean stew (£8). It occupies a lovely space inside a small art gallery and there's seating in the courtyard too.

Opposite, is *West Bay Tea Rooms* (☎ 01308-455697, 🖥 westbaytearooms.co.uk; daily summer 10am-5pm, winter 10am-2.30/3pm) which has a wide tea selection and a good choice of baguettes (£4.95-7.95); note that dogs are not allowed here.

The Cornish Bakery (☎ 01308-458256, 🖥 www.thecornishbakery.com; WI-FI; 🐾; school summer holidays daily 8am-8pm, rest of year to 6pm) serve pasties, pastries as well as interesting breads to take away. Pasty options (from £3.40/£3.70 take out/eat in) may include: pork, apple & Cornish cider; cheese & onion; steak & stilton; as well as traditional.

For **restaurants**, dominating the harbour, *Bridport Arms Hotel* (see Where to stay; food served daily noon-2pm & 6-8.30pm, Aug weekends noon-9pm) has mains ranging from pub classics such as sausage & mash (£11.95) to more substantial fare like rump steak with celeriac remoulade and spiced beetroot (£19).

Just up the road, *Haddon House Hotel* (see Where to stay; daily 11.45am-2pm & 6.15pm-8.45pm) offers one of the more refined dining experiences in the village. Their two-course lunch offer (£13.50) is good value.

Even smarter, *Riverside Restaurant* (☎ 01308-422011, 🖥 thefishrestaurant-westbay.co.uk; mid Feb to end Nov Tue-Sun noon-2.30pm, plus Tue-Thur 6.30-8.30pm, Fri 6.30-9pm, Sat 6.30-9.15pm) has a cracking location, seemingly perched on a river island, overlooking the village and the waterway. This is the town's premier

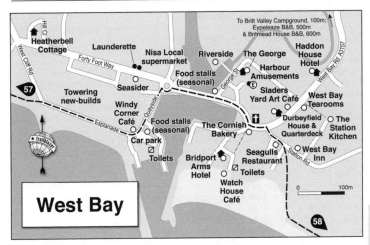

West Bay

seafood restaurant, though it's not cheap (mains from £18).

More affordable, but still a nice place for seafood, **Seagulls Restaurant** (☎ 01308-425099, 🖥 seagullsrestaurant.co.uk; Feb-Nov food served Tue-Sun noon-2pm & 6-8.45pm) is another smart choice for an evening meal, and it also does light lunches (£5-10).

Recently revamped from its previous incarnation as a tea room, *The Station Kitchen* (☎ 01308-422845, 🖥 station .kitchen; Wed-Sat noon-2.30pm & 6-9pm, Sun noon-2.30pm) is a quirky, rustic restaurant, housed inside the disused railway station. The contemporary British menu focuses on locally sourced food, including fresh fish.

For **pubs**, try *The George* (see Where to stay; daily noon-2.30pm & 6-9.30pm), which serves baked potatoes (from £7) and a ploughman's lunch (£9) at lunch time; the main menu includes pie of the day (£11) and Dorset ham, egg & chips (£10) and there are also daily specials.

Round the corner from here is *Quarterdeck* (see Durbeyfield, Where to stay; WI-FI; 🐕 bar; food daily noon-8.30pm) a local boozer with good-value mains. More upmarket is *West Bay Inn* (☎ 01308-422157; WI-FI; 🐕; food Mon-Fri noon-2pm & 6-9pm, Sat noon-3pm & 6-9pm, Sun noon-3pm & 6-8pm, winter Sun noon-3pm only), a Palmers pub with good ale and classic pub-grub mains (lunch £10-13, dinner £12-23).

At the eastern end of West Bay there is more climbing to be done to get over **East Cliff**. There was a dramatic cliff fall here in June 2017, but the path has reopened again, a few metres inland. Be sure to stick to the path here, and not to wander too close to the cliff edge.

From East Cliff, the path follows the cliff line along the edge of a golf course down to the beach at **Burton Freshwater**, where you'll find Freshwater Beach Holiday Park before climbing up **Burton Cliff**. From the top of this cliff you can, by gazing inland, catch your first glimpse of the Saxon settlement of Burton Bradstock. Straight ahead, the terrain flattens out, the ominous edge of Portland's Underhill getting ever closer.

To access **Burton Bradstock** turn left up Cliff Rd (see Map 58, p247).

BURTON BRADSTOCK   [Map 58]

This unspoilt historic stone village is very pleasant, with lovely old buildings, many of them topped with thatch, particularly the old cottages around **St Mary's Church**, a number of which date back to the 16th and 17th centuries. That said, it is probably not worth diverting from the path just to see the village unless you plan to take advantage of its services or to grab a pub lunch. Many of the events in **Burton Bradstock's Festival of Music and Art** (see p14), held in August, take place in the church.

Close to the church you'll find the **Village Stores** (Mon-Fri 8.30am-5pm, Sat 8.30am-12.30pm) which sells local farm produce and houses the **post office** (same hours). Down on the main road out of the village is a petrol station with a Central **convenience store** (daily 6.30am-11pm) that sells coffee and has an **ATM** (£1.75) outside it. For **internet access** (free for 30 mins), the village has a cute little **library** (Mon & Wed-Fri 3-5pm, Tue & Sat 10am-noon).

First's X53 **bus service** (see pp50-4) calls in en route between Axminster and Weymouth; their SLOWcoaster 510 (Bridport to Weymouth) also stops here.

Should you wish to **camp** in the area *Freshwater Beach Holiday Park* (☎ 01308-897317, 🖥 freshwaterbeach.co.uk; mid Mar to end Oct; £5-18 for a tent and up to two hikers; 🐾; WI-FI) is the large family-orientated caravan park at the back of Burton Freshwater. It has a Spar **supermarket** (daily 9am-5pm, closes later in peak season), and campers can use both the indoor swimming **pool** (which has a Jacuzzi, steam room and sauna!) and the outdoor swimming pool free of charge. Be sure to tell them you are a hiker in order to get the cheapest rate for a tent pitch.

B&B is provided at *Bridge Cottage* (☎ 01308-897222, 🖥 bridgecottagebedand breakfast.co.uk; 1D/1T/1Qd; 🛁; WI-FI; 🐾; £35-45pp, sgl occ £45-90), 87 High St. Note that in July and August they have a

minimum two-night stay policy for advance bookings. You can also get B&B at *The Anchor Inn* (☎ 01308-897228, 🖥 anchor innburtonbradstock.co.uk; 2D; WI-FI; £42.50-50pp, sgl occ from £75). Alternatively, on top of Burton Cliff, you can find sumptuous double rooms at *Seaside Boarding House* (☎ 01308-897205, 🖥 theseasideboardinghouse.com; 9D; 🛁; WI-FI; 🐾; £95-125pp, sgl occ from £175), right on the path before it drops down to Hive Beach. Seaside has a bar and a quality restaurant too.

Further beyond the village, *Chesil Beach Lodge* (Map 59; ☎ 01308-897428, 🖥 chesilbeachlodge.co.uk; 1D/2D or T; WI-FI; 🐾; £50-60pp, sgl occ room rate) is on the coast road (B3157). The best way for walkers to reach it is to continue along the coast path for just under half a mile before turning inland before Old Coastguard Holiday Park and following the footpath. They do not accept advance bookings for a one-night stay at the weekend over the summer months.

For **food**, there are two excellent pubs on the main road in the centre of the village. The menu at *The Anchor Inn* (see Where to stay; food Mon-Sat noon-2pm & 6-9pm, Sun noon-3pm & 6-9pm) changes frequently but focuses on fish and shellfish – hand-dived West Bay scallops are £18.95 – but they also have meat and vegetarian options. You sometimes need to book here for evening meals.

Just down the hill, *The Three Horseshoes* (☎ 01308-897259, 🖥 three horseshoesburtonbradstock.co.uk; limited WI-FI; 🐾 bar area; food summer Mon-Sat noon-9pm, Sun noon-3pm, winter Mon-Fri noon-2pm & 6-9pm, Sat noon-9pm, Sun noon-3pm) is more down-to-earth, and welcomes muddy hikers as well as dogs. They offer good homemade food (mains £10-15) with a particular flair for desserts, and have Palmers' ales on tap.

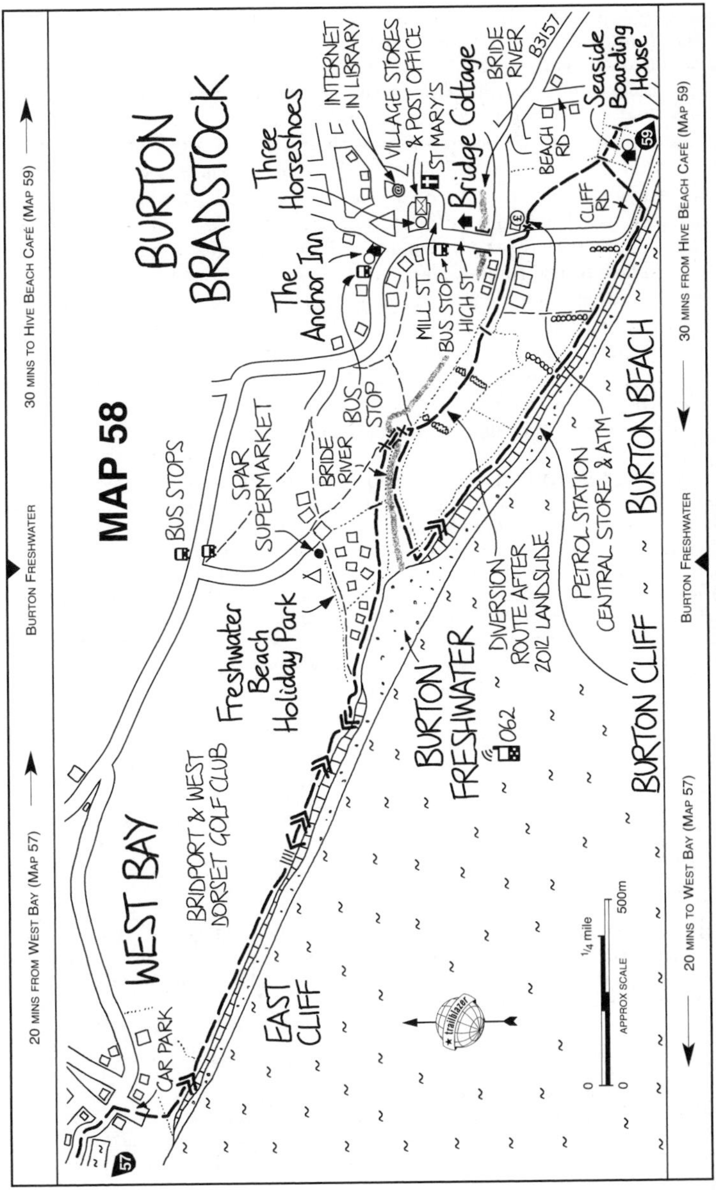
MAP 58
20 MINS FROM WEST BAY (MAP 57)
BURTON FRESHWATER
30 MINS TO HIVE BEACH CAFÉ (MAP 59)
20 MINS TO WEST BAY (MAP 57)
BURTON FRESHWATER
30 MINS FROM HIVE BEACH CAFÉ (MAP 59)
57
59
WEST BAY
CAR PARK
EAST CLIFF
BRIDPORT & WEST DORSET GOLF CLUB
BURTON BRADSTOCK
BUS STOPS
SPAR SUPERMARKET
Freshwater Beach Holiday Park
BRIDE RIVER
BUS STOP
The Anchor Inn
Three Horseshoes
INTERNET IN LIBRARY
VILLAGE STORES & POST OFFICE
ST MARY'S
Bridge Cottage
BRIDE RIVER
B3157
MILL ST
BUS STOP
HIGH ST
BEACH RD
CLIFF RD
Seaside Boarding House
BURTON FRESHWATER
062
DIVERSION ROUTE AFTER 2012 LANDSLIDE
PETROL STATION CENTRAL STORE & ATM
BURTON CLIFF
BURTON BEACH
APPROX SCALE
0
1/4 mile
0
500m
trailblazer

The walking is easy as you pass Burton and then **Hive Beach** where *Hive Beach Café* (☎ 01308-897070, 🖳 hivebeachcafe.co.uk; WI-FI; 🐕; daily 10am-5pm plus summer Thur-Sat 6-8pm) has grown from a seasonal beach shack into a gourmet café-bistro with plastic awnings sheltering diners from the elements. The food's good, but it's not cheap (lunchtime mains £12-20). First's seasonal SLOWcoaster 510 (Bridport to Weymouth) **bus service** calls here (see pp50-4).

More caravan parks and cliffs follow before **Cogden Beach** spreads out on your right and **Burton Common** appears bleak and endless to your left, looking in many ways like Dartmoor (its tors are around 50 miles south-west). The path slices between the two, their contrasting charms changing with each season.

Passing behind **Burton Mere**, you walk through scrub and farmland along the back of a pebble ridge – the sea isn't always visible but the sound of the waves remains therapeutic enough.

Having passed through **West Bexington Nature Reserve** – of importance due to the rare shingle habitat that thrives here – you arrive at the car-park at **West Bexington Beach**. This is also the start of the **South Dorset Ridgeway** (see p251). For the continuation of the main route see p254.

WEST BEXINGTON   [Map 60, p250]

It is hard to imagine that contemporary West Bexington was, before the Romans came, inhabited by the feared and belligerent Durotriges tribe that once occupied much of Dorset; indeed, what with a French raiding party burning and pillaging the tiny village (and destroying its church) in the 15th century, it's fair to say that this sleepy hamlet has had more than its fair share of excitement down the centuries. All this violence in what is now such a tranquil location.

Unfortunately, Tamarisk Farm **shop** (Tue 4-6.30pm, Fri 8.30-11am), the only shop here, has very limited hours.

The only place to stay is at *Manor House* (☎ 01308-897660, 🖳 manorhotel dorset.com; 9D/4D or T; 🛏; WI-FI in public areas; from £52.50pp, sgl occ from £95), a 16th-century manor-house hotel with well-appointed bedrooms. The **restaurant** (Mar-end Oct Sun-Thur noon-2pm & 6.30-8.30pm, Fri-Sat noon-2.15pm & 6.30-9pm,

rest of year Thur-Sun only), which has garden seating on pub benches, and the **bar** (Mon-Thur 11.30am-3pm & 6-9.30pm, Fri-Sun 11.30am-late), which serves real ales, are both open to non-residents, and passing walkers are welcome just to pop in for a cake and some coffee.

Down at the beach is *The Club House Restaurant* (☎ 01308-898302, 🖳 theclub housewestbexington.co.uk; Feb-Nov Tue-Sat noon-9pm, Sun noon-6pm), a fine-dining establishment (mains £16-30) with a lovely sea-facing location, but a slightly stuffy atmosphere. Booking a table is pretty much essential.

The nearest **bus stop** is at Swyre, about 1¼ miles/2km from The Club House. First's X53 **bus** (Axminster to Weymouth; see p51) service stops off by The Bull Inn there. The route is also very handy for the South Dorset Ridgeway (aka The Inland Route), which follows the course of the B3157 road for much of its length.

❏ **Important note – walking times**
All times in this book refer only to the time spent walking. You will need to add 20-30% to allow for rests, photography, checking the map, drinking water etc.

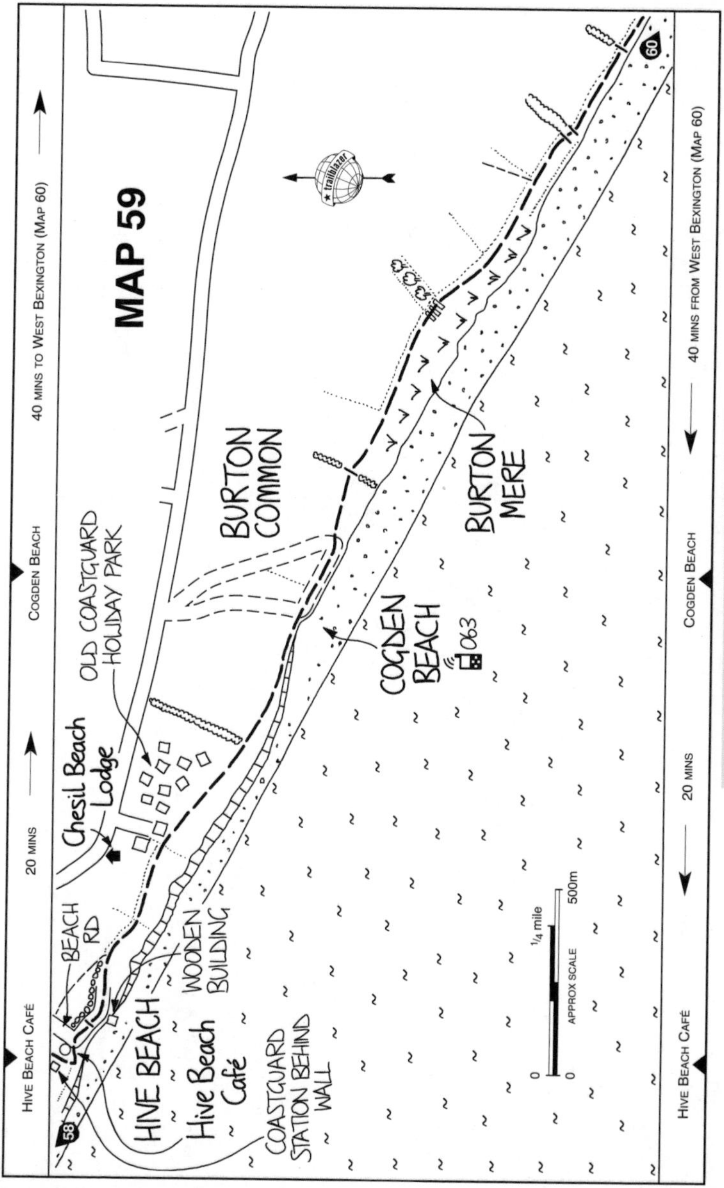

MAP 59

40 MINS TO WEST BEXINGTON (MAP 60)

COGDEN BEACH

20 MINS

HIVE BEACH CAFÉ

BEACH RD

Chesil Beach Lodge

OLD COASTGUARD HOLIDAY PARK

BURTON COMMON

HIVE BEACH

Hive Beach Café

WOODEN BUILDING

COASTGUARD STATION BEHIND WALL

COGDEN BEACH

063

BURTON MERE

trailblazer

¼ mile

500m

APPROX SCALE

40 MINS FROM WEST BEXINGTON (MAP 60)

COGDEN BEACH

20 MINS

HIVE BEACH CAFÉ

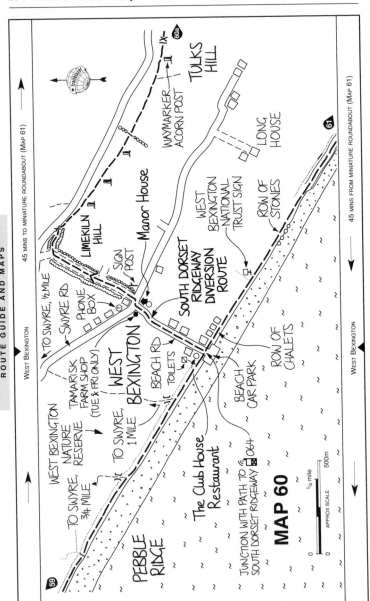

MAP 60

South Dorset Ridgeway (aka Inland Route)
[Map 60, Map 60a & 60b, p252; Map 60c, p253; Map 73, p283]

At its most basic, this walk could be seen as nothing but a short cut, saving the weary trekker about 19¼ miles on the standard route via Weymouth and Portland. Thus those short on stamina and shoe leather, the fatigued and the fed-up, may appreciate this reducing of their expedition. But this **17-mile (27.4km; 5hrs 10 mins)** saunter, **which has been part of the SWCP since its inception in 1978** (and thus 25 years before Portland), offers so much more than just a saving of time. For the South Dorset Ridgeway takes you through one of the most ancient landscapes in the UK. Very few – if any – walks in the UK will take you past such a wealth of **Neolithic, Bronze Age and Roman sites**, from burial chambers and barrows to stare holes and stone circles, not to mention a rash of tumuli like geological pimples pockmarking the ground. (For details of these various sites, see Appendix B, p314.)

It is an incredibly beautiful walk too. Those who have walked on the South Downs Way will find several similarities as they stroll along a chalk ridge with gigantic sweeping views over a terrain that falls away on either side of the trail; indeed, curiously, there are more views of the sea on this route than on the coast path. There is the wildlife, too, particularly birdlife, with raptors especially ubiquitous, including an abundance of buzzards, kestrels and even the odd kite soaring and swooping. There are skylarks aplenty, too, performing a vertical lift-off from the fields as if powered, seemingly, by nothing but song.

Of course, the 'official' coast path is not without its attractions too and we recognise that most people will stick to the seaside route, especially as it takes in the idiosyncratic isthmus of Portland which was added to the official trail in 2003. But we do urge you, if you have the time, to try to fit in at least a section of the Ridgeway as well. You'll find that Weymouth is a good base, with buses from there to Swyre for West Bexington in the morning and buses back from Osmington in the late afternoon and evening; see pp50-4 for details.

Note that there are **no refreshments** on the South Dorset Ridgeway until Osmington, less than a mile from the end of the trail, though a side-trip to Abbotsbury, three-quarters of a mile down the hill, is a viable option. Note, too, that just about the entire trek is on an **exposed ridge** so bring suitable rain-gear and sunblock to cover all weather possibilities.

The route

Leave West Bexington from the beach car park next to The Club House and follow the road up the hill, passing Manor House on your right. Where the road bends away keep heading straight up on a farm track to the summit of **Limekiln Hill** where the path meets and follows the B3157. Crossing several fields, you soon pass the first of a myriad of tumuli, or barrows, on the trail.

Traversing **Tulks Hill**, you cross the road to climb the western end of the ridge up to **Abbotsbury Castle**. Sitting proudly above the surrounding landscape, this triangular hill-fort is the most prominent of the Iron Age sites on the route, one of a string of such fortifications that include nearby Eggardon Hill Fort and much larger Maiden Castle, both of which are visible from here. Excavations have also yielded evidence of a Roman signal tower that was situated here and the site was, for centuries, the location for a warning beacon, used, for example, during the nation's wait for the arrival of the Spanish Armada.

ROUTE GUIDE AND MAPS

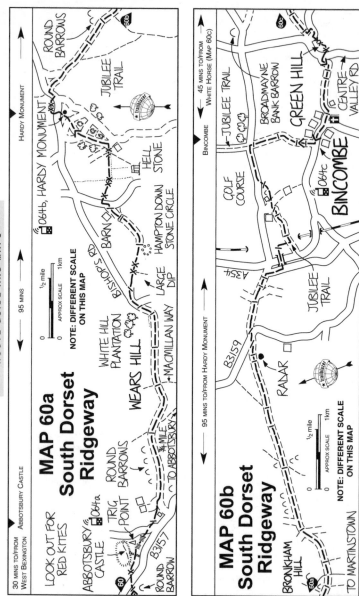

30 MINS TO/FROM WEST BEXINGTON ◀ ABBOTSBURY CASTLE ◀— 95 MINS —▶ HARDY MONUMENT ▶

MAP 60a
South Dorset
Ridgeway

LOOK OUT FOR RED KITES

ABBOTSBURY CASTLE 🏛 064a

TRIG POINT

ROUND BARROWS

TO ABBOTSBURY

¾ MILE

MACMILLAN WAY

WEARS HILL

WHITE HILL PLANTATION

BISHOP'S RD

BARN

LARGE DIP

HAMPTON DOWN STONE CIRCLE

HELL STONE

🏛 064b, HARDY MONUMENT

JUBILEE TRAIL

ROUND BARROWS

0   ½ mile
0   1km
APPROX SCALE
NOTE: DIFFERENT SCALE ON THIS MAP

ROUND BARROW

B3157

60

TO MARTINSTOWN

BRONKHAM HILL

60

MAP 60b
South Dorset
Ridgeway

0   ½ mile
0   1km
APPROX SCALE
NOTE: DIFFERENT SCALE ON THIS MAP

◀— 95 MINS TO/FROM HARDY MONUMENT —▶

RADAR

B3159

JUBILEE TRAIL

A354

GOLF COURSE

🏛 064c

BINCOMBE ◀— 45 MINS TO/FROM WHITE HORSE (Map 60c) —▶

JUBILEE TRAIL

BROADMAYNE BANK BARROW

GREEN HILL

CENTRE VALLEY RD

🏛 064c

BINCOMBE

60c

60c

Crossing a minor road after the castle, the trail dodges through numerous barrows as it heads to the summit of **Wears Hill**, with the western side of The Fleet ever increasing in size below you. St Catherine's Chapel comes into sight and a path offers access to Abbotsbury.

Cross the Macmillan Way (see p38) and continue past **White Hill Plantation** to Bishop's Rd from where you should follow the path to **Hampton Down Stone Circle**, an ancient monument thought to have been used for rituals and constructed around 2000BC.

An even more impressive prehistoric site lies nearby, just south of the path after Hampton Barn Farm. This is the dramatically named **Hell Stone**, a burial chamber or dolmen built around 6000 years ago that was restored, incorrectly by all accounts, in the 19th century. Hell Stone stands just to the south of the path: just before you enter the woods leading up to the Hardy Monument, turn south through the farm gate and walk across the field to the dolmen.

From here it's only a woodland walk to the **Hardy Monument** (🖥 nation altrust.org.uk/hardy-monument; Apr-Sep Wed-Sun 11am-4pm; £2), which commemorates Rear Admiral Sir Thomas Masterman Hardy (1769-1839), captain of *HMS Victory*, part of the fleet that won the Battle of Trafalgar in 1805 and, more famously, the man from whom Admiral Nelson requested a kiss as he lay dying from his wounds (Hardy complied with his friend's wishes, kissing his dying friend on the forehead). Built in 1844-5 the monument stands 22 metres (72ft) high and is owned by the National Trust.

After the monument the Ridgeway joins the Jubilee Trail (see p38) to reach **Bronkham Hill**, passing yet more prehistoric earthworks, before a 3¼-mile stroll amongst numerous barrows brings you to the Roman road between Dorchester and Weymouth, now known, more prosaically, as the **A354**. Excavations near here uncovered a mass grave of some 50 decapitated Scandinavians dating back to the Saxon Age.

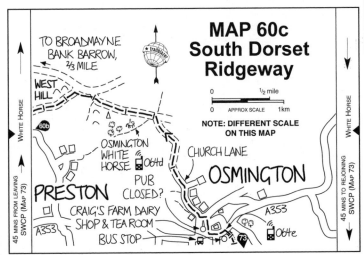

MAP 60c
South Dorset Ridgeway

NOTE: DIFFERENT SCALE ON THIS MAP

Crossing the busy road via a bridge, you follow a gravel path before the Jubilee Trail is again joined briefly, the two trails following the same route as they make their way to a minor road.

The spell on tarmac is brief and you soon leave the road, turning right – and south – on to a farm's driveway, finally leaving the Jubilee Trail behind as it veers away to the north. The path descends to the end of another minor road and on to the settlement of **Bincombe**, leaving it after the church to go through more fields to **Green Hill**.

Carrying on to **West Hill** and back on to the ridge, tumuli again rise peacefully from the earth as you pass a trig point and above the famous **Osmington White Horse** (see p280).

From here you make your last descent to pass through farmland leading to the end of Church Lane in **Osmington.** The local pub, The Sly Fox, recently closed down but there's a chance someone may have bought it and got it going again by the time you pass through the village.

On the way out of the village, *Craig's Farm Dairy Shop & Tea Room* (☎ 01305-834591, 🖥 craigsfarmdairy.co.uk; Mar-late Sep food served Mon-Sat 9am-4.30pm, Sun 10am-4pm, shop open till later, rest of year variable so contact them to check) is a decent little farm shop that sells fruit, cheeses, meats, ice-cream and coffee.

To reach the SWCP from here, head east along the A353, turning right off the road and passing through four fields on your way to **Osmington Mills** and a reunion with the coast path (see p280).

(Main route continued from p248) After more horizontal hiking the pebbles disappear and you're left to stroll on a four-wheel drive track, the scrub hemming you in on both sides.

Having passed **The Old Coastguards**, once a haunt of Thomas Hardy, a minor road (complete with **pill box**) ensues, the epic expanse of **Chesil Beach** now beginning to dominate the view in front of you.

Before you hit the western end of The Fleet (the lagoon behind Chesil Beach), and just after you pass *Beach Café* (daily 9am-4pm), a small café shack, which is open all year and sells bacon baps (£3.95), pasties (£2.95), cakes (£2.20) and coffee, the path takes a left and climbs as if heading towards the 15th-century **St Catherine's Chapel** (Map 62). St Catherine, incidentally, is the patron saint of spinsters and women are said to visit the church in desperate search of husbands. Gentlemen trekkers – you have been warned.

The climb towards the chapel affords your first views of **West Fleet** – and, if you're lucky, the mute swans of **Abbotsbury Swannery** (see p256).

Rounding the hill, the path veers off to the right and you arrive at a junction of two paths: turn left for the village or turn right to cross over a small stream and arrive at a stile next to an impressive plane tree. Turning left here will also lead you into **Abbotsbury** itself; or you can turn right and follow the road onwards along the coastal path, past the entrance to the swannery.

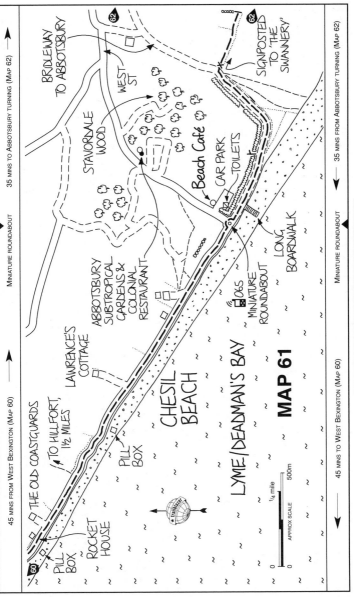

MINIATURE ROUNDABOUT

BRIDLEWAY TO ABBOTSBURY

62

62

SIGNPOSTED TO 'THE SWANNERY'

WEST ST

STAVORDALE WOOD

Beach Café

CAR PARK

TOILETS

MINIATURE ROUNDABOUT

LONG BOARDWALK

ABBOTSBURY SUBTROPICAL GARDENS & COLONIAL RESTAURANT

B3065 MINIATURE ROUNDABOUT

LAWRENCE'S COTTAGE

CHESIL BEACH

LYME/DEADMAN'S BAY

MAP 61

THE OLD COASTGUARDS

TO HILLFORT, 1½ MILES

PILL BOX

PILL BOX

ROCKET HOUSE

60

¼ mile

0   500m
APPROX SCALE
0

trailblazer

ROUTE GUIDE AND MAPS

ABBOTSBURY [map below]

Rich in English history, the pristine little village of Abbotsbury (🖳 abbotsbury.co .uk) is one of the highlights of the whole walk – there's nowhere else along the whole of the coast path quite like it. There is a reasonable amount of accommodation – although booking ahead, especially in summer, is advisable – and it's a great place to stop for lunch, a coffee or a cream tea.

Sight-wise, the most important buildings are the **remains of the Benedictine Abbey of St Peter**, which was founded in the 11th century; the accompanying **Tithe Barn**, which at 272ft is the longest in England (indeed, when they rethatched the roof in 2006, so enormous was the task that it took three years to complete), and which is now part of **Abbotsbury Children's Farm** (☎ 01305-871817, 🖳 abbotsbury-tourism.co.uk/childrens_farm; mid Mar- mid Sep and Oct half-term daily 10am- 5pm, mid Sep to end Oct weekends only; adult/child £11/9.50); and **St Catherine's Chapel** (see p254), which, like Tithe Barn, was a 15th-century addition to the village.

Having survived the Black Death and other invasions, the abbey finally met its match in the Dissolution under Henry VIII and was destroyed in 1538. The barn, however, supposedly resisted the same fate due to its multitude of uses, while the chapel survived due to its importance as a

navigational aid to those sailing in Lyme Bay. Dotted amongst them are several **cottages** that date back to the 16th century or earlier, with many of them incorporating materials from the demolished abbey.

The monks were also responsible for the **Swannery** (☎ 01305-871858, 🖳 abbots bury-tourism.co.uk/swannery; daily 10am- 5pm; £12.50; strictly no dogs), established in the 11th century to supply the fare for their tables. The swans are somewhat luckier today and hundreds reside here. If you're a sucker for a cygnet plan your trip for between mid-May and late June when they are hatching. There's a *café* (daily 11am-4.30pm) by the entrance, which is handy if you're passing through without visiting Abbotsbury.

In the centre of the village, the 14th- century **Church of St Nicholas** remains scarred by the English Civil War – the Grade-I listed tower still bearing the marks of musket fire, shot whilst the Cavaliers had the Roundheads under siege within its walls. Along West St, is the unusual **Clock Work Shop** (☎ 01305-873852, 🖳 dorset antiqueclocks.co.uk; Mon-Fri 9am-5pm, Sat 10am-4pm), which has a first-floor showroom displaying dozens of elegant and largely very rare pieces, including a 1650 balance-wheel lantern clock that is valued at £12,500.

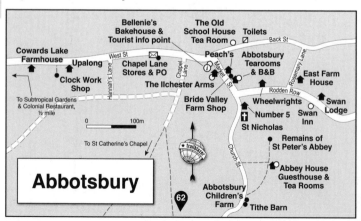

Abbotsbury

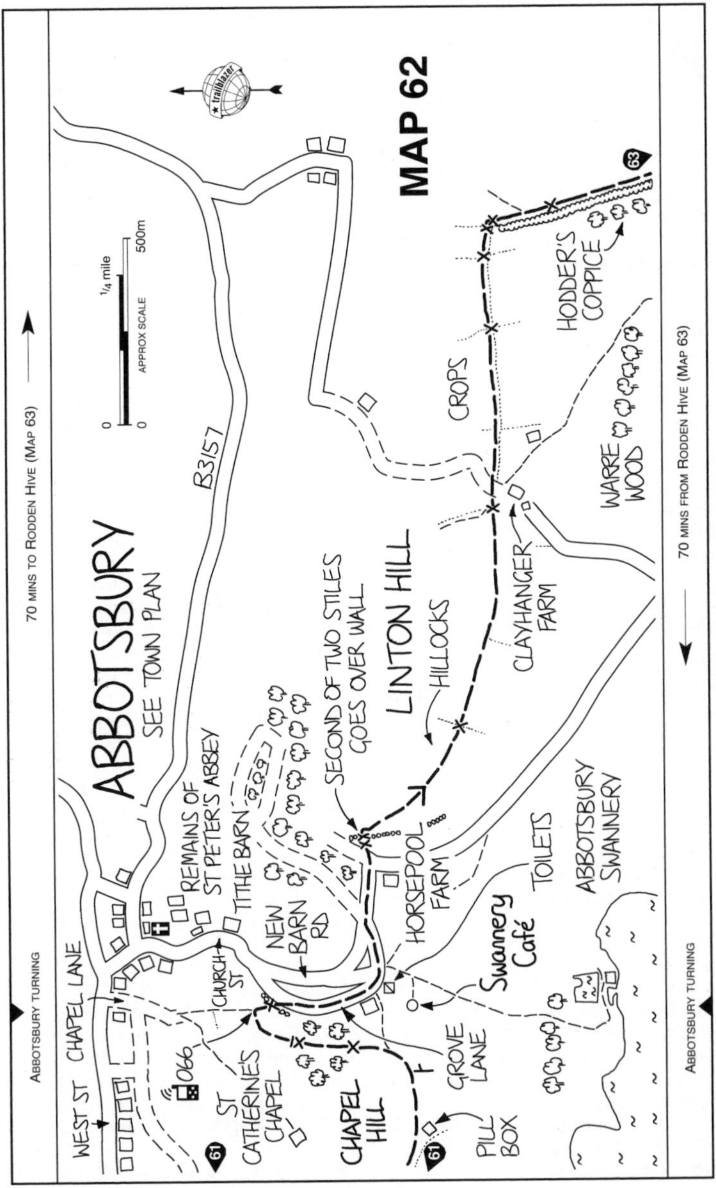
70 mins to Rodden Hive (Map 63)
70 mins from Rodden Hive (Map 63)
Abbotsbury turning
Abbotsbury turning
MAP 62
APPROX SCALE
0
1/4 mile
0
500m
trailblazer
ABBOTSBURY
SEE TOWN PLAN
B3157
WEST ST
CHAPEL LANE
CHURCH ST
REMAINS OF ST PETER'S ABBEY
TITHE BARN
NEW BARN RD
066
ST CATHERINE'S CHAPEL
CHAPEL HILL
GROVE LANE
PILL BOX
HORSEPOOL FARM
Swannery Café
TOILETS
ABBOTSBURY SWANNERY
SECOND OF TWO STILES GOES OVER WALL
LINTON HILL
HILLOCKS
CLAYHANGER FARM
CROPS
WARRE WOOD
HODDER'S COPPICE
61
61
63

About half a mile further west (turn left off West St into Cleverlawns), the **Subtropical Gardens** (Map 61; ☎ 01305-871387, ☐ abbotsbury-tourism.co.uk/gardens; Mar-Oct daily 10am-5pm, Nov-Mar to 4pm, closed mid to end Dec; 🐕 if on a lead; £12.50), on Bullers Way, were originally established in 1765 as the first Countess of Ilchester's kitchen garden. Today the 20 acres are filled with rare and exotic plants – and an eatery, *The Colonial Restaurant* (☎ 01305-871732; daily 10am-4.30pm, food till 3pm).

Services

There is a **tourist information point** (ie a table piled with leaflets) in Bellenie's Bakehouse (see Where to eat). The **post office** is inside the well-stocked **Chapel Lane Stores** (summer Mon-Sat 7am-7pm, Sun 8am-6pm, winter closing earlier).

You can also get supplies such as local cheeses, cold meats, honey and jam, at **Bride Valley Farm Shop** (☎ 01305-871235, ☐ www.dorsetlonghorn.co.uk; Mon 10am-2pm, Wed 9am-2pm, Tue & Thur-Fri 9am-5pm, Sat 8.30am-4.30pm, but best to check as these hours can vary).

Transport

[See pp50-4] First's X53 (Axminster to Weymouth) **bus** service passes through as does the seasonal SLOWcoaster 510 (Bridport to Weymouth); the latter is more expensive than the X53 and of course takes longer.

Where to stay

Abbotsbury has several **B&Bs**, some of which are surprisingly affordable. Those walking with a dog should try either *Cowards Lake Farmhouse* (☎ 01305-871421, ☐ www.abbotsbury.co.uk/cowards-lake-farm-house; 1D/1T; 📶; WI-FI; 🐕; from £40pp, sgl occ from £55) or *Number 5* (☎ 01305-871882, ☐ candcrawlings@gmail.com; 1D, shared facilities; WI-FI; 🐕; from £27.50pp, sgl occ from £50) as both welcome dogs.

At the time of writing new people were taking over *Upalong* (☎ 07775 681081, ☐ bobhure@gmail.com; 1D; 📶; WI-FI; from

£47.50pp, sgl occ rate on request), on West St, and it was due to open in March 2018. The new owners said the B&B's name might change, although any new name will probably still have the word Upalong in it.

Abbey House Guest House (☎ 01305-871330, ☐ theabbeyhouse.co.uk; 2T/3D; 📶; WI-FI; £37.50-62.50pp, sgl occ £75-110) is typical of the kind of accommodation available in the village, being both gorgeous and ancient. The place actually dates back to the 15th century when it was part of the abbey's infirmary and overlooks the abbey today, its grounds (parts of which are now given over to the tearoom – see Where to eat) sloping down to the duck-filled millpond. Do settings get any better? Rooms are individual, as you'd expect, with one attic room and others with king-size or half-tester beds.

Another recommended eatery-cum-B&B is *Abbotsbury Tearooms* (☎ 01305-871757, ☐ abbotsbury-tearooms.co.uk; 1D/2Tr; 📶; WI-FI; Mar-Oct; from £47.50pp, sgl occ rates on request) at 26 Rodden Row. Nearby is *Wheelwrights* (☎ 01305-871800, ☐ wheelwrights.co.uk; 1D or T; WI-FI; from £45pp, sgl occ from £75), a thatched cottage at 14 Rodden Row.

Also very central, at 6 Market St, is the lovely *Peach's* (☎ 01305-871364, ☐ abbotsburybandb.co.uk; 1S/1D; WI-FI; from £35pp, sgl/sgl occ from £50pp).

With a long and interesting history (an arch that can be seen in one of the walls is thought by some to date back as far as the 11th century!), *The Ilchester Arms* (☎ 01305-873841, ☐ theilchester.co.uk; 7D/2T; 📶; WI-FI; 🐕; from £42.50pp, sgl occ rates on request) is an old pub with rooms on Market St in the very heart of the village. Food is also provided (see Where to eat).

Further east the 17th-century Dorset longhouse at *East Farm House* (☎ 01305-871363, ☐ www.eastfarmhouse.co.uk; 2D/1T; WI-FI; from £42.50pp, sgl occ room rate) is now an equine-centric farm on the edge of the village centre, with stables in the back courtyard, while on the eastern extremity of the village is *Swan Lodge* (☎ 01305-871249, ☐ swan-inn.net; 2T/3D; 📶; WI-FI; 🐕; from £42.50pp, sgl occ from

£65) across the road from – and owned by – Swan Inn (see Where to eat).

Where to eat and drink

It probably won't come as any surprise to find that there is no shortage of **tearooms** in Abbotsbury. One of the smartest is *Abbey House Tea Rooms* (see Where to stay; Mar-Oct daily 10am-5pm), with excellent cream teas to gorge on while watching the ducks frolic in the pond below. Nor is it the only B&B with a tearoom attached, with *Abbotsbury Tearooms* (see Where to stay; Mar-Oct daily noon-5pm) also operating a nice little sideline in baked comestibles.

Two more tearooms face each other in the centre of the village. *The Old School House Tea Room* (☎ 01305-871808; school holidays daily 10am-5.30pm, rest of year Tue/Wed-Sun 10.30am-4.30pm but can vary in the winter months; closed mid Dec to end Jan; 🐕) is known for its 'set teas' that include sandwiches, scone, cake and a pot of tea, the exact price depending on the filling in the sandwich (£9.95-14.95). It has a lovely little patio garden out back, a delightful hostess, dogs are welcome and there is also a great selection of cakes. A standard cream tea costs £4.65.

Bellenie's Bakehouse & Tea-Room (☎ 01305-871990; 🐕; Feb to mid Dec Wed-Mon 7.30am-5pm) proudly boasts of its award-winning cakes such as a delicious farmhouse fruitcake but also has a magnificent cream tea; as hosts of the village's tourist information point, they also have a good selection of brochures to browse while you tuck in.

The pubs and inns are the most reliable places to head for dinner. *The Ilchester Arms* (see Where to stay; food daily 8-10.30am, Mon-Fri noon-2.30pm & 6-9pm, Sat noon-9pm, Sun noon-8pm; 🐕) is the focal point of the village come evening and has an à la carte restaurant (mains £11-14) with fish specialities, plus plenty of real ales. It also opens for breakfast each day. On the outskirts of town, *Swan Inn* (see Swan Lodge, Where to stay; food daily summer 11am-9pm, winter 11.30am-2.30pm & 6-9pm; 🐕) has a wide range of fairly simple but filling fare such as braised pork in cider and apple sauce with veg.

ROUTE GUIDE AND MAPS

ABBOTSBURY TO FORTUNESWELL [MAPS 62-68]

This **13-mile (21km; 4hrs 20 mins)** day starts with a 3-mile hike along a ridge and through fields that, at times, can feel a long way from the sea. It is however, good walking. There are great views over the surrounding countryside as you make your way through the farmland, eventually arriving at the western end of The Fleet – the great expanse of water that separates the mainland from the large pebble ridge of Chesil Beach and also a nature reserve.

The rest of the stage is largely spent on the flat. Following the lakeshore, interrupted only by Chickerell Rifle Range (should target practice forbid your passing there is an easy alternative), you eventually arrive at Ferrybridge in Wyke Regis, from where you can either cross the *tombolo* (sand bar) to the Isle of Portland (round hike from Ferrybridge and back 13 miles/21km; 5½hrs), or continue on into Weymouth (3 miles/5km; 1hr 10 mins). There is accommodation in both places and to get to both there are buses.

This may not be the most exciting stage and the relative lack of refreshments until you reach the suburbs of Weymouth/Portland is irksome. Luckily, there are plenty of places along the banks of The Fleet that make great locations for a picnic. Accommodation-wise, there are numerous options for campers, and a pricey manor-house hotel, but little else.

The route

To leave Abbotsbury village head down Church St, passing St Nicholas Church and Tithe Barn, before turning off down a minor road – Grove Lane – signed to The Swannery. Carry on straight down the lane and you are soon on the coastal path again by the gorgeous plane tree.

Passing the entrance to The Swannery (see p256), you leave the road on a bend to cross a stile then, almost immediately cross another to get over a wall, before following the path up over fields with St Catherine's Chapel watching your progress from the rear and the western end of The Fleet now clearly visible to your right. The path follows a ridge with an idyllic pastoral landscape to the right that gently recedes towards Chesil Beach. This ridge is followed until a sharp turn sends you down and right, briefly along the outskirts of **Hodder's Coppice**, before more fields take you to the edges of **Wyke Wood**. Having briefly followed Bridge Lane you pass a house marked 'private' on your right and, crossing a few more fields, you reach **Rodden Hive** and **Fleet Lagoon Nature Reserve**.

Despite the path's occasional brief diversion away from the water's edge (such as at **Herbury**) you never stray too far from The Fleet and its flapping feathery frequenters. Much of the walking is along the edge of farmland, interrupted only by the odd field boundary.

Campers are spoilt for choice along this stretch. They can find a pitch at *Bagwell Farm Campsite* (off Map 63; ☎ 01305-782575, 💻 bagwellfarm.co.uk; WI-FI; 🐾; £11-21/13-23 for a tent and one/two adults), which has its own restaurant (Easter-Oct) and shop and offers £2-5 discounts for sloping pitches. It's signposted half a mile from the path. Close by, and also half a mile from the path, is *West Fleet Holiday Farm* (off Map 63; ☎ 01305-782218, 💻 westfleet holidays.co.uk; WI-FI; 🐾 on lead at all times; Easter-Sep; £10-23/14-27 for a tent and one/two adults), which has an outdoor pool (seasonal), and usually gives hikers a discount. Just beyond this is *Sea Barn Farm* (phone as for West Fleet; 💻 www.seabarnfarm.co.uk; 🍺; WI-FI; 🐾 on lead at all times; mid Mar-early Oct) which charges the same as West Fleet but has better views. Follow the 'farm path' signs from the coast path just after the racecourse.

A little further along, *East Fleet Farm Touring Park* (Map 64; ☎ 01305-785768, 💻 eastfleet.co.uk; from £14 for a pitch plus £2.50-5 per additional person; 🐾; mid Mar-Oct) is right on the path and also very well equipped.

Just before the racecourse you'll pass *Moonfleet Manor Hotel & Restaurant* (☎ 01305-786948, 💻 moonfleetmanorhotel.co.uk; 36 rooms inc 3D/14D or T and rooms sleeping up to six people; 🍺; variable WI-FI; 🐾; from £60pp, sgl occ from £105), a 17th-century manor house that's been converted into a hotel. It's perhaps a touch too expensive to stay here, but passing walkers are welcome to swing by for lunch (noon-2pm), afternoon tea (2-5.30pm) or dinner (7.30-9.15pm). You can even just pop in for a coffee or a cold beer.

Chickerell Rifle Range is eventually reached. **If the red flags are flying do not enter** but follow the short detour to the north instead. You then pass by a caravan park before heading towards an **army training centre**, after which

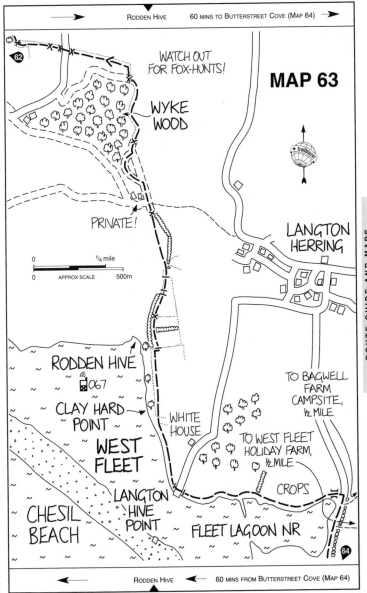

62

WATCH OUT
FOR FOX-HUNTS!

MAP 63

WYKE
WOOD

trailblazer

PRIVATE!

0   ¼ mile
APPROX SCALE
0   500m

LANGTON
HERRING

RODDEN HIVE

067

CLAY HARD
POINT

WEST
FLEET

WHITE
HOUSE

TO BAGWELL
FARM
CAMPSITE,
½ MILE

TO WEST FLEET
HOLIDAY FARM,
½ MILE

CROPS

CHESIL
BEACH

LANGTON
HIVE
POINT

FLEET LAGOON NR

64

ROUTE GUIDE AND MAPS

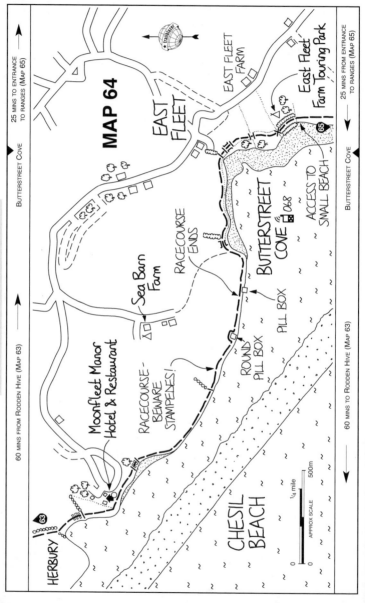

MAP 64

60 MINS FROM RODDEN HIVE (Map 63)

25 MINS TO ENTRANCE TO RANGES (Map 65)

BUTTERSTREET COVE

EAST FLEET

EAST FLEET FARM

East Fleet Farm Touring Park

65

25 MINS FROM ENTRANCE TO RANGES (Map 65)

BUTTERSTREET COVE

ACCESS TO SMALL BEACH

BUTTERSTREET COVE ☐068

PILL BOX

Sea Barn Farm

RACECOURSE ENDS

ROUND PILL BOX

Moonfleet Manor Hotel & Restaurant

RACECOURSE-BEWARE STAMPEDES!

HERBURY 63

CHESIL BEACH

60 MINS TO RODDEN HIVE (Map 63)

¼ mile

APPROX SCALE

0   500m

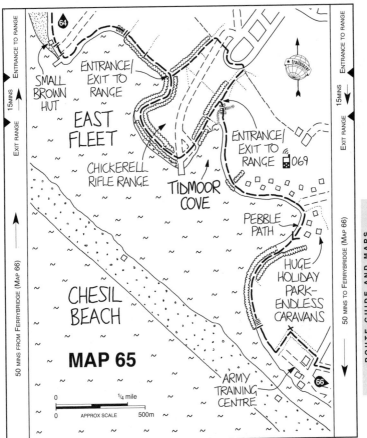

the path turns east by the water's edge to cross level grassland and pasture with the eastern end of Chesil Beach in your sights and with Portland becoming ever clearer. Strolling past chalets on your left you arrive at a minor road where over your left shoulder you'll see the popular *Crab House Café* (☎ 01305-788867, 🖥 crabhousecafe.co.uk; WI-FI; Feb-mid Dec Wed-Sun noon-2.30pm & Wed-Thur 6-9pm, Fri-Sat 6-9.30pm, Sun peak season 6-8.30pm), which specialises in seafood.

From here it's a short hop to **Ferrybridge** where a choice needs to be made; for Portland and the continuation of the path (see p265), or to continue onwards from Ferrybridge, crossing the road and heading into Weymouth. There are **buses**, too, to both Portland and Weymouth from Ferrybridge: First's No 1 (Weymouth–Portland), No 501 (Weymouth–Portland Bill) and their SLOWcoaster 510 (Bridport to Weymouth); see pp50-4. For the trek into Weymouth, see p274.

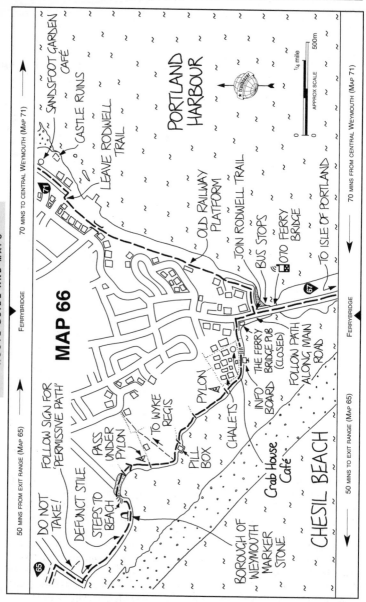

MAP 66

50 MINS FROM EXIT RANGE (MAP 65)

FERRYBRIDGE

70 MINS TO CENTRAL WEYMOUTH (MAP 71)

DO NOT TAKE!

FOLLOW SIGN FOR 'PERMISSIVE PATH'

DEFUNCT STILE

PASS UNDER PYLON

STEPS TO BEACH

SANDSFOOT GARDEN CAFÉ

CASTLE RUINS

LEAVE RODWELL TRAIL

PORTLAND HARBOUR

71

OLD RAILWAY PLATFORM

JOIN RODWELL TRAIL

BUS STOPS

TO TO FERRY BRIDGE

TO ISLE OF PORTLAND

67

THE FERRY BRIDGE PUB (CLOSED)

FOLLOW PATH ALONG MAIN ROAD

INFO BOARD

CHALETS

PYLON

TO WYKE REGIS

PILL BOX

Crab House Café

BOROUGH OF WEYMOUTH MARKER STONE

CHESIL BEACH

¼ mile

APPROX SCALE

0   500m

trailblazer

50 MINS TO EXIT RANGE (MAP 65)

FERRYBRIDGE

70 MINS FROM CENTRAL WEYMOUTH (MAP 71)

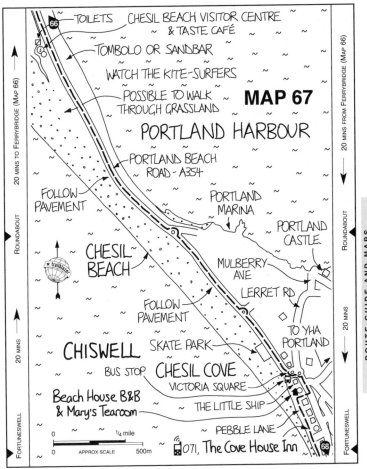

For the continuation to Portland, turn right and follow the tombolo on a dreary 2-mile roadside trudge – it's well worth breaking the journey at the excellent **Chesil Beach Visitor Centre** (Map 67; ☎ 01305-206191, 🖥 chesil beach.org/cbvc; daily 10am-5pm, till 4pm in winter), which houses the award-winning *Taste Café* (☎ 01305-206196, 🖥 tastecafeatchesilbeach.co.uk; WI-FI; same hours), a gift shop, and numerous interactive displays detailing the unique coastline here. They also have free-to-use binoculars for visitors (for use in the centre only).

Back on the path towards Portland, three roundabouts are eventually crossed, the third furnished with a bus stop and The Little Ship pub.

There is a hostel here, **YHA Portland** (off Map 67; ☎ 0345-371 9339, 💻 yha.org.uk/hostel/portland; 1 x 4-/3 x 6-/1 x 8-bed rooms; dorm beds from £13pp, private room from £39) in Hardy House on Castle Rd. One of the 6-bed rooms is en suite. Meals are available but there is also a self-catering kitchen. **Camping** (from £12pp; 🐾) is offered on its back lawn and there are two **bell tents** (mid Apr-Sep; sleep up to 5 people £49-99 inc bedding). It does get busy, though, so book in advance if possible.

Back on the main road, continue past *Beach House B&B & Mary's Tearoom* (☎ 01305-821155, 💻 beach-house-bandb.co.uk; 4D/2T/1Tr; wi-fi; £40pp, sgl occ £55), which has modern rooms and a cute **tearoom** (early Feb to end Nov Tue-Sat 10am-4pm, summer months also Sun 10am-4pm; wi-fi; 🐾), before turning right into Pebble Lane, following it as far as **Chiswell** and *The Cove House Inn* (Map 67; ☎ 01305-820895, 💻 thecovehouseinn.co.uk; wi-fi; 🐾 bar area; food Mon-Fri noon-2.30pm & 6-9pm, Sat & Sun noon-9pm), a friendly pub which serves decent pub grub and real ales; customers spill out onto the promenade on sunny evenings.

From here continue to **Fortuneswell**.

FORTUNESWELL   [Map 68]

Scruffy Fortuneswell isn't the most charismatic of stops on the path. For a night it's fine, but it's much more atmospheric to stay at Portland Bill if you can.

Services on Fortuneswell (the road that runs through the village) include a Co-op **supermarket** (Mon-Sat 7am-10pm) with a free **ATM** inside it, a Boots **pharmacy** (Mon-Fri 9am-5.30pm, Sat 9am-1pm), and a **post office** (Mon-Sat 5am-8pm, Sun 6am-4pm).

Several places here provide accommodation and food; as you come into Fortuneswell, there's *Beach House B&B & Mary's Tearoom* (see above).

Up the hill, at 2-4 Fortuneswell, is the very smart *Queen Anne House* (☎ 01305-820028, 💻 queen annehouse.com; 4D; 🛏; wi-fi; £40-47.50pp, sgl occ £55-70), while higher still, and overlooking the town below, is *The Heights Hotel* (☎ 01305-821361, 💻 heightshotel.com; 66D or T; 🛏; wi-fi; £40-85pp, sgl occ £80-150), on Yeates Rd. It's a modern place which serves decent café and restaurant food all day (daily 7am-9pm; wi-fi) and has panoramic windows to make the most of the great views.

There are numerous other choices for food, but perhaps the most popular for coast path walkers is *The Cove House Inn* (see above). Close by are two cafés: *Mary's Tearoom*, which is attached to Beach House B&B (see above), and the tiny, but very popular *Quiddles* (☎ 01305-820651; daily 9am-sunset but out of school holidays meals only served to 2.30pm, after that only snacks and cakes; in the school holidays also open in evenings Thur-Sat), which has a choice location on the promenade, overlooking West Weare beach. There are a few seats inside but most punters sit on the patio outside; there's also a roof terrace. They specialise in seafood, but do normal café fare too.

There's a good chippy, *Daniel's Fish & Chips* (☎ 01305-821292, 💻 danielsfish andchips.co.uk; Mon-Thur noon-1.30pm & 5-9.30pm, Fri & Sat noon-2pm & 5-10pm, Sun 5-9pm) opposite the Co-op, at 86 Fortuneswell.

For **buses**, First's No 1 service travels regularly between Weymouth and Portland. First also operates a seasonal service (501) between Weymouth and Portland Bill. See pp50-4 for details.

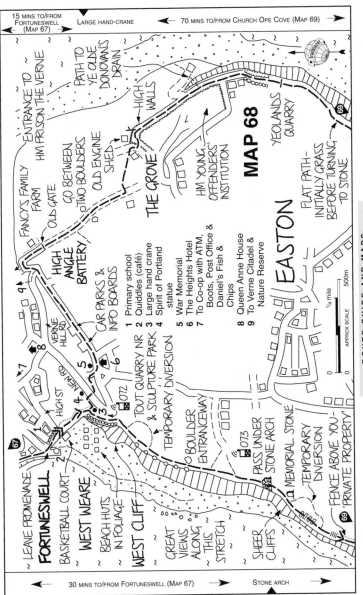

15 MINS TO/FROM FORTUNESWELL (MAP 67)

LARGE HAND-CRANE

70 MINS TO/FROM CHURCH OPE COVE (MAP 69)

PATH TO YE OLDE DONOVAN'S DRAIN

HIGH WALLS

MAP 68

YEOLANDS QUARRY

ENTRANCE TO HM PRISON THE VERNE

GO BETWEEN TWO BOULDERS

OLD ENGINE SHED

HM YOUNG OFFENDERS' INSTITUTION

FANCY'S FAMILY FARM

OLD GATE

THE GROVE

FLAT PATH- INITIALLY GRASS BEFORE TURNING TO STONE

HIGH ANGLE BATTERY

EASTON

CAR PARKS & INFO BOARDS

VERNE HILL RD

1 Primary school
2 Quiddles (café)
3 Large hand crane
4 Spirit of Portland statue
5 War Memorial
6 The Heights Hotel
7 To Co-op with ATM, Boots, Post Office & Daniel's Fish & Chips
8 Queen Anne House
9 To Verne Citadel & Nature Reserve

TOUT QUARRY NR & SCULPTURE PARK

TEMPORARY DIVERSION

NEW RD

HIGH ST

1072

¼ mile

APPROX SCALE

500m

ROUTE GUIDE AND MAPS

FORTUNESWELL

LEANE PROMENADE

BASKETBALL COURT

WEST WEARE

BEACH HUTS IN FOLIAGE

WEST CLIFF

GREAT VIEWS ALONG THIS STRETCH

GO BOULDER ENTRANCEWAY

1073

PASS UNDER STONE ARCH

TEMPORARY DIVERSION

SHEER CLIFFS

MEMORIAL STONE

FENCE ABOVE YOU- PRIVATE PROPERTY

30 MINS TO/FROM FORTUNESWELL (MAP 67)

STONE ARCH

FORTUNESWELL TO WEYMOUTH   [MAPS 68-71]
(VIA THE ISLE OF PORTLAND CIRCUIT)

Today's multifaceted **14¾-mile (23.75km; 5hrs 25mins)** walk around the wild
and intriguing Isle of Portland (see box below) is an adventure like no other on
this trek. Connected to the mainland by two miles of road, the isle feels somehow estranged from the rest of Dorset as if cast away – without ever truly being
able to free itself from the mainland's grasp.

With a landscape that encompasses lonely clifftops, surreal boulders, disused quarries, housing and industrial estates, MoD compounds, prisons and
institutions, nature reserves, a 13th-century church and three lighthouses, there
is little likelihood of you becoming bored on this great slab of limestone.
Wildlife abounds too, with over half of Britain's 57 butterfly species in residence and birdlife visiting the isle in such numbers that one of the three lighthouses has been turned into a bird observatory. Basking sharks, dolphins and
seals also inhabit the waters offshore.

ROUTE GUIDE AND MAPS

❏ The Isle of Portland

Six kilometres long, two-and-a-half kilometres wide and made of limestone, the Isle
of Portland is what is known as a **tied island**, connected to the mainland by a sand-
bar, or tombolo – which, in Portland's case, is better known as the A354. The island
today is most famous for Portland stone, a durable, good-looking material used in the
building of Buckingham Palace and St Paul's Cathedral (the latter, incidentally,
designed by Christopher Wren who was once MP for Weymouth and controlled the
quarries on Portland). The stone was also used for thousands of gravestones during
the two world wars.

The isle is divided into two main areas: the northern, steeply sloping **Underhill**
(which has been visible for many miles) and the flatter, plateau-like southern expanse
of **Tophill**. The isle slopes down from approximately 150 metres above sea-level near
The Verne, atop Underhill, to just above sea-level by the time that you reach Portland
Bill. There are eight settlements, the two most relevant to the walker being Chiswell
and Fortuneswell (for both see p266). Although close enough to be almost indistin-
guishable, Chiswell consists of the flatter area near Chesil Cove and the sea (ie the
home of The Cove Inn) whilst Fortuneswell is made up of the sloping streets that lead
up from the hill.

The most prominent tourist attraction on the island – save, perhaps, for the lighthouse at Portland Bill – is **Portland Castle** (Map 67; ☎ 01305-820539, 🖳 english-
heritage.org.uk; daily Apr-Sep 10am-6pm, Oct 10am-5pm, closed Nov-Mar; £5.70).
Known as a 'Device Fort' or 'Henrician Castle', it was constructed (using Portland
Stone, of course) on the orders of Henry VIII in 1540 in order to defend Weymouth
from attack by the French and Spanish. Possibly due to the quality of the stone it is
one of the best-preserved castles from this era. The fortress can be visited easily
enough from Fortuneswell.

One final tip: whilst a guest on the isle be wary of using the word 'rabbit'.
Records suggest that superstitious quarry workers would always see a bunny emerging from its burrow immediately before a rockfall. Such was their superstition, they
often refused to work if one was spotted! The unusual moniker 'underground mutton'
is how the locals are said to refer to our furry friends.

The path is generally easy on the legs, but with a couple of short ascents around the Underhill area, and there are some places to stop for food, including one excellent café near the isle's southern tip, where you can also find two places with hostel-type accommodation and a pub with rooms. To return to the mainland the coast path suggests you need to walk the tombolo twice – though buses also cross the tombolo frequently between Fortuneswell and Ferrybridge.

The route

From The Cove House Inn the path now briefly follows the edge of Chesil Cove, turning left and then right to head up the steep path to **West Cliff**, with the beach huts and boulders of **West Weare** below you. At the very top of the steps turn back for a great view over Portland Harbour: one of the largest man-made harbours in the world, it was formed by the construction of huge stone breakwaters between 1848 and 1905.

Via a short, signposted, diversion the path now heads through disused **Tout Quarry**, a nature reserve and sculpture park. As you walk alongside the boulders, under stone archways and with some sheer drops to your right, there are marvellous views back down along the whole of Chesil Beach. This exposed cliff-top path contrasts starkly with yesterday's agrarian amble.

After another small diversion, the path gradually bends south and widens, with housing estates interrupting the scenery on the left and a **business park** doing similar work straight ahead. Passing this, you descend gradually across grasslands; watch out for the odd sprouting of barbed wire lying in wait in the scrub to snare the unwary.

On the way you come to a **coastguard's lookout station** and the **Old (Higher) Lighthouse** – the light from which first guided sailors in 1716 – one of three lighthouses at Portland Bill. Just after this you'll pass *Portland Bunkhouse* (☎ 07710-797447, 🖳 portlandbunkhouse.com; 38 beds in rooms with 2/4 bunks sleeping 4/8 people; from £17pp; WI-FI; 🐾), a former transmitter station with windowless rooms, cheap metal-framed bunkbeds and a musty smell throughout. The self-catering kitchen is OK, but the rest of the place lacks natural light so it's only worth staying here if the far nicer bird-observatory dorms (see p271) are full.

Continuing down hill, you soon get to *The Pulpit Inn* (☎ 01305-821237, 🖳 thepulpitinnportland.co.uk; 3D; intermittent WI-FI; 🐾 bar only; from £42.50pp, sgl occ room rate), an old pub that got a refurb in 2014 and which has three simple **B&B** doubles, one of which (from £110) can also sleep two children and now does **food** (summer daily noon-8.30pm, winter noon-3.30pm & 6-8pm but see below). Their pub-grub mains cost £10-15, although they also have fish specials, and do sandwiches and jackets (£5-8) before 5pm. Opening times can be a bit hit and miss, especially in bad weather, so it's worth calling ahead.

From the pub, you soon reach the highlight and focal point of most people's Portland Isle tour: the striking, red-and-white painted **Portland Bill Lighthouse** (☎ 01305-821050, 🖳 trinityhouse.co.uk/lighthouses; visiting hours vary but generally Apr-Sep daily 10am-5pm, Oct & Feb-Mar Tue-Thur & Sat-Sun 10am-3pm, Nov-Jan Sat-Sun 11am-3pm; visitor centre £3, guided tour £7),

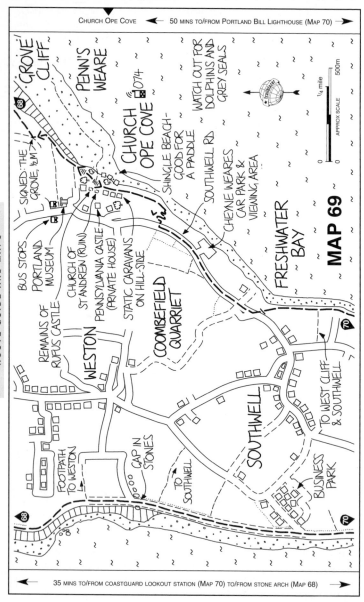

CHURCH OPE COVE ← 50 MINS TO/FROM PORTLAND BILL LIGHTHOUSE (MAP 70) →

GROVE CLIFF

PENN'S WEARE

CHURCH OPE COVE 107+

WATCH OUT FOR DOLPHINS AND GREY SEALS

SIGNED: THE GROVE, ½ M →

SHINGLE BEACH - GOOD FOR A PADDLE

SOUTHWELL RD

CHEYNE WEARES CAR PARK & VIEWING AREA

¼ mile

500m

APPROX SCALE

MAP 69

BUS STOPS

PORTLAND MUSEUM

CHURCH OF ST ANDREW (RUIN)

PENNSYLVANIA CASTLE (PRIVATE HOUSE)

STATIC CARAVANS ON HILL-SIDE

FRESHWATER BAY

REMAINS OF RUFUS CASTLE

WESTON

COOMBEFIELD QUARRIET

SOUTHWELL

TO WEST CLIFF & SOUTHWELL

FOOTPATH TO WESTON

GAP IN STONES

TO SOUTHWELL

BUSINESS PARK

35 MINS TO/FROM COASTGUARD LOOKOUT STATION (MAP 70) TO/FROM STONE ARCH (MAP 68) →

ROUTE GUIDE AND MAPS

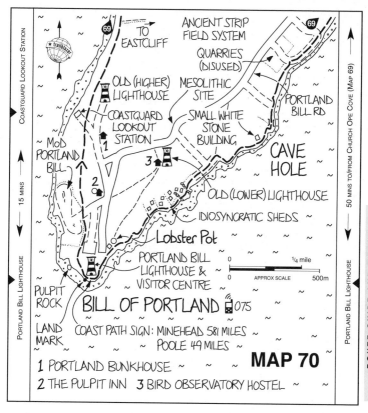

COASTGUARD LOOKOUT STATION

15 MINS

PORTLAND BILL LIGHTHOUSE

50 MINS TO/FROM CHURCH OPE COVE (MAP 69)

PORTLAND BILL LIGHTHOUSE

ROUTE GUIDE AND MAPS

Map content labels:

69

TO EASTCLIFF

ANCIENT STRIP FIELD SYSTEM

QUARRIES (DISUSED)

69

OLD (HIGHER) LIGHTHOUSE

MESOLITHIC SITE

PORTLAND BILL RD

trailblazer

COASTGUARD LOOKOUT STATION

SMALL WHITE STONE BUILDING

CAVE HOLE

MoD PORTLAND BILL

1

3

OLD (LOWER) LIGHTHOUSE

2

IDIOSYNCRATIC SHEDS

Lobster Pot

PORTLAND BILL LIGHTHOUSE & VISITOR CENTRE

0   ¼ mile
0   500m
APPROX SCALE

BILL OF PORTLAND   075

PULPIT ROCK

LAND MARK

COAST PATH SIGN: MINEHEAD 581 MILES
POOLE 49 MILES

MAP 70

1 PORTLAND BUNKHOUSE
2 THE PULPIT INN   3 BIRD OBSERVATORY HOSTEL

which was built between 1905 and 1906, is still a working lighthouse and now houses Portland's **Visitor Centre**. A stone's throw away is **Pulpit Rock**, a remarkably square-looking rock stack, formed during quarrying in the 1870s and which can be climbed.

Close to the lighthouse, and commanding a fabulous seaview location, is the excellent café-restaurant, ***The Lobster Pot*** (☎ 01305-820242, 🖥 lobsterpot restaurantportland.co.uk; WI-FI; daily 9am-5pm), a great spot for breakfast, lunch or just a coffee and ice-cream. It's a bright, big-windowed space and they have picnic tables outside.

A little further along the path the old (lower) lighthouse, built in 1716 (although re-built in 1869), houses an important **bird observatory** and also provides fabulous-value ***hostel accommodation*** (☎ 01305-820553, 🖥 portlandbird obs.blogspot.co.uk; 9 bunk-bed rooms each with 2-4 beds, sleeps 20; £20pp; WI-FI) for ramblers, twitchers, climbers and artists. Meals are not provided but there's a large, well-equipped self-catering kitchen, a lounge area with huge bird-watching bay windows, a small, but well-stocked reading room and simple, but neat and tidy rooms with very comfortable wooden-framed bunk beds and clean shared bathrooms. Most of the rooms are in the ground-floor base of the lighthouse, but three are in the tower itself, at the top of which is an observatory with 360° views. There's a wonderfully laidback atmosphere and outside the main bird-watching seasons (spring and autumn), when it's best to book ahead, you'll often have a dorm to yourself. As well as the dorms, there is also a self-contained **lighthouse keeper's cottage** (1T and a room with a bunk bed; shower; 🐾; £80 for up to four people, sgl occ rates on request).

Keeping to the right of Portland Bill's **idiosyncratic 'sheds'**, you pass through disused and deserted quarries and out of sight of any civilisation. The path gradually rises away from the shoreline to a road, until a second path winds downwards through rocks and scrub to the **remains of Rufus Castle** (Map 69) – also known as Bow and Arrow Castle and built in the late 15th century. The ruins now constitute a Grade-I listed building and unfortunately are deemed too fragile for the public to freely wander. Close by (though off the path) is the site of the 13th-century **Church of St Andrew**, Portland's parish church until the 18th century. Its graveyard remains the eternal resting place of seafarers; the gravestones, made of course of local stone, are worth a look. Not too far away (and also off the path), **Portland Museum** (☎ 01305-821804, 🖥 portlandmuseum.co.uk; Easter-Oct Sat-Thur 10.30am-4pm, rest of year variable as opening days/hours depend on the availability of volunteers so check their website; £3.50) has display sections that include Stone, Sea and Shipwrecks and Famous Portland People.

The path continues through the scrub, above the quarries and boulders of **Penn's Weare** and **Grove Cliff** and through a gate at the far end of the huge **Yeolands Quarry**, with Portland goats grazing nearby. This leads to a Young Offenders' Institution and the **Old Engine Shed**, that housed the locomotives that were used in the quarries. Continue onwards along the road passing **Fancy's Family Farm** and the entrance to **HM Prison The Verne**: formerly a fortress and a barracks for a thousand troops, the Verne Citadel became a prison in 1949, the interior being completed by prisoners themselves. The prison holds an unwanted world record thanks to ex-inmate John Hannan who escaped (by tying bedsheets together to make a rope) in 1955, despite only being given a 21-month sentence in the first place. Assuming he is still alive, he has now been on the run for longer than any person in history. Behind you is **High Angle Battery**, built in 1892 to defend Portland Harbour.

The path follows the road to the left, passing car parks, information boards and a war memorial on the right and *The Heights Hotel* (see p266) on the left.

It then follows a combination of tarmac and trails to the large **hand crane** and stone marked 'Portland, Home of Portland Stone'. The path now drops back to the top of West Weare, with the well-known **Spirit of Portland Statue** just a couple of steps away from the trail.

All that's left to complete your Portland Odyssey is to retrace your footsteps back down into Fortuneswell and across the tombolo.

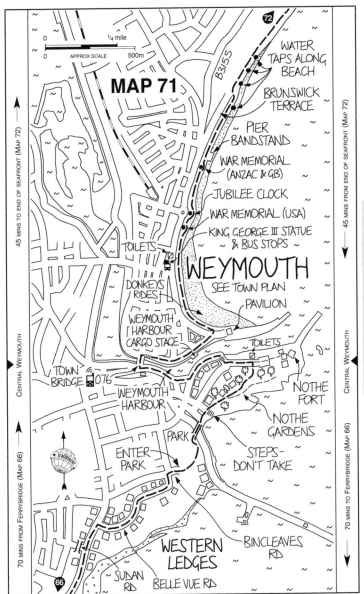

MAP 71

72

WATER TAPS ALONG BEACH

BRUNSWICK TERRACE

B3155

PIER BANDSTAND

WAR MEMORIAL (ANZAC & GB)

JUBILEE CLOCK

WAR MEMORIAL (USA)

KING GEORGE III STATUE ~ & BUS STOPS ~

WEYMOUTH

SEE TOWN PLAN

TOILETS

DONKEY RIDES

PAVILION

WEYMOUTH HARBOUR CARGO STAGE

TOILETS

TOWN BRIDGE   076

WEYMOUTH HARBOUR

NOTHE FORT

PARK

NOTHE GARDENS

ENTER PARK

STEPS- DON'T TAKE

★ trailblazer

BINCLEAVES RD

WESTERN LEDGES

66

SUDAN RD   BELLE VUE RD

0   ¼ mile
0   500m
APPROX SCALE

45 MINS TO END OF SEAFRONT (MAP 72)
CENTRAL WEYMOUTH

45 MINS FROM END OF SEAFRONT (MAP 72)
CENTRAL WEYMOUTH

70 MINS FROM FERRYBRIDGE (MAP 66)
70 MINS TO FERRYBRIDGE (MAP 66)

ROUTE GUIDE AND MAPS

Into Weymouth

For the walk to the centre of Weymouth you join **The Rodwell Trail**, which begins by Ferrybridge (see Map 66, p264). The coast path leaves The Rodwell just before *Sandsfoot Garden Café* (weather permitting summer daily approx 9am-5pm; winter weekends only) near **Sandsfoot Castle** (🖳 www.sandsfoot-castle.org.uk; free), one of Henry VIII's fortifications which, together with Portland Castle (over on the island but away from the coast path), defended the harbour. Most of the ruins have now fallen into the sea but some remain and lottery funding has enabled it to be opened to the public.

From the café follow the road for a distance to **Belle Vue Rd**, where you turn right, then Bincleaves Rd where another right turn and then an almost immediate left leads into a park. That leads, via a bridge, to **Nothe Gardens**, passing the Victorian **Nothe Fort** (☎ 01305-766626, 🖳 nothefort.org.uk; Apr-Sep and school half terms daily 10.30am-5.30pm, mid Feb-Mar & Oct-Dec Sun 11am-4.30pm; £8) on your right. The gardens lead around the pretty little **harbour** where, crossing the **Town Bridge**, you follow the coast path signs down the steps and along the eastern edge of the harbour. You then take up the tram lines, passing **Weymouth Harbour Cargo Stage** on the right, the smell of fish pungent in the air. At the end of the road there's the Pavilion theatre in front of you to the right – and the promenade (Esplanade) along Weymouth seafront ahead.

It's a lovely stroll along the seafront, with arcades and fairground rides on your left and kid-laden donkeys panting in the sun to your right. The promenade is adorned with statues and memorials aplenty to the great and the good including: the grand **George III statue** (situated by the bus stops), a **Jubilee Clock**, a tribute to Queen Victoria, as well as more solemn ones to American GIs, ANZAC forces and home-grown Tommys who perished in World War II. From the Pier Bandstand, follow the blue Coast Path signs and continue along Brunswick Terrace and out of town.

WEYMOUTH   [map p277]

Dubbed 'the Naples of England' by the Victorian tourism industry, and more recently chosen to host the sailing events at the 2012 Olympics, Dorset's fourth largest town was once the favourite holiday destination of His Royal Highness George III following the decision of his brother, the Duke of Gloucester, to build a huge residence here.

Though the townsfolk didn't follow the lead of their fellow south-coast resorts, Lyme and Bognor, in changing their name to celebrate the royal patronage bestowed upon them, there is no doubting they are just as proud of their regal links. Not only are there plaques and place names aplenty in Weymouth that commemorate George's

visits, but there's also the rather gaudy statue of him in the centre and a large white chalk depiction of him atop a horse etched into the hillside just outside the town near Osmington (see p280).

Perhaps, given that Weymouth's prior claim to fame was as the place where the Black Death entered the country in 1348, the locals' desire to celebrate the king's choice of holiday destination is understandable.

There's plenty for walkers to enjoy in the town – including a wonderful sweep of sand that stretches for miles, a great harbour with some lovely cafés and restaurants as well as all the services and facilities you'd expect of a town this size.

Wessex Folk Festival is held here in June and **Dorset Seafood Festival** in July; for details of both see p14. The latter is opened by a rather bizarre race in which participants swim across the harbour before downing oysters and champagne!

Services

Weymouth no longer has a tourist information office, though its tourism website (🖳 weymouth.co.uk) is kept up to date. The town's **library** (Mon 10am-7pm, Tue & Fri 9.30am-5.30pm, Wed 9.30am-1pm, Thur 9.30am-7pm, Sat 9am-4pm) has **internet access**, where the first half-hour is free. As usual, you need to show some form of ID. Nearby is the **post office** (Mon-Thur 8.30am-5.30pm, Fri & Sat 9am-5.30pm) and there are plenty of **banks** with **ATMs** around town.

The town centre also has a branch of Boots the **chemist** (Mon-Sat 8.30am-5.30pm, Sun 10am-4pm), on St Thomas St with another entrance on St Mary St. **Camping suppliers** Mountain Warehouse and Trespass are within a couple of hundred yards of each other on St Mary St and both have the same opening hours (Mon-Sat 9am-5.30pm, Sun 10am-4pm).

There's a Tesco Metro **supermarket** (Mon-Sat 7am-10pm, Sun 10am-4pm) on nearby St Thomas St, and a **launderette** called In a Spin (☎ 01305-778585; Mon-Sat 8.30am-5.30pm, Sun 9am-5pm), further north, at 29 Park St.

If you struggled to find your own ammonites on the beaches around Lyme Regis, you can buy **fossil souvenirs** at a shop called Fossil Beach (daily 9.30am-5pm), at the top of St Thomas St.

Summer walkers should take note of the numerous **water taps**, located at the back of the beach as you leave town heading north.

Transport

[See pp50-4] Weymouth is very well connected by **bus**: both First (Nos 1, 5, 8, 10, X53, X54, X55, 500, 501 & 510) and South West Coaches (No 206) operate numerous services to and from surrounding towns and village. However, the only bus to Durdle Door and Lulworth is the seasonal Breezer 30 service.

South Western Railway operates **train** services from London Waterloo to Weymouth and Great Western Railway from Bristol to Weymouth. To get to Exeter, Torquay or Plymouth by train you need to change in Castle Cary.

Where to stay

There's a **hostel** in Weymouth. *Bunkhouse Plus* (🖳 bunkhouseplus.co.uk; mix of 2-, 3- & 4-bed dorms totalling 19 beds and 2D en suite; WI-FI; bunks £18.50-21pp, dbl rooms £24pp). It's a facility-packed place with a large guest kitchen (with free tea, coffee and toast) and no curfew, but you have to book online; no telephone bookings, no walk-ins.

Just behind the railway station, the very basic *Newlands Guest House* (☎ 01305-785724, 🖳 newlandsweymouth.co .uk; 2S/4D or T; one en suite, rest share facilities; £20-25pp, sgl occ rates on request), at 22 Ranelagh Rd, offers room-only accommodation (no breakfast available) at some of the cheapest rates in town. Similarly cheap, but with a more intriguing location in the narrow lanes near the harbour, *The Cutter Hotel* (☎ 01305-761845; 6D or T/1Tr, one en suite rest share facilities; WI-FI; £20-25pp, sgl occ £25-30) is an old-fashioned drinkers' pub with no-frills rooms. It's at 4 East St, on the corner with St Alban St.

Weymouth has approximately 150 **B&Bs** so there shouldn't be too many issues with finding a bed. They can be fairly helpfully divided into three categories: those that will allow people to book well in advance for one night only; those that do so but not at weekends and/or the peak season (July and August); and those that don't. Ever. That said, most will accept people for just one night if they have availability and you turn up on the day. One that belongs in the first category, on the way into town and perfectly located near harbour-side pubs is *Old Harbour View* (☎ 01305-774633, 🖳 oldharbourviewweymouth.co.uk; 1D/1T; WI-FI; from £49pp, sgl occ from £80); it is not cheap but the location is ideal.

Moving north to the almost unbroken string of establishments on The Esplanade, three more places that accept one-night bookings can be found here with *The Roundhouse Hotel* (☎ 01305-761010, 🖥 roundhouse-weymouth.com; 1T/5D; ▼; WI-FI; £37.50-72.50pp, sgl occ £70-140) at No 1 and, at No 2, *Aaran House* (☎ 01305-766669, 🖥 aaranhouse.co.uk; 4D/2T; ▼; WI-FI; £32.50-40pp, sgl occ £60-75); and their neighbour at No 3, *Beach View Guest House* (☎ 01305-570046, 🖥 beachviewguesthouse.com; 5D/1Tr; ▼; WI-FI in guest lounge; from £35pp, sgl occ from £60).

Still on The Esplanade, *The Anchorage* (☎ 01305-782542, 🖥 theanchorageweymouth.co.uk; 2S shared shower facilities/3D/1T/1Tr/Qd; WI-FI; £42.50pp, sgl occ £48-55), at No 7, accepts a minimum advance booking of two/three nights in the peak season. *The Bedford* (☎ 01305-786995, 🖥 thebedfordweymouth.co.uk; 1S/7D; WI-FI; Mar-Oct; £41-44pp, sgl from £50, sgl occ £36-82), at No 17, accepts one-night bookings except over weekends and in the peak season.

Still good value are *The Bourneville* (☎ 01305-784784, 🖥 bournevillehotel.co.uk; 2S/3D or T/2T/6D/1Tr/1Qd, one room sleeping up to five; ▼; WI-FI; £30-50pp, sgl/sgl occ from £50) at No 31-32, which has a licensed bar, and *Bay View Hotel* (☎ 01305-782083, 🖥 bayview-weymouth.co.uk; 7D/1Tr; WI-FI; £30-32.50pp, sgl occ room rate), No 35, which provides fridges in its rooms as they serve a continental-style breakfast and guests eat in their rooms. Alas, neither of these is likely to take a one-night booking in July or August though both are worth a call on the day if you're stuck.

The Edenhurst (☎ 01305-771255, 🖥 edenhurstweymouth.com; 2S/4D/2T/3Tr; WI-FI; £39-62.50pp, sgl £40-51, sgl occ £50-90), No 122 The Esplanade, requires a minimum booking of two nights between July and mid September (and over bank holiday weekends) and *Langham Hotel* (☎ 01305-782530, 🖥 langham-hotel.com; 9D/3T; ▼; WI-FI; late Feb to early Nov; £35-50pp, sgl occ £45-75), at No 130, requires a minimum stay of three nights between June and September. Some rooms can sleep children and the Langham provides evening meals (three courses £15) if booked in advance.

In contrast and before leaving The Esplanade altogether, right at its heart sits *Gloucester House* (☎ 01305-785191, 🖥 gloucesterhouseweymouth.co.uk; 3S/6D/2T/2Tr/2Qd; ▼; WI-FI; £36-45pp, sgl £47-52, sgl occ rates on request) at No 96, where one-night bookings are generally allowed except for bank holiday weekends and between the beginning of July and the end of August where a minimum of three nights is necessary.

The Esplanade isn't the only street stuffed with accommodation; at the opposite end of town there is another string of B&Bs on Brunswick Terrace. Most of them are great value and some accept one-night stops, at least outside the peak seasons of July and August. *Whitecliff* (☎ 01305-785554, 🖥 whitecliffweymouth.co.uk; 1S/3D/1T/1Tr and one room sleeping up to five; ▼; WI-FI; 🐕; £27.50-50pp, sgl £35-50, sgl occ from £45), at No 7, is a decent and well-run place and, with better rooms, *Sunnyside* (contact details as for Horizon as operated by the same people, see below; 2D/1T share facilities, 2Tr/1Qd, all en suite; ▼; WI-FI; 🐕; £30-40pp, sgl occ £28-38) at No 15.

Also very good value are *Lichfield House* (☎ 01305-784112, 🖥 lichfieldhouse.net; 4D/2T; ▼; WI-FI; £37.50-40pp, sgl occ from £60), at No 8, and *Seaspray*

❏ **Where to stay: the details**

Unless specified, B&B-style accommodation is either en suite or has private facilities; ▼ means at least one room has a bath; 🐕 signifies that dogs are welcome in at least one room but always by prior arrangement, an additional charge may also be payable (see also p83); WI-FI means wi-fi is available in the property, though not always reliably in every room.

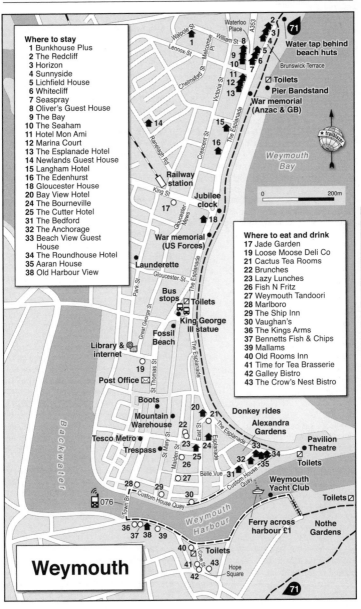

Where to stay
1 Bunkhouse Plus
2 The Redcliff
3 Horizon
4 Sunnyside
5 Lichfield House
6 Whitecliff
7 Seaspray
8 Oliver's Guest House
9 The Bay
10 The Seaham
11 Hotel Mon Ami
12 Marina Court
13 The Esplanade Hotel
14 Newlands Guest House
15 Langham Hotel
16 The Edenhurst
18 Gloucester House
20 Bay View Hotel
24 The Bourneville
25 The Cutter Hotel
31 The Bedford
32 The Anchorage
33 Beach View Guest House
34 The Roundhouse Hotel
35 Aaran House
38 Old Harbour View

Where to eat and drink
17 Jade Garden
19 Loose Moose Deli Co
21 Cactus Tea Rooms
22 Brunches
23 Lazy Lunches
26 Fish N Fritz
27 Weymouth Tandoori
28 Marlboro
29 The Ship Inn
30 Vaughan's
36 The Kings Arms
37 Bennetts Fish & Chips
39 Mallams
40 Old Rooms Inn
41 Time for Tea Brasserie
42 Galley Bistro
43 The Crow's Nest Bistro

ROUTE GUIDE AND MAPS

Weymouth

Waterloo Place
Walpole St
Lennox St
William St
A353
Water tap behind beach huts
Brunswick Terrace
Chelmsford St
Melcombe Pl
Victoria St
Toilets
Pier Bandstand
War memorial (Anzac & GB)
Ranelagh Rd
Crescent St
The Esplanade
Weymouth Bay
200m
Railway station
King St
Jubilee clock
Gloucester Mews
War memorial (US Forces)
Launderette
Gloucester St
Park St
Great George St
Bus stops
Toilets
King George III statue
Library & internet
Fossil Beach
Post Office
St Thomas St
Boots
Mountain Warehouse
Donkey rides
Alexandra Gardens
Tesco Metro
Trespass
St Mary St
East St
Maiden St
Belle Vue
Pavilion Theatre
Toilets
Custom House Quay
Weymouth Yacht Club
Toilets
Backwater
076
Town Br
Custom House Quay
Weymouth Harbour
Ferry across harbour £1
Nothe Gardens
Cove St
Toilets
Hope Square
71

(☎ 01305-786943, 🖳 www.seaspray-guest
house.co.uk; 1S/3D/1D or T/1Tr; WI-FI;
£30-40pp, sgl £42-50, sgl occ rates on
request) at No 6.

Further down the street, *The Redcliff*
(☎ 01305-784682, 🖳 redcliffweymouth.co
.uk; 3S/5D/4Tr; WI-FI; 🐾; £35-50pp, sgl
£48-51, sgl occ rates on request), at No 18-
19, accept advance bookings for a one-
night stay during the week in summer but
not at weekends; while *Horizon* (☎ 01305-
784916, 🖳 horizonguesthouse.co.uk; 1S/
1T share bathroom, 1D/1T/2Qd all en suite;
£30-40pp, sgl occ £28-38), at No 16, are
also unlikely to take one-night bookings
between late July and the whole of August.

One block behind Brunswick Terrace,
so fronted with a road rather than the sea,
Waterloo Place is home to another line of
B&Bs. *Oliver's Guest House* (☎ 01305-
786712, 🖳 oliversguesthouse.co.uk; 2S/3D
all en suite, 1T/1D share facilities; WI-FI;
£25-35pp, sgl occ rates on request), at No
12, though they may not accept a one-night
booking in July/August; *The Bay* (☎
01305-786289, 🖳 thebayguesthouse.co.uk;
3D/2D or T; WI-FI; £32-48pp, sgl occ £42-
96) at No 10; and *The Seaham* (☎ 01305-
782010, 🖳 theseahamweymouth.co.uk;
5D; WI-FI; £34-60pp, sgl occ from £55) at
No 3. This last, incidentally, has kippers,
haddock and salmon on their breakfast
menu.

Also in this area are *Hotel Mon Ami*
(☎ 01305-786917, 🖳 hotelmonami.co.uk;
20T/20D; 🍺; WI-FI in the bar; Apr-Nov;
£30-45pp, sgl occ from £50), No 143-145,
and *Marina Court* (☎ 01305-782146, 🖳
marinacourt.co.uk; 10D/4T; WI-FI; £33-
52.50pp, sgl occ rates on request), No 142,
and *The Esplanade Hotel* (☎ 01305-
783129, 🖳 theesplanadehotel.co.uk; 1S/
6D/1T/1Tr, two rooms sleep up to five; 🍺;
WI-FI; Mar-end Oct; £45-60pp, sgl £50-70,
sgl occ £75-90) at No 141, an award-winning place run by a highly amiable chap; it
offers haddock, kippers, porridge, and a
veggie alternative for breakfast. Will accept
one-night stops in the peak season if
booked near the time. In the winter months
they operate walking tours (Trexx Walking
Holidays; see p29).

Where to eat and drink
The historic harbour area is your best bet
for a meal or a drink, but the most pleasant
place to eat is just off it, to the south, in a
small, quiet, partly tree-shaded plaza called
Hope Square, where three lovely café-
restaurants create a Mediterranean-like
atmosphere with tables spilling out onto the
pavements.

Cafés & delis Right on the Esplanade,
Cactus Tea Rooms (☎ 01305-778933; 🐾;
Mar-Nov daily from 10.30am, they close
when it is quiet or the weather is bad) has
been going for almost 20 years and does
brunches and lunches (£4-8) as well as a
lovely Dorset apple cake. It's similar fare at
the family-friendly café, *Brunches* (Mon-
Sat 9.30am-3pm), hidden in the narrow
lanes behind the harbour.

For sandwich fillers, try *Loose Moose
Deli Co* (☎ 01305-774941; Mon-Fri 7am-
4.30pm, Sat 9am-4pm), on School St just
off St Thomas St, or the very reasonably
priced sandwich bar *Lazy Lunches* (☎
01305-782187; Mon-Sat 9am-4pm, Sun
10.30am-3pm), on St Alban St, with
baguette meals for just £2.40.

Restaurants On a sunny summer's day,
you can't beat Hope Square, where three
charming European-inspired eateries vie
for your attention: best of the lot, thanks
largely to its tree-shaded terrace, is *The
Crow's Nest Bistro* (☎ 01305-786930, 🖳
crowsnestweymouth.com; summer daily
9am-9pm, winter Tue-Thur & Sun 9am-
4pm, Fri-Sat 9am-9pm) which has an
extensive tapas menu (£4-6) as well as
doing lunches (£6-10).

Across the square, *Galley Bistro* (☎
01305-784059, 🖳 thegalleybistro.co.uk;
Mon 10am-2.30pm, Tue-Thur 10am-
2.30pm & 6-9pm, Fri-Sat 10am-2.30pm &
6-10pm, Sun 10am-4pm) has a good selection of breakfasts as well as lunches (£5-10)
and evening mains (£11-15), while *Time
for Tea Brasserie* (☎ 01305-777500; June-
Sep daily 9.30am-5pm, rest of year Wed-
Mon only) serves nothing but home cooking, much of it French (the owner hails
from Paris), and specialises in dishes such

as 'cassoulet au canard confit' (duck cassoulet), though doesn't ignore the cuisine of its new homeland either, baking cakes and scones daily and conjuring up a mean Dorset apple cake.

Also on this side of the harbour, *Mallams* (☎ 01305-776757, 💻 mallams restaurant.co.uk; Mon-Sat 6-9.30pm, also Fri-Sun noon-2.30pm in summer) is a stylish evening-meal bistro, although it does open for lunch on summer weekends. The menu (evening mains £15-25) changes regularly but typically includes local seafood (mussels usually feature highly) plus two vegetarian and two meat options. Their wine list includes some local tipples too. On the other side of the harbour, *Vaughan's* (☎ 01305-769004, 💻 www.vaughansbistro .co.uk; summer Tue-Sun 11am-2.15pm & 6-9pm, winter hours variable check website for details) is similarly refined, and specialises in steak and seafood.

For Chinese food, *Jade Garden* (☎ 01305-778844, 💻 jadegardenweymouth.co .uk; Sun-Thur 5-11.30pm, Fri & Sat 5pm-midnight), on King St near the railway station, is a sit-down restaurant as well as a takeaway. They do some Malay and Thai dishes too.

Pubs & takeaways There are numerous harbourside pubs including *The Kings Arms* (☎ 01305-772200) reopening soon after refurbishment, *The Ship Inn* (food daily noon-9pm; 🐾) and *Old Rooms Inn* (food daily 10am-10pm). Old Rooms Inn has an extensive outdoor seating area. All three serve a selection of real ales.

Of the plethora of **fish & chip shops**, a few stand out: *Fish N Fritz* (Mon-Sat 11.30am-9pm, Sun 11.30am-7pm) does its best to promote less popular fish to try to save the diminishing stocks of cod and other favourites. Similarly, *Bennetts Fish & Chips* (☎ 01305-781237; Sun-Thur 11.30am-10.30pm, Fri & Sat to 11.15pm, winter hours variable); its speciality is its mackerel in a bap (£4.95). *Marlboro* (☎ 01305-785700; restaurant/takeaway daily noon-8pm/10pm) is one of the most established chippies in town and has been going since 1974.

For an Indian takeaway, try *Weymouth Tandoori* (☎ 01305-776744, 💻 thewey mouthtandoori.co.uk; daily 5.30-10.30pm) on Maiden St.

WEYMOUTH TO LULWORTH COVE　　　　　　　　　　[MAPS 71-76]

This **11-mile (17.75km; 4hrs 40 mins) stage** is as splendid as it is strenuous. Reckoned by many to be the most beautiful on the trail, it takes you to the pure white chalky cliffs leading to Lulworth Cove – similar to the chalky cliffs prevalent further east at Beachy Head and the South Downs of Sussex.

Apart from their distinctive colour, the other characteristic of this type of cliffs is the way they rise and fall, sometimes relentlessly so – and this is certainly true of this trail, which starts off with an iron-flat walk along Weymouth seafront (complete with several places serving refreshments) and ends with a real rollercoaster along the cliffs leading to Durdle Door – perhaps the Dorset coastline's most iconic feature. From there it's a comparatively small hop to Lulworth Cove – one of the county's more famous olde-worlde villages, where even the bus shelter is thatched!

The route

The first gradient on this strenuous stage is a small one. Having finally diverted from the seafront at *Café Oasis* (💻 www.cafeoasis.co.uk; peak season daily 8am-late, rest of year Sun-Thur 8am-5pm, Fri & Sat 8am-5pm & 7-9pm), you climb up **Bowleaze Coveway**, past *The Lookout Café* (daily 9am-5pm), with its fine views, and up over Jordan Hill, which is topped by the remains of a **Roman temple**. Not much is known about this once-sacred place other than that it was built in around the 4th century; there's not much now save for the simple square outline of the temple's foundations in the ground. The road continues down to another temple of sorts, this one dedicated to the practice of arcades and sun worshipping: Beachside Leisure Centre with its amusement-park children's rides and rather rundown *café-restaurant* (summer daily 9am-10pm, winter 9am-5pm) is probably best avoided, unless you need to use the **ATM** (£1.75) inside the restaurant. There's a handy Spar **supermarket** (daily 8am-8pm) here, though, at the entrance to Waterside Holiday Park (which doesn't allow camping).

Climbing out of the dip, the path passes the Art Deco splendour of **Riviera Hotel** (🖥 www.rivieraweymouth.co.uk), which looks particularly spectacular at night when lit up in a subtle blue lighting. The hotel's *Bowleaze Bar & Restaurant* (☎ 01305-836600; daily for breakfast, lunch & dinner) is open to non-residents.

You soon climb into the fields at the end of the road – look to your left for the best view from the path of the **Osmington White Horse** (see Map 60c, p253) at Osmington Hill. The figure on the horse is George III and was done in the early 1800s.

Having crossed some fields the path now saunters along – or near – the cliffs and below the perimeter of an activity centre, before dropping, after some simple meandering, to a reunion with the South Dorset Ridgeway (see p251), just before it meets the road running down to **Osmington Mills**.

OSMINGTON MILLS   [Map 73, p283]

There's little to the village save for a place to have lunch but it's perfectly located – and there are some options for accommodation should you wish to linger longer.

For **campers**, the very welcoming *Rosewall Camping* (☎ 01305-832248, 🖥 weymouthcamping.com; Mar/Apr-Oct, weather dependent; 🐾; tent & 1/2 hikers from £8/12) has a **shop** (peak season daily 8am-5/6pm, rest of season hours vary) which is well stocked in the high season – and even serves hot drinks – but has a more limited selection in the low season. The site is right on the path and has a lovely spacious shower block considering it's only a relatively basic campsite.

There's also **B&B** accommodation; *No 1 Old Coastguards* (☎ 01305-832663, 🖥 hope.horvath68@live.co.uk; 1S/1D private facilities; WI-FI; £35-40pp, sgl occ from £50) offers pleasant adjoining rooms which are only let to people who know each other. It's tucked away nicely down a quiet little lane, close to both the path and the pub. At the bottom of the village – and yet also its very heart – is the charming *Smugglers Inn* (☎ 01305-833125, 🖥 smugglersinnosmingtonmills.co.uk; 4D; 🛏; WI-FI; 🐾; £42.50-57.50pp, sgl occ rates on request), a lovely thatched place with origins dating back to the 13th century. It's a Hall & Woodhouse pub and bears the same smart-traditional style of the others in the chain, has great **food** (daily noon-9pm), a large beer garden, and Badger ales on tap.

As for transport, First's X54 and X55 **bus** services stop in Osmington village (see Map 60c) – a 15-minute walk from Osmington Mills – en route between Poole and Weymouth. In summer Damory Coaches operate the Breezer 30 service between Weymouth and Swanage. See pp50-4 for details.

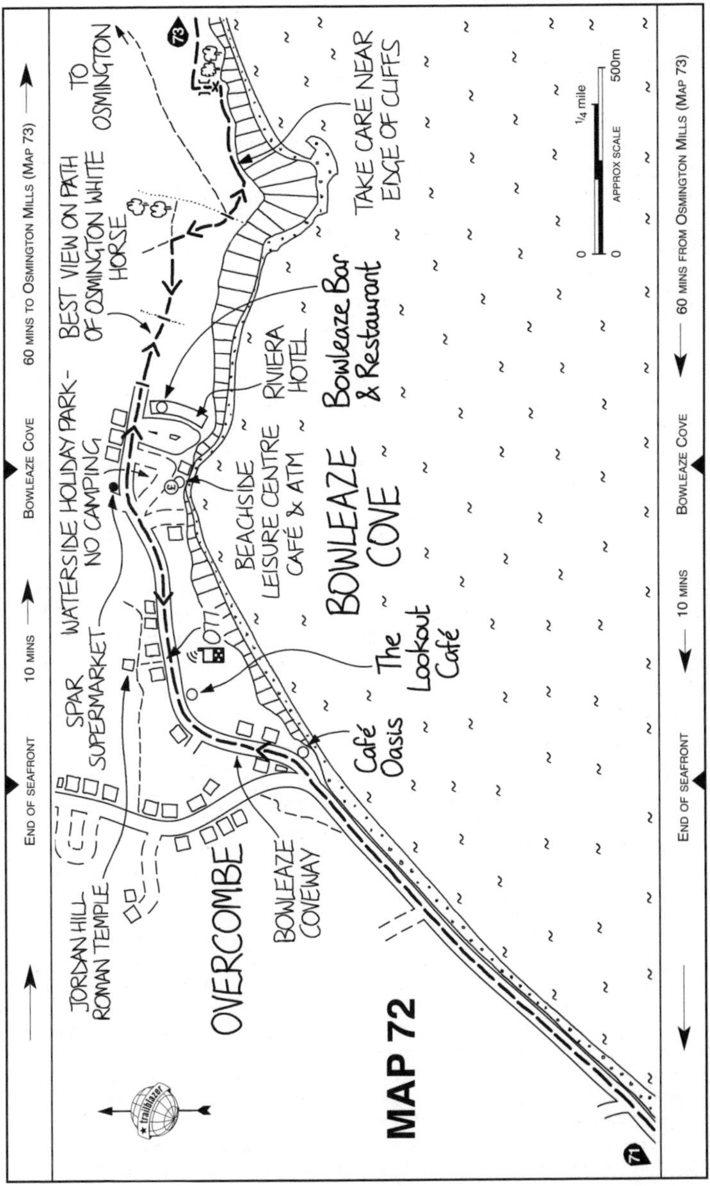

MAP 72

OVERCOMBE

JORDAN HILL ROMAN TEMPLE

BOWLEAZE COVEWAY

SPAR SUPERMARKET

WATERSIDE HOLIDAY PARK – NO CAMPING

Café Oasis

The Lookout Café

BEACHSIDE LEISURE CENTRE CAFÉ & ATM

RIVIERA HOTEL

Bowleaze Bar & Restaurant

BEST VIEW ON PATH OF OSMINGTON WHITE HORSE

TO OSMINGTON

TAKE CARE NEAR EDGE OF CLIFFS

BOWLEAZE COVE

¼ mile

APPROX SCALE

0   500m

END OF SEAFRONT ◀ ── 10 MINS ── ▶ BOWLEAZE COVE ◀ ── 10 MINS ── ▶ END OF SEAFRONT

END OF SEAFRONT ── 10 MINS ── BOWLEAZE COVE ── 60 MINS TO OSMINGTON MILLS (MAP 73) ──▶

◀── 60 MINS FROM OSMINGTON MILLS (MAP 73)

Heading round behind Smugglers Inn, more field walking follows, the path squeezed between fence and cliffs, with a couple of brick shelters as the only significant features before the path cuts through the houses of **Ringstead Bay**, where you'll find ***Ringstead Bay Kiosk*** (☎ 01305-852427; summer generally daily 9am-8pm, winter hours variable) waiting to serve you food and hot drinks (depending on the weather). Turning right along a lane just before the kiosk, you walk round the back of some homes and on, up past the landslips that lie to your right like scruffy terracing, to the tiny wooden **chapel**, dedicated to St Catherine. Some more easy climbing brings you to the remote houses at **White Nothe**. (Note you can also walk along the landslips, known as **Burning Cliff**, though you do so at your own peril and you may not be able to ascend to White Nothe so you may have to return before continuing on the path. The cliff is so-named after a band of bituminous shale caught fire in 1826.)

The tough stuff begins here. Most of the climbs on this section to Durdle Door are both lengthy and steep. The first descent, down to Middle Bottom, is typical. Passing a **stone obelisk** (which, along with a second obelisk nearby, is a 19th-century navigational aid used by sailors), the path descends quickly along the cliffside before climbing, equally rapidly, out of it.

A second descent down to the beach by the **Bat's Hole** rock formation and a third to the wonderfully named **Scratchy Bottom** (which features in the book *Rude Britain: The 100 Rudest Place Names in Britain* by Ed Hurst and Rob Baile) follow in short order before you are finally rewarded with your first view of the famous natural arch at **Durdle Door** (see box below). At the time of research there was a temporary diversion just after Durdle Door, which took walkers inland slightly, up the car park by the entrance to ***Durdle Door Holiday Park*** (see p286) before rejoining the original path soon after, as it climbed over **Hambury Tout**. From here it's a gentle descent to the elegant arc of lovely **Lulworth Cove**. *(cont'd on p286)*

❏ Durdle Door

Geologically speaking, Durdle Door is nothing more than an arch of limestone rock set out at sea but joined to the mainland by a narrow sliver of land or isthmus. Derived from an Old English word *thirl* meaning 'to drill', the door is part of the 12,000-acre Lulworth Estate. Though it appears to have been here forever, the arch was of course formed by the tides eroding the rock away – the same force that now threatens to destroy it and which UNESCO are attempting to counteract to prevent it falling into the sea altogether. (Incidentally, to see what Durdle Door might have looked like once upon a time, neighbouring Stair Hole is an 'infant' cove, the waves having broken through to form an arch and the Wealdon clays behind that which were once protected are now rapidly being eroded.)

So far, so prosaic. Plenty of artists down the years have been inspired by Durdle Door, however, and this curiously carved lump of rock features in many works, from music videos (step forward Billy Ocean, Cliff Richard and Tears for Fears who all shot promotional videos here), to films (Emma Thompson's *Nanny McPhee* and *Wilde*, the biopic of Oscar Wilde starring Stephen Fry, both had scenes filmed here), and, perhaps most famously, it was also used as a location for the 1967 film adaptation of Thomas Hardy's novel *Far from the Madding Crowd*, starring Julie Christie.

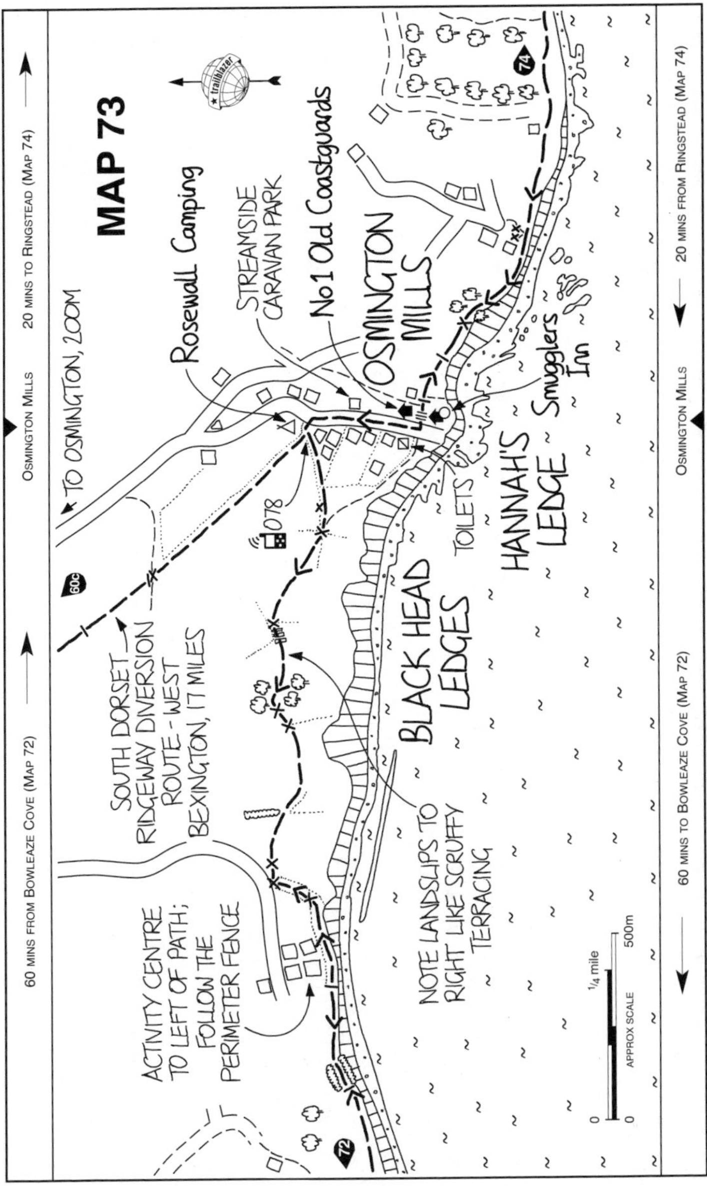
MAP 73
trailblazer
60 MINS FROM BOWLEAZE COVE (MAP 72)
OSMINGTON MILLS
20 MINS TO RINGSTEAD (MAP 74)
TO OSMINGTON, 200M
Rosewall Camping
STREAMSIDE CARAVAN PARK
No 1 Old Coastguards
OSMINGTON MILLS
Smugglers Inn
HANNAH'S LEDGE
TOILETS
BLACK HEAD LEDGES
078
60c
SOUTH DORSET RIDGEWAY DIVERSION ROUTE - WEST BEXINGTON, 17 MILES
NOTE LANDSLIPS TO RIGHT LIKE SCRUFFY TERRACING
ACTIVITY CENTRE TO LEFT OF PATH; FOLLOW THE PERIMETER FENCE
APPROX SCALE
0
1/4 mile
0
500m
72
74
20 MINS FROM RINGSTEAD (MAP 74)
OSMINGTON MILLS
60 MINS TO BOWLEAZE COVE (MAP 72)

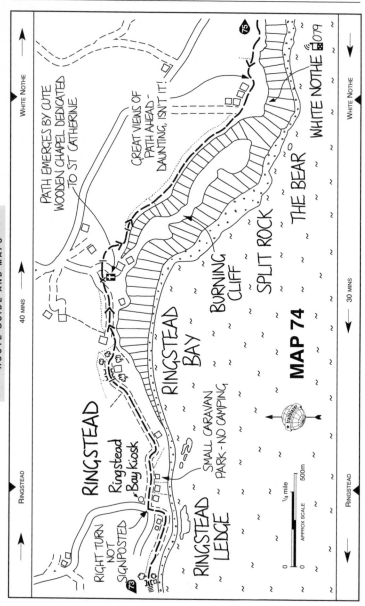

WHITE NOTHE

40 MINS

RINGSTEAD

PATH EMERGES BY CUTE
WOODEN CHAPEL DEDICATED
TO ST CATHERINE

GREAT VIEWS OF
PATH AHEAD -
DAUNTING, ISN'T IT!

RINGSTEAD

Ringstead
Bay kiosk

RIGHT TURN
NOT SIGNPOSTED

75

RINGSTEAD
BAY

SMALL CARAVAN
PARK - NO CAMPING

RINGSTEAD
LEDGE

BURNING
CLIFF

SPLIT ROCK

THE BEAR

WHITE NOTHE

MAP 74

¼ mile

500m

0

0

APPROX SCALE

30 MINS

RINGSTEAD

WHITE NOTHE

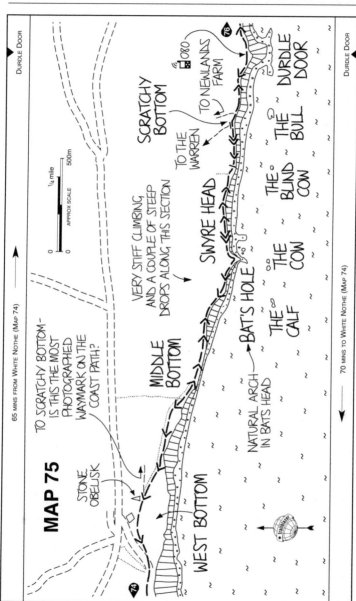

DURDLE DOOR

65 MINS FROM WHITE NOTHE (MAP 74)

MAP 75

STONE OBELISK

TO SCRATCHY BOTTOM – IS THIS THE MOST PHOTOGRAPHED WAYMARK ON THE COAST PATH?

MIDDLE BOTTOM

WEST BOTTOM

NATURAL ARCH IN BATS HEAD

BAT'S HOLE

THE CALF

THE COW

VERY STIFF CLIMBING AND A COUPLE OF STEEP DROPS ALONG THIS SECTION

SWYRE HEAD

SCRATCHY BOTTOM

TO THE WARREN

TO NEWLANDS FARM

THE BLIND COW

THE BULL

DURDLE DOOR

¼ mile

500m

0

0

APPROX SCALE

70 MINS TO WHITE NOTHE (MAP 74)

DURDLE DOOR

ROUTE GUIDE AND MAPS

WEST LULWORTH AND LULWORTH COVE   [Map 76 & map p288]

One of the most picturesque coves on the south coast, inland of which is one of the walk's most idyllic villages, Lulworth Cove, and its accompanying village, West Lulworth, virtually demand that you spend a night here. Add some wonderful nearby scenery, a couple of fantastic pubs, some great B&Bs and an absorbing **visitor centre** (daily 10am-5pm) and it's a strange trekker indeed that decides to breeze through.

Services

There isn't much in the way of amenities in either the cove or the village. There is a **shop**, Hambury Stores (daily 8am-9pm), on Church Rd on the edge of the village, that has a good selection of groceries and baked goods. The visitor centre has an **ATM** (£1.85) as well as a gift shop and a café.

For **tourist information** try 🖳 lulworthonline.co.uk or for the Lulworth Estate see 🖳 lulworth.com.

Transport

[See pp50-4] In summer, Damory Coaches' Breezer 30 (Weymouth to Swanage) **bus** service calls at Durdle Door, West Lulworth and Lulworth Cove and First's X55 calls at Durdle Door and Lulworth Cove.

For a **taxi** try Silver Car (☎ 07811-328281 or ☎ 01929-400409).

Where to stay

There is **camping** just a few minutes back from Durdle Door, immediately behind the car park at the top of the hill. *Durdle Door Holiday Park* (Map 76; ☎ 01929-400200, 🖳 lulworth.com/stay/durdle-door-holiday-park; Mar-end Oct; WI-FI; 🐾) has a café/bar, a shop and a wonderful location. A standard pitch (for up to four people) costs from £26, but walkers may get a discount; booking is recommended. They also have **camping pods** (£50-75, sleep 4, bedding not included). It's a nice place, though spend a night here and you'll understand why a collection of crows is called a murder, because that's exactly what you'll want to do with them at 5am when they wake you up.

Lulworth also boasts a **hostel**, though it's a little way out of the village. *YHA Lulworth Cove* (☎ 0345-371 9331, 🖳 yha.org.uk/hostel/lulworth-cove; 3 x 4-/2 x 5-/2 x 6-bed rooms; dorm beds from £12pp, private rooms from £39) is a pleasant place with helpful staff. One of the four-bed rooms is en suite. Meals are available but there is also a self-catering kitchen. They also allow **camping** (Mar-Oct; from £13pp). To get here follow the road to West Lulworth to a signpost on the right pointing the way to the hostel.

Other accommodation includes *The Castle Inn* (☎ 01929-400311, 🖳 lulworthinn.com), a beautiful, thatched 16th-century establishment which at the time of research was due to close for refurbishment and open again in April 2018. The new room and rate details weren't certain at the time of research.

The village also has a number of charming **B&Bs**. On Main Rd you'll find *Downalong* (☎ 01929-400300, 🖳 downalong.co.uk; 1D/1T; WI-FI; May-early Oct; £42.50-45pp, sgl occ room rate) and *The Old Barn* (☎ 01929-400305, 🖳 theoldbarnlulworthcove.com; 2D/1T/1D or T/1Qd; 🍽; WI-FI; 🐾; Mar-early Nov; £40-55pp, sgl occ rates on request), who do not accept advance bookings for one-night stays at the weekend in summer.

The following B&Bs are also reluctant to accept one-night stays at the weekend and over summer but may do if there is space in their diary. The 400-year-old dog-friendly *Tewkesbury Cottage* (☎ 01929-400561; 1D en suite, 1D/1T shared bathroom; 🍽; WI-FI; 🐾; £40-45pp, sgl occ from £70) is at 28 Main Rd, as is *Bindon Bottom* (☎ 01929-400256, 🖳 bindonbottom.com; 4D/1T; 🍽; WI-FI; Feb-Nov; £45-65pp, sgl occ £85-125), a large Victorian country house built in 1871 opposite the junction of Church Rd and Main Rd, from which there are great views over the surrounding countryside. They only ever accept bookings for a minimum of two nights. The ingredients for breakfast are locally sourced and where possible organic. Next door you will find *Cove House* (☎

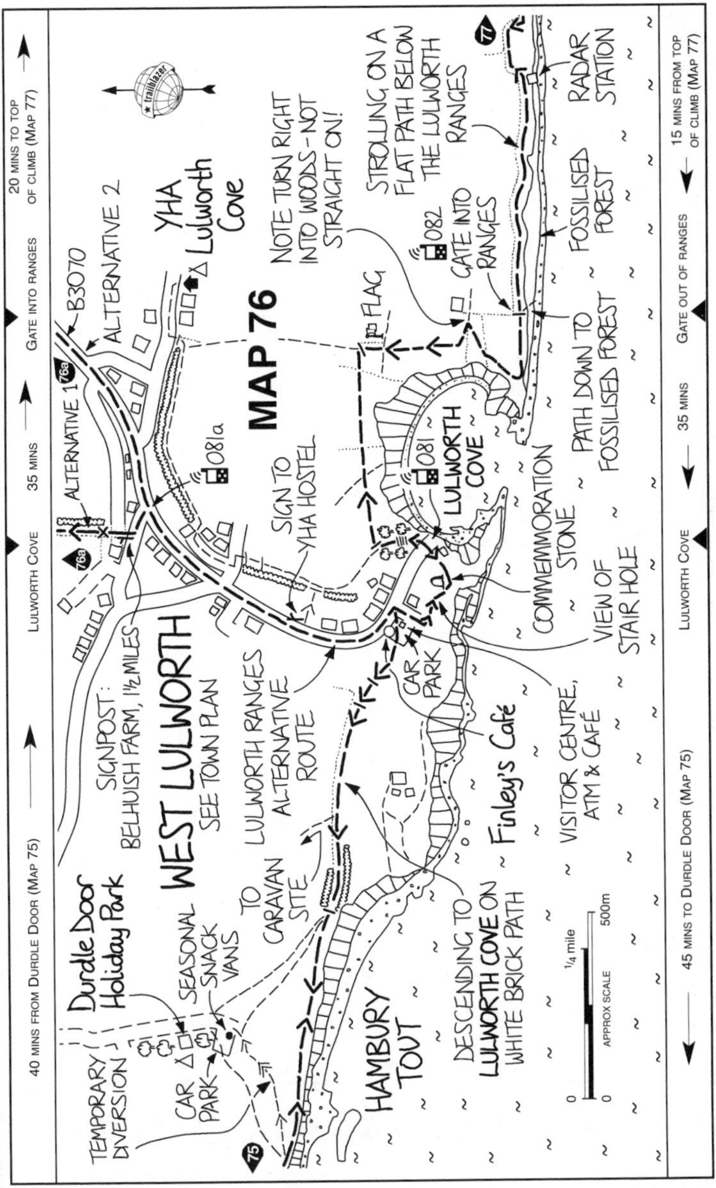

MAP 76

20 MINS TO TOP OF CLIMB (MAP 77)

GATE INTO RANGES

ALTERNATIVE 2

B3070

YHA Lulworth Cove

NOTE TURN RIGHT INTO WOODS – NOT STRAIGHT ON!

STROLLING ON A FLAT PATH BELOW THE LULWORTH RANGES

082 GATE INTO RANGES

FOSSILISED FOREST

RADAR STATION

15 MINS FROM TOP OF CLIMB (MAP 77)

FLAG

PATH DOWN TO FOSSILISED FOREST

081 LULWORTH COVE

081a

SIGN TO YHA HOSTEL

ALTERNATIVE 1

76a

35 MINS

LULWORTH COVE

SIGNPOST: BELHUISH FARM, 1½ MILES

WEST LULWORTH SEE TOWN PLAN

TO CARAVAN SITE

LULWORTH RANGES ALTERNATIVE ROUTE

CAR PARK

COMMEMORATION STONE

VIEW OF STAIR HOLE

VISITOR CENTRE, ATM & CAFÉ

Finley's Café

GATE OUT OF RANGES

35 MINS

LULWORTH COVE

TEMPORARY DIVERSION

CAR PARK

SEASONAL SNACK VANS

HAMBURY TOUT

DESCENDING TO LULWORTH COVE ON WHITE BRICK PATH

Durdle Door Holiday Park

40 MINS FROM DURDLE DOOR (MAP 75)

75

45 MINS TO DURDLE DOOR (MAP 75)

77

¼ mile

500m

APPROX SCALE

0

0

01929-400137, 🖳 covehouse.net; 3D/1T; WI-FI; Feb-Nov; from £52.50pp, sgl occ from £100); they generally only accept bookings for a minimum of two nights.

Apart from *Limestone Lulworth* (☎ 01929-400252, 🖳 www.limestonehotel.co .uk; 6D/2D or T; ☞; WI-FI; 🐾; £55-87.50pp, sgl occ rates on request), which is in the centre of the village, most **hotel**-style accommodation can be found down in Lulworth Cove itself, just a couple of hundred metres or so from the path. *Lulworth Cove Inn* (☎ 01929-400333, 🖳 lulworth-coveinn.co.uk; 12D; ☞; WI-FI; £40-50pp, sgl occ £60-100) is a smart pub with some lovely rooms, many with sea view, and accepts one-night

bookings except at weekends and on bank holidays. Further down, *Lulworth Lodge & Bistro* (☎ 01929-400252, 🖳 lulworthlodge .co.uk; 7D/5D or T; ☞; WI-FI; 🐾; £45-92.50pp, sgl occ from £90) is similarly stylish and is situated where the old mill once stood. It also has some fabulous views of the cove and is owned by the same people as Limestone Lulworth.

Next door, *Bishop's Boutique Hotel* (☎ 01929-400552, 🖳 bishopslulworth.co.uk; 9D; ☞; WI-FI; 🐾; £42.50-95pp, sgl occ £80-150) is housed within two cottages dating back to the 1650s; it has a range of rooms from budget to luxury as well as an outdoor swimming pool overlooking the cove.

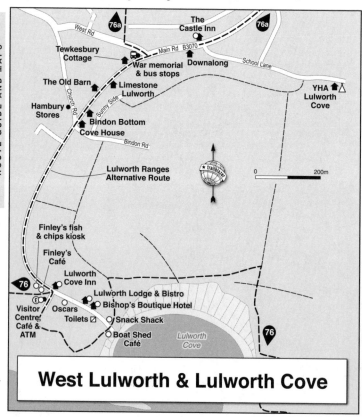

West Lulworth & Lulworth Cove

Where to eat and drink

With the exception of the excellent *Castle Inn* (see Where to stay; food served daily noon-9pm; 🐾), which was undergoing renovations from new owners at the time of research but which traditionally served great ciders (see box p23), beer and food, the rest of the eateries are clustered together, down towards the cove.

Next to the visitor centre, which itself has a small café, is *Finley's Café* (☎ 01929-400711, 🖥 finleyscafe.co.uk; WI-FI; 🐾; daily summer 9.30am-5pm, winter 10am-4pm), which has a self-service canteen system, and is sometimes overrun with school groups, but is an OK choice nonetheless. It has an attached **fish & chips kiosk** (Mar-Oct daily 11.30am/noon-7/8pm) that's also very popular.

Walking downhill from here towards the cove you'll pass a trio of side-by-side establishments, including an ice-cream parlour, a fudge shop and the newly opened café-bistro, *Oscars* (daily 10am-5pm).

On the opposite side of the lane is *Lulworth Cove Inn* (see Where to stay; WI-FI; 🐾; food daily noon-9pm), a Hall & Woodhouse pub, serving good-quality pub grub. Further down the lane are *Lulworth Lodge & Bistro* (see Where to stay; food daily noon-9pm) and *Bishop's Boutique Hotel* (see Where to stay; food daily 8.30-10am, noon-3pm & 6.30-8.30pm), which both have bistro-style restaurants serving good food, including seafood specials, in a stylish atmosphere.

For something more affordable (not that the bistros are overly expensive) walk further down to the *Snack Shack* (Mon-Fri 10am-5pm, Sat-Sun 9am-7pm), a takeaway kiosk that does burgers, baps, sandwiches and coffee. Right by the water is *Boat Shed Café* (daily 9.30am-5pm), a tiny café with a veranda overlooking the famous cove.

LULWORTH COVE TO KIMMERIDGE BAY [MAPS 76-79]

There's a bit of a military theme to this 7¼-mile (**11.75km; 3hrs; Alternative 1: 4hrs 55 mins. Alternative 2: 4½hrs**) stage. In addition to the fact that today you'll be visiting both an Iron-Age fort (which was later used by the Romans) and various fortifications from the Second World War, there is also the small matter that, for almost its entire length, **you'll be walking through a very active firing range**. Indeed, the ranges provide the greatest obstacle to today's stage, for the path through them is open only occasionally (usually only at weekends). This is a shame, for the ranges are a delight, with fortifications, fossilised forests and fascinating flora abounding.

In short, **it's well worth timing your walk to ensure your arrival coincides with the weekend, which is when the ranges are usually open** (call ☎ 01929-404712, Mon-Thur 7.30am-5pm, Fri to 3pm, to double check when the ranges are open); and this is the trek we've described below. (We've also described the alternatives; see pp293-7.)

If you do manage to hike through the ranges you'll actually find this stage rather short – it can be completed in a morning. (That's not to say it's easy, however, for there are several painfully sharp gradients on the way.) This, of course, allows for the possibility – for the fit, at least – of combining this stage and the following one into one long (and exhausting) day to Swanage. This is no bad thing, for accommodation at Kimmeridge is both a little off the trail and in short supply. However, only the fit and fanatical should consider doing this – it's a lot of miles and gradients to squeeze into one day. If you do decide to combine the two stages you should certainly consider bringing lunch with you from Lulworth, unless you're willing to trek uphill to Kimmeridge village from the bay.

ROUTE GUIDE AND MAPS

The route through the ranges

The day begins with a relatively untaxing stroll around the cove that brings you to the no-nonsense fence surrounding the firing range. Once through the **gate**, a short diversion on entering the range also brings you to one of the most unusual sights on the trail: a **fossilised forest**. Don't expect to see stone trees 'growing' out of the cliff-ledge; instead, look for **thrombolites**, which are fossilised rings of algae that thrived around tree trunks when the forest was flooded 150 million years ago. The area used to be known as 'Vairy Vances' or 'Fairy Dances', in reference to these thrombolite rings.

The walk within the ranges can best be described as two very stiff climbs and one long but gentle one, separated by some surprisingly unchallenging sections, all set amongst some fascinating (particularly if rusting military vehicles are your thing) and beautiful scenery.

The first of the big climbs lies about a mile from the fossilised forest; it's an exhausting haul up **Bindon Hill**, usually done to a soundtrack of crashing waves and whistling wind. That climb conquered, a lovely bit of gentle ridgetop rambling follows before a sharpish descent to **Arish Mell** – from where the lengthier climb up to **Flowers Barrow** begins. It's a wearying climb – you can see why Iron-Age man chose the summit of this hill as the location for a **fort** – and why the Romans subsequently used it for their own military purposes. The unexcavated remains of the fort explain the existence of the unusual bumps and folds in the summit.

Amongst these remains are a couple of hut circles and a few ramparts; sadly, however, where the hill forts were designed to protect the inhabitants from invaders, they are helpless against the depredations of the elements and much of the site has fallen victim to erosion.

Also on the Barrow, an old **WWII gun emplacement** shows that, while weaponry and warfare may have changed in the 2500 years since the Iron Age fort was built, a hilltop location is still regarded as invaluable when it comes to looking out for enemy advances. Further down the slopes, the rust-coloured metal ball is actually a WWII **Allen Williams Steel Turret** – of which we've already seen an example in Exmouth.

The path passes more ruins at **Worbarrow** and its accompanying **Tout**, or hill, which resembles a giant geological apostrophe punctuating the sea. You then climb for a third time (though mercifully less steeply now) towards **Tyneham Cap** which, unusually, the path contours round rather than conquers, dropping gently, via unconcerned sheep, to the gate at the end of the ranges.

❏ KEEP TO THE PATH!

More than anywhere else on the coast path it is absolutely vital that you keep to the signposted path through Lulworth Military Range (the yellow-topped posts traditionally point the way). As you can probably tell by all the metalware rusting in the fields, there's a fair bit of unexploded ordnance left lying hereabouts. So keep to the path – and make sure your dog keeps to the path too.

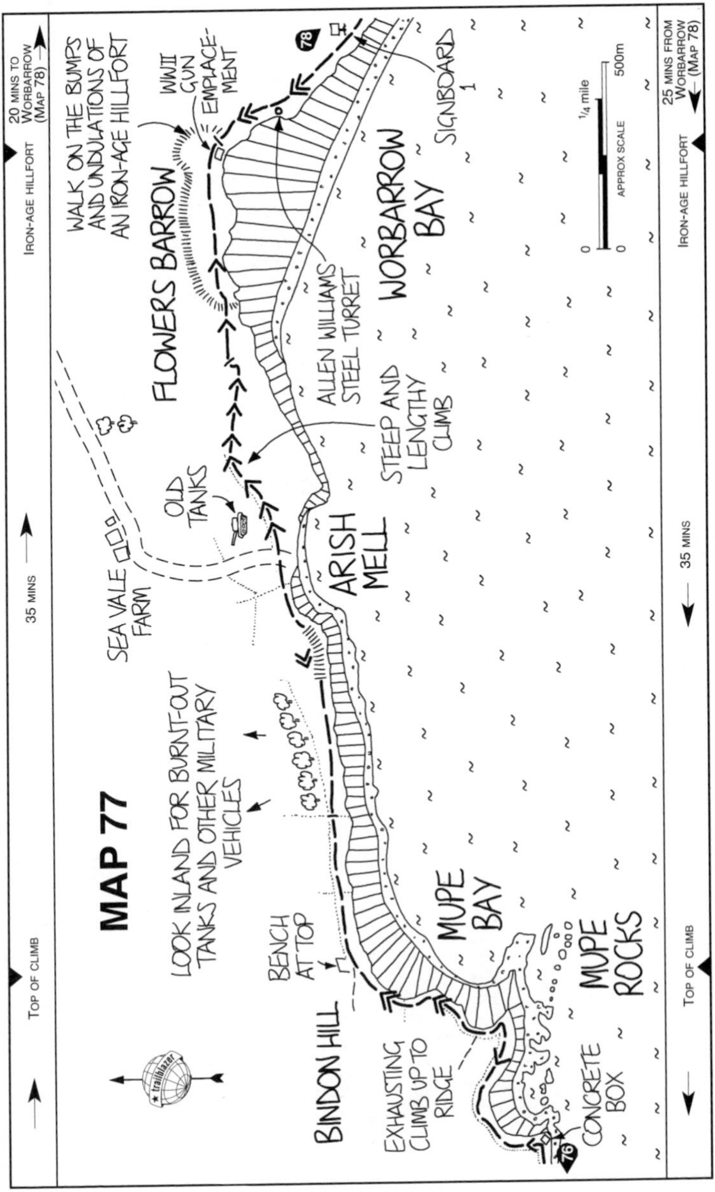

MAP 77

20 MINS TO WORBARROW (MAP 78) →

IRON-AGE HILLFORT

WALK ON THE BUMPS AND UNDULATIONS OF AN IRON-AGE HILLFORT

WWII GUN EMPLACE-MENT

78

FLOWERS BARROW

WORBARROW BAY

SIGNBOARD

ALLEN WILLIAMS STEEL TURRET

STEEP AND LENGTHY CLIMB

¼ mile

APPROX SCALE

0   500m

25 MINS FROM WORBARROW (MAP 78)

IRON-AGE HILLFORT

35 MINS →

SEA VALE FARM

OLD TANKS

ARISH MELL

35 MINS

LOOK INLAND FOR BURNT-OUT TANKS AND OTHER MILITARY VEHICLES

BINDON HILL

BENCH AT TOP

MUPE BAY

EXHAUSTING CLIMB UP TO RIDGE

MUPE ROCKS

78

CONCRETE BOX

TOP OF CLIMB

TOP OF CLIMB

trailblazer

ROUTE GUIDE AND MAPS

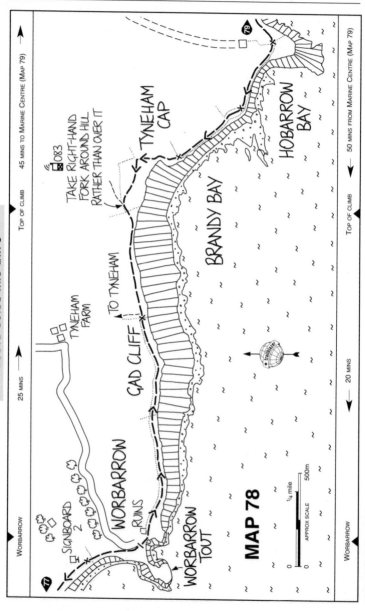

ROUTE GUIDE AND MAPS

WORBARROW — 25 MINS → — TOP OF CLIMB — 45 MINS TO MARINE CENTRE (MAP 79) →

TOP OF CLIMB — 50 MINS FROM MARINE CENTRE (MAP 79) →

TYNEHAM CAP

HOBARROW BAY

083
TAKE RIGHT-HAND FORK AROUND HILL RATHER THAN OVER IT

TYNEHAM FARM

TO TYNEHAM

BRANDY BAY

CAD CLIFF

SIGNBOARD 2

WORBARROW

RUINS

WORBARROW TOUT

MAP 78

¼ mile
APPROX SCALE
0   500m

WORBARROW — 20 MINS → — TOP OF CLIMB — WORBARROW

Incongruously, next-door is a small **oil well** – indeed, Wytch Farm Oil Well is said to be the site of the oldest continually working oil well in the world!

From here it's but a short stroll round to **Kimmeridge Bay**. At first sight there doesn't seem to be much here save for a large car park, some public toilets and a couple of old sheds down on the water's edge. However, these sheds provide the answer to why so many people come to this bay for they house the **Fine Foundation Marine Centre** (Easter-Sep Tue-Sun & bank hols 10.30am-5pm, Oct-Mar Sun noon-4pm) which provides an interactive explanation on the neighbouring bay, its ledges and rockpools, waters that together make up **Purbeck Marine Nature Reserve** – Britain's longest-established Voluntary Marine Nature Reserve – home to sea anemones, crabs, wrasse, mullet, lobster and blennies. The centre has a small souvenir shop and, on display outside, the skull of a juvenile fin whale (the world's second largest type of whale) whose body was washed ashore in 2012.

For the amenities of Kimmeridge (see pp297-8) you have to walk for 10-15 minutes up the hill from the bay.

See p298 for the continuation of the route.

WHEN THE RANGES ARE CLOSED [Map 76a, p295; Map 76b, p296]

Alternative 1

Yes, the walk through the ranges is the kind of stroll that causes writers to write, poets to eulogise, and atheists not only to believe in the existence of a God but also to believe that he loves us dearly and clearly wants us to be happy.

But if the ranges are shut when you arrive, there's no need to plunge head-long into a pit of despair and self-loathing (as long as you choose Alternative 1). Because, simply put, this **13½-mile (21.75km; 4hrs 55mins)** yomp has more than enough compensations. It's much easier (though longer), with fewer of those roller-coaster undulations that are so characteristic of the coastal route.

The scenery, too, is often exquisite (and if you've followed this book from the start – and especially if you began at the beginning of the South West Coast Path in Minehead – your eyes and ears will probably be grateful to gaze upon something other than the sea), with sumptuous bluebell woods, sweeping country estates, neatly cultivated fields, ancient farmhouses and some whopping great country manors to titillate the senses.

There's also more wildlife on this path too, with deer (both roe and the rarer sika, an immigrant from East Asia, thrive in the ranges), hares, pheasants and raptors all dropping by now and again to see who's passing. And overlaying everything is this comforting, life-affirming tranquillity and isolation. It's just lovely. And yes, while there is a good amount of this walk that is undertaken on roads (approximately four miles), much of it is on quiet country lanes edged with lovely cottages or rhododendron forests, where traffic is infrequent and there are grassy verges to hop onto if necessary.

So cease your wailing, silence those gnashing teeth, dry those tears from your eyes and wipe your nose on your Gore-Tex; because you have a lovely walk to complete – and you need to get going...

The route The day begins with a stroll from the official path up to **West Lulworth** (assuming you haven't already visited it), from where the first of the steep climbs begins up through fields to a brief union with the **Purbeck Way** (see p38), a route that you very quickly betray for the **Hardy Way** which leads you down past hare-inhabited pastures to **Belhuish Farm**. Reaching the end of their drive, after the B3071, the path then follows the edge of gorgeous **Burngate Wood**, filled with deer and bluebells, which you leave by its most easterly point to saunter eastwards on a rough track to **Park Lodge**, with Lulworth Castle (see p295) and its domed chapel to your right.

More woodland skirting occurs after crossing another road, with the idyllic looking lake and its 'fort' to your left. Following a hedge-lined country track, it's not long before you hit the range (the border, as you'll soon discover, being marked by a red flag). Follow the path round the ranges' edge and you soon reach **Coombe Heath Nature Reserve** and from there more woodside wandering leading to a small country lane which, in turn, leads to **Holme Lane** (Map 76b), where you turn right.

While it's never a blessing to feel the thud of sole on tarmac, the road is pleasantly quiet and the bucolic views to Holme Priory – after you've passed the crossroads at **West Holme** – are distracting. You eventually leave this road, just after a signposted but badly maintained bridleway, for a road marked 'East Holme Rifle Range', which soon takes you past an unsightly quarry and on to **Dorey's Farm**, after which there's yet more sylvan strolling – at least until the road to Kimmeridge is reached. There now follows the least pleasant couple of miles on this walk, though with some lovely little cottages and the huge **Grange Farm** on the way, it isn't entirely horrid. The road-rambling ends with a steep, uphill gradient, your reward for conquering it being some wonderful sweeping views north and south over lovely, voluptuous Purbeck.

A steep descent, some more road walking, a bisection of *Steeple Leaze Farm* and its **campsite** (see p297), another small climb and descent and a traverse of four or five fields follows before Kimmeridge Bay is reached – and a reunion with the official trail.

Alternative 2

Definitely the inferior of the three routes, basically on this **12-mile (19.3km; 4½hrs)** option you are treading tarmac the whole way. The road in question is the B3070 which is the same road that you join when you hit Lulworth Cove and which passes through West Lulworth and the ranges (but is open even when the ranges are usually shut). Given all the pavement-pounding, you should really consider this option only if you are after a pub, a café, or Lulworth Castle – all of which can be found in East Lulworth.

The route From West Lulworth continue on the B3070 to **East Lulworth**. The pub here, *Weld Arms* (☎ 01929-400211, ☐ weldarms.co.uk; 3D/1D or T/1Qd, all en suite; ☞; WI-FI; ☛ bar only; £32.50-80pp, sgl occ from £60) is a goodie, with decent **food** (Mon-Sat noon-2.30pm & 6-9pm, Sun noon-5pm; mains £11-15), a lovely beer garden and five **B&B** rooms. The only problem with it is that it is probably too near West Lulworth to consider it a lunchtime option; though if you visit the castle first it could fit in with your day's schedule.

Just beyond here is *Past and Presents Café* (☎ 01929-400637, ☐ pastand presents.co.uk; daily summer 10am-5pm, winter 10am-4pm; WI-FI), housed in an old Catholic school, originally built in 1877. You can get tea, coffee and

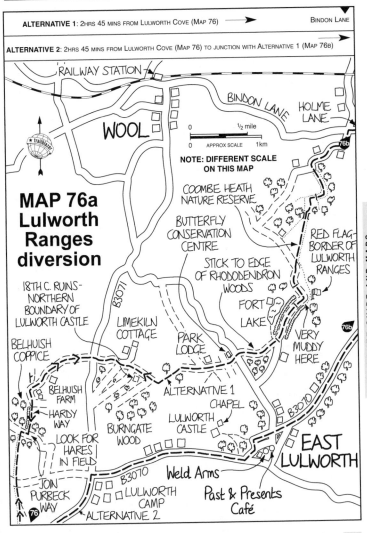

snacks here, and there's an art gallery to peruse and a gift shop selling locally produced handicrafts.

The road passes the entrance of **Lulworth Castle** (Sun-Fri 10.30am-5pm; £6, English Heritage members free); the castle was originally built as a hunting lodge in the early 17th century by Thomas Howard, 3rd Lord Bindon, to entertain hunting parties for the king and his court. Gutted by a fire in 1929, it

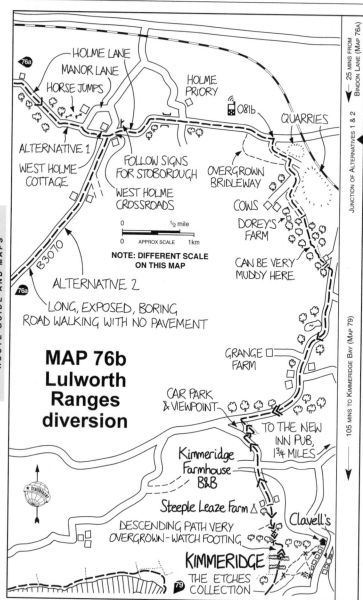

HOLME LANE

MANOR LANE

HORSE JUMPS

HOLME PRIORY

081b

QUARRIES

ALTERNATIVE 1

WEST HOLME COTTAGE

FOLLOW SIGNS FOR STOBOROUGH

WEST HOLME CROSSROADS

OVERGROWN BRIDLEWAY

COWS

DOREY'S FARM

0   ½ mile
0   1km
APPROX SCALE

NOTE: DIFFERENT SCALE ON THIS MAP

CAN BE VERY MUDDY HERE

B3070

ALTERNATIVE 2

LONG, EXPOSED, BORING ROAD WALKING WITH NO PAVEMENT

**MAP 76b
Lulworth
Ranges
diversion**

GRANGE FARM

CAR PARK & VIEWPOINT

TO THE NEW INN PUB, 1¾ MILES

Kimmeridge Farmhouse B&B

Steeple Leaze Farm △

DESCENDING PATH VERY OVERGROWN – WATCH FOOTING

Clavell's

★ trailblazer

KIMMERIDGE
THE ETCHES COLLECTION

79

25 MINS FROM BINDON LANE (MAP 76A)

JUNCTION OF ALTERNATIVES 1 & 2

105 MINS TO KIMMERIDGE BAY (MAP 79)

was restored and is still maintained by English Heritage. Camp Bestival (see box p14), held here in July, is the little sister of the far larger Bestival, held on the Isle of Wight.

From East Lulworth, you now have to walk along the morale-sapping, pavement-less and seemingly never-ending B3070 to the **West Holme crossroads** where this route joins up with Alternative 1 (see p294).

KIMMERIDGE [Map 76b]

As well as the excellent new fossil museum (The Etches Collection, see p298) which opened in 2016, there's a **B&B**, a nearby **campsite** and a good **café** here.

The **campsite**, at *Steeple Leaze Farm* (☎ 01929-480733; £7pp; Easter till Sep/Oct depending on weather; 🐾), is about 20 minutes out of Kimmeridge on the alternative route (see p294). It's a simple place with portacabin showers, toilets without toilet paper, and no food available on site, but it does allow open fires.

Kimmeridge Farmhouse (☎ 01929-480990, 🖥 kimmeridgefarmhouse.co.uk; 1D/2D or T; 🛏; WI-FI; £45-50pp, sgl occ from £80) is a great big 14th-century pile with three smart rooms. The café/restaurant, run by the same people who own Kimmeridge Farmhouse, is called *Clavell's* (☎ 01929-480701, 🖥 clavellscafe.co.uk; Tue-Sun plus school-holiday Mondays 10am-5pm). It's licensed and has a good selection of sandwiches, baguettes, lunchtime mains and desserts. They also open for evening meals on Fridays and Saturdays

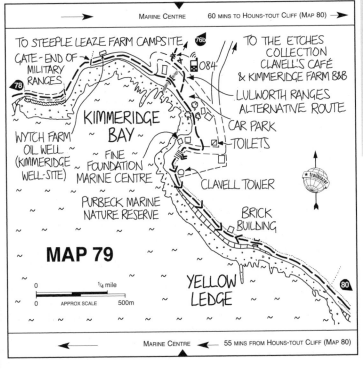

MARINE CENTRE   60 MINS TO HOUNS-TOUT CLIFF (MAP 80) →

TO STEEPLE LEAZE FARM CAMPSITE 76b

GATE-END OF MILITARY RANGES 084

78

TO THE ETCHES COLLECTION CLAVELL'S CAFÉ & KIMMERIDGE FARM B&B

LULWORTH RANGES ALTERNATIVE ROUTE

CAR PARK

KIMMERIDGE BAY

WYTCH FARM OIL WELL (KIMMERIDGE WELL-SITE)

~ FINE ~ FOUNDATION MARINE CENTRE

TOILETS

CLAVELL TOWER

trailblazer

PURBECK MARINE NATURE RESERVE

BRICK BUILDING

MAP 79

0   ¼ mile
0   APPROX SCALE   500m

YELLOW LEDGE

80

MARINE CENTRE ← 55 MINS FROM HOUNS-TOUT CLIFF (MAP 80)

between April and September. The nearest pub, *The New Inn* (off Map 76b; ☎ 01929-480357, 🖥 newinn-churchknowle.co.uk; WI-FI function room; food daily noon-2pm & 6-8pm, till 9.30pm in summer), is a couple of miles away, in Church Knowle.

❏ **The Etches Collection – Museum of Jurassic Marine Life**

Over the last 35 years, local amateur paleontologist and fossil hunter Steve Etches has assembled a unique collection of over 2000 specimens from the late Jurassic period. In 2016 a home was found for this superb collection in a purpose-built museum and workshop that opened in the centre of Kimmeridge.

The fossils are beautifully displayed and labelled; the CGI animations showing them swimming in the sea bring it all to life. Top exhibits include an ichthyosaur with a stomach full of fish, a squid complete with its ink sac, a lobster and a fossilised dragonfly wing. Through the big glass window at the end of the main gallery in the workshop you may see Steve Etches himself hard at work on a new specimen.

The museum (☎ 01929-270000, 🖥 theetchescollection.org, £8) is open daily (except 24-26 Dec) 10am-5pm. It's quite small but well worth a visit.

KIMMERIDGE BAY TO SWANAGE [MAPS 79-84]

[MAPS 79-84]

Just two stages to go, but by now it should have become clear that the coast path is not going to let you complete your trek without a struggle. For though in mileage terms this stage is not too daunting at **13½ miles (21.75km; 4hrs 50 mins)**, those bald statistics hide a couple of pretty hamstring-hammering, calf-creaking ascents. But there are compensations – as always – in the form of some delicious views, an ancient and remote chapel, the penultimate lighthouse on the path, a diverting nature reserve and the former tourist attraction of the Tilly Whim Caves (closed to the public for safety reasons since 1976).

The village of Worth Matravers, about a mile inland, is also a charming place with pretty limestone cottages, a great pub and a cute teahouse – well worth a detour if you're after refreshments. If you're not planning on visiting Worth Matravers, there's nowhere else to stop for food until Durlston, about a mile before Swanage, so make sure you bring your own!

The route

The path leaves Kimmeridge Bay via the 19th-century **Clavell Tower**, a folly built by the 70-year-old Reverend John Richards Clavell in 1830. It was moved back from the cliff edge at great expense and effort in 2002 to avoid the encroaches of the sea and the slips of land. The tower is now available as accommodation – though it's usually booked out years in advance and costs from £466 for a four-night stay! Contact The Landmark Trust (🖥 landmarktrust .org.uk) if you're interested.

The gradients are rather gentle for the first few miles (especially when compared to some of the giants of the previous two stages) but don't be lulled into a false sense of security; you'll soon have to tackle the hill of **Houns Tout Cliff** – the summit of which is only gained after a tough slog. Following the descent, a simple meander inland of **Chapman's Pool** brings you to the point where you could leave the coast path for Worth Matravers.

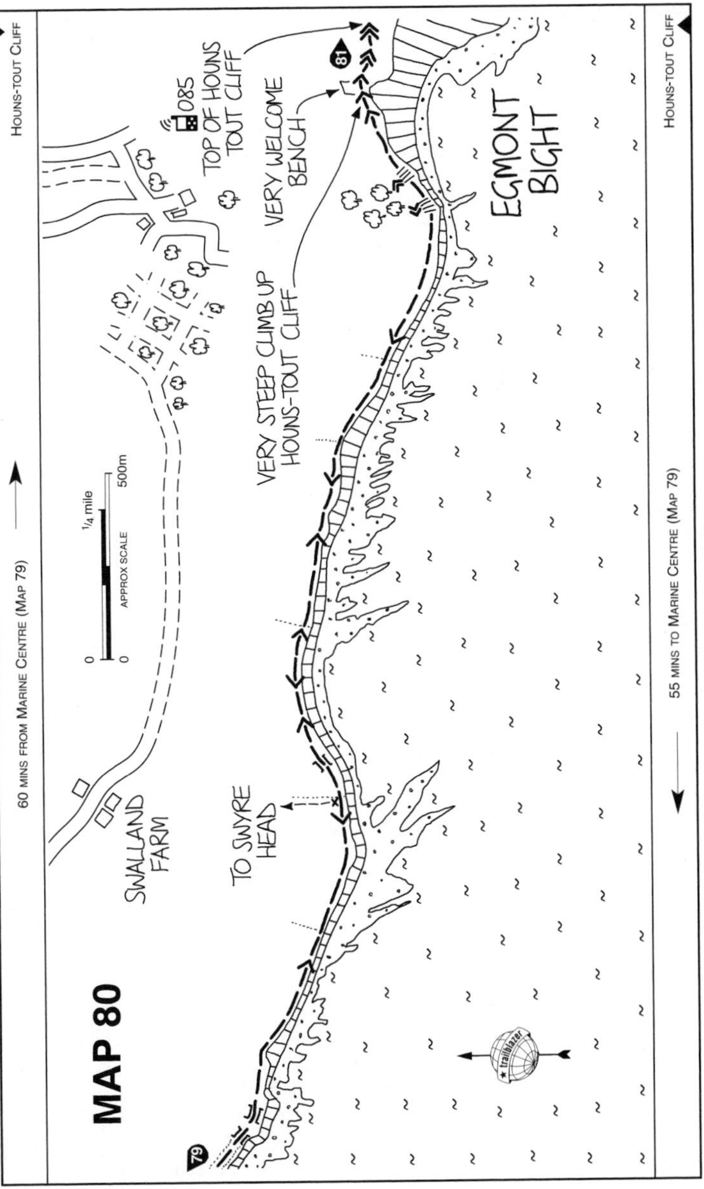
MAP 80
60 MINS FROM MARINE CENTRE (MAP 79)
HOUNS-TOUT CLIFF
55 MINS TO MARINE CENTRE (MAP 79)
HOUNS-TOUT CLIFF
APPROX SCALE
0
0
1/4 mile
500m
SWALLAND FARM
TO SWYRE HEAD
VERY STEEP CLIMB UP HOUNS-TOUT CLIFF
VERY WELCOME BENCH
TOP OF HOUNS TOUT CLIFF
085
EGMONT BIGHT
79
81
trailblazer

WORTH MATRAVERS **[off Map 81]**
Lovers of quaint villages and quirky pubs
may well be tempted to detour inland to the
knot of thatched, limestone cottages built
around a pond that makes up the beautiful
stone-clad settlement of Worth Matravers.

Weston Dairy Campsite (☎ 07757-
159749, 🖳 worthcamping.co.uk; from
£7pp; 🐾) lies on the path between
Chapman's Pool and the village, but is only
open on selected weeks in July and August.
A small catering shed provides campers
with hot drinks, bacon sandwiches and the
like.

For **B&B**, there's the gorgeous *Post
Office Cottage* (☎ 01929-439442, 🖳 www
.worthmytravels.co.uk; 2D/1T; WI-FI; small
🐾; from £45pp, sgl occ from £75), a Grade
II-listed building, built in 1750 and overlooking the village pond. There are three
bedrooms, but they only rent to one guest
(or group of guests) at a time, so even if you
just book one room, you'll get sole use of
the living and dining areas too.

Practically next door, *Worth
Matravers Tea & Supper Room* (☎ 01929-
439368, 🖳 worthmatraverstearoom.co.uk;
🐾; summer Tue-Sun 11am-4.30pm & Tue-

Sat 6.30-9pm but check before going, especially for the winter months, as their opening days/hours can vary even weekly) is a
quintessential, award-winning teahouse
that's perfect for cream teas, but also does
light lunches and evening meals.

Just up the road, *The Square &
Compass* (☎ 01929-439229, 🖳 squareand
compasspub.co.uk; 🐾; daily summer
noon-11pm, winter Mon-Thur closed 3-
6pm, check website for details) is a unique
village pub dating back to 1776. They don't
have a typical food menu. Instead, their
recipe for success is a selection of hot
pasties and pies, washed down with real
ales or homemade cider (see box p23) and
served inside, in an atmospheric low-
ceilinged pub, or outside, on their chunky,
stone-carved garden furniture. They hold a
week-long stone-carving festival here in
July/August (see box p14), and there's a
fossil museum attached to the pub. There's
also live music most Saturday nights. Also
note, they don't accept cards.

Worth Matravers can also be accessed
from Map 82, which you can reach from the
village by following the signposted path to
Winspit.

The slog up Houns Tout Cliff was not the last for, having climbed
Emmett's Hill, a near-vertical descent and ascent follows to **St Aldhelm's
Head** – home to a coastguard hut, a house or two, a radar research monument
and a 12th-century chapel, dedicated to the eponymous saint, that's made of
local Purbeck stone. If you missed the turning to Worth Matravers earlier it is
also accessible by taking the track due north from St Aldhelm's Chapel.

It is no small relief to find that the haul up to St Aldhelm's really is the last
major climb of the day, and though five miles separate you from Swanage, none
of them, thankfully, is that taxing.

The path meanders past old quarries and cliffs – the latter a real draw for
local climbers, for whom the region has plenty – and on via **Dancing Ledge**
(Map 83) to the lighthouse at **Anvil Point** and so on to **Durlston National
Nature Reserve**, home of butterflies, birds and plants galore. Here you will also
find the Victorian **Durlston Castle** (🖳 durlston.co.uk; daily Apr-Nov 10am-5pm,
Nov-Mar 10am-4pm; free), with a visitor centre, gift shop and pleasant *café*
(daily 9.30am-5pm; 🐾). Outside it stands the 40-tonne **Great Globe**, constructed from Portland stone in 1891 and one of the largest stone spheres in the world.

From here the path descends on pretty **Isle of Wight Rd** (yes, that is the
island you can see ahead of you on a clear day) and out into the outskirts of
Swanage, which you reach via a short detour along **Peveril Point**.

(cont'd on p304)

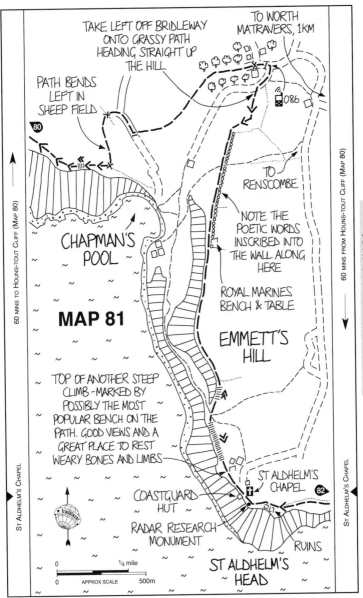

TAKE LEFT OFF BRIDLEWAY ONTO GRASSY PATH HEADING STRAIGHT UP THE HILL

TO WORTH MATRAVERS, 1KM

PATH BENDS LEFT IN SHEEP FIELD

80

086

TO RENSCOMBE

CHAPMAN'S POOL

NOTE THE POETIC WORDS INSCRIBED INTO THE WALL ALONG HERE

ROYAL MARINES BENCH & TABLE

MAP 81

EMMETT'S HILL

TOP OF ANOTHER STEEP CLIMB - MARKED BY POSSIBLY THE MOST POPULAR BENCH ON THE PATH. GOOD VIEWS AND A GREAT PLACE TO REST WEARY BONES AND LIMBS

ST ALDHELM'S CHAPEL

82

trailblazer

COASTGUARD HUT

RADAR RESEARCH MONUMENT

RUINS

ST ALDHELM'S HEAD

0   1/4 mile
0   500m
APPROX SCALE

60 MINS TO HOUNS-TOUT CLIFF (MAP 80)

60 MINS FROM HOUNS-TOUT CLIFF (MAP 80)

ST ALDHELM'S CHAPEL

ST ALDHELM'S CHAPEL

ROUTE GUIDE AND MAPS

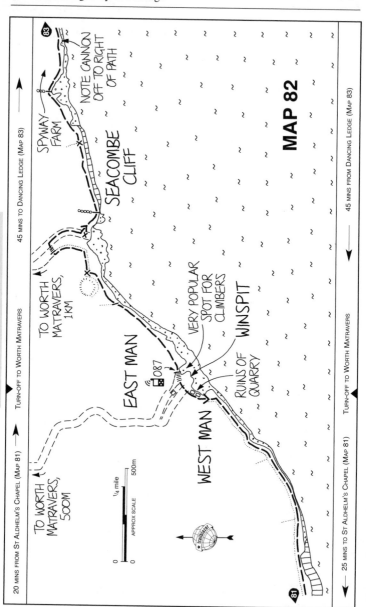

20 MINS FROM ST ALDHELM'S CHAPEL (MAP 81) →

TURN-OFF TO WORTH MATRAVERS →

45 MINS TO DANCING LEDGE (MAP 83)

25 MINS TO ST ALDHELM'S CHAPEL (MAP 81) →

TURN-OFF TO WORTH MATRAVERS →

45 MINS FROM DANCING LEDGE (MAP 83)

MAP 82

NOTE CANNON OFF TO RIGHT OF PATH

SPYWAY FARM

SEACOMBE CLIFF

TO WORTH MATRAVERS, 1KM

VERY POPULAR SPOT FOR CLIMBERS

WINSPIT

RUINS OF QUARRY

EAST MAN

WEST MAN

TO WORTH MATRAVERS, 500M

087

¼ mile

500m

APPROX SCALE

0
0

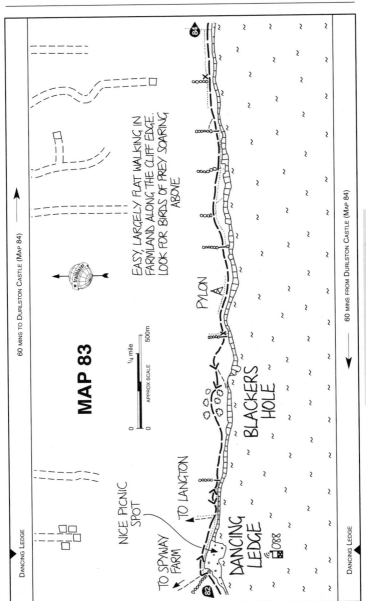

60 MINS TO DURLSTON CASTLE (MAP 84)

DANCING LEDGE

MAP 83

¼ mile
500m
APPROX SCALE

EASY, LARGELY FLAT WALKING IN FARMLAND ALONG THE CLIFF EDGE. LOOK FOR BIRDS OF PREY SOARING ABOVE

NICE PICNIC SPOT

TO SPYWAY FARM

TO LANGTON

DANCING LEDGE

088

PYLON

BLACKERS HOLE

84

82

DANCING LEDGE

60 MINS FROM DURLSTON CASTLE (MAP 84)

SWANAGE [map p307]

The final town on the Jurassic coastline is actually rather a small and unassuming place. With a population of around 10,000 and lacking any major sights or attractions, Swanage is nevertheless the largest settlement on the Isle of Purbeck and another place that survives – and in high summer thrives – on the tourist hordes. What these tourists find when they arrive is a pleasant place with amiable people, a great sweeping arc of sand and just about every amenity a visitor could need.

Swanage Jazz Festival is held here in July and the **Folk Festival** in September; see box p14 for details of both.

Services

Swanage centre is a compact place with everything in easy reach. The **tourist information office** (☎ 01929-766018, 🖳 visit-dorset.com/explore/towns/swanage; Easter-Oct daily 10am-5pm, Nov-Easter Mon-Sat 10am-5pm) is on the seafront overlooking the beach.

On High St you'll find the **library** (☎ 01929-423485; Mon 10am-6.30pm, Wed & Fri 9.30am-5pm, Sat 9.30am-4pm) with **internet**, the local **launderette**, Purbeck Valet (Mon-Wed & Fri 9am-4pm, Thur & Sat 9am-1pm) and, at its eastern end, the **camping outlet** Jurassic Outdoor (☎ 01929-424366, 🖳 jurassicoutdoor.com; Mon-Sat 10am-5pm, Sun 10am-4pm).

Moving to Station Rd you'll find Boots **pharmacy** (Mon-Sat 9am-5.30pm, Sun 10am-4pm) and the **supermarket** Budgens (Mon-Sat 7am-10pm, Sun 11am-5pm), while at the end of the road, by the station, is a second and larger supermarket, Co-op (Mon-Sat 6am-11pm, Sun 10am-4pm).

Near here is the **post office** (Mon-Fri 9am-5.30pm, Sat 9am-5pm). There are also some **banks** with **ATMs** on High St and Station Rd.

Transport

[See pp50-4] Wilts & Dorset's Breezer No 40 **bus** travels to Poole via Wareham whilst their No 50 goes to Bournemouth via Sandbanks and South Haven Point.

In summer, Damory Coaches Breezer 30 service travels to Weymouth stopping at Lulworth Cove en route.

For a **taxi**, try Swanage Associated Taxis (☎ 01929-421122 or ☎ 01929-425350).

Where to stay

Swanage is blessed with two **hostels**. The first is **YHA Swanage** (☎ 0345-371 9346, 🖳 yha.org.uk/hostel/swanage; 101 beds in 2-/3-/4-/6-/7-bed rooms, some en suite; WI-FI in social areas; dorm bed from £13pp, private rooms from £39), on Cluny Crescent. Meals are available but there is also a self-catering kitchen. Note that for individual bookings the hostel is only open Monday to Thursday and in the school holidays between March and the end of October.

There's also the very welcoming **Swanage Auberge** (☎ 01929-424368, 🖳 swanageauberge.co.uk; 1 x 4-bed, 1 x 6-bed Alpine style, 1 x 5-bed dorm; WI-FI; from £20pp inc cereal breakfast), at 45 High St, which is smart, clean, central and friendly; it also has self-catering facilities.

There are several particularly decent **B&Bs** scattered about town. However, note that during festivals (see box p14) and in the peak season many require a two- or three-night minimum stay, particularly for advance bookings.

Climbing the hill on Park Rd you will find the upmarket, award-winning **Clare House** (☎ 01929-422855, 🖳 clare-house.com; 4D/1D or T; ✈; WI-FI; Apr-Sep; £45-57.50pp, sgl occ rates on request) at No 1; **Ocean Lodge** (☎ 01929-422805, 🖳 oceanlodgeswanage.co.uk; 2D/1Tr/1Qd; ✈; WI-FI; Mar-mid Oct; £35-50pp, sgl occ from £55), at No 3, who will not accept one-night bookings in advance during the summer holidays; and the dog-friendly **The Limes** (☎ 01929-422664, 🖳 limeshotel.net; 3S/6D/3Qd; ✈; WI-FI; 🐾; from £49.50pp, sgl £48-60) at No 48.

In the same vicinity but on Manor Rd, **Hermitage Guesthouse** (☎ 01929-423014, 🖳 hermitage-online.co.uk; 2D/2T/3Qd, shared facilities; ✈; WI-FI; Mar-end Oct;

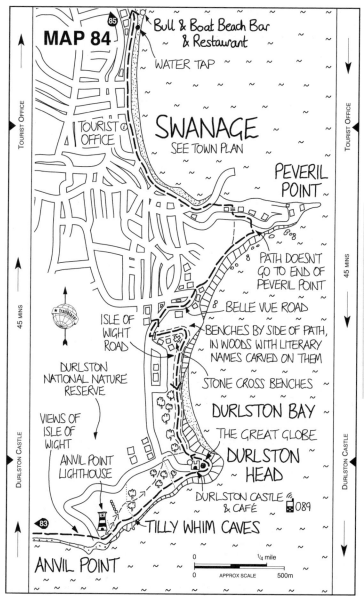

MAP 84

Bull & Boat Beach Bar & Restaurant

WATER TAP

TOURIST OFFICE

TOURIST OFFICE

SWANAGE
SEE TOWN PLAN

PEVERIL POINT

PATH DOESN'T GO TO END OF PEVERIL POINT

BELLE VUE ROAD

ISLE OF WIGHT ROAD

BENCHES BY SIDE OF PATH, IN WOODS WITH LITERARY NAMES CARVED ON THEM

DURLSTON NATIONAL NATURE RESERVE

STONE CROSS BENCHES

DURLSTON BAY

VIEWS OF ISLE OF WIGHT

THE GREAT GLOBE

DURLSTON HEAD

ANVIL POINT LIGHTHOUSE

DURLSTON CASTLE & CAFÉ 089

TILLY WHIM CAVES

ANVIL POINT

TOURIST OFFICE

45 MINS

45 MINS

DURLSTON CASTLE

DURLSTON CASTLE

ROUTE GUIDE AND MAPS

0   ¼ mile
0   APPROX SCALE   500m

from £35pp, sgl occ from £45) overlooks the town.

Moving to the centre of town and closer to the bus and railway stations is ***Firswood*** (☎ 01929-422306, 🖳 firswoodguesthouse.co.uk; 1S/2D or T/4D; ☕; WI-FI; from £40pp, sgl from £40, sgl occ room rate), 29 Kings Rd, though they don't take credit or debit cards.

A short stroll away from the centre and opposite St Mary's Church on Kings Rd are ***Millbrook*** (☎ 01929-423443, 🖳 millbrookswanage.com; 5D/1T/1Qd, 1D/1T share facilities; WI-FI; £35-44.50pp, sgl occ £60-79), at No 56, who do not accept advance bookings for a one-night stay on a Saturday; and ***Rivendell Guesthouse*** (☎ 01929-421383, 🖳 rivendell-guesthouse.co.uk; 3D/2D or T; ☕; WI-FI; £43.50-49pp, sgl occ from £65), No 58, who will take one-night bookings throughout July and August if their diary allows, but not for advance bookings.

If you'd rather stay in a pub, ***The Red Lion*** (☎ 01929-423533, 🖳 redlionswanage.co.uk; 1S/1D/2T/1Tr, futon beds can also be put in some rooms; 🐕; £45-55pp, sgl occ rates on request) and ***The White Swan*** (☎ 01929-423804, 🖳 info@whiteswanswanage.co.uk; 3D/1T/1Tr; ☕; WI-FI; 🐕; from £50pp inc for sgl occ) both do B&B.

North of the centre and a place willing to accept bookings for one-night stays is the dog-friendly ***Railway Cottage*** (☎ 01929-425542, 🖳 railwaycottagehotel.co.uk; 3D/1T/1Qd; ☕; WI-FI; 🐕; room only £32.50-40pp, sgl occ room rate), at 26 Victoria Ave. It's room only, though; no breakfasts.

Closer towards the seafront along the same road is the smart ***Caythorpe House*** (☎ 01929-422892, 🖳 caythorpehouse.co.uk; 2S/2T/1D/2D or T; WI-FI; mid Mar to mid Oct; from £42.50pp, sgl/sgl occ from £52/78), at 7 Rempstone Rd, situated a mere 100 metres from the sands.

Northern Swanage (Map 85) Just after the coast path leaves the beach, are two more options, both on Ulwell Rd: ***Tower Lodge*** (☎ 01929-422887, 🖳 towerlodgehotel.co.uk; 1S/2D/1T/6Qd, most en suite; ☕; WI-FI; £37.50-42.50pp, sgl £35-40, sgl occ from £65) next door at No 17; and ***Sandhaven*** (☎ 01929-422322, 🖳 thesandhaven.co.uk; 1S/4D/2T/1Qd; ☕; WI-FI; £35-50pp, sgl £45-55, sgl occ £65-100) at No 5. As with most places they don't accept advance bookings for a one-night stay in the main season.

Nearby on Highcliffe Rd, ***The Castleton*** (☎ 01929-423972, 🖳 thecastleton.co.uk; 1S/6D/1D or T/1Tr/1Qd; ☕; WI-FI; £42.50-60pp, sgl £50-65, sgl occ rates on request) at No 1, and ***The Rookery*** (☎ 01929-424224, 🖳 therookeryswanage.co.uk; 1S/4D/1T/1Tr/2Qd; ☕; WI-FI; £40-42.50pp, sgl 40-50, sgl occ £60-85) at No 3, are also decent options. The latter is licensed and can serve pizzas and snacks, although an advance booking for a one-night stay in the main season may prove difficult.

Where to eat and drink

Cafés & delis The unusual ***Gee Whites*** (☎ 01929-425720, 🖳 geewhites.co.uk; Easter-Oct daily 9am-9pm) is a thatched open-sided affair that wouldn't look out of place on the white sands of the Caribbean. The extensive menu includes typical British-café fare (breakfasts, toasties, jackets and burgers), but there's also a shellfish bar and a crêpes counter, and they serve booze too. It can look bleak in overcast conditions, but pick a hot day in August and it's a lovely, bubbling place.

Nearby is the no-frills ***High St Café*** (daily 7am-2pm), a good-value place with baps (£2.60) and all-day breakfasts (£4.30-7.50), but no card-payment facilities.

Further along the High St you'll find ***Earthlights*** (☎ 01929-422266, 🖳 earthlightscafe.co.uk; summer Sun-Thur 9am-5pm, Fri & Sat 8.30am-9.30pm; winter Mon-Sat 9am-5pm, Sun 10am-4.30pm), housed in an 1896 building that was constructed by the same stonemason who created the Great Globe (see p300). It's a pleasant place for coffee or a cream tea and they also do a decent line in paninis.

For a traditional café with a sea view, head to ***Brook Tea Rooms*** (daily 9am-5pm, Fri & Sat also 6-9pm) which has a good selection of pasties and pies as well as crab

ROUTE GUIDE AND MAPS

Where to eat and drink
1 Brook Tea Rooms
2 The Salt Pig Too
3 Tawny's
4 Earthlights
5 The Red Lion
6 The White Swan
7 Purbeck Deli
8 Fish Plaice
9 Harlees, The Parade
10 La Trattoria
11 Old Brick Pizza Co
12 Gee Whites
13 The White Horse
14 Masala
15 Rainbow Kebab
16 Cauldron Bistro
17 High St Café

Swanage

sandwiches and, of course, cream teas. If you're just passing through and looking for better-than-average lunchbox fillers, *Purbeck Deli* (☎ 01929-422344; Mon-Sat 9.30am-5pm, Sun Mar-Dec 10.30am-4pm), on Institute Rd, is bursting with cheeses, chutneys and freshly baked breads.

Restaurants For fish & chips, two places stand close to each other: *Fish Plaice* (☎ 01929-423668. ▭ fishplaice.co.uk; generally Mon-Sat 11.30am-8pm, Sun to 7pm but hours vary depending on the season and the weather) serves the usual battered fare –

as well as some renowned homemade fish-cakes (£2) – that has 'em queuing out of the door. *Harlees, The Parade* (☎ 01929-422362, ▭ harlees.co.uk; daily Apr-Oct restaurant noon-2.30pm & 5-7.30pm, take-away 11.30am-8.30pm, rest of year restaurant noon-2pm & 5-7.30pm, takeaway 11.30am-2.30pm & 4.30-8pm) offers a slightly more formal seafood experience with great views over the bay from some tables.

Pizza fans can head to *Old Brick Pizza Co* (☎ 01929-422620, ▭ oldbrickpizza company.co.uk; daily 11.30am-11pm), with decent stone-baked pizzas (£8.85-11.45), or *La Trattoria* (☎ 01929-423784, 🖥 latrat toria.co.uk; Mon-Fri 10am-9pm, Sat & Sun from 9am, limited menu between 3pm and 6/6.30pm), an Italian restaurant that's been here since 1970.

Masala (☎ 01929-427299; daily noon-2pm & 5.30-11.30pm; curries £7.95-11.95), on High St, is a fairly standard Indian that does takeaway (though not deliveries). Close by is *Rainbow Kebab* (☎ 01929-427373; Sun-Wed 3pm-1am, Thur-Sat to 1.30am).

For more upmarket dining, the excellent *Cauldron Bistro* (☎ 01929-422671; Fri & Sat from 6.30pm; booking essential) is a long-established place serving fairly fancy British/European fare (mains £13-27.50) such as honey roast confit of duck (£14.95); the seafood here is high quality. Further up High St, *Tawny's* (☎ 01929-422781, 🖥 taw nys-winebar.co.uk; Tue-Sat noon-2.30pm & 6.30-9.30pm) is a sophisticated restaurant/wine bar with some good value, hearty lunches (around £6.50) and evening dishes (£12.25-19.50) such as beef bourguignon with parsnip crisps, garlic sauté potatoes and roast vegetables (£15.95).

The Salt Pig Too (daily 7.30am-7pm) is a rustic, open-plan, café-restaurant with tasty breakfasts and lunches. The burgers here are particularly good and they do a cracking Sunday roast.

Pubs The best pub-food option is probably *The White Swan* (see Where to stay; food served daily 9am-9pm; 🐾), a deceptively large place in the centre of town. It's a real-ale pub and the home of the popular Piddle Beer, but it's also a very welcoming place. Food-wise, they serve breakfasts from 9am to noon, then baguettes (£8.50) and pub-grub mains (around £10) throughout the day.

Another fine real-ale pub is *The Red Lion* (see Where to stay; WI-FI; 🐾), further up High St. They serve food daily (noon-3pm & 6-9pm) including a Wednesday curry night (curry and a pint for £9.75), a Friday steak night (two rib-eye steaks and a bottle of wine for £25.50) and a Sunday roast (from £7.95).

Also on High St, *The White Horse* (☎ 01929-422469; food daily noon-3pm & 6-9pm) does pub-grub classics such as steak & ale pie and has Sky TV for the football.

Food is also available at *Bull & Boat* (Map 84; ☎ 01929-422222, 🖥 bulland boat.co.uk; WI-FI; 🐾 bar only; food served summer Mon-Fri 9.30-11.30am, noon-3pm & 6-9pm, Sat-Sun 9.30am-9pm, winter Sun-Thur 9am-3pm, Fri & Sat 9am-9pm), a beach bar and bistro that sits conveniently on the coast path at the point where the road leaves the beach to head north out of town.

SWANAGE TO SOUTH HAVEN POINT [MAPS 84-88]

And so to the last stage – and, at **7½ miles (12km; 2hrs 40 mins)** a very pleasant one it is too. After all the ups and downs of the previous few days, it's also a relatively painless one, with only one simple climb, an even more gentle descent – and then, for the first time in the book, a lengthy stretch of beach-combing along the flat sands of South Haven.

It's a lovely, serene end to your journey as you pick your way amongst the sun seekers, sand strollers, naked naturists and other daytrippers to South Haven Point and the finish line, where any aches and niggles that have haunted you for the past few days are suddenly soothed by the most effective balm known to man – the overwhelming sense of achievement and self-satisfaction.

The route

The stage begins with a simple stroll along Swanage seafront, the path eventually abandoning the coast to strike through the northern suburbs. Your last

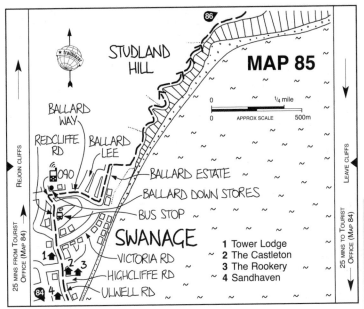

chance to buy **refreshments** before you climb Studland Hill is at Ballard Down Stores (Map 85; Mon-Sat 6am-1pm & 2.15-5.30pm, Sun 6am-1pm) on Redcliffe Rd. For accommodation options here see p306.

The path then embarks on the gentle climb up breezy **Studland Hill**. You don't stay up there for long, however – just long enough, perhaps, to get your first glimpse of Poole – before the even more gentle descent to **The Pinnacles** and **Old Harry Rocks**, where seagulls soar and falcons swoop.

Your path takes a sharp left here to head eventually into the trees then divides: the right-hand (alternative) branch takes you to the beach and the friendly beach shack *Joe's Café* (Easter-Oct daily 10am-4pm up to 8pm depending on the weather; Nov-Easter weekends only); by keeping straight on you'll pass some toilets and the road that runs in front of award-winning 16th-century *Bankes Arms* (☎ 01929-450225, 🖥 bankesarms.com; 1S/7D/1T/1Tr; two rooms share a bathroom, rest en suite; 🛏; WI-FI but weak signal; 🐕; £40-50pp, sgl occ rates on request, minimum two nights at weekends, three nights over bank holiday weekends), the home of the Isle of Purbeck brewery (see box p23), two log fires, some great **food** (Mar/Apr-Nov daily noon-9.30pm, Nov-Mar/Apr Mon-Fri noon-3pm & 6-9pm, Sat-Sun noon-9.30pm) and smart rooms. Wonderful, yes – but it's an unusual trekker who stops now when the finishing line is just a short trudge away, along Studland Beach.

About 50 metres past Bankes Arms, turn right down a marked pathway to rejoin the coastline, then turn left to reach the simple wooden *Middle Beach Café* (Easter/Apr-Sep daily 9am-5pm, Oct 10am-4pm, winter weekends only 10am-4pm), which does some splendid cakes, from where your route is pretty self-evident, the path joining the sands of **Studland Bay** to continue its shore-side saunter. It is tempting here, especially on a hot day, to take off your hiking boots and finish your walk barefoot with the cool waves lapping over your aching feet, but be warned: walking barefoot on fairly rough sand for what amounts to around 4km, whilst carrying a heavy rucksack, is an invitation for some serious blisters. Keep those boots on for now.

Passing the National Trust car park, home to a **visitor centre**, the large *Knoll Beach Café* (daily Apr-June & Sep-Oct 9.30am-5pm, Jul-Aug 9am-6pm, Nov-Mar 10am-4pm) and gift shop, the route continues north through the **naturist beach** (the only one in the National Trust's extensive portfolio). Not even the sight of Dorset's finest in the buff can detract you from your task now, though, as you march ever onwards, rounding the bend to see, in the distance ahead, first the large ferry making the short trip between Sandbanks and **South Haven Point**; then, a few steps further on, the point you've probably been dreaming about for the past 217¼ miles (or, indeed, 630 miles if you've walked all the way from Minehead): the **Coast Path Sculpture**, marking the end of this stage, the end of the path – and the end of your walk.

Congratulations!

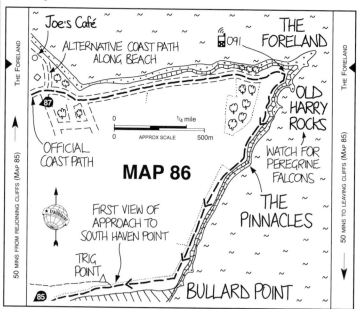

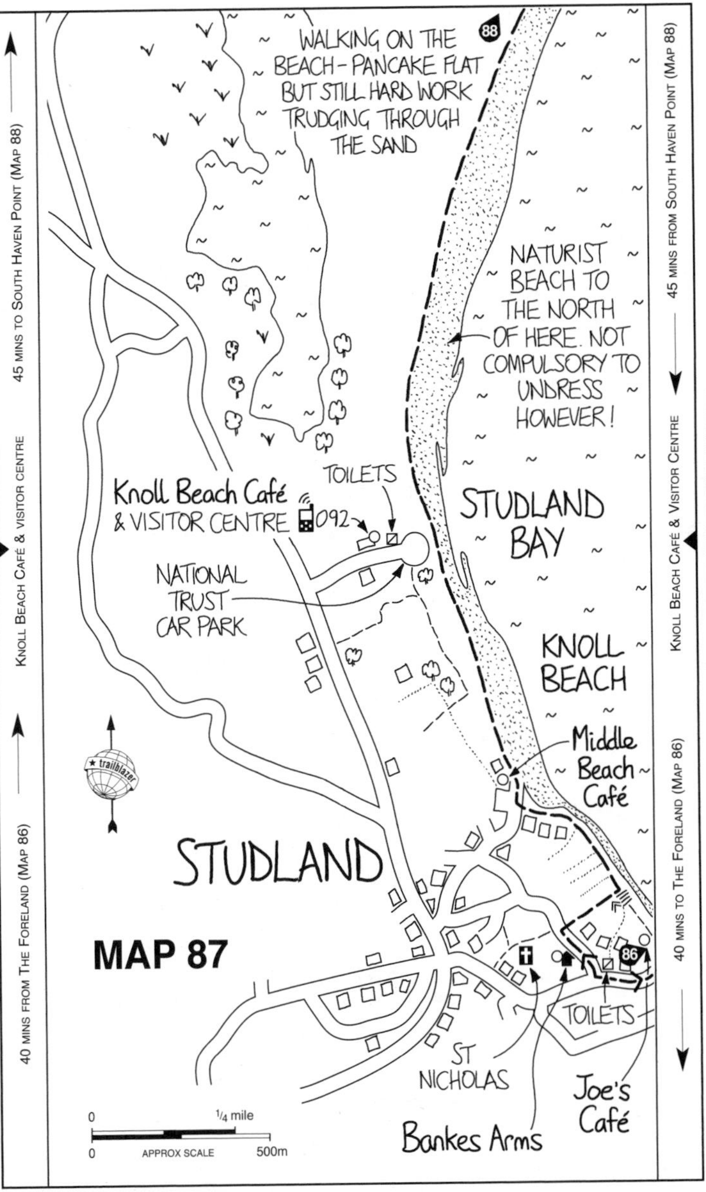

WALKING ON THE BEACH - PANCAKE FLAT BUT STILL HARD WORK TRUDGING THROUGH THE SAND

NATURIST BEACH TO THE NORTH OF HERE. NOT COMPULSORY TO UNDRESS HOWEVER!

STUDLAND BAY

Knoll Beach Café & VISITOR CENTRE 092

TOILETS

NATIONAL TRUST CAR PARK

KNOLL BEACH

Middle Beach Café

STUDLAND

MAP 87

ST NICHOLAS

Bankes Arms

TOILETS

Joe's Café

45 MINS TO SOUTH HAVEN POINT (MAP 88)

KNOLL BEACH CAFÉ & VISITOR CENTRE

40 MINS FROM THE FORELAND (MAP 86)

45 MINS FROM SOUTH HAVEN POINT (MAP 88)

KNOLL BEACH CAFÉ & VISITOR CENTRE

40 MINS TO THE FORELAND (MAP 86)

ROUTE GUIDE AND MAPS

trailblazer

0   ¼ mile
0   APPROX SCALE   500m

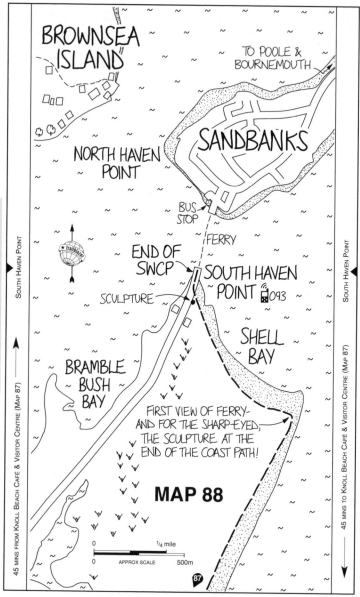

BROWNSEA ISLAND

TO POOLE & BOURNEMOUTH

SANDBANKS

NORTH HAVEN POINT

BUS STOP

FERRY

END OF SWCP

SOUTH HAVEN POINT 📱093

SCULPTURE

SHELL BAY

BRAMBLE BUSH BAY

FIRST VIEW OF FERRY — AND FOR THE SHARP-EYED, THE SCULPTURE AT THE END OF THE COAST PATH!

MAP 88

0   ¼ mile
0   500m
APPROX SCALE

87

ROUTE GUIDE AND MAPS

► SOUTH HAVEN POINT

SOUTH HAVEN POINT ◄

45 MINS FROM KNOLL BEACH CAFÉ & VISITOR CENTRE (MAP 87) ↑

45 MINS TO KNOLL BEACH CAFÉ & VISITOR CENTRE (MAP 87) ↓

APPENDIX A: POOLE & BOURNEMOUTH

Though not on the path, there's a fair chance you'll be visiting Poole or Bournemouth at some point in your trip – probably at the end – in order to catch transport to/from the start/end of the trail. Both offer all the amenities you are likely to need.

Poole

To get to Poole Bus Station (20 mins), which is walking distance from Poole Railway Station, take the **ferry** (🖳 sandbanksferry.co.uk; daily 7am-11pm; 3/hr; £1) across to Sandbanks and jump on Wilts and Dorset's Breezer No 60 **bus** (this stops running at around 6pm; Mon-Sat only in winter). First's X54 bus connects Poole with Weymouth. South Western Railway operates **train services** to London Waterloo; for further details of these bus and train services see pp50-4.

To help you get around pay a visit to the **tourist information centre** (☎ 01202-262600, 🖳 pooletourism.com; Easter-Oct daily 10am-5pm, Nov-Easter Mon-Sat 10am-4pm, Sun noon-4pm) in the flashy modern Poole Museum, at 4 High St.

The most attractive part of town is the harbour area, where you'll also find some **B&Bs** including *Quayside* (☎ 01202-683733, 🖳 quaysidepoole.co.uk; 1S/2D/2T/2Tr, all en suite; WI-FI; from £37.50pp, sgl from £55), 9 High St, which is opposite the museum.

Nearer to the railway and bus stations on Wimborne Rd are *Towngate Guest House* (☎ 01202-668552, 🖳 towngateguesthouse.net; 1D or T/1T/1Qd; ♥; WI-FI; from £35pp, sgl occ from £50), at No 58, who welcome walkers and are willing to put you up for one night only.

For **food**, there are lots of options along The Quay and the High St. *Guildhall Tavern* (☎ 01202-671717, 🖳 www.guildhalltavern.co.uk; Tue-Thur 11.30am-3.30pm & 6-9.30pm, Fri & Sat 11.30am-3.30pm & 5.30pm-10pm), at 15 Market St, is a French restaurant that is a good place for that end-of-trek celebration, pricey and indulgent (mains £18-23.95) but with suitably luxurious dishes such as chargrilled whole seabass flambéed in Pernod (£22.95), or Dorset rack of lamb with fresh rosemary & honey sauce (£23.95).

Bournemouth

Wilts & Dorset's Breezer No 50 stops at South Haven Point on its way between Swanage bus station and Bournemouth railway station (45 mins; £3.60). The **bus**, which runs until around 9.30pm in the main season (rest of year to about 6.45pm), goes on the ferry (see above) itself, stopping to pick up passengers at the bus stops immediately before and after it. South Western Railway operates **train services** to London Waterloo and Cross Country Trains to Birmingham. For further details of these bus and train services see pp50-4.

Bournemouth Tourist Information Centre (☎ 01202-451734, 🖳 bournemouth.co .uk; Apr-Oct daily 9am-5pm, July & Aug to 6pm, Nov-Mar 9am-4pm) is at Pier Approach on the seafront.

Bournemouth has no shortage of **accommodation** options. One place near the railway station is *Lea Hurst Hotel* (☎ 01202-290136, 🖳 leahursthotel.co.uk; 4D/2T/2Qd, all en suite; WI-FI), at 8 Frances Rd, charges £25-35pp (sgl occ £25-45) and is near the railway station. In the peak season they do not accept bookings for one night only. If you want a final night near the sea consider *The Cumberland* (☎ 01202-298350, 🖳 cumberlandhotel .oceana-collection.com; 11S/50D/15D or T, one suite, all en suite or with private facilities; ♥; WI-FI; small 🐾); it is a vast 1930s Art Deco hotel with a wide range of rooms, the best of which have a balcony and sea view. B&B costs £40-110.50pp (sgl/sgl occ £60-142); room only rates also available.

For **food** again there is the usual range of chain restaurants and cafés but one place by the sea that is worth trying is *West Beach* (☎ 01202-587785, 🖳 west-beach.co.uk; daily 9-11am, noon-3pm & 6-9.30pm, winter Sun to 5pm); the menu focuses on fish and may include baked cod fillet with red pesto crust, roasted cauliflower, heritage carrots and jus (£19) but there are also daily specials and meat/vegetarian options.

APPENDIX B: THE RIDGEWAY'S PREHISTORIC SITES

Nobody is quite sure why there is such an abundance of prehistoric sites along the Ridgeway. Many think that this chalky ridge provided the easiest way to travel east–west through this part of Dorset, rather than trying to wade through the boggy forested ground present in the valleys below. The Ridgeway also provides a natural 'plinth', a perfect platform for these early people to design and display their temples, tombs and tumuli so their neighbours could see them. Whatever the reasons, the quantity and variety of prehistoric sites on the Ridgeway puts it on a par with the landscape around Stonehenge. Over 3000 sites have now been discovered, many of them only recently.

These sites fall into four main chronological categories. The oldest finds date back to the **Neolithic Age** (4000-2000BC – note the definitions of each of these ages is very fluid and different books may give different start and end dates for the various eras). These were the first farmers, who cleared the Ridgeway of its forests in order to plant crops and cultivate the land. The monuments they built tend to be found at the western end of the Ridgeway, where they had easy access to their building materials – rocks from the Valley of Stones. This valley lies to the west of the Hardy Monument (see Map 60a) and is where early man would source rocks and boulders for their burial chambers and stone circles that dot the landscape. There are only a couple of examples of these within easy reach of the path. The first is **Hampton Down Stone Circle**, constructed around 2000BC – though it has been moved and altered many times since. It is believed that the stone now sits in its original position, though with only 10 of the original stones (a photograph from 1908 indicates there were 16 at that time). On the other side of the Hardy Monument, and a little off the path, is the more impressive **Hell Stone**, a Neolithic stone burial chamber that resembles a kind of mini Stonehenge. Actually, the chamber was only one part of the structure, for from the chamber ran a mound of earth, the whole construction being known as a **long barrow**. Unfortunately, it is widely believed that the 19th-century antiquarians who restored this one rebuilt it incorrectly – though to the laymen it's still a powerful place and the chamber a mighty structure.

In addition to the 17 long barrows on the Ridgeway there are also three **bank barrows**, of which one, **Broadmayne Bank Barrow**, lies around 500m off the path to the north-east of Green Hill. While it is believed the long barrows had some sort of funerary function – the number of bones excavated within the burial chambers suggest they were used as communal burial places – the function of these bank barrows is unknown.

The practice of constructing barrows continued into the **Bronze Age** (2000-500BC) though the style changed as the mounds became more hemispherical. It is these Bronze Age **round barrows** that are the dominant feature of the path. Once again these definitely had a funerary purpose, the corpses of the deceased being placed within the mounds. **Bronkham Hill**, east of the Hardy Monument on the trail, has the finest collection of round barrows on the path. Some important archeological finds have been found in these tumuli including the beautiful Clandon Lozenge, a decorative gold 'plate' that is now on display in the County Museum in Dorset.

By around the 9th century BC the Britons were using a new metal for the first time, heralding in the **Iron Age**. On the Ridgeway, this epoch is best represented by the giant hillforts scattered hereabouts, of which **Abbotsbury Castle** is typical: there's little to cause the layman's jaw to drop when visiting this hilltop site today, though archaeologists will recognise the curves, folds and bumps in the land that are the telltale signs of such a construction. The castle is just one of three in the area, with Maiden Castle, just outside Dorchester, considered to be the most important Iron Age fort in the UK due to its size and history. By the middle of the 1st century AD, however, the Romans had arrived and the Iron Age was ending – and prehistory, too, with the Romans bringing their practice of writing official documents, notes and letters that recorded their time in the UK.

APPENDIX C: TAKING A DOG

The South-West Coast Path is a dog-friendly path and many are the rewards that await those prepared to make the extra effort required to bring their best friend along the trail. However, you shouldn't underestimate the amount of work involved in bringing your pooch to the path. Indeed, just about every decision you make will be influenced by the fact that you've got a dog: how you plan to travel to the start of the trail, where you're going to stay, how far you're going to walk each day, where you're going to rest and where you're going to eat in the evening.

The decision-making begins well before you've set foot on the trail. For starters, you have to ask – and be honest with – yourself: can your dog really cope with walking 10+ miles (16+km) a day, day after day, week after week? And just as importantly, will he or she actually enjoy it?

If you think the answer is yes to both, you need to start preparing accordingly. For one thing, extra thought needs to go into your itinerary. The best starting point is to study the Village & town facilities table on pp32-3 (and the advice below), and plan where to stop, where to eat, where to buy food for your mutt.

Looking after your dog

To begin with, you need to make sure that your dog is fully **inoculated** against the usual doggy illnesses, and also up-to-date with regard to **worm pills** (eg Drontal) and **flea preventatives** such as Frontline – they are, after all, following in the pawprints of many a dog before them, some of whom may well have left fleas or other parasites on the trail that now lie in wait for their next meal to arrive. **Pet insurance** is also a very good idea; if you've already got insurance do check that it will cover a trip such as this.

On the subject of looking after your dog's health, perhaps the most important implement you can take with you is the **plastic tick remover**, available from vets for a couple of quid. Ticks are a real problem on the SWCP, as they hide in the long grass waiting for unsuspecting victims to trot past. These removers, while fiddly, help you to remove the tick safely (ie without leaving its head behind buried under the dog's skin).

Being in unfamiliar territory also makes it more likely that you and your dog could become separated. For this reason, make sure your dog has a **tag with your contact details on it** (a mobile phone number would be best if you are carrying one with you); you could also consider having it **microchipped** for further security.

What to pack

You've probably already got a good idea of what to bring to keep your dog alive and happy, but the following is a checklist:
● **Food/water bowl** Foldable cloth bowls are popular with walkers as they are light and take up little room in the rucksack. It is also possible to get a water-bottle-and-bowl combination, where the bottle folds into a 'trough' from which the dog can drink.
● **Lead and collar** An extendable one is probably preferable for this sort of trip. Make sure both lead and collar are in good condition – you don't want either to snap on the trail, or you may end up carrying your dog through sheep fields until a replacement can be found.
● **Medication** You'll know if you need to bring any lotions or potions.
● **Tick remover** See above.
● **Bedding** A simple blanket may suffice, or you can opt for something more elaborate if you aren't carrying your own luggage.
● **Poo bags** Essential.
● **Hygiene wipes** For cleaning your dog after it's rolled in stuff.
● **A favourite toy** Helps prevent your dog from pining for the entire walk.

❑ **Packing for your dog**
When it comes to packing, I always leave an exterior pocket of my rucksack empty so I can put used poo bags in there (for deposit at the first bin I come to). I always like to keep all the dog's kit together and separate from the other luggage (usually inside a plastic bag inside my rucksack). I have also seen several dogs sporting their own 'doggy rucksack, so they can carry their own food, water, poo etc – which certainly reduces the burden on their owner!

Henry Stedman

● **Food/water** Remember to bring treats as well as regular food to keep up the mutt's morale.
● **Corkscrew stake** Available from camping or pet shops, this will help you to keep your dog secure in one place while you set up camp/doze.
● **Raingear** It can rain a lot!
● **Old towels** For drying your dog after the deluge.

Dogs on beaches

There is no general rule regarding whether dogs are allowed on beaches or not. Some of the beaches on the SWCP are open to dogs all year; some allow them on the beach only outside the summer season (1st May to 30th Sep); while a few beaches don't allow dogs at all. (Guide dogs, by the way, are usually excluded from any bans.) If in doubt, look for the noticeboards that will tell you the exact rules. See also below.

South Devon's website (💻 visitdevon.co.uk/things-to-do/attractions/beaches/dog-friendly-beaches) says which beaches allow dogs and which don't, as does Visit Dorset (💻 visit-dorset.com/ideas-and-inspiration/dog-friendly/dog-friendly-beaches).

Where dogs are banned from a beach there will usually be an alternative path that you can take that avoids the sands. If there isn't an alternative, and you have no choice but to cross the beach even though dogs are officially banned, you are permitted to do so as long as you cross the beach as speedily as possible, follow the line of the path (which is usually well above the high-water mark) and keep your dog tightly under control **on a lead**.

Whatever the rules of access are for the beach, remember that your dog shouldn't disturb other beach-users – and you must always **clean up after your dog**.

Finally, remember that you need to bring drinking water with you on the beach as dogs can overheat with the lack of shade.

Beaches with restrictions Unless otherwise stated, dogs are not allowed on the beaches listed below between May and September.

● **Devon**: Bigbury-on-Sea; **Blackpool Sands** (1st Mar to 1st Nov); **Bovisand; Challaborough; Coryton's Cove; Hope Cove; Salcombe South Sands; Shaldon Beach; Teignmouth Town Beach; Wembury**.

● **Dorset**: **Lyme Regis** No dogs on the area of beach from Cobb Gate Car Park west to the Lifeboat slipway between 1st April and 31st Oct, though dogs are allowed on East Cliff Beach and Monmouth Beach year-round; **Charmouth West Beach; Charmouth East Beach**: No dogs between 10am and 6pm during July & August; **Seatown** No dogs at any time; **West Bay** No dogs within the East Pier to East Cliffs and West Pier to West Cliffs areas between May & Sep; **Burton Bradstock; West Bexington** Dogs allowed at all times within a restricted area; **Weymouth** No dogs on main beach between May & Sep. Dogs permitted year-round within a restricted area; **Swanage; Studland** Dogs are not allowed on Middle and Knoll beaches (from Red-end point to training bank) between early July and early September.

Dogs are allowed on Shell Bay and South Beach all year provided they are on a lead and that owners clean up after them.

When to keep your dog on a lead

● **On cliff tops** It's a sad fact that, every year, a few dogs lose their lives falling over the edge of the cliffs. It usually occurs when they are chasing rabbits (which know where the cliff-edge is and are able, unlike your poor pooch, to stop in time).

● **When crossing farmland**, particularly in the lambing season (around May) when your dog can scare the sheep, causing them to lose their young. Farmers are allowed by law to shoot at and kill any dogs that they consider are worrying their sheep. During lambing, most farmers would prefer it if you didn't bring your dog at all.

The exception is if your dog is being attacked by cows. There have been deaths in the UK caused by walkers being trampled as they tried to rescue their dogs from the attentions of cattle. The advice in this instance is to let go of the lead, head speedily to a position of safety (usually the other side of the field gate or stile) and call your dog to you.

● **On National Trust land**, where it is compulsory to keep your dog on a lead.

● **Around ground-nesting birds** It's important to keep your dog under control when crossing an area where certain species of birds nest on the ground. Most dogs love foraging around in the woods but make sure you have permission to do so; some woods are used as 'nurseries' for game birds and dogs are only allowed through them if they are on a lead.

Cleaning up after your dog

It is extremely important that dog owners behave in a responsible way when walking the path and all excrement should be cleaned up. In towns, villages and fields where animals graze or which will be cut for silage, hay etc, you need to pick up and bag the excrement. In other places you can possibly get away with merely flicking it with a nearby stick into the under-growth, thus ensuring there is none left on the path to decorate the boots of others.

If your dog is anything like others, it'll wait until you are 300m past the nearest bin – and about four miles from the next one – before relieving itself. Don't be tempted to leave it, but bag it up; this means you're likely to have to carry it for a couple of miles – just look on it as your own personalised little hand warmer.

Staying and eating with your dog

In this guide we have used the symbol 🐕 to denote where a hotel, pub or B&B welcomes dogs. However, this always needs to be arranged in advance and some places may charge extra. Hostels (both YHA and independent) do not permit them unless they are an assistance (guide) dog; smaller campsites tend to accept them, but some of the larger holiday parks do not. Before you turn up always double check whether the place you would like to stay accepts dogs and whether there is space for them; many places have only one or two rooms suitable for people with dogs.

When it comes to eating, most landlords allow dogs in at least a section of their pubs, though few restaurants do. Make sure you always ask first and ensure your dog doesn't run around the pub but is secured to your table or a radiator.

APPENDIX D: GPS WAYPOINTS

MAP	REF	GPS WAYPOINT	DESCRIPTION
Map 1	001	SX 48376 54004	Start of walk/Mayflower Steps
Map 1	002	SX 48974 53954	Turn-off to Breakwater Hill
Map 2	003	SX 50643 53881	Oreston Rhino sculpture
Map 2	004	SX 50350 52914	Radford Castle
Map 3	005	SX 49140 52394	Jennycliff Café
Map 3	006	SX 49141 50716	Cliffedge Café
Map 4	007	SX 49744 48820	Heybrook Bay
Map 5	008	SX 51786 48489	The Old Mill Café (turn-off to Wembury)
Map 6	009	SX 54021 47711	Ferry at Noss Mayo
Map 6a	009a	SX 52858 49645	Knighton Stores & post office in Wembury
Map 6a	009b	SX 55377 52168	Brixton Village Stores and post office
Map 6b	009c	SX 56655 52714	Join lane
Map 6b	009d	SX 57093 51067	Puslinch Bridge
Map 6a	009e	SX 54772 47658	The Ship Inn, Noss Mayo
Map 7	010	SX 54423 45979	Ruined signal station
Map 8	011	SX 59057 47243	St Anchorite's Rock
Map 9	012	SX 61415 47574	Crossing of Erme, Mothecombe side
Map 10	013	SX 64908 44880	Fryer Tucks fish & chips, Challaborough
Map 11	014	SX 65162 44158	Venus Takeaway
Map 11	015	SX 66623 44045	Cockleridge Ham Ferry Landing (River Avon)
Map 11a	015a	SX 69261 47236	Roundabout into Aveton Gifford
Map 12	016	SX 67718 41556	Beachhouse Café
Map 13	017	SX 68734 38504	Turn-off for pathway by wall
Map 14	018	SX 69814 37608	Path left to Bolberry
Map 15	019	SX 72538 36200	Bolt Head
Map 16	020	SX 74148 38087	Mill Bay
Map 17	021	SX 76605 35829	Junction with path by Gammon Head
Map 18	022	SX 79156 36320	Maelcombe House
Map 19	023	SX 80192 37184	Lannacombe Beach
Map 20	024	SX 82456 37221	Turn-off to Start Point Lighthouse
Map 21	025	SX 82334 42016	Torcross
Map 22	026	SX 82888 44346	Slapton Turn
Map 23	027	SX 84075 46876	Strete Post Office & Stores
Map 24	028	SX 85935 47962	Take left fork, uphill to Stoke Fleming
Map 25	029	SX 88664 50280	Dartmouth Castle
Map 26	030	SX 90309 49635	Inner Froward Point
Map 27	031	SX 92234 53402	Man Sands
Map 28	032	SX 93514 54677	Sharkham Point
Map 29	033	SX 94030 56163	Entrance to Berry Head Country Park (NNR)
Map 30	034	SX 89516 57606	Path turns left between row of beach huts
Map 31	035	SX 89460 60284	Paignton Harbour
Map 32	036	SX 89787 62257	Hollicombe Park
Map 33	037	SX 91761 63385	Torquay Marina
Map 34	038	SX 94952 63682	Tip of Hope's Nose
Map 35	039	SX 92154 66031	Join A379
Map 36	040	SX 92656 68475	Maidencombe Beach Car Park
Map 37	041	SX 94041 71961	The Ness
Map 38	042	SX 95496 74828	High- and low-tide routes merge
Map 39	043	SX 97854 78532	Dawlish Warren railway station

MAP	REF	GPS WAYPOINT	DESCRIPTION
Map 40	044	SX 97689 81903	Starcross Ferry
Map 40a	044a	SX 96240 87947	Topsham Ferry
Map 40a	044b	SX 98275 86387	Junction with Station Rd
	044c	SX 98875 84287	Lympstone, cross railway line
Map 41	045	SY 02079 79549	Geoneedle, start of Jurassic Coast
Map 42	046	SY 03594 79851	Straight Point Rifle Range
Map 43	047	SY 06365 81799	Budleigh Salterton; join Marine Parade
Map 44	048	SY 09047 83638	Brandy Head Observation Hut
Map 45	049	SY 10876 86735	Peak Hill
Map 46	050	SY 11977 86946	Clock Tower Café
Map 47	051	SY 16397 87962	Weston Mouth Beach
Map 48	052	SY 19210 88297	Path joins track above Branscombe
Map 49	053	SY 20684 88162	Branscombe Mouth
Map 50	054	SY 25368 90114	Axe Cliff Golf Club clubhouse, Squire's Lane
Map 51	055	SY 27034 89627	Sign: Axmouth–Lyme Regis Undercliffs NNR
Map 52	056	SY 31690 90835	Viewpoint at Pinhay Cliff
Map 53	057	SY 33804 91656	The Cobb, Lyme Regis
Map 54	058	SY 36206 93612	Turn-off for Charmouth Beach
Map 55	059	SY 38315 92966	Westhay Farm
Map 56	060	SY 42011 91776	Seatown
Map 57	061	SY 44782 91079	Eype Mouth
Map 58	062	SY 47487 89729	Burton Freshwater
Map 59	063	SY 50271 88161	Cogden Beach
Map 60	064	SY 53054 86511	Junction with path to South Dorset Ridgeway
Map 60a	064a	SY 55071 86596	Abbotsbury Castle
Map 60a	064b	SY 61306 87616	Hardy Monument
Map 60b	064c	SY 68352 84842	Bincombe
Map 60c	064d	SY 71520 84385	Osmington White Horse
	064e	SY 72839 82931	Turn off road after Craig's Farm Dairy Shop & Tea Room
Map 61	065	SY 55974 84614	Miniature roundabout
Map 62	066	SY 57576 84873	Junction with path to Abbotsbury
Map 63	067	SY 60535 82030	Rodden Hive
Map 64	068	SY 63457 79942	Butterstreet Cove
Map 65	069	SY 64638 78822	Entrance/exit to range (Tidmoor Cove)
Map 66	070	SY 66674 76290	Ferry Bridge
Map 67	071	SY 68327 73505	The Cove House Inn
Map 68	072	SY 68639 72928	Large Hand Crane
Map 68	073	SY 68215 72084	Pass under stone arch
Map 69	074	SY 69712 71084	Church Ope Cove
Map 70	075	SY 67711 68279	Bill of Portland
Map 71	076	SY 67882 78756	Town Bridge, Weymouth Harbour
Map 72	077	SY 69910 81969	Turn-off to Jordan Hill Roman temple
Map 73	078	SY 73556 82056	Reunion with South Dorset Ridgeway
Map 74	079	SY 77221 80962	White Nothe
Map 75	080	SY 80595 80302	Path above Durdle Door
Map 76	081	SY 82425 79934	Lulworth Cove
Map 76	081a	SY 82450 80766	Alternative routes divide
Map 76b	081b	SY 90923 85489	Turn off road to quarries
Map 76	082	SY 82975 79720	Gate into Lulworth Ranges
Map 78	083	SY 88895 79777	Take right-hand fork around hill, not over it

MAP	REF	GPS WAYPOINT	DESCRIPTION
Map 79	084	SY 90803 79304	Stile near end of alternative routes
Map 80	085	SY 94996 77334	Top of Houns-tout Cliff
Map 81	086	SY 96129 77784	Turn-off for Worth Matravers
Map 82	087	SY 97722 76177	Gate at East Man, Winspit
Map 83	088	SY 99686 76962	Dancing Ledge
Map 84	089	SZ 03399 77253	Durlston Castle & café
Map 85	090	SZ 02989 80264	Turn-off Redcliffe Road to Ballard Way
Map 86	091	SZ 05441 82474	Old Harry Rocks
Map 87	092	SZ 03427 83558	Knoll Beach Café
Map 88	093	SZ 03620 86653	South Haven Point

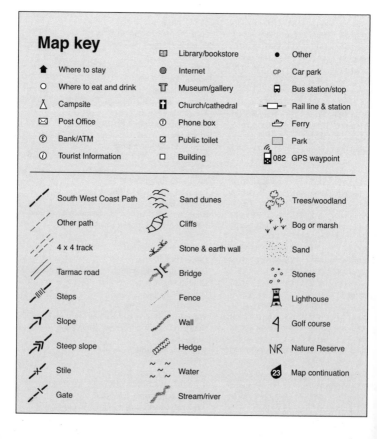

Map key

🏠 Where to stay	📚 Library/bookstore	● Other
○ Where to eat and drink	@ Internet	CP Car park
△ Campsite	🏛 Museum/gallery	🚌 Bus station/stop
⊠ Post Office	🏢 Church/cathedral	Rail line & station
£ Bank/ATM	☏ Phone box	⚓ Ferry
ⓘ Tourist Information	☑ Public toilet	Park
	☐ Building	082 GPS waypoint

South West Coast Path	Sand dunes	Trees/woodland
Other path	Cliffs	Bog or marsh
4 x 4 track	Stone & earth wall	Sand
Tarmac road	Bridge	Stones
Steps	Fence	Lighthouse
Slope	Wall	Golf course
Steep slope	Hedge	NR Nature Reserve
Stile	Water	23 Map continuation
Gate	Stream/river	

INDEX

Page references in **bold** type refer to maps

TRAILBLAZER TITLE LIST

Adventure Cycle-Touring Handbook
Adventure Motorcycling Handbook
Australia by Rail
Azerbaijan
Cleveland Way (British Walking Guide) – due 2018
Coast to Coast (British Walking Guide)
Cornwall Coast Path (British Walking Guide)
Cotswold Way (British Walking Guide)

The Cyclist's Anthology
Dales Way (British Walking Guide)
Dorset & Sth Devon Coast Path (British Walking Gde)
Exmoor & Nth Devon Coast Path (British Walking Gde)
Great Glen Way (British Walking Guide)
Hadrian's Wall Path (British Walking Guide)

Himalaya by Bike – a route and planning guide
Inca Trail, Cusco & Machu Picchu
Japan by Rail
Kilimanjaro – the trekking guide (includes Mt Meru)
Moroccan Atlas – The Trekking Guide
Morocco Overland (4WD/motorcycle/mountainbike)

Nepal Trekking & The Great Himalaya Trail
New Zealand – The Great Walks
North Downs Way (British Walking Guide) – due 2018
Offa's Dyke Path (British Walking Guide)
Overlanders' Handbook – worldwide driving guide
Peddars Way & Norfolk Coast Path (British Walking Gde)
Pembrokeshire Coast Path (British Walking Guide)
Pennine Way (British Walking Guide)

Peru's Cordilleras Blanca & Huayhuash – Hiking/Biking
The Railway Anthology
The Ridgeway (British Walking Guide)
Sahara Overland – a route and planning guide
Scottish Highlands – Hillwalking Guide
Siberian BAM Guide – rail, rivers & road
The Silk Roads – a route and planning guide
Sinai – the trekking guide

South Downs Way (British Walking Guide)
Thames Path (British Walking Guide)
Tour du Mont Blanc
Trans-Canada Rail Guide
Trans-Siberian Handbook
Trekking in the Everest Region
The Walker's Anthology
The Walker's Anthology – further tales
The Walker's Haute Route – Mont Blanc to Matterhorn
West Highland Way (British Walking Guide)

For more information about Trailblazer and our
expanding range of guides, for guidebook updates or
for credit card mail order sales visit our website:

www.trailblazer-guides.com

TRAILBLAZER
British Walking Guides
SEE OPPOSITE FOR FULL TITLE LIST

Great Glen Way

Dales Way

Norfolk Coast Path and PEDDARS WAY
ALEXANDER STEWART

South Downs Way

Thames Path

North Downs WAY
HENRY STEDMAN

★ *trailblazer*

Orkney
Thurso
Inverness
Skye
Mull
Fort William
SCOTLAND
Aberdeen
Milngavie
Glasgow
Edinburgh
Berwick upon Tweed
Kirk Yetholm
Arran
Bowness-on-Solway
Carlisle
Wallsend
Newcastle upon Tyne
St Bees
Bowness-on-Windermere
Robin Hood's Bay
Filey
Helmsley
York
Ilkley
Leeds
Hull
Liverpool
Manchester
Edale
Prestatyn
Crewe
Lincoln
Bangor
Anglesey
Nottingham
ENGLAND
Cromer
Norwich
Great Yarmouth
Knettishall Heath
Birmingham
WALES
Cambridge
Chipping Campden
Kemble
Ivinghoe Beacon
London
Chepstow
Cardiff
Bristol
Bath
Overton Hill
Winchester
Farnham
Canterbury
Dover
Cardigan
Amroth
Minehead
Salisbury
Portsmouth
Brighton
Eastbourne
Bude
Exeter
Poole
Plymouth
Isle of Wight

Scottish Highlands Hillwalking Guide

Great Glen Way

West Highland Way

Pennine Way

Hadrian's Wall Path

Coast to Coast

Dales Way

Pennine Way

Cleveland Way

Norfolk Coast Path & Peddars Way

Offa's Dyke Path

Cotswold Way

The Ridgeway

Thames Path

Pembrokeshire Coast Path

Exmoor & N Devon Coast Path

Cornwall Coast Path

Dorset & S Devon Coast Path

South Downs Way

North Downs Way

Orkney
Lerwick
Stornoway
IRELAND
Belfast
Isle of Man
P. OF LAND
Dublin
IRISH SEA
ISLE of

★ *trailblazer*

ENGLISH CHANNEL

| 0 | 50 | 100km |
| 0 | 25 | 50 miles |

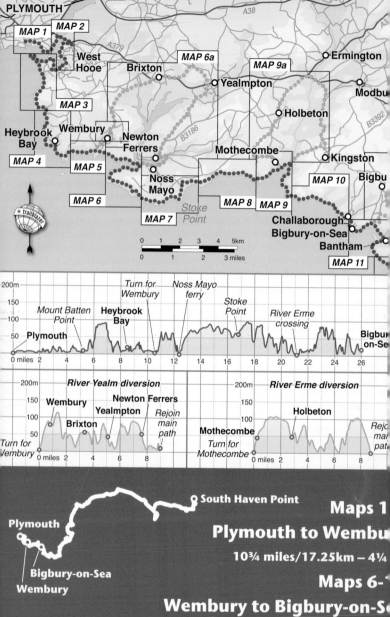

PLYMOUTH

MAP 1   MAP 2

West
Hooe   Brixton

MAP 6a

Yealmpton

MAP 9a

Holbeton

Ermington

Modbu

A379

A38

A3

B3392

MAP 3

Heybrook
Bay   Wembury

Newton
Ferrers

MAP 4

MAP 5

MAP 6

Noss
Mayo

MAP 7

Mothecombe

B3186

Stoke
Point

MAP 8   MAP 9

Kingston

MAP 10

Bigbu

Challaborough
Bigbury-on-Sea
Bantham

MAP 11

0 1 2 3 4 5km
0   1   2   3 miles

200m
150
100
50

Turn for
Wembury

Noss Mayo
ferry

Stoke
Point

River Erme
crossing

Mount Batten
Point

Heybrook
Bay

Plymouth

Bigbur
on-Se

0 miles 2   4   6   8   10   12   14   16   18   20   22   24   26

200m
150
100
50

River Yealm diversion

Wembury

Brixton

Newton Ferrers

Yealmpton

Rejoin
main
path

Turn for
Wembury

0 miles 2   4   6   8

200m
150
100

River Erme diversion

Holbeton

Mothecombe

Turn for
Mothecombe

Rejoi
mai
pat

0 miles 2   4   6   8

South Haven Point

Plymouth

Bigbury-on-Sea
Wembury

Maps 1

Plymouth to Wembu

10¾ miles/17.25km – 4¼

Maps 6-1

Wembury to Bigbury-on-Se

15¼ miles/24.5km – 5hrs 25m

NOTE: Add 20-30% to these times to allow for st